GOVERNING ENGLAND

English Identity and Institutions in a Changing United Kingdom

PROCEEDINGS OF THE BRITISH ACADEMY • 217

GOVERNING ENGLAND

English Identity and Institutions in a Changing United Kingdom

Edited by

MICHAEL KENNY, IAIN McLEAN & AKASH PAUN

Published for THE BRITISH ACADEMY
by OXFORD UNIVERSITY PRESS

Oxford University Press, Great Clarendon Street, Oxford OX2 6DP

First edition published in 2018

British Library Cataloguing in Publication Data
Data available

Library of Congress Cataloging in Publication Data
Data available

Typeset by Mach 3 Solutions Ltd
Printed in Great Britain by TJ International, Padstow, Cornwall

ISBN 978-0-19-726646-5
ISSN 0068-1202

Contents

Foreword

The British Academy was founded in 1902 to be the national academy for the humanities and social sciences across the UK. The Academy exists to demonstrate the great value that scholarly disciplines such as history, law, economics and political science can bring to contemporary policy debates and decision-making processes within government.

As such, the British Academy is delighted to be publishing this volume on the past, present and future governance of England, as part of our long-standing Proceedings of the British Academy series. The Academy is, as its name suggests, a *British* institution, but just as there is no separate English Parliament or Government, there are no English equivalents to bodies such as the Royal Society of Edinburgh, the Royal Irish Academy or the Learned Society of Wales. Like Westminster and Whitehall, therefore, the British Academy is by default also the representative body of the *English* social science and humanities communities, to the extent that these can be distinguished from those of the UK as a whole.

Governing England is the final product of a programme of work instigated by the British Academy in 2015, a year after the Scottish independence referendum and as the potential spectre of Brexit began to loom. The programme included a series of events and publications examining various aspects of English governance and identity, at both national and regional levels. This book draws together the strands of the programme to ask whether England is growing more distinct from Britain than in past years and what that might mean for how England should be governed.

Questions about the nationhood, identity and sovereignty of the different peoples of the UK have come to the forefront of British politics from time to time for well over a century. The first Prime Minister to engage seriously with the question of devolution was William Gladstone, proponent of Irish Home Rule and one-time resident of the building that now houses the British Academy. In the thirty years before the First World War, Scotland's governance was also debated regularly, with four bills to establish home rule for Scotland introduced into Parliament, one receiving a second reading in 1913 before war intervened.

After most of Ireland left the UK in 1922, territorial questions to a large extent faded from the political agenda for half a century, but they have returned with interest since then. After an earlier attempt at devolution faltered in the 1970s, Scotland and Wales gained their own democratic bodies in 1999, since when they have grown considerably in strength and prominence. Equally historic was the

Northern Ireland peace agreement and the new cross-community and cross-border institutions created. Devolution in the form of a mayor and an assembly came also to London, increasingly a world apart from its English hinterland in economic and cultural terms.

But England as a nation was left essentially untouched, if not deliberately ignored, by these waves of reform. The English have appeared largely immune to the lure of nationalism and, for the most part, uninterested in questions of governance and constitutional reform. However, devolution to the other nations appears to have sparked a new realisation that to be British and English is not necessarily the same thing. Many English voters and MPs also regard devolution as unfair, both because non-English MPs can vote on English business at Westminster and because of the perceived English subsidies for higher public spending in the other nations.

Over the past five years, two seismic constitutional events have shaken the foundations of the UK and have raised serious questions about England's relationship with its neighbours. The first was the 2014 Scottish independence referendum, which almost broke apart the 300-year-old Anglo-Scottish Union, and the second was the 2016 EU referendum, in which England and Wales voted Leave while Scotland and Northern Ireland backed Remain. Brexit has destabilised relations between Westminster and the institutions in Edinburgh and Cardiff, as well as threatening to undermine the achievements of the Northern Ireland peace process.

On the face of it, England as a nation is unrepresented and unrecognised in the Brexit process. Yet the decision to hold the referendum was a product of English political calculations, including the Conservative desire to counter the rise of the United Kingdom Independence Party (UKIP). Further, the vote to leave the EU was driven disproportionately not just by English voters, but by those who defined their national identity as English as opposed to British. Brexit can therefore be seen as very much an English political project, albeit one cloaked in the familiar colours of the Union Jack rather than the Cross of St George.

These recent events have shaken up the kaleidoscope of the UK constitution, leaving in flux the future of the Union and England's place within it. This book represents the British Academy's contribution to the debate on these questions. We are grateful to all those who contributed to or otherwise supported the production of this volume.

The contributors include Professor Sir John Curtice FBA FRSE FRSA, who writes on English public opinion; former Cabinet Minister Rt Hon John Denham, who writes on the Labour Party's complicated relationship with English identity; Professor Tony Travers, who examines the place of the London 'city state' within England; and Professor Meg Russell, who considers whether an English Parliament would be a feasible model for governing England. The volume has been compiled and edited by Professor Michael Kenny, Professor Iain McLean FBA FRSE and Akash Paun, supported by the British Academy Public Policy team. Finally, we thank the Carnegie UK Trust for their support of this project.

It is my hope that this book will make a serious contribution to the burgeoning debate about who the English are, what they want and how their choices might affect the UK as a whole. The Academy does not advocate a particular way forward—that is a task for others. What the Academy is well placed to do is to draw upon the best expertise from across the social science and humanities to analyse and provide insight into where the English are as a nation, why we are here and where we might be heading. I therefore hope this volume will assist and inform decision-makers and opinion-shapers engaged in the important debate about how England should be governed within a changing United Kingdom.

Alun Evans
Chief Executive of the British Academy
April 2018

Acknowledgements

The editors of this volume are grateful to a large number of people who have contributed in different ways to the making of this book.

First, we would like to thank the British Academy for sponsoring the two-year Governing England research and events programme out of which the idea for this volume emerged. In particular, we are grateful to Alun Evans, Chief Executive of the Academy, for his personal commitment to this work, and to the members of the British Academy Public Policy Committee for their support.

Secondly, we must thank several current and former members of the British Academy Public Policy team—in particular Natasha McCarthy, Lisa Davies, Barbara Limon, Helen Gibson and Martin Rogers—for their invaluable contributions and advice. Also, James Rivington and Brigid Hamilton-Jones of the Academy's publications team have been instrumental in bringing this volume to completion.

Thirdly, we would like to thank the Carnegie UK Trust for their financial contribution to the Governing England research programme, although we note that the views presented here do not necessarily reflect the views of the Trust, its officers, staff or trustees.

And, fourthly, we very much appreciate the efforts and commitment of all our contributors and the patience and judgement they have shown in responding to several rounds of editorial comments. We also express our gratitude to the various anonymous reviewers who generously took the time to offer their views and have helped improve the book as a result.

All errors, as ever, are the responsibility of the editors.

Finally, we would like to pay a personal tribute to Professor Mick Moran, lead author of Chapter 9, who tragically passed away in April 2018 as the book was going to press.

Michael Kenny, Iain McLean and Akash Paun

April 2018

List of Figures

List of Tables

Notes on Contributors

Arthur Aughey is Emeritus Professor of Politics at Ulster University, Senior Fellow at the Centre for British Politics at the University of Hull and Fellow of the Academy of Social Sciences. He has published widely on Northern Irish politics, British Conservatism and constitutional change in the United Kingdom. Publications include: *Nationalism, Devolution and the Challenge to the United Kingdom State* (2001), *The Politics of Englishness* (2007), *The British Question* (2013) and *The Conservative Party and the Nation: Union, England and Europe* (2018).

Sir John Curtice is Professor of Politics at Strathclyde University and a Senior Research Fellow at NatCen Social Research. He has written extensively about public attitudes towards constitutional reform, including towards devolution (and independence) across the UK. He has been a co-editor of NatCen's annual British Social Attitudes (BSA) reports series for over twenty years and is a regular contributor to British and international media coverage of politics in the UK. He is a Fellow of the British Academy, the Royal Society of Edinburgh and the Academy of the Social Sciences and an Honorary Fellow of the Royal Statistical Society.

John Denham is a visiting professor at the University of Winchester and Director of the Centre for English Identity and Politics. As Labour MP for Southampton Itchen (1992–2015), he held several ministerial offices in the 1997–2010 Government and served in the Cabinet from 2007 to 2010, having previously chaired the Home Affairs Select Committee. He is also Director of the English Labour Network and Chair of the Southern Policy Centre.

Alun Evans has been Chief Executive of the British Academy since July 2015. Prior to his appointment, Alun was Director of the Scotland Office, which represents Scottish interests in the UK Government and the UK Government in Scotland. Before taking up his role as head of the Scotland Office, Alun was Secretary of the Detainee Inquiry from 2010 to 2012 and prior to that he held a series of senior Civil Service posts across various UK Government departments.

Robert Ford is a Professor of Political Science at the University of Manchester. He works broadly in the areas of public opinion, electoral choice and party politics. He has published on the radical right, electoral forecasts, support for the welfare state and attitudes towards immigration. His book about UKIP with Matthew Goodwin, *Revolt on the Right*, was named Political Book of the Year in 2015. He also co-edited short essays for a general audience looking at voter behaviour and public opinion: *Sex, Lies and the Ballot Box* and *More Sex, Lies and the Ballot Box*.

Jim Gallagher CB was the UK's most senior civil servant dealing with devolution and a member of the Number 10 Policy Unit under Tony Blair and later Gordon Brown. Later, Professor Gallagher advised the (winning) 'Better Together' Campaign in the Scottish independence referendum. He is now a member of Nuffield College, Oxford, and writes on devolution, the UK territorial constitution and Brexit as well as the Scottish Question.

Daniel Gover is a researcher in the School of Politics and International Relations at Queen Mary University of London. Much of his research has focused on the UK Parliament. He worked on a major project analysing the introduction and operation of 'English votes for English laws' (EVEL) in the House of Commons, and he has given evidence to several parliamentary select committees on this topic. He is also co-author of *Legislation at Westminster* (2017).

Michael Kenny is Professor of Public Policy at the University of Cambridge. He has written extensively on British politics and political ideas and is the author of *The Politics of English Nationhood* (2014), which won the W. J. M. Mackenzie Prize awarded by the Political Studies Association of the UK in 2015. He is currently working on a project, funded by the Economic and Social Research Council (ESRC), examining the implications of Brexit for the UK's territorial constitution.

Iain McLean is a Fellow of Nuffield College, Oxford, and a specialist in UK devolution since his time as a senior member of Tyne & Wear County Council in the 1970s. He has published widely on the Barnett formula and alternative transfer mechanisms, including those used in Australia. He has served on the Independent Expert Group advising the Calman Commission in Scotland and an expert group advising the Minister of Finance in Wales on local taxation.

Mick Moran FBA was Emeritus Professor of Government at the University of Manchester and worked in the Alliance Manchester Business School. His work addressed British politics. His most recent publication was *The End of British Politics?* (2017). Mick sadly passed away in April 2018, as this book was going to press.

Akash Paun is a Senior Fellow of the Institute for Government in London, leading research on devolution and constitutional change. He was Expert Adviser to the British Academy Governing England programme, out of which this book emerged. Recent publications include *Four Nation Brexit: How the UK and Devolved Governments Should Work Together on Leaving the EU* (2016) and chapters on devolution to four English regions in *Governing England: Devolution and Mayors in England* (2017).

Meg Russell is Professor of British and Comparative Politics in the Department of Political Science, University College London. She began at UCL in 1998 as a researcher in the Constitution Unit and is now the Unit's Director. She leads its research on parliament and is best known for her work on the British House of Lords, bicameralism and parliamentary policy influence. In 2016–18 Meg led a Nuffield Foundation-funded project on Options for an English Parliament.

Jack Sheldon is a Research Assistant in the Bennett Institute for Public Policy at the University of Cambridge, where he is working on an ESRC-funded project—'Between Two Unions: The Constitutional Future of the Islands after Brexit'. He was previously a Research Assistant at the Constitution Unit, UCL, where he worked on a Nuffield Foundation-funded project on Options for an English Parliament.

Maria Sobolewska is a Senior Lecturer in Politics at the University of Manchester and a member of the Centre on Dynamics of Ethnicity. Dr Sobolewska has published articles on the political integration and representation of ethnic minorities and British Muslims, public perceptions of ethnicity, immigrants and integration, as well as a book with Oxford University Press, *Political Integration of British Ethnic Minorities*. She was part of the team conducting the Ethnic Minority British Election Survey in 2010 and is part of PATHWAYS, an eight-country study of the descriptive and substantive representation of immigrant-origin minorities. She currently leads an ESRC-funded project on Brexit and Identity.

John Tomaney is Professor of Urban and Regional Planning in the Bartlett School of Planning, UCL. His work addresses local and regional development, urban and regional planning and governance, and questions of local and regional identity. Among his publications is *Local and Regional Development* (2nd edn, 2017).

Tony Travers is Director of the Institute of Public Affairs at the London School of Economics & Political Science, where he is also a professor in the Department of Government. His research interests include subnational government, local taxation and public finance. He has published two books about the current system of London government: *The Politics of London: Governing an Ungovernable City* (2004) and *London's Boroughs at 50* (2015).

Karel Williams is Professor of Accounting and Political Economy in the Alliance Manchester Business School at the University of Manchester. He works mainly on alternative economic policies for Wales and the devolved English city regions. His most recent article is 'How Cities Work' in the July 2017 issue of the *Cambridge Journal of Regions Economy and Society*.

Part I

England and the Union State

1

Introduction: English Identity and Institutions in a Changing United Kingdom

MICHAEL KENNY, IAIN McLEAN & AKASH PAUN

We cannot readily disentangle Englishness from Britishness in our history or in our institutions. It is better to accept them for what they are, deeply intertwined, and allow the English to celebrate being English and British. Their political allegiance is to Westminster.

Hazell, 'The English Question'

In whichever direction they look, the English find themselves called upon to reflect upon their identity, and to re-think their position in the world. The protective walls that shielded them from these questions are all coming down.

Kumar, *The Making of English National Identity*

I have long believed that a crucial part missing from this national discussion is England. We have heard the voice of Scotland—and now the millions of voices of England must also be heard.

Cameron, 'Scottish independence referendum: statement by the Prime Minister'

1.1 English Questions

ENGLAND, ALONE AMONG the nations of the UK, has no legislature or executive of its own and remains one of the most centralised countries in Europe. It is ruled directly from Westminster and Whitehall by a parliament, government and political parties that simultaneously represent the interests of the UK and England—although this distinction is rarely publicly acknowledged or discussed. Correspondingly, at the level of identity, the English have a greater propensity than the Scots and Welsh to conflate their own nationhood with a sense of affiliation to Britain and its state. As Robert Hazell noted, 'in our history and in our institutions the two identities [of English and British] are closely intertwined, and cannot easily be unwoven' (2006a: 12).

Proceedings of the British Academy, **217**, 3–26, © The British Academy 2018.

This willingness to subsume England into the UK has been seen by many commentators (e.g. Bogdanor 2009: 98–110) as key to the success and stability of the post-1707 union state, which required a new 'invented nation' of Britons to be 'consciously and officially constructed' to bind together the older nations of England, Scotland and Wales (Colley 2009).

With a considerable number of domestic social policy and public service responsibilities devolved to Edinburgh, Cardiff and Belfast, Westminster and Whitehall frequently oversee legislation that applies entirely, or predominantly, to England—albeit with various kinds of indirect or secondary implications for other parts of the UK. But the Government and most politicians at Westminster tend to elide these territorial complexities, talking of setting policy or legislating for 'the nation' or 'the country', whatever the precise territorial application of the announcement in question. Governing England is rarely considered as an enterprise separate from the wider governance of the UK. The key fiscal arrangements underpinning devolution, not least the Barnett formula, which adjusts the budgets of the devolved nations in line with decisions about domestic spending in England and provides for higher public spending in the three devolved nations, further reflect the continued inclination of the political establishment in the UK to fold England's interests into a broader unionist project.

Devolution to the other nations, since the late 1990s, has sparked intermittent debate about whether England should acquire its own representative institutions and whether England's distinct nationhood should be more formally recognised within the institutions of the union state. For many constitutional thinkers and practitioners, however, 'the fundamental difficulty is the sheer size of England by comparison with the rest of the UK' (Hazell 2006a: 9). If the English lion should awaken, it has long been argued, this would disturb the stability of the Union due to England's demographic preponderance and relative economic strength. The post-1999 devolution project was therefore not extended to the largest of the UK's nations (except through weak and often abortive decentralisation initiatives), as part of a strategy of 'territorial statecraft' which prioritises the stability of the union state over the goals of constitutional symmetry or procedural fairness. For the *Economist*'s correspondent 'Bagehot', England's quiet dominance of the UK is its historic prize for willingly subsuming its identity and institutions into those of the wider British nation. This he termed 'England's sensible slumber' (Bagehot 2015).

This line of thinking rests upon established understandings of the British state that have developed over several centuries, including through the writing of the original Bagehot, whose book *The English Constitution* famously used England and Britain effectively as direct synonyms (Bagehot 1867). England gained a majority share in the multinational country that was created through successive unions with its neighbours and this guaranteed that its distinctive interests could never be ignored. But to prevent English dominance from becoming too overt or overbearing, and to reduce the possibility of a nationalist backlash, the English were encouraged to regard themselves first and foremost as part of the new 'imagined community' of Britons.

However, several recent trends and developments have served to erode the assumptions underlying these sentiments, leading to rising tensions over questions of territorial governance and identity across the UK. Devolution to England's smaller neighbours, and particularly the rise of Scottish nationalism in the past decade, has made the English aware, arguably for the first time, that the UK is a union of nations, not a unitary state governed from London. It has also fed a narrative of unfairness towards England, given the absence of a distinct English 'voice' and the visible signs of higher public spending in the devolved nations. At a deeper level, Krishan Kumar argues, the loss of empire, relative economic decline, the challenge of multiculturalism and 'the promise, or threat, of "Europe"', have brought down the 'protective walls that shielded' the English from having to reflect upon their nationhood for so long (2003: 16).

This volume explores these processes and their implications from several perspectives. It includes chapters from leading academic experts on territorial politics, national identity, political parties, public opinion and local government. Through these contributions we aim to offer the most comprehensive scholarly treatment of the English Question since the 2006 volume of that title (Hazell 2006b). In this introduction we draw together the threads of the twelve chapters that follow and explore the key issues—about the governance and identity of the English—which have reanimated the English Question. We also sketch the outlines of a prospective research agenda on these issues. We conclude that the traditional conflation of England and Britain *is* growing harder to sustain, because of the growing politicisation of English national identity and political divergence between the nations of the UK. This has become particularly salient after Brexit, which was 'made in England' (Henderson et al. 2017) in the sense that it was English voters who were the most pro-Leave and, further, because Brexit was backed disproportionately by those who emphasise English over British national identity (Henderson et al. 2016, 2017).

However, the evidence on these issues is far from unambiguous. Within this volume there are competing interpretations of what, if anything, has changed in terms of English nationhood. Trying to capture the collective aspirations and affiliations of 50 million people in singular or simple ways requires enormous simplification and over-reliance upon survey averages and imaginary median voters. And for two additional reasons, the task of interpreting prevalent patterns of national identification is especially challenging in the case of England.

This is, first, because of the deep and widening cleavages running through its political landscape. Even before the EU referendum, it was argued that relative economic decline and the impact of globalisation had brought about a 'bifurcation' of England between so-called 'cosmopolitan' and 'backwater' areas, with the latter more likely to oppose the EU and immigration and to identity as 'English' rather than 'British' (Jennings & Stoker 2016). Brexit appears to have widened these cleavages and, since 'cultural differences are less easily reconciled or subject to political compromise' (ibid.: 372) than the distributional questions that animate traditional left–right politics, a unifying national story has slipped even further out of reach. At the referendum itself, it has been argued, it was not 'England' that delivered the victory for Brexit, but rather the distinct entity of 'England-without-London', where the margin of victory for Leave was a decisive 11 percentage points (Barnett 2017).

Secondly, England—unlike Scotland, Wales and both parts of Ireland—has yet to engage in an extended, reflective national conversation about its place in the post-devolution UK. Even if Brexit did mark the long-anticipated revolt by G. K. Chesterton's 'people of England, that never have spoken yet', it is far easier to identify what the English spoke against than what they spoke in favour of. Amidst the political turmoil that followed the referendum, journalist Fintan O'Toole (2017) echoed Kumar's earlier analysis, concluding that having been 'wrapped up for so long in the protective blankets of Britishness and empire', England 'has not been forced to rethink itself and imagine how it might work in a world where collective identities have to be complex, ambiguous, fluid, and contingent'. England is an ancient nation, but its national consciousness is today both fragmented and conflicted.

1.2 Disentangling England?

In the dozen years that have passed since the publication of Hazell's edited collection *The English Question*, there has been a great deal of change to the constitutional arrangements and territorial politics of the UK. Devolution has been entrenched and extended further in Scotland, Wales and Northern Ireland (until the 2017 breakdown of power-sharing in Belfast). The vote of June 2016 to leave the European Union foreshadows a further period of change and threatens to destabilise further the complex relations between the four nations of the UK, two of which voted to Remain and two, including England (though not London), to Leave.

The question of England's place within the Union has risen in salience in recent years, in both academic and policy terms (Aughey 2007; Cameron 2014; Kenny 2014; McKay Commission 2013 *inter alia*), amidst debates about whether, how and with what implications English national identity has grown more politicised.

Various academic studies report evidence that a distinct and self-conscious form of Englishness has grown in strength (Kenny 2014; Wyn Jones et al. 2012 *inter alia*), although British Social Attitudes (BSA) survey data suggests that, having risen in the early years of devolution to the other nations, attachment to English national identity has not altered much since (Park, Bryson & Curtice 2014: iii). The 2011 Census, meanwhile, found that 60 per cent of respondents in England selected English as their sole identity, compared to 19 per cent for British (ONS 2012: section 7). This headline result in fact obscures an even wider gulf among 'white British' voters, 72 per cent of whom identified as English only. By contrast, 56 per cent of Asian British and 48 per cent of Black British respondents in England identified themselves as British only (ONS 2011, data analysed by authors). This question had not been asked in any previous census, however, so this particular evidence cannot tell us what has changed over time and it does not itself inform us about what weight people place on their sense of national identity. Many respondents appear also to have mistakenly believed they could select only one option, leading to a very low proportion of people identifying as *both* English and British, which several other surveys have found to be the preference of a majority of English residents (Curtice, Devine & Ormston 2013: 148; What Scotland Thinks 2016).

Other studies, meanwhile, have found clear evidence of dissatisfaction in England about the post-devolved union, particularly about levels of public spending in Scotland and the ability of non-English MPs to vote on legislation for England (Jeffery et al. 2014). But, once again, it remains a matter of debate whether or not this reflects a trend of *rising* English discontent.

There is also mixed evidence about the depth of public support for the introduction of devolution to cities and local authorities within England. Few parts of England have a strong sense of regional identity, while regionalism as a serious political force is notable for its absence across most of the country. When asked, voters often express support in opinion polls for the broad principle of passing powers away from Westminster, but they are less likely to vote in favour of creating new political institutions when offered the chance. This was apparent in the 2004 rejection of an elected assembly for the North East. The Greater London Authority (GLA) is an exception to this trend, however. Introduced following a referendum in 1998, giving the office an enhanced degree of legitimacy, the London mayoralty has acquired new powers over time and has given the capital a stronger voice in national debate (Blick & Dunleavy 2017).

Recent electoral trends offer additional evidence that a more distinctively English political culture and system may be emerging. This is reflected in the increased party political differentiation between the four nations of the UK, each of which has been led by different parties since 2010 (albeit that, at time of writing, Northern Ireland is without a government). Perhaps the most dramatic development in this respect has been the rise of the Scottish National Party (SNP), which won a majority in the Scottish Parliament in 2011 and all but three of Scotland's fifty-nine Westminster seats in a 2015 landslide. The Labour Party has retained a dominant position in Wales. In England, the Conservatives have won a majority of seats in three consecutive elections since 2010—by as early as 2005 the party had won more votes than Labour. The rise and subsequent fall of United Kingdom Independence Party (UKIP) was also a predominantly English (and to a lesser extent, Welsh) phenomenon, raising the question of whether the party should be interpreted as a de facto outlet for a resurgent English nationalism (Hayton 2016).

However, institutional responses to these developments have been minimal thus far. The introduction of 'English votes for English laws' (EVEL) in the House of Commons in October 2015 marked a small (and little noticed) move away from the entanglement of Britain and England within the legislature. This reform is of symbolic importance and may come to be seen as the start of a wider phase of English constitutional development (Denham 2015), but on its own it is far from transformational. If English nationalism is a genuine phenomenon, more profound change will surely be demanded, whether through the creation of new English representative bodies, or by redressing other English grievances, for instance by reforming arrangements for funding devolution elsewhere in the UK.

Meanwhile, an incremental form of decentralisation to England's cities and city regions offers the potential for different kinds of answers to any nascent demand for new English representative institutions. The London mayoralty has both profited from and strengthened London's sense of being a place apart from the rest of the country. Time will tell whether the 'metro mayors' elected in seven further English city regions in 2017 and 2018 have a similar impact. The roles were created without referendums, giving the mayors a weaker starting point in terms of profile and legitimacy. Their powers also fall far short of those devolved to the non-English nations, which suggests that despite a willingness in Westminster to let the other nations enjoy greater autonomy, England is still 'regarded as the core of the traditional UK state' and should therefore remain under 'direct rule' from the centre (Sandford & Mor forthcoming). Nonetheless, the history of devolution since the 1990s suggests that, once established, subnational institutions often accrue additional powers, create a focus for the expression of alternative political identities and find creative ways to influence national debate beyond their formal responsibilities.

Debate has also begun in the main UK parties about whether to move to a more decentralised or federal structure, involving greater autonomy for the party at regional or devolved levels, and whether to develop a distinct English party structure. Within the Labour Party, the latter idea has been advocated as necessary to counter 'the sense that Labour did not really believe in England or the English' (Hunt 2016: 1). On the Conservative side, David Cameron made a direct appeal to the English on the day after the Scottish independence referendum, when he announced plans to heed the 'millions of voices of England' and, specifically, to move ahead with the introduction of EVEL (Cameron 2014). These developments have led some scholars to identify a 'revival of an English Toryism which is happy to discard the older clothes of Empire and Union once so important to Conservative identity' (Gamble 2016: 359).

The EU referendum seems almost certain to bring about a profound change in how England is governed. Brexit has already generated an intense focus on constitutional questions across the UK. With Scotland voting heavily in favour of Remain, the Scottish Government raised the spectre of a second independence referendum, while the Scottish and Welsh governments formed an alliance to challenge Westminster over the form that Brexit should take, the impact it should have on devolution arrangements and the role of the devolved bodies in the Brexit process. The future of Northern Ireland has also been rendered uncertain. A majority voted to remain in the EU, but there was a significant pro-Brexit vote amongst unionist supporters. The UK Government has struggled to resolve the question of how Brexit will impact on the Irish border and the UK–Irish relationship.

Faced by these pressures, the UK Government appears to face a choice between the decisive split with the EU that a large number of English voters appear to favour and the stability of the domestic union. Reaching agreement with the devolved governments, and avoiding a hard border in Ireland, points towards a 'softer' form of Brexit. That might in turn provide a conducive environment for powerful appeals to English nationalist sentiment, whether by elements within the major parties or by UKIP (or some potential successor), by channelling disaffection with a deal that allows continued mass migration and maintains England's legal and political entanglement with the EU.

The centre also faces pressure from large English cities concerned about the impact of Brexit on their global economic competitiveness. After the EU referendum, the Mayor of London revived a campaign for powers to raise and retain an increased share of tax revenue (LFC 2013, 2017), while the new cadre of city-regional metro mayors quickly showed willingness to work as a bloc to press Whitehall for further resources and powers (BBC News 2017).

1.3 England and the Union State

Part I of this volume includes four chapters examining England's place in a changing union state. Each employs a different lens to consider evidence for growing public desire and new political incentives to disentangle England from Britain in institutional terms. These chapters also consider the impact of devolution to other parts of the UK and the emergence of the European Question in British politics.

In Chapter 2 Arthur Aughey argues that the stability of the UK has in part rested upon the willingness of unionists to view the constitution through a 'soft focus double vision' that manages to 'see the country as singular while also acknowledging it to be multiple' and that a sharpening of focus upon particular, exclusive national identities within these islands would erode the foundations of the union state. The traditional constitutional orthodoxy has been that 'to differentiate consistently between what is English and what is British is to play a separatist game'.

Unionist statecraft has never required the extirpation of the individual UK nations' distinct identities, which may carry 'powerful and possibly divisive emotional or ethnic meanings' (a similar pattern can be perceived in recent events in Catalonia). Instead, the trick has been to build an inclusive—emphatically civic, rather than ethnic—identity of Britishness, which Aughey has elsewhere called the UK's 'fifth nation' (2010: 272). This was forged from a shared identification with the *institutions* of the UK state and, in particular, with the Parliament at Westminster. Thus 'the British governing wisdom was that identity could look after itself so long as fifth nation allegiance was secure' (ibid.). The success of this unionist 'double vision' for most of the post-1707 period underpins the historian Colin Kidd's observation, referenced by Aughey, that 'unionism [in Scotland] was never the antithesis of Scottish nationalism but was a distinctive form of it'. This enabled Scotland and Wales (less so Northern Ireland) to build a relationship with England in the 'middle ground between the extremes of anglicising unionism and Anglophobic nationalism' (Kidd 2008: 300). But, he asks, are there signs now of 'that ground becoming narrowed, on one direction by English self-interest and in the other by nationalist self-assertion'? The rise of the SNP, the introduction of EVEL and the Brexit vote are all indications, for Aughey, that this may be so.

For Akash Paun, in Chapter 3, the UK territorial constitution is the product of a deliberate strategy of 'constructive ambiguity' so far as the nature and location of sovereignty are concerned. The English doctrine of unlimited parliamentary sovereignty within a unitary state has long co-existed with appeals to popular sovereignty in the other nations of the UK. Devolution since 1999 reflected and further entrenched these alternative constitutional doctrines, admitting the right of the non-English nations to determine their own forms of government and creating, on the island of Ireland, a settlement rooted in non-majoritarian governance and a pluralist conception of sovereignty.

Yet Westminster has never formally conceded that its power to make and unmake any law has been abridged by devolution. Ambiguity has been artfully retained at each step, he suggests, allowing each nation to develop its own constitutional discourse rather than creating a new narrative for the Union as a whole. Making sense of the post-1999 constitution therefore requires a form of 'doublethink', according to legal expert Mark Elliot (2012). Nor did the new settlement recognise the nationhood of England, which became the UK's 'last stateless nation' as a result (Weight 2002: 726, cited in Chapter 2). England was left to slumber on the assumption that it was still satisfied to be governed by 'hybrid Anglo-British institutions in Westminster and Whitehall, which were English before there was a Britain, and remained as such in the eyes of many' (Paun, Chapter 3).

While Aughey posits the narrowing of the unionist middle ground, Paun identifies a widening gap between constitutional theory and practice since 1999. He suggests that the EU referendum result, brought about in part by a more assertive and politicised sense of English national identity, calls into question the ability of constructive ambiguity to continue to bridge this gap. This is illustrated by the various political and legal disputes that have opened up since 2016 between the UK and devolved governments concerning Brexit. Prime Minister Theresa May reflects a traditional Westminster perspective when she maintains that: 'Because we voted in the referendum as one United Kingdom, we will negotiate as one United Kingdom, and we will leave the European Union as one United Kingdom' (May 2017). Yet the Scottish and Welsh governments, and nationalists on the island of Ireland, have made the case that the terms of exit must be agreed between Westminster and the devolved governments due to the impact this process will have on the domestic constitutions of the devolved nations. There is here an appeal to the alternative notion of the UK as a 'family of nations', albeit with Westminster assumed to speak for a still voiceless England.

The two subsequent chapters explore some of the ways in which England and Britain are still elided within the core institutions of the central state. Both examine new pressures for a clearer institutional delineation of England's identity. In Chapter 4, Jim Gallagher searches for signs that an English 'ghost' exists within the Whitehall 'machine', in the sense of a de facto English executive operating within the confines of the British Government. The British Government is comprised of a collection of departments with a varied and confusing set of different territorial remits, reflecting the asymmetrical nature of the devolution settlements created for the other nations within the UK since 1999.

In principle, ministers from departments with remits that are primarily English might operate as an embryonic English Cabinet, for instance by meeting as a subcommittee of the UK Cabinet to consider specifically English affairs. Yet Gallagher finds no evidence that the Government is organised in this way or will be in the near future. Rather, ‘priority is given to policy coherence around topics rather than reflecting the territorial constitution division of power’. The ‘deep entanglement of the government of England and that of the UK’ is most visible in the realm of economic and fiscal policy, he argues. English economic development policy cannot be delineated from the Government’s overall UK economic strategy. Furthermore, fiscal devolution since 2014 notwithstanding, there remains a largely unitary UK-wide system of taxation and resource allocation, with revenue collected by HMRC and distributed to the devolved nations by the Treasury. This system provides that devolved budgets are determined (via the Barnett formula) by choices taken by the UK Government about public spending in England.

Within England itself, there is no equivalent to the Barnett formula and block grant funding mechanisms. Departments such as health and education instead distribute resources according to various formulae and on the basis of differing administrative geographies. Yet data presented in Chapter 4 reveals a clear relationship between social protection spending (pensions and benefits) and public services expenditure at the level of the English regions (although London is an outlier). Gallagher concludes that Whitehall overall ‘sees need for public spending through the same lens for its English responsibilities as its UK-wide ones: no special “domestic English” assessment of need is seen in the numbers’. He concludes that the English ghost ‘remains firmly locked’ within Whitehall’s functionally, rather than territorially, focused machine.

But he also identifies two potential sources for change in this area. One is Brexit, which, as Paun shows, is causing significant conflict between Whitehall and the devolved administrations, particularly on the question of where EU powers returning to the UK should land. Resolving this issue might require Whitehall to distinguish more clearly between English and UK responsibilities in areas such as agriculture and the environment. Yet such a move would run directly against Whitehall’s deep-wired functionalist instincts. A second potential catalyst for change might come from reform of the legislature, either in the form of the new EVEL procedures in the House of Commons, which are considered in more depth in Chapter 6, or from the more radical proposal to create an English Parliament of some kind (the focus of Chapter 5).

In their chapter on this topic, Meg Russell and Jack Sheldon argue that there is significant public dissatisfaction with the perceived unfairness of the UK’s devolution arrangements and some desire for a greater recognition of England within the Union, although support for an English Parliament has not shown a sustained rise in recent years. Nonetheless, a growing number of politicians from both of the main UK parties, as well as UKIP, have backed the idea of a separate English legislature. Consequently, Russell and Sheldon argue, an English Parliament 'can no longer be considered an entirely fringe proposal'.

Two distinct models for an English Parliament have been proposed, but Russell and Sheldon illustrate that proponents have not convincingly set out the implications of either. The more intuitively appealing version is a wholly new 'separately elected' legislature, with similar law-making powers to those of the Scottish Parliament. This would require the parallel creation of a separate English Government to take on responsibility for major public services such as education, health, transport, local government and potentially also policing and justice if these functions were devolved to Wales. Given the huge size of England relative to the other nations, the most common criticism of this model is that made by the Royal Commission on the Constitution in 1973: that 'a federation consisting of four units—England, Scotland, Wales and Northern Ireland—would be so unbalanced as to be unworkable' (Royal Commission on the Constitution 1973: para. 531). This argument leads to the familiar conclusion that England's nationhood cannot be given political recognition if the wider union is to survive.

The alternative model is a so-called 'dual mandate' system whereby MPs for English seats sit separately as an English Parliament for part of the time. This approach can be seen as 'a natural next step from English votes for English laws', in which non-English MPs would be excluded completely from consideration of English business. Instead of the upheaval of creating a wholly new legislature, this model therefore 'appears consistent with the piecemeal and pragmatic way in which the British constitution has often developed'. However, by keeping England and the UK entwined in this way, the dual mandate model would create 'a parliament without a government … creating significant complexity and an apparent accountability gap'. It would also fail to give England a distinct voice in political debate, including, for instance, the Brexit negotiations, the absence of which is a central grievance of many English Parliament advocates. In considering the case for a clearer delineation of English functions within Whitehall, Gallagher likewise concludes that if 'the pressures of English identity politics' are not satisfied by the terms of Brexit, then 'meat much redder' than the 'internal reorganisation of the UK Government' would be needed.

This analysis implies that if the English do wake from their constitutional slumber and begin to demand recognition and equal standing to the other parts of the UK, then only a separately constituted national parliament and government will suffice. It is not clear, however, that they have arrived at this point. The 'soft focus double vision' of traditional unionist statecraft, in which the distinction between England and Britain is intentionally blurred, remains a persistent habit of mind for much of the governing elite. Ultimately, however, unionist statecraft cannot be sustained if the voters demand an answer, or if the major political parties perceive a political advantage in proposing an answer, which is the focus of the subsequent section of this volume.

1.4 Speaking for England? The Political Parties

In Part II of this volume, various authors consider the different ways in which the UK's political parties have begun to engage with a gathering debate about the meaning and salience of English national identity. And they examine some of the dilemmas in terms of public policy and political mobilisation that have arisen as a result. These chapters look in some depth at the relatively neglected, but immensely important, question of whether the Conservative and Labour Parties have shifted their intellectual anchorage away from long-established modes of constitutional thinking and statecraft since the late 1990s. And they explore whether some of the key political and constitutional events that have contributed to the turbulence that has afflicted British politics since 2014 have resulted in parties that are more responsive in their outlook to the divergent political cultures of the different territories within the UK than those of the past. If the political organisations that contest power at the state level are increasingly reflective of national and intra-national differences, what implications does this carry for the UK's political system?

In Chapter 6 Daniel Gover and Michael Kenny offer a historical overview of the evolution of the Conservative Party's thinking towards England in constitutional terms. For much of its history the party has exhibited a deep-seated commitment to the merits of the British system of parliamentary government and a unitary model of sovereignty, a stance which was honed through its uncompromising opposition to various schemes for home rule for Ireland and—more recently—Scotland. Against this backdrop, the party's apparent shift to articulate and appropriate a heightened sense of English grievance, in the aftermath of the Scottish independence referendum of 2014, looks like a departure from a historical pathway in order to pursue a particular tactical goal. Many critics have indeed heaped blame upon the then Prime Minister, David Cameron, for jeopardising the integrity of the UK as a result.

Gover and Kenny query this interpretation. They call upon several important scholarly accounts of the development and character of the Conservative Party's territorial politics to present a rather different picture of how both evolution and change have characterised Conservative thinking on these questions. They consider, in particular, Andrew Gamble's (2016) emphasis on the integral commitment to England underpinning the Tory tradition and the creeping tendency of English Conservatives to regard the domestic union from a decidedly Anglo perspective, a trend which has become all the more prominent in recent times. They rehearse too some of the powerful insights of the late Jim Bulpitt, whose historically grounded account of the successive models of statecraft through which the central state has preserved its hegemony over the different territories and peoples gathered within the UK continues to inform the analysis of territorial politics. His framework, they argue, helps explain the major consequences for the legitimacy of both state and constitution of the rising sense of disenchantment and anger that has arisen from the English 'provinces', a resentment that is directed most powerfully against London and the 'establishment', but which also finds expression in a growing sense of grievance about England and where it sits within the wider union. This deep-seated and slow-burning trend was illuminated by the vote to leave the EU in June 2016 and is the source of major dilemmas for and divisions within the contemporary Conservative Party.

Having sketched these larger historical arguments, these authors delve into one very recent and under-analysed policy episode—the decision by Cameron's new administration in 2015 to pursue the introduction of the complex set of procedures known as EVEL, despite the opposition of every other party represented in the House of Commons. These new rules were introduced through a single vote of the House and are now integral to the legislative process. They carry in their wake various practical and constitutional implications. Gover and Kenny conclude that this complicated and opaque set of arrangements represents a somewhat uncomfortable attempt to reconcile two different political imperatives: the desire to engage and assuage a rising sense of English national consciousness and an intuitive adherence to the institutions and traditions of the United Kingdom. This uneasy fusion, they conclude, has shaped an institutional innovation which is unlikely either to satisfy the audiences it is intended to appease or to gather the wider political support it needs if it is to endure over time. Rather than signalling a decisive shift towards English nationalism, as critics claim, EVEL is in many ways a symptom of an increasingly divided and uncertain Conservative Party faced with a multitude of conflict territorial dynamics and dilemmas, a situation which is likely to be accentuated by Brexit.

In Chapter 7, former Cabinet Minister John Denham offers a unique reflection on the challenges which England posed for the Labour Party during its time in office from 1997 to 2010. He identifies a deep-seated commitment to the idea of delivering a more equitable pattern of distribution and greater social investment through the allocation of resources by the central state as the overriding ethos shaping Labour's territorial politics during this period. This shaped an unyielding belief within the party that England was best governed by the institutions of the British state, an idea that sustained its consistent opposition to the idea that England too deserves devolution.

Turning its face against such an idea, Labour sought to advance a more effective system of regional administration outside London and at times aspired to dress this up as a form of regional government and perhaps even as an answer to the increasingly insistent English Question. This enterprise was undertaken incrementally, and was driven primarily, he reports, by a concern for regional inequality rather than democratic expression. Drawing upon a new set of interviews with some of the key architects and advisors associated with Labour's policy in these years, Denham tracks the development and character of these ideas and charts some of the key debates about governance and policy which they generated. This regional discourse was, he notes, offset by an alternative vision of localism which promoted the merits of city regions and limited forms of delegation to them, an idea which gained some notable adherents from the Blairite political camp. But this perspective was no more able to create a persuasive vision for how England as a whole should be governed.

Denham draws particular attention to the unreflective nature of the orthodoxies that underpinned this ultimately unsuccessful programme; he concludes that Labour's inability to address the democratic deficit which its stance on English devolution entailed has had fateful electoral consequences for the party and may indeed result in long-term damage to the Union itself given that Labour has in recent decades been the only political party that can credibly present itself as a 'national' force in England, Scotland and Wales. Labour was on the defensive too as a result of important changes to English national identity in the early years of the millennium, and it failed to respond to the opportunity to shift its stance and tone on these issues in the wake of the Scottish referendum campaign of 2014.

These chapters suggest that both of the major UK parties were discomfited in different ways by the emergence onto the political agenda of new questions and claims about the governance and identity of England. But one political party appeared—for a while at least—to be a beneficiary of them. This was UKIP, which rose to unexpected prominence but has subsequently fallen back to the margins of British politics. UKIP is commonly viewed as the portal through which the kind of xenophobic and exclusivist nationalism, which the mainstream parties have marginalised, managed to enter British politics. But its relationship with an emergent form of English national sentiment is more complex than this suggests, according to Robert Ford and Maria Sobolewska, writing in Chapter 8. Drawing upon a range of polling data, they highlight the way in which UKIP mobilised a very particular segment of English national identity—but never came to shape or speak to the entirety of this complex phenomenon.

The party was especially adept, they show, at speaking to culturally conservative voters who were disaffected for various reasons with both of the other main parties in British politics. The majority of those drawn to UKIP were from the 'white working class' living outside the largest cities in towns and communities that have acquired the label 'left behind'. They provided the core audience for an increasingly angry and 'ethnic' form of English nationalism. But, importantly, this form of identity politics has produced a strong counter-mobilisation among younger cosmopolitan city-dwellers and many members of ethnic minority groups who remain committed to a liberal and civic ideal of Britishness. In the 2017 general election, these authors suggest, the Conservatives were drawn to competing with UKIP for the loyalties of this 'English' demographic and were therefore increasingly unattractive to those parts of the population who turned to Jeremy Corbyn's Labour Party. Standing back from these very recent trends, they observe how Britishness has long been the form of national identity promoted by the mainstream political parties and the state and has provided a relatively successful vehicle for integrating immigrant communities.

For the English populace as a whole, blurred and overlapping forms of national identity remain the preference of the majority, as most citizens continue to choose to identify as both 'British' and 'English'. But among those who are adamantly 'English', Ford and Sobolewska argue, a distinctive political identity began to form and harden over the past decade. This coheres broadly around the themes of leaving the European Union, restricting inward immigration into the UK and a developing preference for some kind of reform to the existing constitutional settlement so that England is more clearly recognised and indeed protected than at present.

UKIP became an influential and effective carrier for these sentiments, despite various internal tensions associated with its official insistence upon a British model of parliamentary sovereignty. The authors conclude their chapter with an analysis of the way in which this developing pattern of national sentiment played out in the vote to leave the European Union, arguing that 'exclusively English national identity and the radical right nationalism associated with it' was a crucial part of the vote in support of Brexit. The latter, they maintain, was 'thus a powerful expression of the disruptive potential of Englishness'. This was one of the main forces which the new Prime Minister, Theresa May, felt compelled to assuage once she assumed office in the aftermath of the Conservative Party leadership election of 2016, and it is an important attitudinal element within the coalition of support in the Conservative Party for a 'hard Brexit'. In these authors' judgement, this particular form of political Englishness remains difficult to satisfy in the realm of constitutional policy. There is every prospect that the kind of Brexit deal which ultimately emerges will fail to satisfy this constituency. And so, they conclude, we should not write off the prospect of a revival of UKIP.

Despite their different subjects and approaches, each of these chapters sheds light on one of the key—but still relatively under-examined—interpretative questions associated with the politics of English national identity. Have the political parties been predominantly reactive in their attempts to respond to deep-seated changes in the national mood of the English and, if so, have they read the nature and implications of political Englishness correctly? Or, is it the case that they have been more preference-shaping than chasing in terms of this brand of territorial politics? Were, first, UKIP and then, after 2014, the Conservatives, agents of a novel collision between national mood and political behaviour at the mass level? And was it the parties, not the people, who brought the English Question back to the forefront of political life?

1.5 An England of Cities and Regions

In Part III, three chapters explore a different facet of this question—recent and ongoing attempts to introduce devolution to different parts of England, particularly some of its larger urban areas, rather than to the nation as a whole. These chapters examine the patchwork of English local government in the light of recent reforms. They illustrate that these build upon previous changes, a point that has been underplayed in much commentary on them. In London, the GLA (comprising a mayor and an elected assembly) created by the first Blair administration in 2000 represented in essence the re-creation of the Greater London Council (GLC), established in 1965 and abolished in 1986. It was now reconstituted with the same external boundary but with fewer powers and a much slimmer structure than the old GLC. Sadiq Khan, representing Labour, is the third Mayor of London, following Ken

Livingstone and Boris Johnson, who served two terms each. Going back further still, the Local Government Act of 1972 extended the London pattern of a conurbation-level authority with boroughs beneath it to some of the other main urban areas of England: Tyne and Wear, West Yorkshire, South Yorkshire, Merseyside, Greater Manchester and the West Midlands. And at the same time three new counties were formed in other conurbations: Avon (greater Bristol), Cleveland (greater Teesside) and Humberside (greater Hull).

All nine of these authorities had strategic planning, transport and economic development responsibilities. Avon, Cleveland and Humberside also had significant responsibilities for education, social services and highways. The six metropolitan counties were abolished in 1986, at the same time as the GLC, and Avon, Cleveland and Humberside followed in 1996. Most passed unmourned—except perhaps by their staff and elected members[1]—and there has been no attempt to bring back Humberside (the Humber Bridge has proved to be a bridge too far). But in the wake of the reforms introduced by central government in 2017 and 2018, six of these authorities have, in effect, been re-created. Merseyside, Greater Manchester, West Midlands and South Yorkshire have been reborn on precisely their 1973 boundaries, each now with a directly elected 'metro mayor'. The new metro mayoral authority of Tees Valley is similar, but not identical, to the old Cleveland (and does not include most of the valley of the river Tees). The new West of England regional authority would have had identical boundaries to Avon if one of the Somerset suburban districts had not pulled out of the deal. The new authority covers three-quarters of the administrative area of Avon and more than three-quarters of the population.

How and why this re-creation of the local governance architecture of a previous era has happened is one of the central questions addressed in Part III.[2] The main political catalyst for this recent wave of decentralisation was George Osborne, Chancellor of the Exchequer from 2010 to 2016 and MP for a suburban area just outside the Greater Manchester boundary. Together with his junior minister, Jim (Lord) O'Neill, Osborne became an enthusiast for giving more autonomy to dynamic urban areas that were defined, in the new jargon, as 'Functional Economic Areas'. Ministers, and some academic economists, noticed that some conurbations enjoyed faster economic growth than their surrounding areas—an insight first aired in the work of American statistician Harold Hotelling (1929).[3] Subsequent scholars have also observed the phenomenon of 'agglomeration' and noted how experts benefit from the proximity of others, which can create a

[1] Full disclosure: Iain McLean was an elected member and committee (vice-)chair of Tyne and Wear Metropolitan County Council from 1973 to 1979.

[2] This question has also been explored in some depth in the course of the British Academy's Governing England project (British Academy 2017a, 2017b), which convened meetings with local leaders and stakeholders in five regions of England where the Government had offered devolution deals.

[3] Credit should perhaps go to A. A. Cournot, who in 1838 had produced a model in which two owners of mineral springs could exist in a stable duopoly. But nobody understood his work for almost a century.

virtuous economic circle. Associated skills, including in training and recruitment, feed into the further concentration of these centres of expertise. Examples cited by the UK Government (see, for instance, HM Treasury 2016) include media and materials in Manchester, bioscience in Cambridge and motorsport and physical science in Oxfordshire.

In Chapter 9, Mick Moran, John Tomaney and Karel Williams study the case closest to Osborne's heart—the establishment of the Greater Manchester Authority. 'Devo Manc', they say, 'is the product of a deal between symbiotically entwined elites in Whitehall and Manchester City Council' which somehow managed to bring along the nine other boroughs of the former Greater Manchester to support its reincarnation with an elected metro mayor. Both central and local government have published studies of the agglomeration benefits of urban growth in Manchester. The reclamation of derelict land around the Ship Canal afforded three boroughs—Manchester, Salford and Trafford—a good opportunity to allow intensive development (including 'Media City' in Salford and a major new tram extension). There were no direct benefits to the outer boroughs, but their support was required for the successful metro mayoral bid. These authors chart these developments and the networks which shaped them, and they express considerable scepticism about their economic benefits and potential for civic renewal.

Like Greater Manchester, London contains pockets of wealth and poverty in close juxtaposition and its mayor faces a powerful mixture of opportunities and challenges, as Tony Travers demonstrates in Chapter 10. It is now the region with the highest GDP per head of any in the UK, by some margin (see Table 11.1, in Chapter 11). Its size and wealth afford its mayor the opportunity to exert considerable influence beyond his formal responsibilities. But what about those responsibilities themselves? The most important powers of the metro mayors (including the Mayor of London) are transport and policing. As Travers notes, the chief office of Transport for London (TfL) has 'managed the operation of the city's massive urban rail and bus systems, the introduction of congestion charging, the Oyster card, cashless payments, delivering a bike hire scheme, the transfer of the Overground, a series of major station improvements and the construction of Crossrail'. And in comparison with other parts of the national rail system, 'official statistics suggest TfL has been significantly more effective at service and infrastructure delivery than the national rail operating companies'.

At the time of writing it is too early to say whether the powers of the other newly created metro mayors will be deployed to make significant improvements to the transportation systems of their areas. One problem is that the integrated transport networks of the former metropolitan counties, including the four that are now back in existence, were dispersed after 1986. Tees Valley, West of England and Cambridge–Peterborough have never had integrated transport. Indeed, if significant and overdue transport investment is to come to Cambridge and Peterborough, it is likely to arrive from a separate source—the National Infrastructure Commission's (NIC) proposals for development of the Oxford–Cambridge corridor (NIC 2016).

The proposed remedy in this instance comes from an unelected body, not a metro mayor. Oxfordshire is one area where the local authorities could not agree on a bid, while none was offered to Milton Keynes, Northamptonshire or Bedfordshire.

The wider fiscal aspects of devolution are at the heart of Chapter 11. Here, Iain McLean shows that public expenditure per head is spread very unevenly across the regions of England, with apparently little relationship to relative need. London—the wealthiest part of England—receives more public expenditure per head than any other and, notably, more per head than any of the five northern and Midlands regions which are all considerably poorer. Whatever lies behind these relative differentials, they do not reflect a calculation of relative need. And since they have almost exactly the same geography as the Leave and Remain votes in the 2016 referendum, these differences are potentially extremely significant.

McLean explores an alternative perspective upon territorial spending, which focuses on incentives rather than need. Spatial redistribution might be attempted in a way that encourages growth and does not reduce the incentive to tax efficiently. Here, the main problem is the very low proportion of locally raised tax in the UK. In England, the only local tax is the council tax, yet, even with this, national politicians cannot resist interfering. The ratio between the tax rate in each band is fixed in law and councils cannot alter them. Councils have little incentive to grow their council tax base in the most obvious way—by granting planning permission for new housing to be built on their patch. But the planning system is fundamentally asymmetrical: those who already have houses have a voice to use against development and those who do not, lack one. The other main property tax in the UK—business rates—was nationalised in 1989. There are proposals to relocalise it, either for areas with devolution deals or for everywhere. Either approach would be desirable, he suggests, but the two options tend to work against each other. If they are relocalised only for areas with devolution deals, then only they have an incentive to grow their local business tax bases. If they are relocalised everywhere, then what was the point of creating the metro mayor authorities?

Indeed, one striking part of the recent story of devolution in England is the slender nature of the financial incentives offered to 'Devo Manc' and the other areas that agreed these deals. In return for taking on some expensive liabilities—such as some health care in Greater Manchester—they were offered tax transfers (which may grow more slowly than their spending needs) and a fairly trivial lump of extra revenue.

The geography of local government in England is now extremely uneven, McLean concludes, and potentially unsustainable. There are areas with devolution deals and areas without. Most, though not all, of the former are urban areas, but not all the conurbations outside London have them. The 'Northern Powerhouse' policy was designed to encourage growth in the densest parts of large cities. But what about the rest of the country and the citizens of places such as Cumbria, Lincolnshire and Devon? Recent initiatives have created an uneven patchwork and the patches are poorly sewn together.

1.6 English Identity and Attitudes

The two final chapters, in Part IV of this volume, probe some of the existential questions which have surfaced in recent debates about the English Question. Who now are the English? Is their nationhood of ancient vintage or expressed through a new kind of political nationalism? And what do we know about what the English want in constitutional terms. In Chapter 12 Sir John Curtice scrutinises data from a range of public attitude surveys and opinion polls to analyse the interconnection between English identity and constitutional preference. And then, finally, Michael Kenny in Chapter 13 considers the case for 'a stronger sense of history as crucial to generating a deeper understanding' of English national consciousness.

Curtice notes that the case for devolution in the UK has tended to invoke three quite distinct arguments, drawing respectively on the concepts of *fairness*, *identity* and *good governance*. One might devolve power to tackle unfairness in how a particular territory is treated, to create institutions that better reflect people's sense of identity, or to improve the quality of government—for instance by ensuring that policy decisions are taken closer to those affected rather than by an overburdened central state. In the case of Scotland, Wales and Northern Ireland, all three arguments pointed towards the same solution: the establishment of new 'national' devolved institutions.

But in the case of England, these different arguments may well pull in different directions. If the problem to be solved is over-centralisation, then devolution to cities and regions seems the sensible response. But if the issue is that the post-1999 constitution is 'unfair' to England, because of the lack of English institutions and legislative autonomy, then options such as an English Parliament or a strengthened form of EVEL may be appropriate. And if we want institutions that better align with underlying patterns of identity, we must first establish the strength of popular affiliation with Britishness, Englishness and other local and regional identities within England, and then respond accordingly.

Curtice cautions in particular against hyperbolic claims about the impact in England of devolution to the other nations. His analysis of various polling sources leads him to suggest that 'there may well have been some increase in English identity in the early years of devolution', but 'there is no evidence of any continuing trend thereafter'. When asked by pollsters to choose between the two competing national affiliations, around two-fifths of people tend to opt for Englishness over Britishness. When offered a wider range of choices (using the so-called Moreno methodology),[4] the choice of 'equally British and English' is the most popular. This, he thinks, suggests that 'for many the two identities are still regarded as largely interchangeable'.

[4] The 'Moreno Question' offers respondents five options to best describe the balance of their affiliation with two identities. Applied in England, the options are: 'British not English'; 'More British than English'; 'Equally British and English'; 'More English than British'; 'English not British'.

On the key question of whether the English are in favour of devolution, Curtice argues that 'at first glance, the answer to this question is a straightforward "Yes"', but pro-devolution sentiment is rather shallow. Voters tend overwhelmingly to favour the *principle* of more decisions being taken locally, but they are reluctant to embrace its logical corollary: that policy in areas such as housing, transport or education might vary between parts of the country. There is little data that allows comparisons between different parts of England. That which exists suggests 'perhaps a slight hint that support for some form of regional government may be a little higher in the North of England'. Curtice also finds that, London aside, it is residents of the North of England who express greatest pride in their own region.

When asked about the governance of England as a whole, around 50 per cent of English voters prefer England to be 'governed as it is now, with laws made by the UK parliament', a finding that seems broadly in line with Hazell's cautionary argument that seeking to disentangle the English from Britain is misguided, since 'their political allegiance is to Westminster' (2006a: 12). And yet, if half of respondents are content with the status quo, it follows that the other half are not. The latter group are quite evenly split between those preferring regional and all-England solutions, Curtice reports. He concludes that 'there is far from widespread support for major institutional change in England, but equally … there is a substantial current of discontent with existing arrangements'. There is also consistent evidence of strong support for barring non-English MPs from voting on English matters (EVEL), in line with the case for institutional reform that hinges on the notion of territorial 'fairness'.

Curtice also finds that support for reforms such as regional devolution and an English Parliament has 'oscillated in response to the changing public policy agenda'. The evidence of a relationship between elite and public attitudes raises some significant questions. If, as some of the other authors in this volume have attested, the mainstream political parties are now more willing to appeal directly to English national sentiment, and if high-profile 'metro mayors' spark a new kind of local civic pride, might we see public attitudes move further away from support for the status quo? At the same time, given the strength of populist sentiments, might attempts to shore up the old union state provoke a nationalist backlash rooted in a sense of English grievance—perhaps channelled against a future Brexit deal?

In the final chapter of this volume Kenny argues against the recent tendency to view English nationalism as the main 'culprit' in relation to Brexit and calls instead for 'an appreciation of how fractured and contested the interpretation of English nationalism has always been, and remains'. Assertions of English national pride have become increasingly associated with 'a discernible pattern of thinking about sovereignty, national self-determination and self-government' and support for Brexit may well be one manifestation of this sentiment. Yet there are real dangers of over-generalisation and of reducing a complex set of social and cultural motivations to simplistic slogans about English nationalism: 'in both conceptual and empirical terms, debate about this phenomenon is in its infancy', he concludes. Undoubtedly for some voters in England—and indeed elsewhere—the idea of Brexit did come to embody a 'sense of righteous commitment', allowing the disgruntled to reject the 'policies and priorities of the governing elites and to signal major concerns about the erosion of national sovereignty'. But it is less clear precisely what these sentiments mean in institutional terms. Did the English vote for a reassertion of the traditional Westminster-centred constitution, or was this a call for 'a more bounded and delineated conception of an English polity', more clearly separated from the other nations of the UK?

The idea of English national self-assertion has long been dismissed and denounced for its 'lingering association with Enoch Powell', a connection which 'served to make many progressives distant from, and wary of, nearly all actual manifestations of Englishness'. Kenny takes the thinking of progressive intellectual Tom Nairn (1977, 2000) to be a particularly influential embodiment of such an approach. He considers other interpretations too, notably the idea that Englishness is a manifestation of an enduring post-imperial crisis—a theme developed in the work of historical sociologist Krishan Kumar (2003, 2006, 2016). The British imperial project had in large part relied upon the readiness of the English to pour their nationhood into the more inclusive conception of Britishness, a thinner national construct which allowed space for the other nations of the UK and the peoples of Britain's global empire. As a result, the English fell out of the habit of celebrating their nationhood or telling their own national story as distinct from that of the empire they ruled. The loss of empire, on this reading, has led to an extended identity crisis and Englishness has become 'necessarily more exclusive, resentful and anxious' in comparison with nationalisms elsewhere (including elsewhere in these islands). Kenny challenges this reading, pointing out that one could equally argue that it is the English who are 'turning against the ethos and assumptions of "Greater Britain", rather than seeking comfort from a nostalgic reincarnation of it'. Brexit, in other words, might be viewed as 'the expression of a national consciousness directed against the policy priorities and approaches of a British establishment which still hankers after great power status'.

The unwillingness of the governing elite to engage with ideas of English nationhood, he concludes, has resulted in very little extended public debate about the traditions and characteristics of England's nationhood. The rather confused picture of public opinion painted by Curtice may indeed be a reflection of this absence, rather than evidence that the English are broadly content with their current constitutional position.

1.7 Conclusion

Governing England is a relatively under-studied subject in comparison with the governance of the smaller UK nations and of the UK as a whole. As Henderson et al. argue, 'to focus explicitly on England and its national identities goes against the grain of conventional understandings of UK politics' (2017: 632). As part of what these authors call a 'triple effacement' of the complexities of contemporary territorial governance, studies of British politics often ignore Northern Ireland altogether, leave Scotland and Wales to area specialists and fail to treat England as a separate 'unit of analysis', thus studying 'the United Kingdom as a fictive country: Anglo-Britain' (ibid.).

One of the core aims of this volume, and the British Academy programme from which it emerged, has been to correct this imbalance. In particular, this collection examines the complex relationship between changing patterns of identity and questions of institutional legitimacy. England is a divided nation and debate about its nationhood is embryonic. We therefore do not offer simple, overarching conclusions about what the English want, but in each of the four parts of this book we explore signs of change at the level of both identity and institutions and highlight several key shifts.

First, England's relationship with the other nations of the UK has been transformed by devolution, leaving England as the only nation subject to 'direct rule' from Westminster, while also undermining the ability of the English majority at Westminster to shape the governance of the UK as a whole. This has become ever more apparent since the EU referendum, as the complications of the Irish border and the determination of Edinburgh and Cardiff to defend their interests in the Brexit process have frustrated the ability of the UK Government to 'take back control' from Brussels on its own terms. As Brexit proceeds, there will be a strong need for in-depth research into the changing relations between the four nations of the UK and the extent to which the English remain willing to accept the compromises necessary to maintain the stability of the union state.

Secondly, there are signs of change in the attitudes struck by the main UK parties towards England as a political community. The Conservatives appealed directly to English national sentiment in the aftermath of the Scottish independence referendum and during the 2015 general election campaign. This was in part a response to the UKIP insurgency, arguably the closest England has come to a serious nationalist movement of its own. UKIP's rapid decline since 2016 raises another crucial question, which we hope that future research will explore: Will departure from the EU address the root concerns of the millions of English voters who turned out to vote for Brexit, and if not, what will be the political outlet for this latent discontent? Labour's response will be significant. The party's deep aversion to Englishness appears to have undermined its position in its English heartlands without preventing decline in Scotland, where, despite a partial revival at the 2017 general election, Labour has fallen to third place behind both the SNP and the Conservatives. How Labour should adapt to the shifting sands of English identity politics will be a crucial question both for those on the progressive side of politics and for academics seeking to make sense of changing patterns of political affiliation.

Thirdly, the excessively centralised nature of England's polity has been recognised for some time, but attempts by successive governments to redress this have been half-hearted and often undermined by countervailing tendencies to reinforce central control. The weakness of regional identities across most of England is one explanation for the absence of genuine devolution within England. It is no coincidence that London has been the major exception to this trend. The more recent devolution initiatives are built on weaker foundations, but now that they are established, they may create a valuable opportunity to learn more about how identity and institutions interact at the subnational level. Will the new metro mayors and combined authorities facilitate the emergence of new city-regional political communities and what implications might this have for English governance and identity as a whole? And, finally, will London further evolve into a distinct political entity within the UK and how will that affect its relationship with the rest of England and the central state?

Fourthly, underlying these various sets of questions is a more fundamental quandary of how to conceive of contemporary forms of political Englishness. This volume includes competing views including the contentions that little has changed, that Englishness has been captured by populist nationalism, and that a more progressive and inclusive Englishness is struggling to emerge. English—and British—politics in 2018 is in a state of flux and there is real danger that observers mistake temporary tremors for a more profound tectonic shift. It will be for future researchers to determine whether or not this recent period has marked a turning point in the governance and national consciousness of England.

Whatever change there has been in recent years, England and Britain *are* still deeply intertwined in terms of both governance and identity and are likely to remain so for the foreseeable future. It remains true, as Hazell concluded, that 'we cannot readily disentangle Englishness from Britishness in our history or in our institutions' (2006a: 12), but equally apt is Kumar's prescient observation that 'In whichever direction they look, the English find themselves called upon to reflect upon their identity, and to re-think their position in the world' (2003: 16). As Kenny concludes in Chapter 13, there are 'momentous decisions that lie ahead for the English and their political representatives' as England refashions its relations with Europe and the wider world and, in all probability, with the other nations of these islands; and, also, as some of England's most powerful urban regions seek a new relationship with the centre.

We hope in this volume to have shown the value of the academic contribution to emerging debates about England and the UK's constitutional future and to have made the case for sustained scholarly and political consideration of the dilemmas facing the English over the coming years. As recent events have shown, predictions about politics are for the foolhardy. We cannot be certain how the English will come to feel about their nationhood and system of governance. What we can say is that the English are not at ease with how they are currently governed, even though it is not yet clear how they would like to be.

References

Aughey, A. (2007), *The Politics of Englishness* (Manchester, Manchester University Press).

Aughey, A. (2010), 'Fifth Nation: the United Kingdom between definite and indefinite articles', *British Politics*, 5(3): 265–85.

Bagehot (2015), 'England's sensible slumber', *The Economist*, 18 June.

Bagehot, W. (1867), *The English Constitution* (London, Chapman & Hall).

Barnett, A. (2017), *The Lure of Greatness: England's Brexit and America's Trump* (London, Random House).

BBC News (2017), 'England mayors call for more tax control', 1 November, http://www.bbc.co.uk/news/uk-england-41832231, accessed 21 January 2018.

Blick, A. & Dunleavy, P. (2017), 'Audit 2017: how democratic is the devolved government of London?', Democratic Audit, 26 June.

Bogdanor, V. (2009), *The New British Constitution* (Oxford, Hart Publishing).

British Academy (2017a), *British Academy Governing England Conference 2017* (London, British Academy), https://www.britac.ac.uk/sites/default/files/Governing%20England%20July%20Conference%20Write%20Up.pdf, accessed 8 November 2017.

British Academy (2017b), *Governing England: Devolution and Mayors in England* (London, British Academy), https://www.britac.ac.uk/sites/default/files/Devolution%20and%20mayors%20in%20England.pdf, accessed 8 November 2017.

Cameron, D. (2014), 'Scottish independence referendum: statement by the Prime Minister', Gov.UK, 19 September, https://www.gov.uk/government/news/scottish-independence-referendum-statement-by-the-prime-minister, accessed 17 January 2018.

Colley, L. (2009), *Britons: Forging the Nation 1707–1837*, 3rd rev. edn (New Haven, CT, Yale University Press).

Cournot, A. A. (1838), *Recherches sur les principes mathématiques de la théorie des riches* (Paris, Hachette).

Curtice, J., Devine, P. & Ormston, R. (2013), 'Devolution: identities and constitutional preferences across the UK', in A. Park, C. Bryson, E. Clery, J. Curtice & M. Phillips (eds), *British Social Attitudes 30* (London, NatCen Social Research), 139–72.

Denham, J. (2015), 'The Anglicisation of English politics', *Demos Quarterly*, 6, https://quarterly.demos.co.uk/article/issue-6/on-devolving-power/, accessed 2 July 2018.

Elliott, M. (2012), 'The British constitution, devolution and "doublethink"', *Public Law for Everyone*, https://publiclawforeveryone.com/2012/09/13/the-british-constitution-devolution-and-doublethink/, accessed 15 June 2018.

Gamble, A. (2016), 'The Conservatives and the Union: the "New English Toryism" and the origins of Anglo-Britishness', *Political Studies Review*, 14(3): 359–67.

Hayton, R. (2016), 'The UK Independence Party and the politics of Englishness', *Political Studies Review*, 14(3): 400–10.

Hazell, R. (2006a), 'The English Question' (London, Constitution Unit), https://www.ucl.ac.uk/political-science/publications/unit-publications/130.pdf, accessed 2 July 2018.

Hazell, R. (ed.) (2006b), *The English Question* (Manchester, Manchester University Press).

Henderson, A., Jeffery, C., Wincott, D. & Wyn Jones, R. (2017), 'How Brexit was made in England', *British Journal of Politics and International Relations*, 19(4): 631–46.

Henderson, A., Jeffery, C., Lineira, R., Scully, R., Wincott, D. & Wyn Jones, R. (2016), 'England, Englishness and Brexit', *Political Quarterly*, 87(2): 187–99.

HM Treasury (2016), 'Northern Powerhouse strategy', https://www.gov.uk/government/uploads/system/uploads/attachment_data/file/571562/NPH_strategy_web.pdf, accessed 8 November 2017.

Hotelling, H. (1929), 'Stability in competition', *Economic Journal*, 39(153): 41–57.

Hunt, T. (ed.) (2016), *Labour's Identity Crisis: England and the Politics of Patriotism* (Winchester, Centre for English Identity and Politics).

Jeffery, C., Wyn Jones, R., Henderson, A., Scully, R. & Lodge, G. (2014), *Taking England Seriously: The New English Politics* (Edinburgh, Centre on Constitutional Change).

Jennings, W. & Stoker, G. (2016), 'The bifurcation of politics: two Englands', *Political Quarterly*, 87(3): 372–82.

Kenny, M. (2014), *The Politics of English Nationhood* (Oxford, Oxford University Press).

Kidd, C. (2008), *Union and Unionisms: Political Thought in Scotland, 1500–2000* (Cambridge, Cambridge University Press).

Kumar, K. (2003), *The Making of English National Identity* (Cambridge, Cambridge University Press).

Kumar, K. (2006), 'Empire and English nationalism', *Nations and Nationalism*, 12(1): 1–13.

Kumar, K. (2016), *The Idea of Englishness: English Culture, National Identity and Social Thought* (London, Routledge).

LFC (London Finance Commission) (2013), *Raising the Capital: The Report of the London Finance Commission* (London, GLA).

LFC (London Finance Commission) (2017), *Devolution: A Capital Idea* (London, GLA).

McKay Commission (2013), *Report of the Commission on the Consequences of Devolution for the House of Commons* (London, HM Government).

May, T. (2017), 'Prime Minister: Britain after Brexit: a vision of a global Britain', speech at Conservative Party Conference, 2 October, http://press.conservatives.com/post/151239411635/prime-minister-britain-after-brexit-a-vision-of, accessed 8 September 2017.

Nairn, T. (1977), *Break-Up of Britain* (London, New Left Books).

Nairn, T. (2000), *After Britain: New Labour and the Return of Scotland* (London, Granta).

NIC (National Infrastructure Commission) (2016), 'Cambridge—Milton Keynes—Oxford Corridor: interim report', https://www.gov.uk/government/uploads/system/uploads/attachment_data/file/569867/Cambridge-Milton_Keynes-Oxford_interim_report.pdf, accessed 8 November 2017.

ONS (Office for National Statistics) (2011), 'LC2202EW—National identity by ethnic group', https://www.nomisweb.co.uk/census/2011/lc2202ew, accessed 9 April 2018.

ONS (Office for National Statistics) (2012), 'Ethnicity and national identity in England and Wales: 2011', https://www.ons.gov.uk/peoplepopulationandcommunity/culturalidentity/ethnicity/articles/ethnicityandnationalidentityinenglandandwales/2012-12-11, accessed 9 April 2018.

O'Toole, F. (2017), 'Brexit's Irish Question', *New York Review of Books*, 28 September, http://www.nybooks.com/articles/2017/09/28/brexits-irish-question/, accessed 6 April 2018.

Park, A., Bryson, C. & Curtice, J. (eds) (2014), *British Social Attitudes: The 31st Report* (London, NatCen Social Research).

Royal Commission on the Constitution (Kilbrandon Commission) (1973), *The Report of the Royal Commission on the Constitution* (London, The Stationery Office).

Sandford, M. & Mor, F. (forthcoming), 'England plus? Territory, identity and fiscal devolution in the UK', *British Politics*.

Weight, R. (2002), *Patriots: National Identity in Britain 1940–2000* (Basingstoke, Macmillan).

What Scotland Thinks (2016), 'What is your national identity? (English views, "Moreno" Question)', http://whatscotlandthinks.org/questions/what-is-your-national-identity-english-views-moreno-question#table, accessed 9 April 2018.

Wyn Jones, R., Lodge, G., Henderson, A. & Wincott, D. (2012), *The Dog that Finally Barked: England as an Emerging Political Community* (London, IPPR).

2

England and Britain in Historical Perspective

ARTHUR AUGHEY

2.1 Introduction

FOLLOWING A DECADE of intense constitutional debate in the 1970s about accommodating nationalism, the logic of devolution and the possible break-up of Britain, Richard Rose (1982: 4–5) wrote that too many books and articles had been published explaining events that did not happen. Written in another period of constitutional uncertainty like our own, it is wise to keep Rose's caveat in mind and to be careful not to confuse contingent and significant trends. How one can avoid doing so is not self-evident. In retrospect, Rose's *Understanding the United Kingdom* can be read as anticipating a transition in modern British history, announcing the re-emergence of the 'territorial dimension in government', though it can be understood otherwise as the return of the 'national question'. To grasp its implications, Rose argued that it was necessary to understand what he awkwardly called 'the present meaning of past history'. Twenty-five years later, Robert Colls (2007: 525) put it more felicitously: national identity is based on historical relationships, not on 'national values', and is intimately connected to constitutional practice. His interpretation of the 'present meaning' of the past was more radical than Rose's. It was that relationships 'of the British people are now so much more diverse' such that older forms of constitutional history and political identity could be relied upon no longer. That insight informs the discussion in this chapter. It considers the relationship between England and Britain from distinct, if related, angles of historical and constitutional vision.

The first of these angles of vision is national. One looks out from England to other parts of the United Kingdom and the other looks in to England from other parts of the UK. The second is constitutional. One looks out from Westminster to other parts of the UK and the other looks in to Westminster from other parts of the UK. The argument of the chapter is that the historical bias of the English/Westminster angles of vision have been singular and uniform; the bias of those looking in have been multiple and diverse. 'Bias' is used deliberately because these angles of

Proceedings of the British Academy, **217**, 27–44, © The British Academy 2018.

vision are both unionist. Britishness may involve blurring national and regional distinctions, ignoring national and regional distinctions or celebrating national and regional distinctions. The problem which Rose thought central to understanding—and defending—the integrity of the United Kingdom remains today. It is a matter of 'double vision': how to see the country as singular while also acknowledging it to be multiple. Indeed, one can argue (to adapt an expression of W. H. Greenleaf) that singularity and multiplicity delimit the boundaries to which Britishness is confined. And the practical challenge for unionist politics has been to do justice to territorial diversity while maintaining the unity of the country. To adapt a line from Seamus Heaney, the object has been to make nation and constitution rhyme. Doing so involved a question of perspective which replicated politically the tension between singularity and diversity (Boyce 1998: 8–9): 'was the United Kingdom inhabited by a single nation, however much regional or even patriotic differences might distinguish its component parts'; or was it 'one whose national distinctions made it essential that they should be given some constitutional recognition?' Boyce was referring to the Irish Home Rule crisis. That crisis had demonstrated the danger of nation and constitution, unity and diversity, failing to rhyme because of partisan commitments and polarised positions. After 1921, Boyce's question was not so much answered as blurred in unionist constitutional 'double vision'.

In the Scottish case, Colin Kidd (2008: 300) has argued convincingly that Scotland's relations with England have been conducted mainly 'in the vast yet variegated terrain which constitutes the middle ground between the extremes of anglicising unionism and Anglophobic nationalism'. That middle ground could be found not only in Scotland but also in Wales (it is vanishingly small in Northern Ireland). Kidd described its character as 'banal unionism' while Rose had called it 'unthinking unionism'. Both terms identified the possibility of that ground becoming narrowed, in one direction by English self-interest and in the other by nationalist self-assertion. The chapter explores this variegated terrain, the forces which have sustained and the forces which threaten it, in order to bring contemporary debate about England and Britain into more fruitful dialogue with political history. It begins with a reminder of disagreement between two eminent historians on the matter of these angles of vision and what that disagreement revealed about England's relationship with Britain. It considers, secondly, the intersection of the national and the institutional in what Colls referred to as constitutional 'personality'. The chapter concludes with some reflection on whether unionist 'double vision' can continue to plot a stable path for England and Britain.

2.2 Cranks and Rows

The date is 1975, the year when the United Kingdom had its first referendum on membership of what was then called the European Communities, when Northern Ireland's place within the Union was being debated in a constitutional convention and when the Labour Government published its White Paper 'Our Changing

Democracy: Devolution to Scotland and Wales'. The occasion was the publication of J. G. A. Pocock's landmark essay 'British History: A Plea for a New Subject'. That essay had been provoked by Pocock's realisation that perspectives on English and British history had to be rethought as the UK joined the European Community. Here was another example of double vision, looking in from New Zealand, a tangential, 'antipodean perception', reminding readers of a 'greater', formerly imperial, British identity (Pocock 2005: 3). The correlation of contemporary constitutional change—actual or prospective—and historical reflection was not coincidental but intentional. Pocock's argument (1975: 603) was stated concisely: 'no true history of Britain has ever been composed'. Instead there were mainly histories of England (looking out), in which the Welsh, Scots and Irish appeared as 'peripheral peoples when, and only when, their doings assume power to disturb the tenor of English politics' and 'histories of Wales, Scotland, Ireland, and so forth, written as separate enterprises' (looking in to England). By contrast, the new historical subject which Pocock (1975: 620) wanted to explore would be neither 'monolith' (singular, English) nor 'fragment' (diverse, Welsh, Scots or Irish), but their complex interrelationship or what was to become known as 'four nations history' (Kearney 1995). The success or otherwise of that enterprise is not the concern of this chapter, but it is worth considering the sort of 'monolithic' English mentality against which Pocock was writing.

The subject of his criticism was A. J. P. Taylor's (1965: v) provocative statement, in the preface to his Oxford *English History: 1914–1945*, that he intended to use English as an all-embracing term for things British. As Pocock observed (1975: 602–3)—especially with regard to Taylor's habit of using 'Scotch' for 'Scots'—there are parts of the world in which men are killed for less. Taylor's use of language, he thought, revealed an eminent English historian willing to declare that the word 'Britain' had no meaning for him and that he had 'no more than an obligatory sense of identity with any of the peoples of his island group other than his own'. Taylor (1975: 622–3) was given the opportunity to comment on Pocock's article and his reply disclosed a certain 'English idea of Britain'. It is noteworthy that he brought together both national and constitutional perspectives, observing that everyone knew the important historical institution was Parliament, 'which can be called English or British according to choice'. The difference in wording was trivial, Taylor thought, and of interest only to people who wanted a row, whom he dismissed summarily as 'nationalist cranks'. Taylor always enjoyed a bit of coat-trailing but it is interesting that Roy Hattersley (2006) shared a similar view of nationalist crankiness more or less the same time as the publication of *English History: 1914–1945*, remarking that '50 years ago, when I first went to Edinburgh, Scottish nationalism was an old lady giving away leaflets in Princes Street on a Saturday night'. If Taylor proposed that it was irrelevant to distinguish English from British, he also identified what once was the pragmatic solution for those who held his certain 'English idea of Britain' (looking out from England and Westminster). If confusion arose about what was English and what was British, then one should avoid having a row. This, of course, is a very *English* way of looking at things.

The style of *British* politics which it informed assumed that the UK was stable and enduring such that questions of national identity could be deemed trivial. Even in 1975 Taylor's Anglocentricity seemed at odds with contemporary political trends.

Pocock thought Taylor's use of language betrayed a monolithic English perspective, but one can deploy a more inclusive, British, defence of his argument: that to differentiate consistently between what is English and what is British is to play a separatist game fit only for nationalist troublemakers. If, in the Taylor version, England had become Britain (and vice versa) it was also true that Britishness relied upon the political solidity of England. According to Margaret Canovan (1996: 79; also Stapleton 2005) the key to stability in the United Kingdom is not only that the Scots, Welsh and Northern Irish feel comfortable being British but also that the English do. The relationship requires this sort of soft-focus double vision. If the English had become British in a fit of absence of mind, so too had things English become part of the common British inheritance. If one anxiety of the non-English has been the appropriation by the English of things British, one benefit has been the reciprocal appropriation of things English by those who are not English. To think in that manner does not necessarily weaken any local sense of identity; rather it can enhance that belonging by participating in a larger collective identity. That was certainly the traditional intellectual understanding of the Union. Considering Scotland's relationship with England, Dicey & Rait (1920: 320) argued that the Union had caused no problem for England—indeed its identity had achieved Canovan-like 'perfect security' in Britishness (a harmonious rhyming of the national and the constitutional)—but that this had been more difficult for Scotland. Yet in accepting their common British identity, both nations had preserved 'as much of the noble spirit and traditions of their separate nationality as may be compatible with the wider sense and the extended patriotism which ought to bind together all the citizens of one politically united country' (1920: 326). In sum, Dicey & Rait (1920: 362) held that the Union secured political unity (singularity) while keeping alive what they called 'the nationalism both of England and Scotland' (diversity). These were complementary angles of that British 'double vision'. In that same tradition, Ernest Barker (1927: 17) also believed that the United Kingdom had become a state 'both multi-national and a single nation', which—in language which recalled George III—enabled 'its citizens at one and the same time to glory both in the name of Scotsmen or Welshmen or Englishmen and in the name of Britons'. That melodious rhyming can be called 'high unionism' and it assumes political harmony to be the norm. It has been an enduring historical perspective even if (Northern) Ireland, for good reason, rarely featured in it—though Mrs May (2016) made a pointed exception when becoming Prime Minister. In this perspective, 'nationalism', or self-interest, should be contained by 'extended patriotism' or mutual solidarity.

For example, thirty years after *English History: 1914–1945*, Noel Malcolm (1998: 50–3) articulated an intelligent, non-confrontational, version of the Taylor doctrine. Any journalist, he wrote, knows that he or she will get a letter of complaint 'from some hyper-sensitised Scot who says you wrote "England" when you should have written "Britain"'. Nevertheless, Malcolm believed that English journalistic confusion—or mental laziness—helped to hold the UK together. He supposed that most people (he meant the English) do not classify politicians into national categories. Yet he went on to argue that once 'separate primary political consciousnesses have been developed that make people think of themselves first of all as English as opposed to Scottish, and so on', then real problems would emerge for the stability of the Union. Malcolm conceded that if the Scottish National Party (SNP) could persuade 'Scots that they are primarily Scots' then a very large step would have been taken towards the dissolution of the UK. When he wrote, that concern appeared to be a constitutional cloud no bigger than a man's hand, for the middle ground of British politics still seemed secure. Two decades later and the cloud of competing national mandates hanging over an extended British patriotism has become much darker and larger—and not only from the angle of looking in to England. It could also affect the English angle of vision. Indeed, Malcolm had been writing for a Conservative readership and was particularly exercised by the history of Conservative Party temptation to exploit Englishness for electoral gain. In 1894, for example, one party pamphlet (McKenzie & Silver 1968: 54–5) argued that Conservatives had won a majority of English seats but were denied office 'entirely due to Irish, Welsh and Scotch votes'. England had been denied its rights and its affairs controlled by other parts of the country 'while these are free from the interference of Englishmen'. Here was intimated not only the West Lothian Question but also the warnings of Conservative general election campaigns in 2015 and 2017.

Again looking out from England, in his famous address to the Royal Society of St George, Stanley Baldwin had wished (1927: 1) he could use the word 'English' in his speeches without someone at the back of the hall always interjecting 'British'—though one suspects that the reverse would be true today, especially at Conservative Party meetings (Goodman 2017). Of course, Baldwin was not seeking a 'row', he was not trying to encourage 'nationalist cranks', he had no intention of questioning the enduring value of the UK—especially when it had just lost most of Ireland—and he was the author of the integrative idea of 'one nation' Conservatism (Lexden 2016). He was joking. Today one can find similar examples, only this time without the humour and with a subversive English nationalist edge. When, as Prime Minister, Gordon Brown tried to define his 'British Way'—a Labour version of Baldwin's 'one nation'—it was pointed out by one academic critic (Lee 2011: 160) that most of his references and quotations were not British at all but *English*, as also noted by John Denham in Chapter 7. Those seeking a row in this case were not the usual ('Scotch') suspects of Taylor's and Malcolm's experience but those English who believed Brown's Britishness meant the 'negation of England'. In short, the 'nationalist cranks' now seeking 'a row' were no longer those looking in to England and Westminster but those looking out—something which Taylor had considered inconceivable. Views from within or without which differentiate absolutely 'ours' from 'yours' radically disturb the double vision of high unionism—exactly as Malcolm feared.

2.3 Constitutional Alternatives

In the first two decades of the 20th century it appeared likely that the second of Boyce's alternatives—national distinctions should be given constitutional recognition—would become established in British constitutional thought and practice. In response to the Irish Question, the prospect of a federal, 'home rule all-round' arrangement was widely canvassed immediately before and after the First World War. If the damnable question was Ireland (looking in to England), then the vexatious question for any symmetrical answer was England (looking out to Britain). In 1911, Churchill's proposal in the cabinet committee had ruled out an English Parliament because it would be too powerful in relation not only to the other home rule parliaments but also to Westminster, although this idea may yet come back onto the agenda, as discussed in Chapter 5 by Russell and Sheldon. This was also the question for which the Speaker's Conference on Devolution 1919–20 found no resolution and where the same judgement was made about the imbalance of a distinctive English mandate in the affairs of the United Kingdom (Evans 2015). It continued to be the judgement of the Royal Commission on the Constitution (1973) half a century later as well as of the Constitution Unit (Hazell 2006a: 241) thirty years after that.

If these convictions were based on a *British* perspective of constitutional order, there was an *English* political disposition at work. Linda Colley (2014: 153) recounted how, in 1911, one journalist had pronounced: 'If Home Rule for England presents serious problems we had better face them at once. They are not going to be solved by either postponing them or ignoring them.' Here one can detect a pattern in constitutional politics from an English and Westminster angle of vision. If the moment always involves urgency, the longer view always suggests inaction. Vernon Bogdanor (2015) suggested a reason why English politicians did postpone, and then ignore, the question: 'home rule all round' got nowhere mainly because it required 'pulling up the British constitution by its roots to solve the Irish problem and imposing upon England a form of government it did not want purely to satisfy the Irish nationalists'. It was always better to avoid those problems, especially when that meant avoiding rows with nationalist cranks. Therefore, Lord Irvine's famous remark—the best way to deal with the West Lothian Question is to stop asking it—actually has sound historical pedigree. Furthermore, Bogdanor (2015) suspected that there would be a similar (English) response today, because any proposal for federalism would require imposing a 'probably unwanted system of government in England purely to accommodate the Scots'. The English Question is not a recent phenomenon but a historical problem (Evans 2015: 30), yet even as the claims of English nationhood (Kenny 2015) move up the political agenda the obstacles to its satisfactory resolution still seem formidable.

The *political* history of the 20th century confirmed the first of Boyce's constitutional perspectives: that the United Kingdom was 'a single nation, however much regional differences distinguished its component parts'. It was a perspective which the Conservative Party continued to defend until Tony Blair's electoral landslide in 1997. It held that the cultural uniqueness of each part of the country was worth recognising and its symbols worth cherishing—John Major's (1996) justification for returning the Stone of Scone from Westminster Abbey to Scotland—but that it was axiomatic that the whole, defined in terms of parliamentary sovereignty, remained far greater than the sum of its parts. It admitted bureaucratic differentiation—for example conceding the establishment of the Scottish and Welsh Offices—but considered national democratic institutions a threat to the Union. Here is yet another connection to the Taylor/Pocock debate. Taylor (1965: 236) famously argued that in 1921 Lloyd George had conjured the Irish Question 'out of existence'. If one ignored Northern Ireland's self-government—and Westminster, on the basis of the ruling of the Speaker of the House of Commons in 1923 which excluded devolved matters being discussed in Parliament, was happy to do just that (Bogdanor 1998: 10)—Lloyd George's conjuring act appeared to have settled the English as well as the British Question, removing both national and constitutional questions in one fell swoop.

Thus the historian G. M. Young (1947: 86) observed that for his generation, Ireland had become the great unknown: 'It is difficult for a generation like ours, which probably does not think of Ireland once in a month, to recover the atmosphere, the sentiment, of a generation which thought of nothing else.' And when in 1927 Barker had wondered at the 'somehow' of British stability, reconciling its nations to singularity and diversity, amnesia about Ireland was clearly an important element of that 'somehow'. A suitably sceptical note was later entered by Anthony King (2007: 2) who thought it quite remarkable that constitutional historians, when writing of the British constitution's evolutionary character, paid little attention to the secession of most of Ireland from the Union. The traditional approach, according to King (2001: 41) had suffered—as Young had conceded a half century earlier—to a 'truly breathtaking extent from selective amnesia'. Amnesia was conducive to the complacency of that English idea of Britain we find in Taylor and of a certain intellectual complacency that all angles of vision had a common focus on Westminster. Despite his scepticism, even King (2001: 40) conceded that, as a rule of thumb, the British 'were confident in their national identity, confident in the cohesion of the United Kingdom and confident in the country's ultimate social cohesion. The traditional constitution did not address the question of national unity for the simple reason that the question did not arise.' One major reason for this absence of the national question was party political.

The resolution of the Irish Question emphasised the sovereignty of Parliament as well as the authority of central government and coincided with the interests of the major political parties. Maurice Cowling (1971) has written of a political transition in this period from an era of constitutional obsession, about which Young wrote, to what in 1922 *The Spectator* (cited in Evans 1998: 24–5) called the 'maintenance of the moral, political and commercial fabric of the nation'. For Cowling, the 'impact of Labour' in 1920–4 announced 'the beginning of modern British politics', where the emphasis shifted, as *The Spectator* advised, to issues of class, wealth creation and its redistribution. It was now convenient *not* to think about national questions and thus convenient *not* to think about the Union. This became Rose's (1982: 67) era of 'unthinking' unionism, one in which it was assumed—apart from a few nationalist cranks on Edinburgh's Princes Street—that the state could be taken for granted because there existed cross-party agreement on the constitution (see Harvie 2000). If there was such a thing as a 'post-war consensus' it was to be found here. According to Bogdanor (2011: 59), the major parties had different concerns but their positions broadly coincided in support of Westminster sovereignty and opposition to constitutional recognition of national distinctions (or devolution). Conservatives opposed devolution, fearing 'it would lead to the break-up of the kingdom'. By contrast, the Labour Party argued that 'devolution would deprive Westminster not so much of sovereignty, as of power: the power to correct territorial disparities', contributing to the party's centralist instincts discussed by John Denham in Chapter 7.

Where sovereignty and power intersected, there could be found agreement on the value of the 'traditional' constitution, even if the traditional practices celebrated were not ancient at all, but relatively novel and sometimes controversial (Hailsham 1978). To adapt Pocock's distinction, it appeared that the 'monolith' of parliamentary sovereignty had absorbed the peripheral fragments into what scholars came to call 'the Westminster model'. From this angle, national identity was defined politically—representation in Parliament—the definition the Royal Commission on the Constitution had favoured in its 1973 report. That integrative relationship of nation with constitution was expressed in the carefully chosen words of Lewis Namier (1958: 47) as one which had 'produced a British island nationality which comprises the English, Scots and Welsh, and to which Ulster adheres', one which meant that the 'political life of the British island community centres in its Parliament at Westminster which represents men rooted in British soil'. Here was identified the 'vast yet variegated' middle ground of England *and* Britain.

Another of Taylor's points (1976: 21–2) captures succinctly this state of mind. He thought that conventional wisdom on the constitution, found in works of historical and constitutional authority, was based 'on the principle that Whig plus Tory equals eternal truth'. He identified a correspondence of interest between political stability and material progress, which was expressed in any number of great speeches on the constitution. Disraeli's (1872) address at Manchester Trade Hall set the tone for all those platform speeches which followed by celebrating the constitution in the traditional Tory language of 'Queen, Lords, and Commons' but justifying it in the Whig language of progress—'the unbroken application of scientific discoveries to your welfare, and the comfort and convenience of men'. It proved to be also a potent, cross-party combination and marked another intellectual middle ground. As the philosopher Michael Oakeshott (2014: 339) confided to his notebook in 1944: 'Progress & continuity. So firmly grounded in our non-doctrinaire system of politics, we were not tempted' to throw over continuity for abstract perfection. Twenty years later, however, Oakeshott (2014: 485) introduced a note of caution into that historical perspective: 'England, on the whole, has come to terms with its memories of wrongs. Not so Scotland or Ireland.' The trope of nationalist grievance looking in to England and Westminster is revealed as an irritant to harmony in the state. Such qualification notwithstanding, scholars as well as politicians replayed a great rhyming melody, often forgetting that there were different historical perspectives and that these perspectives were capable of changing. Lord Salisbury had warned of sentimental illusions in politics and that one should never consider 'rhapsody' (constitutional myths, for example) 'an adequate compensation for calculation' (Roberts 1999: 2). Yet how did the UK function if the Irish—and later Northern Irish—case revealed its fragile potential when nationalists were determined to have a serious row?

2.4 Constitutional Angles of Vision

Colls provided one persuasive answer to that question (2002: 43). He argued that there have been two connecting wires running through the history of the UK. The first of these wires is 'being British' and, because 'being British' is not particularly ethnic, 'it was the nearest the United Kingdom got to a concept of citizenship'. The second of these wires is being Scottish or English, Welsh or (Northern) Irish, identities with powerful and possibly divisive emotional or ethnic meanings. To avoid serious constitutional rows, Colls identified a distinctive British governing strategy. 'It was vitally important to the United Kingdom not to get the wires crossed' and he thought the fact that those in power were generally successful in keeping the wires apart demonstrated that there were, and are, more ways than one to be national, 'even in the same nation' (the point which Barker had made earlier about unity in diversity). As J. C. D. Clark (2000: 275–6) put it, membership of the UK seldom meant 'demanding of its members a deeper acknowledgement of kinship with their neighbours than they were willing, informally, to give', the relationship between the nations displaying the resilience of diverse identities rather than the rigidity of a unitary one: 'This produced a polity with strengths and weaknesses; although it could not mobilize an ethnically homogeneous "people", it had the strength of accommodating regional differences in a system which imposed on England, Scotland, Ireland, and Wales no novel, abstract formula.' If the English, looking out, could think of themselves as part of a unitary state under Westminster sovereignty and others, looking in, could believe that they had (at least in part) a contractual relationship with Westminster, well and good (Keating 2010: 379–81; see also Akash Paun in Chapter 3). Constructive ambiguity can be—well—constructive. So, when David McCrone (2013: 473) asks: 'Might it be, however, that the Scots and the English have different conceptions of what "British" means?' the clear answer is 'yes'—to which one can add the Welsh and the (Northern) Irish.

From the English and Westminster angle of vision, historians, journalists and constitutional lawyers—for example, Bagehot and Dicey—rarely talked of the British but mostly of the English constitution: 'Nineteenth-century English constitutionalism was essentially a story of the triumph of liberty over tyranny, a story extended by English beneficence to Scots and others' (Colls 2002: 45–6; also

Bogdanor 1996: 183–6). When Taylor defended his position on the historical irrelevance of distinguishing British and English, his starting point had been this tradition of constitutional thought. The official description of constitutional practice as the Crown-in-Parliament, Colls thought (2002: 53), remained the 'English constitutional way of seeing the nation whole' and did its duty as a powerful 'integrationist myth'. An important aspect of that integration was blurring distinctions between English and British, ironically the very thing which irritated the non-English. This blurring was more administrative convenience than national arrogance because, looking out from England, the simplest thing to do was to assume that the UK was a single homogenous nation (Rose 1982: 29). The perspective was that of the British post-war centralised state and it became deeply ingrained culturally. When devolution was debated in the 1970s, Hugh Seton-Watson (1979: 272) complained that civil servants 'think in bureaucratic categories, use bureaucratic language and are on a different wavelength' from those looking in from Scotland, Wales and Northern Ireland. Seton-Watson's lament about Westminster corresponded with a later English grievance. According to Jim Bulpitt (1983: 237), the British Government 'attempted to relate to (or distance itself from) all parts of the country in a similar fashion' and, when looked at from Westminster, England was not the centre but just another 'part of the periphery'. One may call this angle of vision the highest of high unionism, so very high in its transcendent sovereign unity that Nevil Johnson (1977) believed the British political elite incapable of thinking seriously about either nation or constitution. It was an accusation later made of Tony Blair's approach to reform (Norton 2007; also Hazell 2006b: 6). What was that accusation? It was that New Labour's devolution policy subscribed to Boyce's second option—conceding constitutional recognition to the nations looking in to England and Westminster—but assumed still—looking out from England and Westminster—the UK remained, as before, a single (political) nation. In short, with devolution, one can argue that Colls' lines did get crossed. Ambiguity can also be unhelpful and provoke disagreement between England and Britain.

Take one famous political exposition of the English and Westminster angle of vision: Enoch Powell's speech to the Royal Society of St George in 1961. When he spoke of England's identity it was to institutions that he referred and Powell (1969: 339–40) was certain that what bound the nation together were its traditions of 'government and lawgiving'. He argued that institutions 'which elsewhere are recent and artificial creations appear in England almost as works of nature, spontaneous and unquestioned'. Unquestionably for him, those institutions were—in their *fons et origo*—English and not British. Even that symbol of national unity, the monarchy, remained English despite all the multinational leeks and thistles and shamrocks that had been grafted onto it: 'The stock that received all these grafts is English, the sap that rises through it to the extremities rises from roots in English earth, the earth of England's history.' Powell was also announcing, a decade before Pocock's 1975 essay, the end of the Greater Britain vision or what one Ulster Unionist once called 'the world mission of the British Empire in the interests of civil and religious freedom' (Sinclair 1912: 173). Half a century after Powell it was

'England's structure' which took the central role in Robert Tombs' monumental history (2014: 881), detailing England's powerful central government, ancient tradition of representation, effective common law and sovereign parliament. One finds reference (Tombs 2014: 330) to Englishness as 'the root-stock of Britishness onto which the others were grafted', even though Tombs considered England also to be—in a rather unflattering analogy of the United Kingdom—'the front legs of the pantomime horse, taking the main part in setting the common direction in domestic, foreign and imperial matters'. Such an arrangement could gallop along well enough so long as the back legs and the front legs wished to go in the same direction according to the same rules. Unthinking unionism (Rose 1982: 214) and the centrality of Westminster in political life assumed that, as the gallop continued, 'what is important for England will never be overlooked'.

On both counts—setting a common direction and securing particular interests—this is now in doubt. When Lee had challenged Brown's Britishness as a 'denial' of England he was stating an ever-growing view. For example, Richard Weight (2002: 726) had concluded *Patriots* with reference to a stubborn, self-serving British political elite who left the English 'the last stateless nation in the United Kingdom' adrift and silenced. In short, England's interests *were* being overlooked and its identity disregarded. That great institutional inheritance, bequeathed by English to the British, was now being operated to their disadvantage. What was being disturbed—albeit expressed as an emergent public mood rather than a distinctive nationalist movement—was the stabilising intimacy of England's unthinking Britishness (Aughey 2010). The grievance articulated was national—who spoke for England now?—as well as constitutional—how was England, the 'gaping hole' (Hazell 2006a) in the devolution settlement, to be justly governed?

The second angle of vision, which looks in at England from the rest of the UK, inverts the institutionalism of Powell and Tombs. Though he appreciated the political and cultural weight of England's influence in the United Kingdom, Krishan Kumar (2003: 256) wrote that very few institutions are English as opposed to British and this was 'true of Parliament, the monarchy, the law courts, the civil service, the armed forces, the broadcasting system and practically every other important national institution'. In his view, participation in the UK by what was once called the 'Celtic fringe' served to guide the front legs of the pantomime horse for everyone's mutual benefit. Colin Kidd demonstrated convincingly how the 'nationalism', about which Dicey & Rait had written, functioned in the history of a wider British patriotism. As he argued (Kidd 2008: 6–8), Scotland's relationship with England was compatible with depths of cultural nationalism and its 'grammar of assent did not preclude criticism of England', most evident in the *Schadenfreude* whenever English teams do badly at sport. The characteristic tone of Scottish politics was often 'incomprehensible or even offensive to English ears' and much the same may be said about the historical relationship between the Welsh or even loyal Northern Irish Unionists and England. Indeed, one of the central insights to be found in Kidd (2008: 20–1) is that unionism, again echoing Dicey & Rait, was never the antithesis of Scottish nationalism but was a distinctive form of it. Britishness was an expression of defensive national self-interest in relation to England (again, something similar may be said of Wales and Northern Ireland). What distinguishes this version of nationalism from that of the SNP is that it has been comfortable with British patriotism. Sporting *Schadenfreude* and its variants, which so annoy the English, should not be confused with hostility either to being British (nationhood) or to the UK (constitution). Indeed, Kidd (2008: 24) thought that, for two centuries after the 1707 Act of Union, if a Scottish Question existed it was something of a non-question. In the modern era, both Labour and Conservative Parties were happy that it should remain that way: in short, no rows please, we're British. This was Kidd's 'banal unionism', casual and generally unquestioned.

Looking in to England and Westminster, of course, banal unionism was not the only perspective. The year 1975 was equally significant for the publication of another academic work, Michael Hechter's *Internal Colonialism: The Celtic Fringe in British National Development*. This book came from a very different academic tradition than Pocock's but it also pointed to what the latter thought to be absent in modern historical scholarship—attention to how the 'multiple peripheries' of the UK interact with each other and with England. Hechter's significance was to throw down a challenge to the received model of post-war British politics which had mainly occluded questions of national identity. Though most academic critics dismissed Hechter's distillation of history into England *versus* the rest—Anthony Birch (1976: 232), for example, gave 'little credence to the notion that the Celtic regions could be usefully compared to colonies' exploited by the English—the book was in tune with an emerging discourse which integrated radicalism, nationalism and anti-imperialism, a mixture to be found in Tom Nairn's influential *The Break-Up of Britain* (1977) published two years later. Nairn's book appeared in the same year as the Queen's Silver Jubilee, while in her Address to Parliament on 4 May even Her Majesty (HM The Queen 1977) had detected an awakening 'awareness of historic national identities in these islands'.

The question which Hechter asked was: Why has nationalism not been *more* assertive in British history? It was a question—as well as an invitation to action—which fitted neatly into an increasingly influential nationalist world view which not only questioned but also rejected 'banal unionism' and believed unionist double vision a suitable case for treatment. One historian claimed that Scotland has been important to English ideas of Britishness, yes, but there could never be what the Irish had learned to call national 'parity of esteem'. For Pittock (2009: 302)—with intimations again of the general election campaigns in 2015 and 2017—'Scottish behaviour perceived to challenge existing arrangements, or even to take perceived advantage of them, is met with an outbreak of negative stereotyping intended to stress English solvency, responsibility, civility, temperance, balance, and generosity by highlighting Scots as possessed of the opposite characteristics.' And from a Welsh angle of vision, John Osmond (cited in Rose 1982: 30) thought that history demonstrated the 'refusal of the English to participate in the idea of Britishness' if that meant taking seriously the claims to equal recognition of the other nations in the United Kingdom. Three recent examples illustrate the forces which threaten to disrupt the middle ground which Kidd, Rose and others believe has sustained the UK.

The first is the 2014 Scottish referendum which compelled the 'variegated terrain' to separate into the binary positions of yes and no to independence. The consequent polarising effect in politics did not do justice to the complexity of perspectives, which is why so many Scots have felt wary about a second poll, a wariness which helped the Scottish Conservative Party at the expense of the SNP in the 2017 UK general election. Linda Colley (2014: 93) observed astutely that the change over the last fifteen years has been 'not so much a rise in Scottish nationalism, as the emergence of a different kind of Scottish nationalism', one not complementary to—but antagonistic to—Britishness. Moreover, she was struck by how many Scots she met (interpreting history in Hechter's terms) who complained of being 'colonised' by the English or by London.

The second is the European Union referendum in 2016. The Scottish journalist Chris Deerin (2017) employed the image of three small nations tied to the back of an English elephant and observed that because 'Jumbo wants something different' on Brexit 'Jumbo is going to have what it wants', irrespective of the views of the rest of the UK. This was both an unfair characterisation of the vote (Wales also voted Leave) and a fair expression of the political fallout. To use Tombs' image, the pantomime horse no longer looked in step. A United Kingdom referendum (in which the decisive weighting is English) and the sovereignty of Westminster (in which the majority of MPs are English) can be defended as constitutionally just but it comes up against that alternative legitimacy which had so worried Malcolm: people thinking of themselves as primarily Scots or English rather than British. On Europe the people have spoken, yes—but who are the people? Kidd's response (2016) to the EU referendum result was to revisit the unionist slogan of 2016 and ask: 'Better Together with whom?' The common ground of England and Britain, he thought, had narrowed dangerously.

The third illustrates well a clash between these two angles of vision. It can be found in the debate over 'English votes for English laws' (EVEL), discussed by Gover and Kenny in Chapter 6. For those advocating EVEL, here was an opportunity to address England's democratic deficit by way of modifications in House of Commons' procedures. It was proposed as a pragmatic way to rebalance the Union and to address that 'gaping hole' in the devolution settlement, even if many thought it inadequate (Montgomerie 2015). For those opposing it, mainly non-Conservative MPs from Scotland, Wales and Northern Ireland, EVEL was an infringement of the equal status of electoral representatives from all parts of the UK and a further threat to its integrity (as the Royal Commission on the Constitution had defined it).

2.5 Conclusion

After the Second World War, the intention of the organising committee of the Festival of Britain (1948)[1] was to emphasise 'that diversity within unity which is an essential ingredient of our democracy'. That is a fair statement of the intersection of the national and the constitutional angles of vision which focus on the Union's common ground. It was restated by Gamble & Wright (2009: 7) sixty years later when they argued that Britishness does not only mean membership of a political association, national identity meaning something else: 'Britishness is about both, but they are not the same.' Traditionally, Britishness for Scots, Welsh and Northern Irish (Unionists) has asserted affinities with the English but without the requirement to become English. In England, Britishness being interchangeable with Englishness secured the solidarity of 85 per cent of the population with the interests of the other parts of the United Kingdom. The relationship has been an enduring one, though, as this chapter has argued, a changing one. History suggests the paradoxical notion of 'elective affinity' (Aughey 2016), a notion which referendums in Northern Ireland (1973) and Scotland (2014) confirm. In short, nations elect (consent) to stay in constitutional relationship with one another and that relationship exhibits affinity (connection) which gives substance to being British. That paradox has required unionist double vision such that nation and constitution appear stable. Major constitutional challenges—Scotland, Europe and demands for greater recognition of England's political voice—intimate greater difficulties in reconciling those two angles of vision.

References

Aughey, A. (2010), 'Anxiety and injustice: the anatomy of contemporary English nationalism', *Nations and Nationalism*, 16(3): 506–24.

Aughey, A. (2016), 'The elective affinity of the New Elizabethan nation', in I. Morra & R. Gossedge (eds), *The New Elizabethan Age: Culture, Society and National Identity after World War II* (London, I.B.Tauris), 95–115.

Baldwin, S. (1927), *On England* (London, Philip Allan).

Barker, E. (1927), *National Character and the Factors in its Formation* (London, Methuen).

Birch, A. H. (1976), 'The Celtic fringe in historical perspective', *Parliamentary Affairs*, 29(2): 230–3.

Bogdanor, V. (1996), *Politics and the Constitution* (Aldershot, Dartmouth).

Bogdanor, V. (1998), 'Devolution: the constitutional aspects', in The University of Cambridge Centre for Public Law, *Constitutional Reform in the UK: Principles and Practice* (Oxford, Hart Publishing), 9–20.

Bogdanor, V. (2011), *The Coalition and the Constitution* (Oxford, Hart Publishing).

[1] I would like to thank Dr Carol-Ann Barnes for this reference.

Bogdanor, V. (2015), 'The crisis of the constitution', *New Statesman*, 23 April, http://www.newstatesman.com/politics/2015/04/vernon-bogdanor-crisis-constitution, accessed 3 March 2017.

Boyce, D. G. (1988), *The Irish Question and British Politics 1868–1986* (Basingstoke, Macmillan).

Bulpitt, J. (1983), *Territory and Power in the United Kingdom* (Manchester, Manchester University Press).

Canovan, M. (1996), *Nationhood and Political Theory* (Cheltenham, Edward Elgar).

Clark, J. C. D. (2000), 'Protestantism, nationalism and national identity, 1660–1832', *Historical Journal*, 43(1): 249–76.

Colley, L. (2014), *Acts of Union and Disunion* (London, Profile Books).

Colls, R. (2002), *The Identity of England* (Oxford, Oxford University Press).

Colls, R. (2007), 'After Bagehot: rethinking the constitution', *Political Quarterly*, 78(4): 518–26.

Cowling, M. (1971), *The Impact of Labour 1920–1924: The Beginning of Modern British Politics* (Cambridge, Cambridge University Press).

Deerin, C. (2017), 'Why Scotland needs two more referendums', *CapX*, 20 March, https://capx.co/why-scotland-needs-two-more-referendums/, accessed 20 March 2017.

Dicey, A. V. & Rait, R. S. (1920), *Thoughts on the Union between England and Scotland* (London, Macmillan).

Disraeli, B. (1872), 'Speech of B. Disraeli at the Free Trade Hall', Manchester, 3 April, *Bristol Selected Pamphlets*, http://www.jstor.org/stable/60249422, accessed 15 August 2016.

Evans, A. (2015), 'Back to the future? Warnings from history for a future UK constitutional convention', *Political Quarterly*, 86(1): 24–32.

Evans, S. (1998), 'The Earl of Stockton's critique of Thatcherism', *Parliamentary Affairs*, 51(1): 17–35.

Festival of Britain Committee (1948), 'Transcript of statement made by Mr Gerald Barry', Minutes, 31 May, COM/4/A/7.

Gamble, A. & Wright, T. (2009), 'Introduction', in A. Gamble & T. Wright (eds), *Britishness: Perspectives on the British Question* (Oxford, Wiley-Blackwell), 1–7.

Goodman, P. (2017), 'Scotland, independence—and our survey finding: Are Conservative Party members just about unionist?', *ConservativeHome*, 2 March, https://www.conservativehome.com/thetorydiary/2017/03/scotland-independence-and-our-survey-finding-are-conservative-party-members-just-about-unionist.html, accessed 2 March 2017.

Hailsham, Lord Q. (1978), *Dilemma of Democracy: Diagnosis and Prescription* (London, Collins).

Harvie, C. (2000), 'The moment of British nationalism, 1939–1970', *Political Quarterly*, 71(3): 328–40.

Hattersley, R. (2006), 'Home rule all round', *The Guardian*, 13 March.

Hazell, R. (2006a), 'Conclusion: What are the answers to the English Question?' in R. Hazell (ed.), *The English Question* (Manchester, Manchester University Press), 220–41.

Hazell, R. (2006b), 'Wave upon wave: the continuing dynamism of constitutional reform', The Constitution Unit, https://www.ucl.ac.uk/political-science/publications/unit-publications/129.pdf, accessed 18 July 2017.

Hechter, M. (1975), *Internal Colonialism: The Celtic Fringe in British National Development* (London, Routledge and Kegan Paul).

HM The Queen (1977), Silver Jubilee address to Parliament, 4 May, http://news.bbc.co.uk/1/hi/uk_politics/1959535.stm, accessed 19 June 2018.

Johnson, N. (1977), *In Search of the Constitution: Reflections on State and Society in Britain* (Oxford, Pergamon).

Kearney, H. (1995), *The British Isles: A History of Four Nations* (Cambridge: Cambridge University Press).

Keating, M. (2010), 'The strange death of unionist Scotland', *Government and Opposition*, 45(3): 365–85.

Kenny, M. (2015), 'The return of "Englishness" in British political culture: The end of the unions?', *Journal of Common Market Studies*, 53(1): 35–51.

Kidd, C. (2008), *Union and Unionisms: Political Thought in Scotland, 1500–2000* (Cambridge, Cambridge University Press).

Kidd, C. (2016), 'Where are we now? Responses to the referendum', *London Review of Books*, 38(14), https://www.lrb.co.uk/v38/n14/on-brexit/where-are-we-now, accessed 19 July 2017.

King, A. (2001), *Does the United Kingdom Still Have a Constitution?* (London, Sweet & Maxwell).

King, A. (2007), *The British Constitution* (Oxford, Oxford University Press).

Kumar, K. (2003), *The Making of English National Identity* (Cambridge, Cambridge University Press).

Lee, S. (2011), 'Gordon Brown and the negation of England', in A. Aughey and C. Berberich (eds), *These Englands: A Conversation on National Identity* (Manchester, Manchester University Press), 155–73.

Lexden, Lord A. (2016), 'Stanley Baldwin and the birth of one-nation conservatism', 17 August, https://www.alistairlexden.org.uk/news/stanley-baldwin-and-birth-one-nation-conservatism, accessed 2 March 2017.

McCrone, D. (2013), 'Whatever became of the British?', *Political Quarterly*, 84(4): 470–7.

McKenzie, R. & Silver, A. (1968), *Angels in Marble: Working Class Conservatives in Urban England* (London, Heinemann).

Major, J. (1996), 'The text of Mr Major's speech on the British constitution, made on 26th June', http://www.johnmajor.co.uk/page846.html, accessed 20 March 2017.

Malcolm, N. (1998), 'A reply', in J. Barnes, *Federal Britain: No Longer Unthinkable?* (London, Centre for Policy Studies), 50–3.

May, T. (2016), 'Statement from the new Prime Minister Theresa May', https://www.gov.uk/government/speeches/statement-from-the-new-prime-minister-theresa-may, accessed 19 August 2016.

Montgomerie, T. (2015), 'Never mind Scotland. What about the rest of the UK?', *CapX*, 10 February, http://www.capx.co/ten-parts-of-the-uk-even-more-deserving-of-attention-than-scotland/, accessed 12 December 2016.

Nairn, T. (1977), *The Break-Up of Britain: Crisis and Neo-Nationalism* (London, New Left Books).

Namier, L. B. (1958), *Vanished Supremacies: Essays on European History, 1812–1918* (London, Hamish Hamilton).

Norton, P. (2007), 'Tony Blair and the constitution', *British Politics*, 2: 269–81.

Oakeshott, M. (2014), *Notebooks, 1922–86*, ed. L. O'Sullivan (Exeter, Imprint Academic).

Pittock, M. (2009), 'To see ourselves as others see us', *European Journal of English Studies*, 13(3): 293–304.

Pocock, J. G. A. (1975), 'British history: a plea for a new subject', *Journal of Modern History*, 47(4): 601–21.

Pocock, J. G. A. (2005), *The Discovery of Islands: Essays in British History* (Cambridge, Cambridge University Press).

Powell, E. (1969), *Freedom and Reality*, ed. J. Wood (Kingswood, Elliot Rightway Books).

Roberts, A. (1999), *Salisbury: Victorian Titan* (London, Weidenfeld & Nicolson).
Rose, R. (1982), *Understanding the United Kingdom* (Harlow, Longman).
Royal Commission on the Constitution (1973), *Volume I: Report*, Cmnd 5460 (London, HMSO).
Seton-Watson, H. (1979), 'History', in C. Maclean (ed.), *The Crown and the Thistle: The Nature of Nationhood* (Edinburgh, Scottish Academic Press), 272–305.
Sinclair, T. (1912), 'The position of Ulster', in S. Rosenbaum (ed.), *Against Home Rule: The Case for the Union* (London, Frederick Warne & Company), 169–81.
Stapleton, J. (2005), 'Citizenship versus patriotism in twentieth-century England', *Historical Journal* 48(1): 151–78.
Taylor, A. J. P. (1965), *English History; 1914–1945* (Oxford, Oxford University Press).
Taylor, A. J. P. (1975), 'Comment', *Journal of Modern History*, 47(4): 622–3.
Taylor, A. J. P. (1976), *Essays in English History* (Harmondsworth, Penguin).
Tombs, R. (2014), *The English and their History* (London, Allen Lane).
Weight, R. (2002), *Patriots: National Identity in Britain 1940–2000* (Basingstoke, Macmillan).
Young, G. M. (1947), 'Government', in E. Barker (ed.), *The Character of England* (Oxford, Clarendon Press), 104–17.

3

Sovereignty, Devolution and the English Constitution

AKASH PAUN

3.1 Introduction

SOVEREIGNTY IS A DUSTY old subject. The very word carries unmistakeable echoes of the pre-democratic era of monarchical rule. Yet its nature and location have become highly contested questions in contemporary discourse about the UK constitution and England's relationship with the other nations of these islands, not least in the aftermath of the 2016 EU referendum.

This chapter argues that the constitution of the United Kingdom, formed by successive unions between England and its neighbours, rests upon a profound ambiguity about its central principles. The English doctrine of unlimited parliamentary sovereignty, in which the Westminster Parliament can make or unmake any law and cannot be overruled by the courts, remains at the heart of orthodox accounts of the constitution. Yet this perspective, premised on the idea of the UK as a unitary entity, fails to account sufficiently for the distinct cultural and institutional identities of the component nations of the UK that made the country a 'union state' rather than a true 'unitary state' long before devolution (Rokkan & Urwin 1982: 11, 15, 19–68). From a legal perspective, the absence of a codified constitution means that parliamentary sovereignty cannot be limited, but in terms of 'constitutional practice', it has been persuasively argued, the 'constitution's unitary character is a thin concept' (McHarg 2016: 3).

Since 1999, devolution to Edinburgh, Cardiff and Belfast has appeared to imply that the people of Scotland, Wales and Northern Ireland have the right to determine their own form of government. Successive governments also upheld the Sewel convention by which Westminster does not legislate in devolved areas without consent. The Scottish independence referendum of 2014 went still further, in conceding the right of Scotland to secede from the Union, just as the UK accepts the right of the two parts of Ireland to reunite (Northern Ireland Office 1998: Article

Proceedings of the British Academy, **217**, 45–68, © The British Academy 2018.

1(1)). Legislation passed since 2014 also declared the Scottish and Welsh devolved institutions to be 'a permanent part of the United Kingdom's constitutional arrangements' that cannot be abolished without a referendum in the respective nation (Scotland Act 2016: section 1; Wales Act 2017: section 1).

These reforms, in parallel with other changes such as the Human Rights Act and EU integration, appear to have moved the UK far from the archetypal 'majoritarian' system of old (Lijphart 2012: 9–29) towards something more like a quasi-federal state with an entrenched multilevel system of government. Arguably, devolution since 1999 can only be read as a renunciation of the idea of the UK as a unitary state with Westminster as the single locus of sovereignty, and as an embrace of the alternative conception 'that the United Kingdom is a "family of nations", with equal status for each of the family members' (Douglas-Scott 2015: 6). The regular recourse to referendums has also arguably transformed the nature of parliamentary democracy. For Bogdanor, the country's old constitution has been 'crucially and almost certainly permanently undermined' (2009: 271).

And yet, paradoxically, Westminster has managed to travel all the way down this path of reform without ever conceding that parliamentary sovereignty has been curtailed. Constructive ambiguity has been retained at every step. The devolution statutes assert the ability of the UK Parliament to legislate on any matter, devolved or not. The legislative consent doctrine is carefully expressed as one that Parliament will adhere to 'normally' rather than invariably and, notwithstanding its statutory 'recognition' in the Scotland Act 2016 and Wales Act 2017, it is still just a convention, not a matter for the judicial system to enforce, as the Supreme Court ruled in 2017 (Miller 2017), and as was demonstrated by the passage, without Scottish consent, of the EU Withdrawal Act 2018. Even the 'permanence' of the devolved bodies could in theory be revoked by future legislation.

The architects of devolution have purposefully elected not to reconcile the differences between these competing doctrines. We might even speculate that theory and practice have been encouraged to diverge as part of a strategy of deliberate territorial statecraft. This has permitted the peripheral nations to indulge in their own discourses of sovereignty while the English majoritarians remain safe in the knowledge that if it came to the crunch, the hard power of the law, as well as the arithmetic of the House of Commons, would likely be on their side.

Until recently, that crunch never came. Yet after two decades of devolution, the strategy of constructive ambiguity may no longer be sustainable. The stability of the Union has always rested upon what Bernard Crick called 'an astonishing restraint in the exercise of parliamentary sovereignty towards Ireland, Scotland and Wales' (Crick 1983: 379). It was, to be clear, the *English* majority at Westminster that had exercised this restraint, and Crick was writing before the deterioration of territorial relations that occurred during the latter Thatcher era. Today, at a time when English political identity appears to have grown in strength (Jeffery et al. 2014), and with the UK and Scottish governments at odds over Brexit, the stability of the UK may again depend upon how the English majority chooses to exercise its power.

3.2 The Premature Obituary of Parliamentary Sovereignty?

Writing in 2001, Anthony King declared the country's 'power-hoarding archetype' (2001: 38) of a constitution to be 'dead' (ibid: 81). With power increasingly shared upwards with European institutions, downwards with devolved bodies and horizontally with the courts, many writers have followed suit in dismissing traditional accounts of the constitution. In particular, the classical understanding of unlimited parliamentary sovereignty is dismissed as an 'essentially metaphysical doctrine' (Bogdanor 2012: 179), 'mythical' (Mitchell 2011: 12), 'illusionary' (Toubeau & Murkens 2016) and an idea that 'must be abandoned' (McLean & Peterson 2014: 1134). Keating, meanwhile, has called for a new discourse of 'post-sovereignty' that recognises that sovereignty need not be 'absolute and indivisible' but rather that it has 'multiple sources' and is best understood as a 'relationship' rather than a commodity possessed by a certain people or institution (2012: 11–12).

Yet the momentous reforms King described were all designed to allow defenders of Westminster orthodoxy to argue that nothing fundamental had changed. As the first wave of Labour constitutional reforms came into effect, Norton concluded that 'The Westminster model has been modified, perhaps vandalised but it has not been destroyed' (cited in Flinders & Curry 2008: 104). Crucially, in the absence of a codified constitution, these reforms could not be entrenched, meaning that in principle a future parliamentary majority at Westminster would retain the ability to turn back the constitutional clock, whether by taking back power from Brussels, Holyrood or the Middlesex Guildhall (home of the Supreme Court).

Bogdanor was surely right to claim that in the UK's 'new constitution' the practical exercise of parliamentary sovereignty had been qualified, but it has become less certain that the momentous changes of recent decades can be deemed permanent or irreversible. Consequently, Goldsworthy cautioned against issuing a 'premature obituary' of parliamentary sovereignty and suggested that in the absence of a referendum endorsing a new constitutional settlement it would be 'dangerously destabilizing to declare that parliamentary sovereignty is dead' (2012).

3.3 Taking Back Control: Sovereignty and Brexit

The debate over the nature and location of sovereignty entered a new phase following the June 2016 vote to leave the European Union, presented by pro-Brexit advocates as a way to restore a lost age of unquestioned Westminster supremacy. As discussed in Chapter 8 by Ford and Sobolewska, the vote in favour of Brexit was driven in large part not just by voters *in England*, but by voters who disproportionately *self-identify as English* rather than British and who are also more likely to express dissatisfaction with the perceived favourable treatment given to the other three nations of the Union since 1999 (Jeffery et al. 2014: 11).

Many writers have highlighted a long-established reluctance in the UK, and England in particular, to reflect upon questions of constitutional principle. In Nevil

Johnson's terms, the UK's 'customary' constitution 'lays great store by a capacity to leave principles inexplicit, relying instead on what people feel from past experience to be appropriate in the circumstances' (2004: 19). The absence of a codified constitution, however, meant that fundamental changes such as devolution, which in other places 'would have been the subject of constitutional amendments and, no doubt, considerable discussion and debate' (Bogdanor 2009: 271) across the whole country, could be made without the English having to consider the implications for their own place in the Union. The absence of constitutional self-reflection also meant that the UK has stumbled towards the EU exit door, driven primarily by English (and Anglo-Welsh) political considerations and voters, without serious consideration beforehand of the consequences of Brexit for devolution and the Union. In this light, it is unsurprising that the referendum destabilised the UK territorial constitution.

The Scottish and Welsh governments opposed from the outset major planks of the British Government's Brexit strategy, for instance withdrawal from the single market. Both devolved governments asserted that the consent of the devolved legislatures should be sought under the Sewel convention for legislation both to commence and to implement the Brexit process, since leaving the EU will have a direct impact upon the terms of devolution (Scottish Government 2016; Welsh Government 2017c).[1]

With Scotland having voted by 62 per cent to Remain, the Scottish Government has been particularly assertive, arguing that 'While the referendum resulted in a mandate for England and Wales to leave the EU, that was not the case for Scotland and Northern Ireland' (Scottish Government 2016: 1). The Welsh Government has sought a seat at the negotiation table and wider constitutional changes to strengthen Wales's position within the UK. In Northern Ireland, which also voted Remain, divisions over Brexit were one contributory factor behind the collapse of cross-community power-sharing in early 2017.

The British Government, dominated to an unusual extent by English voices, took a different perspective. It has made plain that while the devolved governments would be 'fully engaged in our preparations to leave the EU' (HM Government 2017b: 17), engagement would be on Westminster's terms and would not imply joint decision-making, let alone a federal-style veto power for Edinburgh, Cardiff and Belfast. The Government has approached Brexit informed by the distinctively English conception of the UK as a unitary entity. For instance, Prime Minister Theresa May has declared that: 'Because we voted in the referendum as one United Kingdom, we will negotiate as one United Kingdom, and we will leave the European Union as one United Kingdom' (May 2017).[2] The English Tory instincts

[1] The UK Government rejected this claim with regard to the legislation that authorised the triggering of Article 50 in March 2017, but recognised that the consent convention should apply to the main enabling legislation for Brexit—the EU (Withdrawal) Act 2018—although when agreement could not be reached, this legislation was enacted without Scottish consent.

[2] Somewhat oddly, the Government has also asserted that while Brexit will enable Westminster to 'take

of the Conservative leadership could also be seen in manifesto commitments to move the country back towards the 'majoritarian' end of the constitutional spectrum, for instance by repealing the Fixed Term Parliaments Act 2011 and the use of alternative electoral systems for some local elections (Conservative Party 2017: 43). The party also kept open the possibility of repealing the Human Rights Act 1998 after Brexit (ibid.: 37), which would be fiercely resisted at the devolved level.

Brexit has thus created significant tensions in the relationship between central and devolved governments. We argue in Sections 3.4 to 3.8 that the roots of these tensions can be traced through the long history of England's constitutional development and its successive unions with Wales, Scotland and Ireland.

3.4 England and the Powerful Integrating Myth of the Unitary State

In 1973, the Royal Commission on the Constitution, established to consider options for devolution, set out its conclusions on the premise that 'it is necessary for the undivided sovereignty of Parliament to be maintained' (Royal Commission on the Constitution 1973: para. 539). Devolution was thus defined as the (implicitly reversible) 'delegation of central government powers without the relinquishment of sovereignty' (ibid.: para. 543). This was an uncontentious position, particularly in England. The two main parties at Westminster, Aughey notes in Chapter 2, shared a 'support of Westminster sovereignty and opposition to constitutional recognition of national distinctions'. But the Royal Commission had been established precisely because the simple assumptions of unitary statehood were being challenged by Scottish and Welsh nationalism and the re-emergence of the Irish Question. For Harvie, Harold Wilson's failed top-down economic modernisation project after 1966 may have marked 'the unitary state's final throw' (Harvie 2000: 338).

Even during the high point of British centralism in the two decades after the Second World War, it can be argued that the 'unitary' label was misapplied. In the classic definition of Rokkan & Urwin, a unitary state is one in which a single and dominant political centre 'pursues a more or less undeviating policy of administrative standardization' across the entire country (1982: 11). This is a description of the English rather than the UK constitution. England has been described as a 'prototypical unitary state' (Mitchell 2011: 6) in which power was centralised early in its history, following the unification of competing Saxon kingdoms prior to the Norman Conquest. The power of the English monarch was then eventually and gradually ceded to the Parliament at Westminster, which claimed for itself the unconstrained power to make and unmake any law. As Dicey put it, 'England

back control', parliamentary sovereignty was never in fact compromised by EU membership: 'Whilst Parliament has remained sovereign throughout our membership of the EU, it has not always felt like that' (HM Government 2017b: 13).

has, at any rate since the Norman Conquest, been always governed by an absolute legislator' (1915: 25). Thus, the English constitution emerged from 'an incremental process in which the principle of parliamentary sovereignty was continuous with monarchical sovereignty' (Gifford 2010: 324).

For these reasons, Dicey described the doctrine of parliamentary sovereignty as having roots that 'lie deep in the history of the English people and in the peculiar development of the English constitution' (1915: 25). Drawing a contrast with the federal system of the USA, Walter Bagehot argued that 'the English is the type of simple constitution, in which the ultimate power upon all questions is in the hands of the same persons', those persons being the majority in the House of Commons (Bagehot 1873: 175).

The series of unions between England and its three neighbours are traditionally interpreted as a gradual expansion of England's constitutional order westwards and northwards. Robert Tombs notes how, for the English political elite, 'the creation of the United Kingdom was de facto a process of political attachment to England' in which 'the Scots were expected to conform to the "ancient constitution" of England' (Tombs 2014: 312). The implication was that Westminster acquired unlimited sovereignty across the entire United Kingdom as it expanded, before contracting in 1922 with the secession of five-sixths of the island of Ireland. As Jennings concluded, in passing the Acts of Union with Scotland and Ireland, what Parliament did 'was to ratify two treaties whereby its own power was extended to neighbouring territories' (1959: 170).

However, this narrative has been widely challenged as an accurate depiction of the constitution of the UK as a whole. Writing in 1983, Bernard Crick criticised constitutional scholars ever since Bagehot for 'ignoring the formula "the United Kingdom", treating it as synonymous with the English constitution, government or politics, and moreover describing this system as centralised and unitary under a sovereign Parliament' (Crick 1983: 378). Arthur Aughey has likewise argued that 'There is no doubting the Anglocentricity of this understanding of constitutional orthodoxy' (Aughey 2016: 352).

Aughey highlights that the narrative of the historical continuity of English institutions from pre-modern to contemporary times cannot be dismissed as ignorance. Rather, it has served an instrumental purpose as 'a powerful integrating myth for the whole of the United Kingdom' (ibid.). But just as the 'forging of the British nation' between the Anglo-Scottish Union and the dawn of the Victorian age (Colley 2003: 1) did not erase the component national identities of the UK, nor was this myth powerful enough to prevent alternative conceptions of the constitution from flourishing across these islands.

The strength of this myth depends upon the English pouring their nationhood into the larger vessel of Britishness. Should the English grow less willing to do so, and less accepting of a constitution that grants recognition only to the three smaller nations of the UK, then the stability of the union state may be called into question. Chapters elsewhere in this volume consider the evidence for such a change in English attitudes.

3.5 The Sovereign Right of the Scottish People

Scotland has a particularly powerful thread of constitutional thinking that runs counter to the narrative of the UK as a unitary state. As Douglas-Scott argued prior to the EU referendum, in anticipation of the destabilising impact that Brexit would have upon the Union, 'the Diceyan orthodoxy of parliamentary sovereignty has never held as much weight north of the border' (Douglas-Scott 2015: 8). In place of English parliamentary sovereignty, it is often argued that Scotland adheres to the doctrine of popular sovereignty, as expressed in the 1989 Claim of Right for Scotland,[3] which 'acknowledge[d] the sovereign right of the Scottish people to determine the form of Government best suited to their needs' (cited in Priddy 2016: 3). The Claim was signed by 160 politicians and civil society leaders and marked the launch of the Constitutional Convention that drew up Scotland's devolution blueprint. It had been inspired by a report, published a year earlier, which explicitly targeted English constitutionalism: '[Scots] have the opportunity ... to start the reform of the English Constitution; to serve as the grit in the oyster which produces the pearl' (Owen Dudley Edwards 1989, cited in Marquand 2008: 338).

From this perspective, the Anglo-Scottish Union of 1707 was not a matter of assimilation of Scotland into Greater England but a voluntary union of two sovereign nations, whose right to self-determination was not extinguished. The Treaty (and Acts) of Union that created the new state indeed explicitly preserved central pillars of the pre-Union Scottish state, including its legal system, church, local government and educational institutions. Some clauses of the 1707 Treaty, for instance the preservation of the status of the High Court of Justiciary as the highest criminal court in Scotland, were described in the treaty as applying 'in all time coming' (McLean & Peterson 2014: 1118). This can be interpreted as reflecting an intention to entrench elements of Scotland's constitution and place these beyond the reach of the new British Parliament to amend on the basis of a House of Commons majority.

In 1884, as the scope of government expanded, a separate Scottish Office headed by a Secretary of State was created to oversee various aspects of government in Scotland. This took on various functions over the subsequent decades and by the 1990s was responsible for health, education, law and order, local government and most other domestic policy spheres with the exceptions of social security, fiscal and monetary policy. These were the functions subsequently transferred to the new devolved parliament and government. Mitchell argues that the existence of the old pre-devolution Scottish Office had 'encouraged a conception of Scotland as a political and not merely a cultural entity' (Mitchell 2003: 2).

From this perspective, the UK has never been a truly unitary state, at least in terms of the definition presented in Section 3.4. The preservation of Scotland's distinct legal system throughout the history of the Union alone belies the suggestion that undeviating administrative standardisation was ever the policy of the British

[3] The 1989 initiative was so-called to echo two previous Claims of Right (in 1689 and 1842).

state. In fact, Kellas concluded that following the Union 'the Scottish system of government did not ossify or lead to the assimilation of Scotland to England. Instead, it grew steadily, with the Scottish part getting in some senses stronger with time' (Kellas 1989: 522). In line with Crick, he further noted that the success of the Union for most of the post-1707 period had rested upon the consistent adoption of a 'hands-off approach by London where important Scottish interests were concerned. Thus, Scottish legal, educational and local government reforms were essentially the product of a consensus arrived at within Scotland and not dictated by London' (ibid.: 523).

However, it is doubtful that the English majority at Westminster—or the English school of constitutional thought—ever accepted that parliamentary sovereignty was qualified by the terms of the 1707 Union, let alone that the growing size and role of the Scottish Office was anything more than an administrative convenience—freeing the centre from direct responsibility for local administrative matters as the scale and complexity of government increased. For Bulpitt (1983), this formed part of a deliberate strategy that sought to liberate the Anglo-dominated centre from entanglement in matters of peripheral public policy, while ensuring that 'matters of high politics or English domestic policy were shielded from interference or negotiation with the periphery' (Convery 2014: 28). The union state preserved English dominance when it mattered and allowed the smaller nations a long leash when it did not.

The unresolved ambiguities of the UK territorial constitution ensured that 'England and the Westminster elite could believe that they inhabited a unitary state governed by parliamentary sovereignty, while the Scots flattered themselves that they had a contractual relationship with the centre' (Keating 2010: 379). The Union therefore rested from the outset upon constructive ambiguity about its terms, but if the principles ever were to come into conflict, the hard power of the law was assumed to lie on the side of the majority at Westminster.

McLean & Peterson show how it took less than five years before the English parliamentary majority disregarded some of the supposed permanent protections granted to the Church in Scotland, when the new British Parliament passed legislation that reformed how ministers of the Church of Scotland were appointed (McLean & Peterson 2014: 1124). Much more recently, the governments led by Margaret Thatcher, who was described as 'intransigently opposed to any weakening of the Westminster Parliament' and as embodying a reversion to traditional English Tory constitutional thinking (Gamble 2016: 360), imposed policies such as the poll tax and contentious economic reforms that lacked majority support in Scotland. This marked a reversal of the 'astonishing restraint' Crick had remarked upon. For Kellas, the Thatcher administrations had 'exploited the English doctrine of the sovereignty of Parliament and have taken to an extreme the centralising, confrontational politics hinted at in earlier periods' (1989: 523). This contributed directly to the emerging pro-devolution consensus in Scotland and the 1997 wipeout of Conservative MPs outside England.

3.6 The (Re)convening of the Scottish Parliament in 1999

When devolution finally occurred a decade later, Westminster had from one perspective conceded 'the sovereign right of the Scottish people to determine the form of Government best suited to their needs' (Priddy 2016: 3). At the very first sitting of the new Parliament in May 1999, the chair Winnie Ewing MSP declared that 'the Scottish Parliament, which adjourned on 25 March 1707, is hereby reconvened' (Scottish Parliament Official Report, 12 May 1999). This was a grand and memorable phrase, appropriate to the occasion, but it spoke more to poetic licence than legal reality. There had been no formal change in the ultimate locus of sovereignty. While the new body was imbued with the legitimacy stemming from the 1997 referendum result, it was at the same time a creature of statute, owing its existence to the Scotland Act 1998, which had been crafted to avoid qualifying the supremacy of Westminster. The Act contained a still-valid provision asserting that its passage 'does not affect the power of the Parliament of the United Kingdom to make laws for Scotland' (Scotland Act 1998: 28(7)). Stating this was redundant, in any case, since the preservation of parliamentary sovereignty could be assumed.

This historic moment in Scottish political history was therefore a textbook case of constructive ambiguity in action—and it would not be the last. Every subsequent step of Scotland's constitutional journey has been framed so that adherents to the rival doctrines of parliamentary and popular sovereignty could each claim vindication. The stability of the new settlement would rely upon traditional willingness to allow theory and practice to part ways. This was made clear during the passage of the Scotland Act 1998, when the Labour Government committed not to legislate in areas of devolved competence without consent, in what became known as the Sewel convention. The convention was extended to also cover legislation that amended the powers of the devolved institutions (Gallagher 2017: 3). This was no more than a political commitment and, in principle, the post-2010 Conservative-led governments could have rejected its constraints, agreed at a time of Labour dominance across Great Britain. But Westminster's self-denying ordinance had taken root and Sewel continued to be used regularly, and largely without controversy, to regulate relations between the UK and Scottish Parliaments.

More recently, the convention was given statutory recognition in the Scotland Act 2016, following a commitment made by the UK Government after the 2014 Scottish independence referendum. The Act was itself subject to Sewel and its passage was held up until the Scottish Government was satisfied with the terms of a new funding settlement. That the UK Government accepted the de facto veto power of Holyrood illustrated the strength of the convention. And yet when it came to the clause referring to Sewel, the legislation asserted merely that '*it is recognised that* the Parliament of the United Kingdom will *not normally* legislate with regard to devolved matters without the consent of the Scottish Parliament' (Scotland Act 2016: section 2, emphasis added). The highlighted phrases were carefully crafted to avoid once again any legal dilution of parliamentary sovereignty. The UK Supreme Court backed this interpretation in 2017, in the context of whether devolved consent was required for the legislation starting the Brexit process, stating that the convention 'has an important role in facilitating harmonious relationships between the UK Parliament and the devolved legislatures. But *the policing of its scope and the manner of its operation does not lie within the constitutional remit of the judiciary*' (Miller 2017: 49, emphasis added).

The Scotland Act 2016 also included a provision stating that the devolved institutions in Edinburgh are 'a permanent part of the United Kingdom's constitutional arrangements' that may not be abolished without a referendum in the territory in question. Even more than the 'recognition' of Sewel, this appeared to mark a historic concession. If the UK Parliament could no longer reverse the 1999 devolution reforms without the express consent of the Scottish people, what else could this be but a victory for popular over parliamentary sovereignty? Yet in the absence of an entrenched constitution, there is no watertight legal barrier that would prevent a future majority at Westminster from changing its mind and legislating to remove the reference to institutional permanence.

In an interesting discussion of this issue, Elliott (2014) argued that any statutory commitments to the permanence of devolution 'ring rather hollow' since 'being sovereign [Parliament] cannot surrender its sovereignty'. Yet he also questioned whether, if the unlikely scenario of Westminster seeking to abolish devolution came to pass, the courts would automatically retreat to the comfort of Westminster model orthodoxy. Potentially, he speculated, the permanence clause might be interpreted as 'a codification of the underlying constitutional value of the autonomy and enduring nature of devolved institutions' implying '*in extremis* limitations upon the UK Parliament's authority'. He noted, however, that one could not predict what the Supreme Court would decide should it be asked to make a decision on this matter.

A final example of the instinct for ambiguity relates to the independence referendum itself. When the Scottish National Party (SNP) won a majority of seats in the Scottish Parliament election of 2011, this was widely interpreted as a mandate for the referendum to take place and the British Prime Minister swiftly confirmed that he would not seek to prevent this from happening. However, under Schedule 5 of the Scotland Act 1998, 'the Union of the Kingdoms of Scotland and England' is a reserved matter, with regard to which the Scottish Parliament may not legislate. This was interpreted by many as meaning that without the agreement of Westminster, even a non-binding vote on independence would be ruled illegal (House of Lords Constitution Committee 2012: paras 23, 30). This point was not explicitly conceded by the Scottish Government and, since David Cameron agreed that the referendum could take place, the question was moot. Instead, agreement was reached that the power to legislate to hold a referendum would be *temporarily* devolved to the Scottish Parliament, on the basis of certain agreed conditions (HM Government & the Scottish Government 2012).[4]

[4] Specifically, the agreement between the two governments was that the Scottish Parliament would be empowered to legislate for a referendum that would have to be held before the end of 2014, that the

By allowing Scotland to vote on independence—and committing to respect the result—the English majority at Westminster appeared once more to concede the principle of Scottish self-determination and the associated idea of the Union as a voluntary partnership. Yet the reverse case could also be made: that the legal path to the 2014 referendum established that sovereignty over the constitution remained unambiguously with Westminster. That the question had not been settled became apparent in 2017 when the Scottish Government put the issue of independence back on the agenda following the EU referendum, again claiming a democratic mandate based on an SNP election manifesto (SNP 2017). On this occasion, Prime Minister Theresa May took a different view to her predecessor and refused even to discuss authorising another such vote while the terms of Brexit remained undecided (ITV News 2017).

What this shows is that the terms of the Anglo-Scottish relationship have been subject to competing interpretations ever since 1707. Developments since 1999 have not helped to clarify the principles of the Union: in contrast, the reluctance to formulate core constitutional principles has enabled these incompatible doctrines to thrive and the divergence of theory and practice to grow wider. As Brexit adds to the strain, the risk is that the old strategy of constructive ambiguity may no longer be capable of bridging the gulf.

3.7 The Pooling of Sovereignty on the Island of Ireland

Following its own Union with Westminster a century after Scotland, Ireland was less fully integrated into the British state, although (or perhaps because) it had long been subject to English and then (after 1707) Anglo-British political dominance—enforced when necessary at the point of a bayonet. As Mitchell notes, 'There never was a serious effort to integrate Ireland with the rest of the state; it was treated more as a colony than an integral part' (Mitchell 2011: 12). The 1801 Union of Ireland and Great Britain abolished the separate Irish Parliament, but other existing institutions of state were preserved. Ireland retained a form of local administration including its own executive departments, courts and the posts of Lord Lieutenant and Chief Secretary, who retained responsibility for public administration in Ireland on behalf of the British Crown (ibid.: 11).

The British imperial state thus delegated to a trusted local elite in Dublin oversight of domestic political issues of little concern to Westminster—'low politics' in Bulpitt's terms—but there was no right of self-government for Ireland, nor religious freedom for the majority of its inhabitants. Catholic emancipation came only three decades after the Union and disestablishment of the Anglican Church in Ireland later still, in 1869. Most significant was the failure of William Gladstone to legislate for Irish Home Rule, largely due to English Tory opposition. Having

---

referendum would be regulated by the Electoral Commission, that there would be only two options on the ballot paper and that the franchise could be extended to 16- and 17-year-olds.

lost the southern part of Ireland as a result, the Westminster Parliament was then content to legislate for home rule in the north in the shape of the Northern Ireland Parliament at Stormont. With an in-built unionist majority, the loyalty of Stormont to the Crown and to Westminster could be taken for granted, so devolution to Ulster created a useful bulwark against competing nationalist appeals to the sovereignty of the Irish people. As Guelke has noted: 'Westminster was only too glad to delegate the problem of dealing with Irish nationalism' (2017: 43).

When Northern Ireland's Troubles erupted in the early 1970s, the British Government stepped in to suspend devolution and reassert direct rule. In one sense, this underlined that the hard power of parliamentary sovereignty remained intact. Yet at the same time, the suspension of devolution can be associated with a historic recognition that majoritarian rule—that core pillar of the Westminster model—was inappropriate in the special circumstances of Northern Ireland, whether by a majority at Westminster or Stormont (Guelke 2017). Instead, the British Government moved towards a new governing doctrine: that any restoration of devolution to Northern Ireland must enjoy the consent of both the Protestant majority and the Catholic minority and, furthermore, that this would require 'that the Republic of Ireland be involved as a guarantor' of the rights of the minority community (Guelke 2017: 44).

Notably, this evolution in British constitutional practice with regard to the island of Ireland coincided with the UK accession into the European Economic Community (EEC) (Meehan 2014), itself predicated on the transcending of traditional Westphalian conceptions of indivisible state sovereignty (Caporaso 2000). With Ireland having entered the EEC alongside the UK, Europe helped facilitate a new relationship between the two states, as both softened their claim to unilateral sovereignty over the six counties. In this period, Gamble (2016: 365) notes, 'the Conservatives temporarily renounced their Tory instincts for preserving undiluted the principle of Westminster sovereignty in relation to both the Union and Europe'. This was spelt out by Prime Minister Edward Heath, who defended his pro-European stance with the memorable phrase: 'If sovereignty exists to be used and to be of value, it must be effective' (cited in Meehan 2014: 61). Sovereignty is here understood as instrumental and contextual rather than absolute.

In the years that followed the resumption of direct rule, one can perceive a growing divergence between constitutional theory and practice. England, at that time the most pro-European of the four UK nations (Henderson et al. 2016), acceded to these historic changes in 'how [the UK] "does" sovereignty', yet it once again did so without reflecting upon their impact upon the constitution, permitting a 'continuing attachment to the old language of sovereignty' (Meehan 2014: 58). Even the phrase 'direct rule'—never used in reference to Scotland or Wales before the 1999 devolution reforms—suggests that Ulster was already regarded as a semi-detached annex to the core British state (Meehan 2014: 68).

By contrast with Heath, Margaret Thatcher is regarded as instinctively antipathetic towards the pooling of sovereignty in both the Irish or European contexts (Meehan 2014: 64). For Gamble, Thatcher's constitutional sensibilities fit comfortably within the traditions of English Tories, for whom the Union is 'desirable, but it comes second in their thinking to the need to protect the sovereignty of the British state, the core of which is England and its traditional institutions' (2016: 359). Nonetheless, under the pressure of events, Thatcher steered the UK towards even greater pooling of sovereignty both in Europe, with the passage of the Single European Act, and in Ireland, with the 1985 Anglo-Irish Agreement (AIA), whose name implied a new relationship between Ireland and *England*, rather than Britain.

The AIA created a new intergovernmental conference through which London and Dublin would seek to resolve political, security and other problems facing the north, thus 'institutionalizing the principle of bilateral cooperation in managing the conflict' (Guelke 2017: 46). Although the Irish Government was not granted 'joint sovereignty' or 'joint authority' over the north, merely a more nebulous notion of 'joint responsibility' (Meehan 2014: 64), the enhanced cross-border role of the Republic triggered huge protests from the unionist community. The treaty also entrenched the 'principle of consent', which established that the reunification of Ireland could lawfully take place but only with the agreement of the people of both parts of Ireland. This was in fact a concession by the Irish, whose constitution still claimed sovereignty over the entire island, and given the demographic dominance of the unionist community this clause appeared to secure Ulster's position within the UK. Nonetheless for the British state to sign up to this principle illustrates its willingness to depart in practice from the unitary conception of the UK, which would imply that Northern Ireland could no more choose to leave the UK than could North Finchley.

Writing two years earlier, Bernard Crick had recognised the need for a new constitutional dispensation in Ulster: 'Since it faces both ways … it will have to develop institutions that face both ways', noting further that 'The normal theory of the sovereign state will not help much here, any more than it is helping to understand what is happening in the EEC' (Crick 1983: 381). The normal theory of the sovereign state was of even less value in explaining the 1998 Good Friday Agreement, which brought to an end the era of armed conflict over the constitutional status of Northern Ireland. The 1998 Agreement created a new multilevel constitutional order of mandatory cross-community power-sharing in Belfast and a web of north–south and east–west intergovernmental institutions to tie in both London and Dublin.

The Good Friday Agreement reiterated the principle of consent, stating that 'it is for the people of the island of Ireland alone, by agreement between the two parts respectively and without external impediment, to exercise their right of self-determination on the basis of consent' (Northern Ireland Office 1998: Article 1(2)). This was accompanied by constitutional change in the Republic that removed its claim to unilateral sovereignty over the north. However, as Guelke notes, 'the implicit assumption of continuing British and Irish participation in Europe was woven into the terms of the Belfast Agreement' (2017: 42). The vote to leave the European Union has been greatly disruptive to the political order in Northern Ireland as a result. There was significant support within the unionist community for Brexit, while the main unionist parties have supported the right of ministers at Westminster to lead the exit process and the Democratic Unionist Party (DUP) explicitly agreed to back the Government's Brexit legislation as part of its 2017 'confidence and supply' agreement with the Conservatives (HM Government 2017c). By contrast, nationalists argued that Brexit would be a breach of the consent principle: 'Dragging us out of Europe against the will of our people and while we have no Executive isn't just an affront to the principles of devolution, it's an act of democratic savagery' (SDLP 2017).

In late 2017, the attenuated nature of Westminster sovereignty in Northern Ireland was made plain, as the Republic of Ireland threatened to derail the UK's Brexit deal without certain guarantees over the Irish border and the rights of Irish citizens in Northern Ireland. With the rest of the EU standing behind him, Irish Prime Minister Leo Varadkar asserted that it was Dublin rather than Westminster that spoke for the nationalist community: 'To the nationalist people in Northern Ireland, I want to assure you that we have protected your interests throughout these negotiations' (Varadkar 2017). In December 2017, the UK and EU published a progress report on the Brexit negotiations, yet the section on Ireland (European Commission 2017: paras 49–50) left unanswered fundamental questions about the future of the Irish border, allowing varying interpretations over what each side had conceded.

This chapter has argued that an already fragile co-existence between competing constitutional doctrines has been destabilised by the vote to leave the EU. This is truest in the divided society of Northern Ireland, where nationalist and unionist identities are rooted in competing visions of sovereignty. The peace process was founded on an attempt to replace these incompatible doctrines with a new constitutional dispensation that 'looks both ways'—to Westminster and Dublin. The English majority at Westminster has discovered that it cannot fully 'take back control' from Brussels without undermining the political settlement across the Irish Sea.

3.8 The Slow Rebirth of Wales

Having been integrated into a single kingdom ruled from London in the pre-modern age, Wales was more extensively assimilated than either of the other nations, such that it was commonly regarded as just another part of England. Drawing a contrast with the 1707 Anglo-Scottish Union, Morgan concluded that 'Modern Wales is the product of an act of conquest, imposed on a fragmented people by Edward I over 400 years earlier' (Morgan 1999: 24). This was followed by the 16th-century Acts of Union under Henry VIII which resolved that Wales 'shall be, stand and continue for ever from henceforth incorporated, united and annexed to and with this his Realm of England' (Jones, Turnbull & Williams 2005: 140). These Acts abolished an existing feudal system of local administration and imposed 'a uniform administration of English common law' across the whole of Wales for the first time (Roberts 1972: 53).

With the remnants of Welsh institutional distinctiveness abolished, Wales came to be seen as a mere 'geographical expression' that 'bore the same relationship to the England of which it formed a part as did the Highland zone to the rest of Scotland' (Morgan 1981: 3). Wales was left with few of the pillars of statehood Scotland and Ireland had retained after union and was in most respects integrated into a Westminster-centred unitary state. Morgan (1981) depicted the revival of Welsh identity as the 'rebirth of a nation' that begun in the late 19th century after the Reform Acts had widened the franchise significantly in Wales: 'Welsh national consciousness in its modern form is a function of mass democracy' (Morgan 1999: 25). There were some significant early victories for the renascent nation, including reforms to secondary and tertiary education in Wales, an 1881 law requiring all pubs to close on Sundays (the first Act of Parliament to apply solely to Wales) and the 1920 disestablishment of the Anglican Church in Wales (ibid.). But while the cultural revival gathered momentum, the institutions of the central state took longer to adapt.

As Brazier notes of the Anglo-Welsh Union: 'So complete, indeed, was the annexation in practice that the word "England" in Acts of Parliament was later deemed to include Wales, a slur which was not removed until 1967' (Brazier 1999: 97). Three further decades passed until 'and Wales' was added to the official title of the Lord Chief Justice of England: 'belated recognition at the very moment of devolution!' according to Rawlings (1998: 496). These were symbolically important moments: official acknowledgement of the simple fact that Wales and England are two different places, so one cannot be part of the other. More significant in governance terms was the 1964 creation of the Welsh Office, eighty years after its Scottish counterpart and initially with significantly fewer powers. Once established, however, 'the story is of a gradual accretion of administrative functions' until the department was responsible for the bulk of non-social security public expenditure in Wales (Rawlings 1998: 466). The growth of Welsh quangos after 1979, as well as the unitarisation of local government in 1994, also created a semi-delineated Welsh governance landscape that was subsequently transferred, in terms of political control, from the Welsh Office to the new Assembly in 1999 (ibid.: 468).

Having been more comprehensively assimilated into England than Scotland and Ireland, and lacking its own legal system to this day, Wales has been slower to develop an alternative constitutional doctrine to define its position within the Union. Its nationalist movement was long associated with defending Wales as a cultural rather than a constitutional entity. The nation's weak position within the Union has led to the conclusion that 'In Wales, devolution remains largely a defensive project. Welsh political institutions are seen as providing a degree of protection against the depredations of Westminster rather than an embodiment of an alternative politics' (Wyn Jones 2016). Devolution to Wales has also often emerged as a weaker derivative of Scottish developments, rather than as the reflection of a national constitutional movement of its own.

In its 1979 referendum, Wales soundly rejected the limited devolution offer made reluctantly by Prime Minister (and Cardiff MP) James Callaghan. Scotland voted Yes, but with turnout below the legally required threshold, so both nations had to wait a generation for another chance. In the interim, Scotland engaged in a long national debate about its constitutional future, culminating in the Claim of Right and Constitutional Convention discussed in Section 3.5. There were no such initiatives in Wales. Instead, when Labour took power in 1997 its offer to Wales rested on an uneasy internal compromise within a party still divided on the very principle of Welsh devolution and unwilling to work with rivals such as Plaid Cymru to develop a broader-based movement (Morgan & Mungham 2000: 87–8).

The original National Assembly held circumscribed executive (not legislative) powers and was modelled on a local authority leadership structure, leading to the jibe that it was just a 'glorified county council', while Scotland had a parliament in name and form. Even the Welsh devolution referendum of 1997 took place a week after that of Scotland as a gambit to borrow momentum from the expected pro-devolution landslide north of the border. Wales then voted Yes by the narrowest of margins—50.3 per cent voted in favour, on a turnout of just 50.2 per cent. This appeared to provide a shaky foundation for devolution that might be eroded by a hostile majority at Westminster. As late as 2005, the Conservative Shadow Welsh Secretary (by necessity an English MP, since Wales was then a Tory-free zone) openly favoured abolition of the devolved bodies (BBC News 2005).

However, for all its unpromising beginnings, it quickly became unthinkable that Westminster would wield the power of parliamentary sovereignty to scrap devolution unilaterally. In 2005, the Conservative position was simply to hold another referendum in which abolition was one option, and since its defeat at that election the party has accepted devolution. In practice, the wafer-thin vote in favour of devolution in the 1997 referendum was sufficient to ensure the survival of the new institutions. Rawlings noted at the dawn of devolution (1998: 474) that 'As a tool of (political) entrenchment, the referendum is the best available means within the Westminster tradition of sovereignty.' Arguably it is the only available means of entrenchment.

Since 1999, Welsh devolution has advanced significantly, with the National Assembly gaining additional powers in legislation passed in 2006, 2014 and 2017, as well as at a further referendum in 2011. The initial council-style assembly has been replaced by a traditional separation of power between legislature and executive, and it will soon be legally renamed as the Welsh Parliament. It is already commonly described as the Senedd, reflecting the strengthened position of the Welsh language, another sign not just of national rebirth but of its coming of age. The next milestone may well be the creation of a separate Welsh jurisdiction, which is being considered by a Commission on Welsh Justice created in 2017 and chaired by the outgoing Lord Chief Justice (Welsh Government 2017b).

Reflecting on Wales' three devolution referendums, Jones underlines the significance of gaining a direct popular mandate for the establishment and enhancement of the Welsh Assembly: 'The use of the referendum emphasizes the sovereignty of the people in determining the legislative powers of the National Assembly' (2012: 153). The Wales Act 2017 marked a further step towards a new understanding of Welsh sovereignty. Once again following Scotland's footsteps, this legislation copied and pasted the clauses that 'recognise' the existence of the Sewel convention (in the Welsh case known simply as the 'Convention about Parliament legislating on devolved matters') and declare the devolved bodies to be 'a permanent part of the United Kingdom's constitutional arrangements', which may not be abolished without a referendum (Wales Act 2017: sections 1–2).

All the same caveats apply as in the Scottish case: namely that the Westminster Parliament could in principle bypass, amend or repeal these provisions in future and would *probably* have the backing of the courts in the case of any legal challenge. Nonetheless, after two decades of devolution, one can speak of the gradual emergence of a new doctrine of Welsh popular sovereignty, which is transforming Wales' sense of nationhood and its relationship with England. The Welsh Government has explicitly invoked this alternative conception of sovereignty on a number of occasions. For instance, in evidence to a parliamentary committee in 2015, it asserted that: 'Whatever its historical origins, the United Kingdom is best seen now as a voluntary association of nations' and asserted in conclusion that 'Parliamentary sovereignty as traditionally understood will need in the longer term to be recognised as incompatible with this evolving constitution' (Welsh Government 2015: 727).

More recently, in 2017, it was confident enough to assert Wales' right 'to participate on equal terms with the UK Government, representing the interests of England' in negotiations over the creation of common policy frameworks to replace EU structures from which the UK intends to depart (Welsh Government 2017c: 26). Notable also was the fact that this claim was made in a White Paper jointly produced with Labour's nationalist rivals Plaid Cymru—the old reluctance to work on a cross-party basis now eclipsed by commitment to defend the Welsh national interest. The Welsh Government has also become a proponent of a reformulated relationship between Westminster and Cardiff, drawing upon federal principles such as pooling of sovereignty and 'shared executive governance' in policy areas currently governed at the EU level (Welsh Government 2017a: 13).

The rebirth of Wales may have taken some time, and its status within the Union remains weaker than Scotland, but it too can now mount a credible challenge to the English constitutional orthodoxy of rule by the majority at Westminster. The strength of this challenge is now being put to the test as the Brexit process continues.

3.9 Conclusions: An Unsettled Constitution

Even before devolution, the depiction of the UK as a unitary state was questionable. In each of the smaller nations distinct institutional arrangements were either retained or emerged over time. For the dominant nation of these islands, there was no perceived need to delineate its national institutions. The central pillars of the pre-1707 English state—Westminster, the Crown, the Privy Council, the Lord Chancellor and the English courts, the currency and the Bank of England—remained intact and recognisable, even as they were absorbed into the larger union state. England was at once invisible within the Union and omnipresent within it.

Due to the conflation of English and British institutions, the centre was also the domestic government for England and this curious settlement—combined with England's political and economic dominance—made it easier for the myth of the unchanging unitary state to survive, even as it grew increasingly divorced from the reality of constitutional practice.

When devolution took place in 1999, the new arrangements were designed to preserve this ambiguity, leaving Westminster formally supreme while enhancing the claims of alternative and more pluralistic accounts of sovereignty in the devolved nations. The 1999 settlement was in fact notable for its combination of radicalism and conservatism. It created significant potential for the three smaller nations to take their own paths, but limited the impact upon the central state. The functions devolved were predominantly already administered separately via the Scottish, Welsh and Northern Ireland Offices. The financial arrangements for devolution were unchanged too, with all significant fiscal levers controlled by the UK Treasury and the devolved bodies funded via central government block grants. Nor was there any reconfiguration of Parliament, other than—belatedly—the little-noticed introduction of 'English votes for English laws' (EVEL) (see Gover and Kenny in Chapter 6). Crucially, there was no formal change in the locus of sovereignty. Despite their democratic mandates, the devolved institutions were legally subordinate to Parliament. The empire sought to retain the capacity to strike back should circumstances require.

It was assumed that the English, meanwhile, were satisfied with the hybrid Anglo-British institutions in Westminster and Whitehall, which were English before there was a Britain, and remained as such in the eyes of many. Today, this assumption is far more questionable: indeed, as discussed elsewhere in this volume, dissatisfaction among English voters with how their nation is governed can be perceived as a root cause of the vote for Brexit. Yet in the early years of devolution the consensus was that 'The English regard it [Westminster] as their parliament, and do not want a separate parliament' (Hazell 2006: 12) and that: 'England fits easily enough in Britain for the English not to feel the need for an English parliament to safeguard an English national identity' (Bryant 2010: 251). Neither were there any serious regionalist movements to challenge the centralised and unitary nature of the English polity, with limited exceptions in more culturally distinct regions such as Cornwall and Yorkshire.

In keeping with the traditions of the 'customary constitution', there was thus no attempt to impose a standard constitutional schema across the UK, nor any explicit consideration of the principles underpinning the reformed union. It was 'as if each nation comprising the UK has embarked on a journey with an uncertain destination' (Leyland 2011: 252). The preference for minimising the impact upon existing institutions and constitutional doctrine made devolution 'a deceptively simple thing to do' (Jeffery & Wincott 2006: 3). However, it also meant that the implications of devolution for the Union as a whole were under-considered and that the contradictions of the constitution lay unreconciled.

The divergence between Westminster orthodoxy and constitutional practice at the devolved level contributed to what Flinders & Curry call 'bi-constitutionality', in which there is 'an attempt to apply different meta-constitutional orientations at different levels of governance' (2008: 100). Even in 2008, these authors wondered whether constitutional change since 1997 had 'eviscerated the malleability of the Westminster Model' thus necessitating 'an explicit debate regarding the country's dominant meta-constitutional orientation' (ibid.: 117).

A decade later such a debate appears more necessary than ever, despite the continued lack of interest at Westminster in reconciling constitutional theory and practice. But Britain's customary constitution, Nevil Johnson pointed out, 'was always premised on elite rule' and on the willingness of the nation at large to trust the wisdom of those in authority (2004: 19). Constructive ambiguity and leaving principles inexplicit may only work so long as deference to elite rule continues, so long as the composite parts of the country are not pulling in opposite directions and so long as the English continue to acquiesce to a settlement that subsumes their nationhood into the wider sovereignty of the British state. The EU referendum result, the mood of English political disaffection Brexit has tapped into and the intergovernmental disputes it has caused all call into question whether these conditions for constitutional stability can be relied upon any longer.

References

Aughey, A. (2016), '"Never reflective, because so obviously a fact": institutions and national identity in English political thought', *Political Studies Review*, 14(3): 349–58.

Bagehot, W. (1873), *The English Constitution*, 2nd edn, https://socialsciences.mcmaster.ca/econ/ugcm/3ll3/bagehot/constitution.pdf, accessed 31 August 2017.

BBC News (2005), 'Wiggin backs scrapping assembly', 21 January, http://news.bbc.co.uk/1/hi/wales/4193425.stm, accessed 1 September 2017.

Bogdanor, V. (2009), *The New British Constitution* (Oxford, Hart Publishing).

Bogdanor, V. (2012), 'Imprisoned by a doctrine: the modern defence of parliamentary sovereignty', *Oxford Journal of Legal Studies*, 32(1): 179–95. DOI 10.1093/ojls/gqr027.

Brazier, R. (1999), 'The constitution of the United Kingdom', *Cambridge Law Journal*, 58(1): 96–128.

Bryant, C. (2010), 'English identities and interests and the governance of Britain', *Parliamentary Affairs*, 63(2): 250–65.

Bulpitt, J. (1983), *Territory and Power in the United Kingdom: An Interpretation* (Manchester, Manchester University Press).

Caporaso, J. A. (2000), 'Changes in the Westphalian order: territory, public authority, and sovereignty', *International Studies Review*, 2(2): 1–28.

Colley, L. (2003), *Britons: Forging the Nation 1707–1837* (London, Pimlico).

Conservative Party (2017), 'Forward Together: Our Plan for a Stronger Britain and a Prosperous Future', Conservative and Unionist Party Manifesto, https://s3-eu-west-1.amazonaws.com/2017-manifestos/Conservative+Manifesto+2017.pdf, accessed 18 December 2017.

Convery, A. (2014), 'Devolution and the limits of Tory statecraft: the Conservative Party in coalition and Scotland and Wales', *Parliamentary Affairs*, 67(1): 25–44. DOI 10.1093/pa/gst020.

Crick, B. (1983), 'Rose of England', *Political Quarterly*, 54(3): 378–81.

Dicey, A. V. (1915), *Introduction to the Study of the Law of the Constitution*, 8th edn (London, Macmillan).

Douglas-Scott, S. (2015), 'A UK exit from the EU: the end of the United Kingdom or a new constitutional dawn?', *Cambridge Journal of International and Comparative Law*, Oxford Legal Studies Research Paper No. 25/2015, https://ssrn.com/abstract=2574405, accessed 7 September 2017.

Edwards, O. D. (ed.) (1989), *A Claim of Right for Scotland* (Edinburgh, Polygon).

Elliott, M. (2014), 'A "permanent" Scottish Parliament and the sovereignty of the UK Parliament: four perspectives', UK Constitutional Law Association blog, https://ukconstitutionallaw.org/2014/11/28/mark-elliott-a-permanent-scottish-parliament-and-the-sovereignty-of-the-uk-parliament-four-perspectives/, accessed 7 September 2017.

European Commission (2017), 'Joint report from the negotiators of the European Union and the United Kingdom Government on progress during phase 1 of negotiations under Article 50 TEU on the United Kingdom's orderly withdrawal from the European Union', 8 December, https://ec.europa.eu/commission/sites/beta-political/files/joint_report.pdf, accessed 19 January 2018.

Flinders, M. & Curry, D. (2008), 'Bi-constitutionality: unravelling New Labour's constitutional orientations', *Parliamentary Affairs*, 61(1): 99–121.

Gallagher, J. D. (2017), 'Conventional wisdom: Brexit, devolution and the Sewel convention', Gwilym Gibbon Centre Working Paper (Oxford, Nuffield College), https://www.nuffield.ox.ac.uk/media/1975/2017-01-conventional-wisdom-brexit-devolution-and-the-sewel-convention.pdf, accessed 19 June 2018.

Gamble, A. (2016), 'The Conservatives and the Union: the "New English Toryism" and the origins of Anglo-Britishness', *Political Studies Review*, 14(3): 359–67.

Gifford, C. (2010), 'The UK and the European Union: dimensions of sovereignty', *Parliamentary Affairs*, 63(2): 321–38. DOI 10.1093/pa/gsp031.

Goldsworthy, J. (2012), 'Parliamentary sovereignty's premature obituary', UK Constitutional Law Association blog, https://ukconstitutionallaw.org/2012/03/09/jeffrey-goldsworthy-parliamentary-sovereigntys-premature-obituary/, accessed 31 August 2017.

Guelke, A. (2017), 'The risk to Northern Ireland', *Journal of Democracy*, 28(1): 42–52.

Harvie, C. (2000), 'The moment of British nationalism, 1939–1970', *Political Quarterly*, 71(3): 328–40.

Hazell, R. (2006), 'The English Question' (London, Constitution Unit), https://www.ucl.ac.uk/political-science/publications/unit-publications/130.pdf, accessed 3 July 2018.

Henderson, A., Jeffery, C., Lineira, R., Scully, R., Wincott, D. & Wyn Jones, R. (2016), 'England, Englishness and Brexit', *Political Quarterly*, 87(2): 187–99.

HM Government (2017a), 'Prime Minister's letter to Donald Tusk triggering Article 50', 29 March, https://www.gov.uk/government/uploads/system/uploads/attachment_data/file/604079/Prime_Ministers_letter_to_European_Council_President_Donald_Tusk.pdf, accessed 8 September 2017.

HM Government (2017b), *The United Kingdom's Exit from and New Partnership with the European Union*, Cm 9417 (London, HM Government).

HM Government (2017c), 'Confidence and Supply Agreement between the Conservative and Unionist Party and the Democratic Unionist Party', https://www.gov.uk/government/publications/conservative-and-dup-agreement-and-uk-government-financial-support-for-northern-ireland/agreement-between-the-conservative-and-unionist-party-and-the-democratic-unionist-party-on-support-for-the-government-in-parliament, accessed 30 January 2018.

HM Government & the Scottish Government (2012), 'The Edinburgh Agreement' ['Agreement between the United Kingdom Government and the Scottish Government on a referendum on independence for Scotland'], London, http://webarchive.nationalarchives.gov.uk/20130102230945/http://www.number10.gov.uk/wp-content/uploads/2012/10/Agreement-final-for-signing.pdf, accessed 1 December 2017.

House of Lords Constitution Committee (2012), *Referendum on Scottish Independence*, 24th Report of Session 2010–12, HL Paper 263 (London, The Stationery Office).

ITV News (2017), '"Now is not the time": May rules out Sturgeon's call for IndyRef2', ITV Report, 16 March, http://www.itv.com/news/2017-03-16/may-rules-out-sturgeons-call-for-second-scottish-referendum-saying-now-is-not-the-time/, accessed 19 August 2018.

Jeffery, C. & Wincott, D. (2006), 'Devolution in the United Kingdom: statehood and citizenship in transition', *Publius*, 36(1): 3–18.

Jeffery, C., Wyn Jones, R., Henderson, A., Scully, R. & Lodge, G. (2014), 'Taking England seriously: the new English politics', Centre on Constitutional Change, Edinburgh, http://www.centreonconstitutionalchange.ac.uk/sites/default/files/news/Taking%20England%20Seriously_The%20New%20English%20Politics.pdf, accessed 31 August 2017.

Jennings, W. I. (1959), *The Law and the Constitution*, 5th edn (London, University of London Press).

Johnson, N. (2004), *Reshaping the British Constitution: Essays in Political Interpretation* (Basingstoke, Palgrave Macmillan).

Jones, T. H. (2012), 'Wales, devolution and sovereignty', *Statute Law Review*, 33(2): 151–62. DOI 10.1093/slr/hms023.

Jones, T. H., Turnbull, J. H. & Williams, J. M. (2005), 'The law of Wales or the law of England and Wales?', *Statute Law Review*, 26(3): 135–45, https://doi.org/10.1093/slr/hmi015, accessed 24 May 2018.

Keating, M. (2010), 'The strange death of Scottish unionism', *Government and Opposition*, 45(3): 365–85. DOI 10.1111/j.1477-7053.2010.01317.x.

Keating, M. (2012), 'Rethinking sovereignty: independence-lite, devolution-max and national accommodation', *Revista d'estudis autonòmics i federals*, 16 (October): 9–29.

Kellas, J. G. (1989), 'Prospects for a new Scottish political system', *Parliamentary Affairs*, 42(4): 519–32.

King, A. (2001), *Does the United Kingdom Still Have a Constitution?* (London, Sweet & Maxwell).

Leyland, P. (2011), 'The multifaceted constitutional dynamics of U.K. devolution', *International Journal of Constitutional Law*, 9(1): 251–73. DOI 10.1093/icon/mor021.

Lijphart, A. (2012), *Patterns of Democracy: Government Forms and Performance in Thirty-Six Countries*, 2nd edn (New Haven, CT, and London, Yale University Press).

McHarg, A. (2016), 'The future of the United Kingdom's territorial constitution: Can the Union survive?', SSRN, https://ssrn.com/abstract=2771614, accessed 7 September 2017.

McLean, I. & Peterson, S. (2014), 'Transitional constitutionalism in the United Kingdom', *Cambridge Journal of International and Comparative Law*, 3(4): 1113–35. DOI 10.7574/cjicl.03.04.282.

Marquand, D. (2008), *Britain since 1918: The Strange Career of British Democracy* (London, Weidenfeld & Nicolson).

May, T. (2017), 'Prime Minister: Britain after Brexit: a vision of a global Britain', speech at Conservative Party Conference, 2 October, http://press.conservatives.

com/post/151239411635/prime-minister-britain-after-brexit-a-vision-of, accessed 8 September 2017.

Meehan, E. (2014), 'The changing British–Irish relationship: the sovereignty dimension', *Irish Political Studies*, 29(1): 58–75. DOI 10.1080/07907184.2013.875002.

Miller, R. (2017), 'R (Miller) v Secretary of State for exiting the European Union (2017) UKSC 5', https://www.supremecourt.uk/cases/docs/uksc-2016-0196-judgment.pdf, accessed 31 August 2017.

Mitchell, J. (2003), *Governing Scotland: The Invention of Administrative Devolution* (Basingstoke, Palgrave Macmillan).

Mitchell, J. (2011), *Devolution in the UK* (Manchester, Manchester University Press).

Morgan, K. (1981), *Rebirth of a Nation: Wales 1880–1980* (Oxford, Oxford University Press).

Morgan, K. (1999), 'Divided we stand', *History Today*, 49(5): 24–6, https://www.questia.com/magazine/1G1-54700556/divided-we-stand, accessed 24 May 2018.

Morgan, K. & Mungham, G. (2000), *Redesigning Democracy: The Making of the Welsh Assembly* (Bridgend, Seren).

Northern Ireland Office (1998), 'The Belfast Agreement' ['The Agreement: agreement reached in the multi-party negotiations'], London, https://www.gov.uk/government/uploads/system/uploads/attachment_data/file/136652/agreement.pdf, accessed 24 May 2018.

Priddy, S. (2016), *Claim of Right for Scotland*, Debate Pack, Number 2016-0158 (London, House of Commons Library), http://researchbriefings.files.parliament.uk/documents/CDP-2016-0158/CDP-2016-0158.pdf, accessed 7 September 2017.

Rawlings, R. (1998), 'The New Model Wales', *Journal of Law and Society*, 25(4): 461–509.

Roberts, P. R. (1972), 'The union with England and the identity of "Anglican" Wales', *Transactions of the Royal Historical Society*, 22: 49–70.

Rokkan, S. & Urwin, D. (eds) (1982), *The Politics of Territorial Identity: Studies in European Regionalism* (London, Sage).

Royal Commission on the Constitution (1973), *The Report of the Royal Commission on the Constitution* (London, The Stationery Office).

Scotland Act (1998), c.46, https://www.legislation.gov.uk/ukpga/1998/46, accessed 19 June 2018.

Scotland Act (2016), c.11, http://www.legislation.gov.uk/ukpga/2016/11/contents/enacted, accessed 2 December 2017.

Scottish Government (2016), 'Scotland's Place in Europe', Edinburgh, http://www.gov.scot/Resource/0051/00512073.pdf, accessed 2 December 2017.

Scottish Parliament Official Report (1999), 12 May, http://www.parliament.scot/parliamentarybusiness/report.aspx?r=4160&i=26584&c=703406#ScotParlOR, accessed 18 June 2018.

SDLP (Social Democratic and Labour Party) (2017), 'Eastwood calls for united front on Brexit', 29 March, http://www.sdlp.ie/news/2017/eastwood-calls-for-united-front-on-brexit/, accessed 2 December 2017.

SNP (2017), 'Nicola Sturgeon's speech on Scotland's referendum', 13 March, https://www.snp.org/nicola_sturgeon_speech_scotland_s_referendum, accessed 19 August 2018.

Tombs, R. (2014), *The English and their History* (London, Allen Lane).

Toubeau, S. & Murkens, J. (2016), 'The illusion of sovereignty: the UK's power-sharing experience can play a constructive role in the EU', LSE British Politics and Policy blog, http://blogs.lse.ac.uk/politicsandpolicy/the-illusion-of-sovereignty/, accessed 31 August 2017.

Varadkar, L. (2017), 'Statement on Brexit negotiations by Taoiseach Leo Varadkar', 8 December, https://merrionstreet.ie/en/News-Room/News/Statement_on_Brexit_negotiations_by_the_Taoiseach_Leo_Varadkar_T_D_.html, accessed 18 December 2017.

Wales Act (2017), c.4, http://www.legislation.gov.uk/ukpga/2017/4/enacted, accessed 2 December 2017.

Welsh Government (2015), 'Evidence to the House of Lords Constitution Committee Inquiry, "The Union and Devolution"', in Select Committee on the Constitution, *The Union and Devolution: Oral and Written Evidence* (London, House of Lords), 726–31.

Welsh Government (2017a), 'Brexit and devolution: securing Wales' future', Cardiff, https://beta.gov.wales/sites/default/files/2017-06/170615-brexit%20and%20devolution%20%28en%29.pdf, accessed 2 December 2017.

Welsh Government (2017b), 'First Minister establishes a Commission on Justice in Wales', 18 September, Welsh Government Press Release, http://gov.wales/newsroom/firstminister/2017/170918-first-minister-establishes-commission-on-justice-in-wales/?lang=en, accessed 6 December 2017.

Welsh Government (2017c), 'Securing Wales' future: transition from the European Union to a new relationship with Europe', Cardiff, https://beta.gov.wales/sites/default/files/2017-01/30683%20Securing%20Wales%C2%B9%20Future_ENGLISH_WEB.pdf, accessed 2 December 2017.

Wyn Jones, R. (2016), 'Why did Wales shoot itself in the foot in this referendum?', *The Guardian*, 27 June, https://www.theguardian.com/commentisfree/2016/jun/27/wales-referendum-remain-leave-vote-uk-eu-membership, accessed 19 June 2018.

4

The Ghost in the Machine? The Government of England

JIM GALLAGHER

4.1 Introduction

ENGLAND IS BY FAR the largest part of the United Kingdom, with 85 per cent of the population and nearly two-thirds of the land area, but does it have a government of its own? The purpose of this chapter is to explore whether, and to what extent, such a government exists and how much this matters. Is the Government of England the 'Ghost in the Machine' of the UK Government?[1] Can its traces be seen in the organisation of government departments, the working of the Cabinet and cabinet committees, the nature of decision-making in social, economic or fiscal policy or, very topically, in the tasks which the UK Government now faces in planning for life after European Union membership? Alternatively, as the philosopher Gilbert Ryle implied when he used this phrase to describe the mind–body problem, are the ghost and the machine one and the same thing (Ryle 1949)? Is England's Government the UK Government and is that all there is to it?

In the minds of many, including many in England, no real distinction is made between the United Kingdom, Great Britain and England. Sir John Fortescue, the important early English jurist and arguably one of England's earliest political scientists, wrote both *The Governance of England* and *De Laudibus Legum Angliae* (Fortescue 1825), but by the time they were published in the 1540s Wales had been ruled by English kings for two centuries and the second of Henry VIII's Laws in Wales Acts had applied English law in Wales. Even more egregiously, when Walter Bagehot wrote *The English Constitution* in the 1860s (Bagehot 1873), he knew he was writing about the constitution of the United Kingdom (he mentions the United Kingdom, Scotland and Ireland exactly once each, for rhetorical purposes, and

[1] I am indebted to Akash Paun for this conceit.

Proceedings of the British Academy, **217**, 69–90, © The British Academy 2018.

once references the British constitution, apparently by accident). But throughout his account, the constitution, parliament and government are described as that of England, or of the English nation or people. Similarly, when Harold Wilson appropriated and amended Fortescue's title for his 1976 book *The Governance of Britain*, he was perhaps acknowledging that he governed the Welsh and Scots, but ignoring the fact that Northern Ireland had been under direct Westminster rule for the previous four years. Wilson's book, which is, to be fair, primarily about the role of the Prime Minister and Cabinet, makes no territorial distinctions within the UK at all. This conflation of England with the whole UK wasn't just an English habit. When John Buchan's heroic Scottish spy, Sandy Arbuthnot, has implausible adventures all across the Middle East in *Greenmantle* he does it for 'England'.

The somewhat cavalier approach to the naming of the parts of the Union may have irritated some in Wales, Northern Ireland and Scotland over the years, but it has seldom been an issue in England. It has been perhaps a sign of supreme self-confidence and, if so, present concerns about it may be evidence of insecurity, as Aughey suggests in Chapter 2. Feelings of identity in England have changed in recent decades, most probably as a result of devolution to Scotland and Wales (see, for instance, Kenny (2014) and discussion elsewhere in this volume). English residents are now more likely than they were to describe themselves as English rather than British, although this English identity is as much concerned with relations with mainland Europe as relations within the UK. English identifiers are more likely to support leaving the EU, as Ford and Sobolewska discuss in Chapter 8.

4.2 Identity and Political Structure

This is not just a question of inaccurate labelling. Identities matter for the political structures which reflect them, and the ambiguity about English or British identity is also reflected in UK constitutional structures. The UK is famously described as a union state (Rokkan & Urwin 1982) and this matters greatly from the point of view of the smaller nations of the Union (as discussed in Chapter 3 by Akash Paun). It gives them a protected status, which they guard jealously. But the UK's political institutions make no special provision for the largest nation, England, save for the cautious 'English votes for English laws' (EVEL) reforms discussed in detail in Chapter 6 by Gover and Kenny. So far at least, they have never needed to: just as England's Parliament is Westminster, the UK Government is also England's Government.

The confusion of identity may largely be down to relative size. Eighty-five per cent of the UK population lives in England, which cannot avoid being economically and culturally dominant. But it also reflects the history of the development of the UK as a union (see Chapter 3). At each stage the extension of the state has taken place with little or no disturbance of how England was governed. Wales was incorporated into English territory in pre-modern times: the monarchy simply extended its power and later England's laws. The Union with Scotland was of huge constitutional and political significance north of the border, even though the Scottish elite continued to run Scotland. For England, it secured both the Protestant succession and the northern border, but barely altered the government of the country. Some Scottish members were added to the English Parliament, but otherwise English institutions were unchanged. Ireland is a different case, in that at the end of the 19th century Irish members threatened to make England ungovernable by making Parliament unmanageable; but after partition Northern Ireland ran itself and the few Ulster MPs were seldom relevant to the Government of England.[2] Ironically, in 2017 it was Democratic Unionist Party (DUP) MPs who ensured that Mrs May's English Conservative majority was (just) able to form a UK Government.[3]

This development illustrates how the most visible disturbance to the governance of England from its membership of a larger union has been at the parliamentary rather than the governmental level: the West Lothian Question (see Gallagher 2012; Gover & Kenny 2016).[4] Having a parliament which was both domestic and imperial perplexed Gladstone as he tried to answer the Irish Question. Now that there are separate legislatures for Scotland, Wales and Northern Ireland the West Lothian Question matters, at least in principle. Members of Parliament for each of these places sit in what is also England's Parliament and (in theory at least) can influence legislation that only applies in England; thus they do not reflect the balance of English opinion as represented by English MPs. This is clearly an anomaly. If it is a problem—and a good case can be made that it is not much of a problem—it is one for England rather than the smaller nations.[5]

Broadly speaking, the West Lothian Question has been a problem of parliamentary representation rather than government formation, but the different solutions proposed to it have differing implications for Government. The first is what Gladstone eventually proposed for Ireland: a cut in the number of MPs, applied from 1923 to 1972 in respect of Northern Ireland. This reduces the size of the problem but leaves the principle unresolved and implies nothing about the organisation of the executive. The second, creating a separate English Parliament, would have very radical implications for how England and the UK are governed, but despite the existence of a Campaign for an English Parliament (CEP) for some years now, the idea remains on the fringes of politics. But if it were to happen in the full-strength form favoured by the CEP it would imply creating a separate English executive accountable to that legislature, as Russell and Sheldon discuss in Chapter 5.

[2] They briefly annoyed Harold Wilson by objecting to his plans on steel nationalisation. See Straw (2007).

[3] After the June 2017 general election DUP members offered confidence and supply to Mrs May's Conservative Government. Her party had an overall majority in England, and in Great Britain, but not the UK.

[4] As posed by Tam Dalyell, MP for West Lothian, the question runs as follows: 'For how long will English constituencies and English Honourable members tolerate … at least 119 Honourable Members from Scotland, Wales and Northern Ireland exercising an important, and probably often decisive, effect on English politics while they themselves have no say in the same matters in Scotland, Wales and Northern Ireland?' (HC Deb., 14 November 1977: col. 122).

[5] As long ago as the 1920s it was a problem for the government of the Church of England: see Machin (2000).

A devolved English Parliament with powers comparable to Edinburgh or Belfast now was considered by the Royal Commission on the Constitution in 1973. It would make the UK a substantially symmetrical, federal state rather than a union. England would have an executive, an English Government like the Scottish Government or Welsh Government. The main problem with this is the one the Royal Commission identified. The English Government would be the focus of English political life, just as the Scottish Government is for Scotland. But England makes up the vast majority of the UK and so that Government would become the focus of most of the UK's political life as well. The federal level of government might be soon become vestigial and irrelevant, and the Union between England and the rest of the UK the same. It is hard to imagine how to create a viable federal UK executive in those circumstances, nor indeed how to reconcile it with the doctrine of (Westminster) parliamentary sovereignty. However, there is no room here to consider this issue.

The third answer to the West Lothian Question, advocated by this author (Gallagher 2012) and now implemented by the Conservative Government (discussed by Gover and Kenny (2016) and in Chapter 6), is to alter parliamentary procedure dealing with legislation that relates only to England, to give English MPs an identifiable voice over it and, in certain circumstances, a veto. This reform—EVEL—does not, in itself, affect the nature or responsibilities of government. England has the same government as the whole United Kingdom, albeit this is inevitably dominated by England as a result of the population and hence parliamentary arithmetic. The present Cabinet, for example, contains only two MPs representing non-English constituencies—the Secretaries of State for Wales and Scotland. That is an unusually English bias, but even the Labour governments at the beginning of the century, which contained a number of senior Scots, were still dominated by English MPs.

But as time goes on, will being held separately accountable to English MPs for English legislation and perhaps English policy decisions reveal where the UK Government is English and where not? Together with English identity politics, will this create pressure for a more identifiably English face of government? Accordingly, this chapter looks hard for the ghost in the machine—in government departments, cabinet committees, taxation and spending decisions and elsewhere. It then asks whether something could be done to separate the two roles more clearly and make the ghost manifest itself.

4.3 Ghost Hunting: English Departments

Government as a whole may deal simultaneously with both the UK and England, but the approach clearly varies from department to department. Some are clearly UK in their responsibilities, others England only, England and Wales, Great Britain or some mixture. The picture is an untidy one, not least because of the habit British prime ministers have of reorganising government departments to meet policy and political priorities with little regard for the geographical division of responsibilities.

Responsibility for higher education, for example, seems to shuffle between whatever department is responsible for business (largely UK focused) and the one dealing with English education, with little regard for the fact that it is a devolved responsibility. (It now seems to be split, with UK-wide research funding in the former and English student finance in the latter.) Another example would be how Prime Minister Blair used Dr John Reid, representing a Scottish seat, as a utility English minister for health and home affairs, and when at Reid's behest he reorganised the Home Office chose to leave it a mixed UK and England and Wales department as it is today.

Nevertheless the following departments (as at December 2017) are clearly UK wide and UK only in their responsibilities. The first four are long-standing Whitehall institutions, though of the latter at least one (the Department for Exiting the EU) is likely to be ephemeral.

Table 4.1 UK-Only Departments

UK-Only Departments
Foreign & Commonwealth Office
Ministry of Defence
Agencies dealing with national security
Department for International Development
Department for International Trade
Department for Exiting the EU

One way to get a picture of the extent to which other departments operate for England only is to look at their spending and the extent to which it is regarded as 'comparable' for Barnett formula purposes, for Scotland, Wales and Northern Ireland, meaning that the spending functions in question are devolved in one or more of the other nations. The Barnett formula operates by identifying UK Government spending, usually for England only but sometimes for England and Wales, which is comparable to devolved spending, and applying a population share to changes in it. In each spending review the Treasury Statement of Funding Policy, of which the most recent was published in November 2015 (HM Treasury 2015), sets out what percentage of each department's spending is comparable. Government departments keep changing (for instance, two of the departments in Table 4.1 did not exist in 2015) but those numbers can still be used to devise a plausible picture of English Government spending responsibilities.

Table 4.2 is the summary of comparability percentages for each department. In short, a comparability percentage close to zero indicates a UK department, or one which is predominantly so. (The Ministry of Defence, the Foreign Office and the Department for International Development are not included in the published table, as their percentage is exactly zero.) A comparability percentage at or close to 100 per cent in respect of Scotland, Wales and Northern Ireland indicates a wholly or predominantly English department. Other departments will be mixed, or differ across the different devolved nations. This will reflect different spending programmes in the department in question and different responsibilities in each of the devolved nations.

The Statement of Funding Policy contains a breakdown of individual departmental spending programme lines and the extent to which each is comparable for Barnett purposes. As for the differing responsibilities amongst the devolved administrations, broadly speaking Northern Ireland's devolved responsibilities are the widest, at least in principle, then Scotland, then Wales. The major differences are that social security is formally devolved in Northern Ireland, and justice in both Northern Ireland and Scotland, while neither is devolved in Wales.

Table 4.2 Summary of Departmental 'Comparability Factors' (in %, departments as at 2015)

Department	Scotland	Wales	Northern Ireland
Business, Innovation and Skills*	66.4	66.3	66.7
Cabinet Office and Security and Intelligence Agencies (SIA)	6.5	6.5	10.3
Chancellor's Departments	0.4	0.0	0.3
CLG: Communities	99.7	99.7	99.7
CLG: Local Government	100.0	100.0	100.0
CLG: Business Rates	100.0	100.0	100.0
Culture, Media & Sport	76.9	76.9	77.6
Education	100.0	100.0	100.0
Energy & Climate Change*	1.8	1.8	15.3
Environment, Food & Rural Affairs	99.8	99.0	99.8
Health	99.4	99.4	99.4
Home Office	91.7	0.0	91.7
Justice	100.0	0.0	99.9
Law Officers' Departments	100.0	0.0	91.6
Transport	91.0	80.9	91.3
Work & Pensions	1.4	1.4	100.0

* Departments that no longer exist.

So, for example, the Department for Work and Pensions (DWP), on the basis of spending allocations in 2015, is properly a GB department (social security is, formally speaking, devolved in Northern Ireland, so spend is 100 per cent comparable there, but in 2015 was almost wholly reserved in Scotland and Wales). By contrast, the Departments of Health and Education are English departments: their responsibilities are fully devolved in each of the three devolved nations. The picture, however, requires more detailed examination, for several reasons. Most departments are a mixture in spending terms and spending isn't the only thing they do. On top of that, departmental responsibilities have changed more than once since 2015. Each department is briefly discussed in turn, broadly in order of decreasing 'Englishness'.

Departments of Health and Education: these are in substance purely English departments. Health and education are both fully devolved in each of Scotland, Wales and Northern Ireland. The Secretaries of State, however, have some minor UK responsibilities for international relations connected with health and education matters.

Department of Communities and Local Government, including Business Rates: this too is an English department, as one would expect given that it deals only with English local government. Business rates are separately identified as they are an 'English' tax and discussed along with other taxes in Section 4.6.

Department of Environment, Food and Rural Affairs: in purely spending terms this is an England-only department, as agriculture and similar issues are devolved in each of the three devolved nations. But it also plays a major international role on behalf of the UK, discharged in liaison with the devolved administrations. For as long as the UK remains in the EU it will lead on agriculture, fisheries and environment negotiations, and quite possibly thereafter it will have a continuing international role in respect of these matters. The immediate Brexit implications are discussed in Section 4.7.

Department of Transport: this is very largely an English department, but it retains some UK-wide responsibilities. These relate, among other things, to aviation and maritime issues and the legal framework for road and rail traffic, although not spending on roads or railway franchising (or, in Scotland and Northern Ireland, rail infrastructure).

Department for Culture, Media and Sport: this is largely an English department but with some important UK responsibilities. They include, notably, broadcasting, broadband and telecommunications issues, as well as the National Lottery. But its arts, museums, sport and tourism responsibilities all relate to England only. Again, it has some minor international UK representative responsibilities.

Three departments are substantially England and Wales departments, thanks to Henry VIII, as noted in Section 4.1:

Ministry of Justice: running prisons, courts and so on, is an England and Wales department, as justice is devolved in Scotland and Northern Ireland.

Law Officers' Departments: small bodies offering advice on the England and Wales legal jurisdiction and dealing with prosecution issues.

Home Office: over the years this has changed from being an all-purpose home (as opposed to foreign) ministry with a wide ragbag of responsibilities, to become a ministry of immigration and the interior, dealing largely with policing and border control. Its immigration and border control responsibilities are, naturally enough, for the whole UK. Its policing responsibilities relate to England and Wales, though it takes the lead on terrorism matters for the whole UK. Despite this, it might be that Home Secretaries see themselves as essentially UK interior ministers.

Department of Business, Innovation and Skills: this was perhaps more of an English than a UK department, but it had significant UK responsibilities. Those for international trade have now been transferred to the new department set up for that purpose. The department dealt with only English higher education and skills development, but it retained responsibility for the UK research councils, funding arts and humanities as well as medicine and the social and natural sciences. In 2016, higher education policy, but not research, was transferred back to the education department. The rest of the department was merged into a new Department for Business, Energy and Industrial Strategy, also incorporating energy and climate change policy.

Department of Energy and Climate Change: this department had a mix of UK, GB and England spending functions before being merged with the business department in 2016. It fulfilled a range of energy, climate change and nuclear decommissioning responsibilities for the entire UK, but some functions relating to renewable energy (for instance the Green Deal) were devolved to Northern Ireland, which is not part of the GB-wide single energy market and national grid. The department also had a few England-only responsibilities relating to energy efficiency and fuel poverty.

Department for Work and Pensions: as noted earlier in this section, DWP is primarily a GB department, at least formally speaking. Social security in Northern Ireland is devolved de jure but operates under a so-called parity principle, under which Northern Irish benefits are, to the extent that they match GB benefits, fully funded by the UK Government. Consequently, DWP de facto operates like a UK department for decision-making, but as a GB department for benefits administration. This is changing to some degree with the devolution of some benefit powers to Scotland by the Scotland Act 2016, although those changes have had, as yet, little practical effect.

Cabinet Office: the Cabinet Office is a UK department, though it runs a few small programmes relating to civil society in England only.

Chancellor's Departments: HM Treasury and HM Revenue and Customs are UK-wide departments. HM Treasury is both an economics and finance ministry for the UK and HMRC collects taxes across the whole UK, including devolved income tax on behalf of the Scottish (and, from 2019, the Welsh) governments. But HM Treasury is also England's finance ministry, making spending decisions and in recent decades substantial related policy decisions across English spending programmes. It is therefore, to that extent, a very important English department.

For the sake of brevity this analysis ignores a large number of minor departments and agencies. It can be mapped onto major government departments (as at July 2017) reasonably readily, as Table 4.3 shows.

4.4 Ghost Hunting: England's Domestic Government?

We have, therefore, a list of wholly or largely English departments. Do they add up to England's domestic government and if so who forms it? At the time of writing, Theresa May is certainly Prime Minister of England as well as of the UK. The Chancellor is also England's finance and economics minister, though in practice much of his involvement in English domestic spending will be delegated to the Chief Secretary to the Treasury. England does not have a domestic Cabinet, but if it did, the members (using the offices existing at July 2017) are listed in Table 4.4.

Table 4.3 UK, GB and English Departments, 2017

July 2017 Department	2015 Precursor Department(s)	Territorial Coverage of Department	Comments
Foreign & Commonwealth Office	Foreign & Commonwealth Office	UK department	
Ministry of Defence	Ministry of Defence	UK department	
Agencies responsible for national security	Agencies responsible for national security	UK departments	
Department for International Trade	Created in 2016, with responsibilities in part taken from Department of Business, Innovation and skills	UK department	
Department for International Development	Department for International Development	UK department	
Department for Exiting the European Union	N/A—created in 2016	UK department	
Cabinet Office	Cabinet Office	UK department	
Chancellor's Departments	Chancellor's Departments	UK departments	HM Treasury is also England's finance ministry
Home Office	Home Office	England and Wales department principally	Significant additional UK responsibilities
Ministry of Justice	Ministry of Justice	England and Wales department	Minimal additional UK responsibilities
Law Officers' Department	Law Officers' Department	England and Wales department	Minimal additional UK responsibilities
Department for Education	Department for Education, plus higher education policy from business department	English department	Minimal additional UK responsibilities

July 2017 Department	2015 Precursor Department(s)	Territorial Coverage of Department	Comments
Department for Business, Energy and Industrial strategy	Department for Business, Innovation and Skills, plus Department for Energy and Climate Change	Mixed UK and English department	English economic development and substantial UK energy, research and trade responsibilities
Department of Health	Department of Health	English department	
Department for Work and Pensions	Department for Work and Pensions	GB department	De facto UK department since Northern Ireland replicates most GB social security policy. Some change in prospect as welfare functions devolved to Scotland
Department for Transport	Department for Transport	English department	Some additional UK responsibilities
Department for Communities and Local Government	Department for Communities and Local Government	English department	
Scotland, Wales and Northern Ireland Offices	Scotland, Wales and Northern Ireland Offices	UK departments	
Department for Environment, Food and Rural Affairs	Department for Environment, Food and Rural Affairs	English department	UK representative responsibilities
Department for Digital, Culture Media and Sport	Department for Culture, Media and Sport	English department	Significant additional UK responsibilities

Table 4.4 England's (Hypothetical) Domestic Cabinet

Minister	**Territorial Responsibilities**
Prime Minister	Very significant additional UK responsibilities
Chancellor of the Exchequer	Very significant additional UK responsibilities
Chief Secretary to the Treasury	Additional UK responsibilities
Home Secretary	Additional Welsh and UK responsibilities
Lord Chancellor	Additional Welsh responsibilities
Secretary of State for Education	English responsibilities almost solely
Secretary of State for Business etc.	Additional UK responsibilities
Secretary of State for Health	English responsibilities almost solely
Secretary of State for Transport	Some additional UK responsibilities
Secretary of State for Communities and Local Government	English responsibilities only
Secretary of State for Environment, Food and Rural Affairs	Some additional UK responsibilities
Attorney General	Additional Welsh responsibilities

Additionally, the Cabinet Office provides not merely a secretariat, but political coordination, so a Cabinet Office Minister (such as a Deputy Prime Minister, when there is one) might plausibly be added to this list.

Such a group of ministers does not, of course, meet as England's domestic Cabinet and certainly does not see itself as an English Government. Ministers, however, do regularly meet to consider the business of government outside the Cabinet, in cabinet committees. So are some UK cabinet committees de facto meetings of this hypothetical English Government? The meetings and agendas of cabinet committees are, of course, confidential (save occasionally when a meeting is said to have happened, for example in relation to civil contingencies matters), but it is possible to deduce from the list of committees and their membership which are likely to deal with substantially English issues.

4.5 Cabinet Government for England?

Each Prime Minister and government forms a set of cabinet committees, in response to external circumstances and political priorities. Like government departments, cabinet committees change and the list that follows is correct as of July 2017. It would have been significantly different before the European referendum and different even before the 2017 election. Broadly speaking, they can be divided into committees dealing with defence and international relations, with economic policy and with domestic policy. This has been reflected in the structure of the Cabinet Secretariat for many years, with an Economic and Domestic Secretariat separate from international affairs secretariats. Some committees have a finite life, dealing with particular issues as they emerge (the present administration uses the quaint name 'implementation task forces' for some). Others tend to continue, sometimes under slightly different descriptions which reflect the political priorities of the administration. The present Government has broadly followed this pattern, although committees to deal with exiting the European Union are a unique phenomenon. The full list of committees can be found in an official government publication (Cabinet Office 2017).

The group of international affairs committees is, of course, solely UK in focus. It includes:

- The European Union Exit and Trade Committee and its subcommittees on Negotiations, on International Trade and on European Affairs (dealing with day-to-day EU issues).
- The National Security Council and its subcommittees on Nuclear Deterrence and Security and on Threats, Hazards, Resilience and Contingencies.

These are UK committees, although some ministers with purely or largely English responsibilities sit on many of them. They do not form in any sense part of the domestic government of England but are very clearly the UK Government discharging its 'federal' role.

The cabinet committees dealing with economic issues are also primarily UK in focus, though, as one would expect, a number of ministers with largely English responsibilities attend and focus on English issues. They comprise:

- The Economy and Industrial Strategy Committee with its subcommittees on Airports (*English, dealing with the South East*); on Economic Affairs (*largely UK*); on Reducing Regulation (*largely UK*).

On the other hand, the committees dealing with domestic policy are, as one might expect (given how much domestic policy is devolved elsewhere in the UK), more English in focus. English ministers dominate:

- The Social Reform Committee and its subcommittee on Home Affairs.

They nevertheless consider some UK and GB issues, such as migration and aspects of social security.

The group of 'implementation task forces', with what is expected to be a limited life, have a mixture of territorial application:

- Housing (*English and membership in substance*).
- Digital (*a mixture of English and UK responsibilities*).
- Tackling Modern Slavery and People Trafficking (*UK*).

The final cabinet committee listed, dealing with *Parliamentary Business and Legislation*, is a UK Government committee and contains few departmental ministers. But it is highly influential in determining the programme of legislation that applies to England.[6]

From this pattern of committee membership, it is clear that no cabinet committee is anything like England's domestic government. Although in social policy English Government can be seen to be a little separate from the Government of the UK, the management of England's domestic economic policies remains deeply entangled with the economic policies of the UK as a whole—hardly surprising, given England has 85 per cent of the UK population. In the creation of cabinet committees, priority is given to policy coherence around topics rather than reflecting the territorial constitution division of power; there is no sign whatsoever of organising government on distinct English and UK lines to meet the pressures of parliamentary scrutiny of English legislation.

4.6 Getting and Spending: England's Taxation and Expenditure

It is in taxation and spending that the deep entanglement of the government of England and that of the UK is most clearly seen. Despite tax devolution to Scotland and Wales (and to some degree a possibility for Northern Ireland) most taxes are set and collected on a UK basis. There are three main taxes—national insurance, VAT and income tax. The first two are set and collected by the UK Government and used to support both reserved and devolved expenditure (although from 2019 a fixed share of VAT revenue in Scotland is to be assigned to the devolved Scottish budget). Income tax is devolved in Scotland, so that its rates and bands are set by the Scottish Parliament, and a less thoroughgoing devolution of income tax is in prospect for Wales. English income tax, however, is set by the UK Chancellor. Indeed, although most Scottish income tax is used to support only devolved expenditure (the exception being income tax on dividends and interest payments, which are collected on a UK basis), income tax collected in England goes to support expenditure across the whole UK, including devolved expenditure in Wales and Northern Ireland and to some degree even in Scotland.[7]

Some minor taxes are also devolved in different parts of the UK,[8] including stamp duty land tax in Scotland and Wales (and there has been much discussion of devolving corporation tax for Northern Ireland) but the budgets of the devolved administrations are still principally supported by shared UK taxes.

[6] The committees dealing with civil contingencies are different in nature, have operational responsibilities and can include the devolved administrations.

[7] For an explanation of the latter point see Gallagher (2016).

[8] The following taxes are or are soon to be devolved: in Scotland, Wales and Northern Ireland, local property taxes, i.e. council tax and rates; in Scotland, additionally, income tax rates and bands, stamp duty land tax—now called land and buildings transaction tax there—landfill tax and air passenger duty; in Wales, stamp duty land tax and landfill tax; in Northern Ireland, air passenger duty for long-haul flights.

Taxation decisions are taken by the Chancellor of the Exchequer in the budget, which is a quintessential piece of UK political theatre. Indeed it is wholly unrealistic to talk of an English Government taking English tax decisions, as there are almost no purely English taxes. The one exception is business rates and council tax (devolved elsewhere in the UK). They support English local council expenditure only. These two taxes are an instructive example, because they are linked directly to England-only spending programmes. No other taxes are so hypothecated: all UK taxes are paid into the Consolidated Fund and allocated to UK-wide, English or devolved responsibilities by HM Treasury. The mechanism by which this is done includes, as is well known, the Barnett formula, which allocates to devolved budgets population shares of changes in the comparable English budgets. On the face of it, therefore, English spending choices determine devolved spending, illustrating the deep entanglement of UK public finances. There is no overall English spending budget to which English taxes are allocated and which an English Government could be seen to be managing. All expenditure and the taxation which supports it is, apparently, mixed together in the UK financial system and it is therefore similarly unrealistic to talk of an English Government taking English spending decisions.

Without a wholesale reconstruction of the territorial financial system to identify UK 'federal' taxes, English taxes and devolved taxes, together with federal, English and of all spending programmes, it makes little sense to think of an English administration taking specifically English tax and spending decisions. Instead, the UK Government takes tax and spending decisions which are overwhelmingly about English taxation and spending, but entangled with the devolved administrations' budgets.

Indeed, this connection between English spending on comparable functions and devolved expenditure is often used as an argument against any alterations to parliamentary procedure to deal with the West Lothian Question: after all, on the face of it, English legislative choices could influence spending and hence devolved budgets. While it is true that radically different approaches to spending programmes north and south of the border could make the Barnett formula much more difficult to defend (e.g. if the UK Government stopped funding health services in England out of general taxation, the consequential effects through the Barnett formula would be a significant reduction in the devolved budgets) this argument is not in fact a strong one.

First of all, formally speaking, English legislation does not of itself provide supply: that is to say it does not authorise expenditure. That is done by the legislation dealing with appropriations, which is, of course, UK legislation. And in fact, although the Barnett formula appears to deal only with comparable spending on health and other devolved issues, the function it discharges is rather a different one. Only the United Kingdom Government can make the choice between expenditure on UK spending programmes such as defence and social security and expenditure such as health and education. Therefore, when allocating its spending resources (i.e. the resources derived from UK taxation) the UK Government has to make a choice between, as it were, guns and butter, or more likely old age pensions and health spending. When UK resources are allocated to programmes such as health and education, the Government then has to make a choice regarding how much of this goes to England and how much to the devolved administrations: that is all that the Barnett formula does. Other mechanisms might be used—such as a more sophisticated assessment of relative need than simply incremental population change—but there is still the question of how much resource should be allocated to UK-wide programmes and that is a political choice for UK ministers, independent of Barnett.

In its budgeting process, however, the UK Government does not make this set of choices explicit. Instead, departmental budgets are a mixture of UK, GB, England and Wales and England-only spending programmes (to which the Barnett formula is applied, as it were, retail) rather than an all-England budget (to which Barnett might be applied, as it were, wholesale, with the same overall effect). Eighty-five per cent of the UK Government's budget is, in one way or another, for England.

It is also worth asking whether the UK Government shows any differentiation in spending policies when it acts as the Government of England. The obvious difference is between how the UK Government allocates money to devolved issues like health and education in the devolved nations and how it allocates money across the regions of England. The former is done by the Barnett formula, now adjusted for devolved tax responsibilities, while the latter is a set of UK decisions based on the Government's assessment of relative need. The overall effect in both cases is substantial geographical redistribution, most obviously to the devolved nations, but also to the poorer regions of England. The fiscal transfers to the North East and North West, for example, are proportionately higher than to Scotland, though not than to Wales or Northern Ireland.[9]

These fiscal transfers are an outcome of how much revenue is raised locally and how much the Government thinks needs to be spent in a particular region. It is interesting to consider whether the Government's assessment of spending need for devolved services in England is related to its assessment of need for reserved services across the UK, notably social security. For the largest domestic spending programmes in England—health, education and local government—expenditure is distributed substantially by formulae, with a substantial addition of political judgement. Other programmes may have more ad hoc distribution methods. Comprehensive figures for public spending by region are regularly published in the Public Expenditure Statistical Analysis series (HM Treasury 2017). No detailed data is published for the spending effects of 'England-only' spending decisions, but rough approximations can readily be made, to give an indication of whether the Government, as Government of England, has distinctive views about need in England.

The Public Expenditure Statistical Analysis deals with so-called 'identifiable' expenditure. That is expenditure which is identifiably for the benefit of a particular part of the country. It therefore excludes substantial amounts of UK Government expenditure which are for the benefit of the whole nation—such as defence, foreign relations and expenditure on debt interest. The remaining public spending is on

[9] The first full analysis of these transfers is in ONS (2017).

Figure 4.1 Domestic and Social Protection Expenditure by English Region, £ per Head, 2015–16

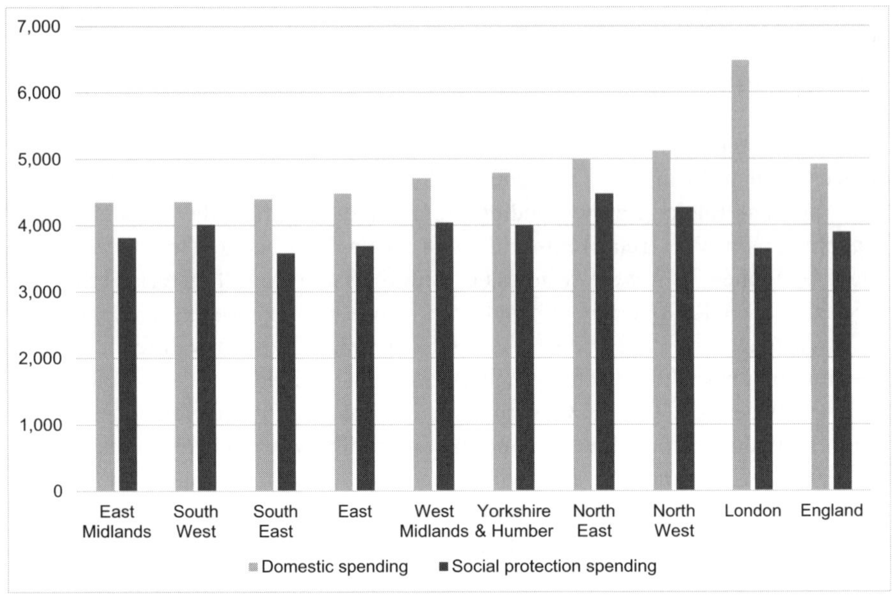

Source: HM Treasury (2017: tables 9.2 and 9.15).

Figure 4.2 Correlation between Domestic and Social Protection Expenditure, £ per Head, 2015–16

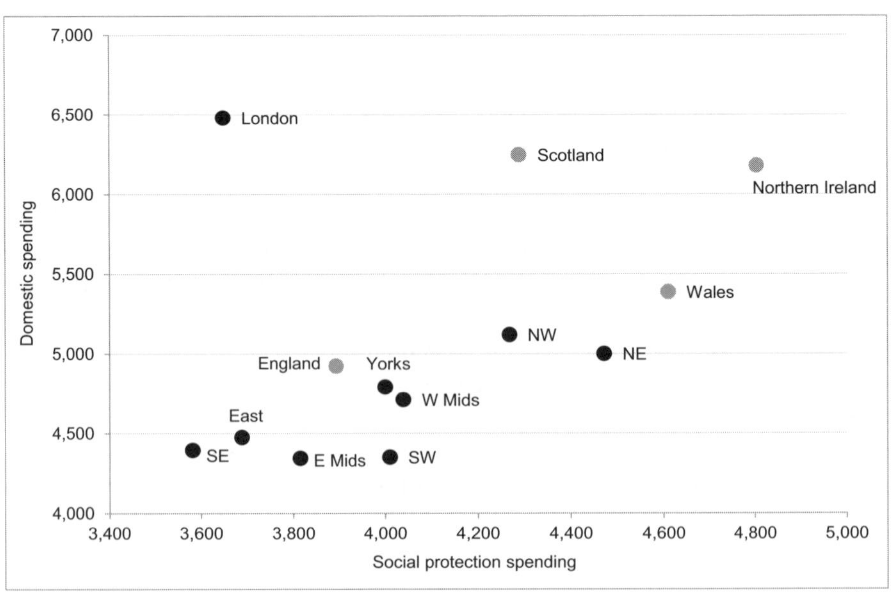

Source: HM Treasury (2017: tables 9.2 and 9.15).

public services, pensions and benefits. The latter two are UK 'federal' functions, but the majority of public services are devolved in Scotland, Wales and Northern Ireland and so might be described as 'domestic' spending for them and so for England. Accordingly, a rough estimate of that domestic spending can be made by subtracting from total identifiable spending in each region expenditure classified as 'social protection', of which the majority is pensions and benefits spending (it also includes a small amount of some service spending on social welfare). The results for the English regions are shown in Figure 4.1.

It will be seen that expenditure on domestic public services ranges between £4,000 and just over £5,000 per head for English regions other than London, but is markedly higher in London, at nearly £6,500 per head. A striking feature of the distribution is confirmed in Figure 4.2—that there is a strong correlation between spending on social protection and spending on other public services in every region of England other than London. In other words, in England outside London the UK Government's assessment of need for public services is strongly correlated with its assessment of need for pensions and benefits. It seems to look at need in England in exactly the same way as it looks at need in the UK as a whole.

This may not be surprising, as the number of elderly people and the incidence of poverty are strong drivers of service spending need. The major exception, of course, is London, where public expenditure on services is over 25 per cent higher than in the rest of England and higher even than in Scotland and Northern Ireland. This may be attributable to the problems of congestion, rather than deprivation, and some evidence for that hypothesis is seen in the very high transport and housing spends (the cost of providing public housing in London is high). It may also reflect the political salience of London (just as public spending levels in Scotland and Northern Ireland reflect the different political leverage of their populations).

In Chapter 11, Iain McLean sets out the fiscal federalism questions for the UK more widely. It is interesting, however, to note here that if the UK Government applied the same (implicit) assessment of spending need to 'domestic' spending as in the regions of England, Welsh expenditure would not change substantially but spending in London would be reduced by over 30 per cent, in Scotland by about 20 per cent and in Northern Ireland by about 15 per cent. But the data show that UK Government generally sees need for public spending through the same lens for its English responsibilities as its UK-wide ones: no special 'domestic English' assessment of need is seen in the numbers.

We can therefore detect little sign of the UK Government acting distinctly as the Government of England in its economic or fiscal policies.

4.7 Brexit and the Territorial Distribution of Responsibilities

One further area, however, merits examination. The process of leaving the European Union has thrown up issues about the distribution of responsibilities between the UK and devolved administrations, which, arguably, suggest the Government should make a greater distinction between its UK and English responsibilities. This has been a matter of major controversy between the Government and the devolved administrations in Scotland and Wales (unresolved at the time of writing). In short, there are a substantial number of policy areas where at present UK-wide consistency is provided by European Union legislation, even though the policy responsibilities are otherwise not reserved to the UK Parliament or Government in the devolution settlements. An obvious example is agriculture, which is largely today concerned with the implementation of the Common Agricultural Policy. Responsibility rests with the Department for Environment, Food and Rural Affairs (Defra) for England and with the devolved administrations for the other three territories. As noted, Defra has apparently few non-English responsibilities, when measured in spending terms, but takes a lead (in consultation with the devolved administrations) in EU negotiations. The list of policy responsibilities that fall into this category is, however, much wider than simply agriculture. A UK Government assessment published by the Scottish Government concluded that over 100 policy areas are affected as far as Scotland is concerned (Scottish Government 2017) but this includes subjects where the EU law interest is marginal or peripheral.

A good argument can be made that the UK's territorial constitution, that is to say the devolution settlements for Scotland, Wales and Northern Ireland, should mean that once EU law no longer applies these matters simply default to being devolved and so become part of the Government's English, not UK, responsibilities. The Scottish and Welsh settlements say that anything not reserved to Westminster is devolved. So in the absence of EU constraint such matters would fall automatically to the responsibility of the devolved administrations and to the UK Government in respect of England. The UK Government's initial approach, however, was to legislate to reserve to Westminster anything which is currently within European competence, so that UK-wide frameworks can be agreed when necessary to replace European ones. Thus, for example, the UK Government department dealing with agriculture would cease to be an English department with international responsibilities and become a UK department determining (not merely leading) UK agricultural policy.

At the time of writing, when it is still unclear what the UK's future relationship with the EU will be and what, if any, EU law will continue to apply in the UK and for how long, an argument can certainly be made for caution in planning for wholesale devolution of these responsibilities. And there is also a good case that the devolved institutions should be obliged to implement whatever EU and other international obligations might be substituted for EU law in due course—it is highly likely that any trade deal would involve constraints on agricultural subsidies, for example, or more generally, rules equivalent to the EU state aid rules. So unfettered devolution is unlikely to be possible. This is, however, already provided for in the devolution settlements, where the UK Government has power to enforce international obligations. By seeking to reserve all of the relevant law, the UK Government in effect assumed that what had been its purely English responsibilities became UK responsibilities, despite devolution. (The UK and Welsh Governments, but not the Scottish Government, have now agreed an approach more respectful of devolution.) This makes little difference to the Government of England, but demonstrates that there is no clear distinction inside the UK administration between devolved and non-devolved responsibilities, between the Government of England and the Government of the UK.

4.8 Is there a Ghost in the Government Machine, and Could it Be Made Manifest?

Gilbert Ryle was essentially saying that the machine and the ghost were one and the same: Similarly, are the English and UK governments one and inseparable? On this evidence, it is hard to say they are not. As the analysis shows, some government departments are largely English, but few are wholly so. Most Cabinet ministers who deal with English domestic issues have some additional Welsh or UK responsibilities. There is no evidence that the distribution of ministerial responsibilities pays any regard to separating English and UK issues into different departments. Taxation and macroeconomic policy-making are indistinguishable between England and the UK. There is no evidence that the Government's understanding of need for public spending is differentiated between its UK and English responsibilities. If anything, they seem to be driven by the same factors. Economic policy for England is deeply entangled with economic policy for the UK. Most English economic development policy is also an integral part of the UK Government's overall economic approach. On the other hand, some degree of separateness can be identified in English social policy. The cabinet machinery which deals with it consists largely of English departments and ministers, but significant non-English issues continue to be discussed alongside English ones and the organisation of cabinet committees makes no attempt to distinguish English from UK domestic business. There is nothing to suggest that the pressures of English identity, nor the creation of specifically English parliamentary procedures, have caused the Government to reorganise itself on any distinct English and UK basis. If anything, most notably in response to Brexit, the trend is in the opposite direction.

The constitutional changes in recent decades, for Scotland in particular, have served to promote the notion of England as a political community distinct from the political community of the United Kingdom. But to borrow a phrase from the Scottish debate, England is a nation without a state of its own. Instead it has very much the majority share in the state of the United Kingdom. For the devolved nations, this absence of distinct statehood is addressed through the mechanism of devolution, providing each with a domestic legislature and executive. For the reasons in Section 4.1 a separate parliament for England is, however, both unlikely and arguably undesirable. Instead, the Government has promoted identifiable parliamentary procedures to deal with English legislation. There has been little demand for explicit institutional recognition of England within the UK Government machine, although a somewhat quixotic call from the CEP for the creation of a Secretary of State for England has now been adopted by some in the Labour Party, despite the party's traditional reluctance to create governance structures for England as a whole (discussed by John Denham in Chapter 7).

This or any similar idea would face some formidable challenges. First there is the untidy distribution of devolved functions across the three other devolved nations, which leads to an apparently random mixture of English, England and Wales, and UK government departments. Two things might be done about this. First, there is some obvious scope for altering the devolved responsibility boundary, most notably in relation to Wales. Discussion has sometimes focused on the creation of a Welsh legal jurisdiction (reversing Henry VIII's changes), which would imply the devolution of policing and justice. This would tidy up the responsibilities of the Home Office and associated departments. It is, however, something which will happen, or not, according to considerations of Welsh devolution rather than English governance. In any event, it would still leave 'English' departments, including the Home Office, with mixed UK and English responsibilities.

Secondly, explicit consideration could be given to the geographical distribution of functions in the allocation of departmental responsibilities. In other words, English departments could be consciously created and UK functions allocated to UK departments—UK economic policy matters could be associated more with HM Treasury or the UK Department of International Trade, say. This would be an additional constraint on prime ministers constructing governments, but it is arguably something they ought always have had an eye to. Such changes would, however, be of little benefit unless the group of 'English' ministers acted and were seen to act as the Government of England. It is conceivable, although contrary to the long tradition of closed cabinet government in the UK, that one or more committees of the UK Cabinet might be explicitly English, and that one might even become and be presented as the 'English Cabinet', a subcommittee of the UK Cabinet. As we have seen, this might be achievable if it dealt substantially with English domestic social policy issues. The Labour Party's 2017 manifesto proposed a Minister for England, but this appeared to be a junior ministerial job in the Department for Communities and Local Government (Labour Party 2017: 103). If there is a more substantial job for a 'Secretary of State for England' it would be to chair an English cabinet committee, but the price would be to set up an artificial boundary inside social policy, between domestic policy on health and education, and on social security, which would still have to be dealt with.

Separating English Government is more difficult in relation to economic policy, for two reasons. First, the fact that England's economy approaches 90 per cent of the UK economy means that English and UK economic development matters are inextricably linked and the separation between UK macroeconomic and English microeconomic policy choices would inevitably be an artificial one. Even more problematic, the fact that UK devolution finance and UK Government finance are considered together, and that despite the recent changes UK and English taxation remain inextricably linked, makes such a change problematic. There is no English cabinet committee which could make English tax and spending decisions. Without a wholesale reconstruction of the UK's fiscal federalism to separate English domestic spending and English taxation from UK spending and taxation, the economic governance of England and of the UK will remain closely bound together.

Nor is there likely at present to be much call for this as the UK Cabinet is overwhelmingly English. Just as the West Lothian Question is an untidy anomaly rather than a political problem when the UK Government enjoys a substantial English as well as UK majority, so a Cabinet in which only the Secretaries of State for Wales and Scotland do not represent English seats hardly needs to demonstrate its Englishness. More speculatively, one might wonder whether responding to the pressures of English identity politics by internal reorganisation of the UK Government is the wrong kind of answer. It is to a large degree the politics of English identity which have driven the Brexit debate, as Ford and Sobolewska explore in Chapter 8. Whether those pressures will be satisfied by the outcome of the EU negotiations remains to be seen, but if they are not, meat much redder than a ministerial title and a modest restructuring of cabinet committees might be demanded. For now at least, it seems reasonable to assume that the ghost remains firmly locked in the machine. It shows little sign of emerging and would do little good if it did.

References

Bagehot, W. (1873), *The English Constitution*, 2nd edn, https://socialsciences.mcmaster.ca/econ/ugcm/3ll3/bagehot/constitution.pdf, accessed 31 August 2017.

Cabinet Office (2017), 'List of cabinet committees', https://www.gov.uk/government/publications/the-cabinet-committees-system-and-list-of-cabinet-committees, accessed 25 May 2018.

Fortescue, J. (1825), *De Laudibus Legum Angliae*, English edn, https://archive.org/stream/delaudibusleguma00fortuoft/delaudibusleguma00fortuoft_djvu.txt, accessed 25 May 2018.

Gallagher, J. (2012), 'England and the Union: how and why to answer the West Lothian Question', IPPR, London, https://www.ippr.org/files/images/media/files/publication/2012/04/west-lothian-question_Apr2012_8954.pdf?noredirect=1, accessed 25 May 2018.

Gallagher, J. (2016), 'Algebra and the constitution: the fiscal framework of the Scotland Act', Gwilym Gibbon Centre for Public Policy Working Paper, Oxford, https://www.nuffield.ox.ac.uk/media/1752/gallagher-wp-algebra-and-the-constitution.pdf, accessed 25 May 2018.

Gover, D. & Kenny, M. (2016), 'Finding the good in EVEL: an evaluation of English votes for English laws in the House of Commons', Centre on Constitutional Change, http://mei.qmul.ac.uk/assets/publications/190095.pdf, accessed 25 May 2018.

HM Treasury (2015), 'Statement of funding policy: funding the Scottish Parliament, National Assembly for Wales and Northern Ireland Assembly', https://www.gov.uk/government/uploads/system/uploads/attachment_data/file/479717/statement_of_funding_2015_print.pdf, accessed 25 May 2018.

HM Treasury (2017), 'Public Expenditure Statistical Analyses', https://www.gov.uk/government/statistics/public-expenditure-statistical-analyses-2017, accessed 21 August 2018.

Kenny, M. (2014), *The Politics of English Nationhood* (Oxford, Oxford University Press).

Labour Party (2017), *For the Many, Not the Few: The Labour Party Manifesto 2017* (London, Labour Party).

Machin, G. I. T. (2000), 'Parliament, the Church of England, and the Prayer Book Crisis 1927–8', *Parliamentary History*, 19(1): 131–47.

ONS (Office for National Statistics) (2017), 'Country and regional public sector finances: year ending March 2016', https://www.ons.gov.uk/economy/governmentpublicsectorandtaxes/publicsectorfinance/articles/countryandregionalpublicsectorfinances/2015to2016, accessed 25 May 2018.

Rokkan, S. & Urwin, D. (eds) (1982), *The Politics of Territorial Identity: Studies in European Regionalism* (London, Sage).

Royal Commission on the Constitution (1973), *The Report of the Royal Commission on the Constitution* (London, The Stationery Office).

Ryle, G. (1949), *The Concept of Mind* (London, Hutchinson).

Scottish Government (2017), 'Defending devolution: justice, farming, fishing, environment and rail among "power grab" list', 19 September, https://news.gov.scot/news/defending-devolution, accessed 25 May 2018.

Straw, J. (2007), 'Living with West Lothian', *Prospect*, 127 (October), https://www.prospectmagazine.co.uk/magazine/livingwithwestlothian, accessed 19 June 2018.

Wilson, H. (1976), *The Governance of Britain* (London, Weidenfield & Nicolson).

5

An English Parliament: An Idea whose Time Has Come?

MEG RUSSELL & JACK SHELDON

5.1 Introduction

CALLS TO CREATE an English Parliament, in order to bring England's constitutional arrangements more closely into line with those elsewhere in the UK, have been made ever since the devolved legislatures were established in Scotland, Wales and Northern Ireland in the late 1990s. But the idea has commonly been dismissed by academics and mainstream politicians. Many argue that a devolved parliament covering almost 85 per cent of the UK's total population would destabilise the Union (e.g. Bogdanor 1999: 192; Constitution Committee 2016: para. 376). Critics also suggest that England is already dominant in the UK Parliament (Hazell 2006b: 14), that an English Parliament would achieve little in the way of decentralisation (Blick 2016: 18) and that establishing a new layer of government in England could cost the taxpayer dear (Bryant 2008: 674). Among elites, devolution to units within England rather than to England as a whole has tended to be the preferred option. Voters, meanwhile—as discussed in Section 5.5—have shown no strong enthusiasm for the creation of a new elected body.

Yet, as we chart in Section 5.2, interest in the possibility of establishing an English Parliament has gradually grown among political actors in recent years. This can be seen as a consequence of the various developments, described throughout this book, which have increased the salience of England's place in the devolution settlement. They include the gradually greater powers of the existing devolved legislatures, challenges to the future of the Union following both the 2014 Scottish independence referendum and 2016 EU referendum, and a growth, identifiable through public opinion surveys, in the relative strength of English national identity (Jeffery et al. 2014: 8–10). This has been accompanied by a growing recognition among some in the mainstream political parties, especially Labour, as discussed in

Proceedings of the British Academy, **217**, 91–114, © The British Academy 2018.

Chapter 7 by John Denham, of a need to improve their appeal to patriotic English voters (Hunt 2016a). In this context the increasingly wide range of political actors who have expressed an interest in the possible creation of an English Parliament suggests that it can no longer be dismissed as a wholly fringe idea.

In this chapter we seek to explore objectively the history of the English Parliament idea, summarising the questions that have been addressed by proponents and those which remain unanswered.[1] We begin with a summary of growing interest in the idea among the political class, broadly defined to include politicians, commentators and activists. We then explore what has driven this change. Having done so, we tease out the alternative models that supporters have proposed, concluding that there are two main models: a 'separately elected' or a 'dual mandate' English Parliament, each with different potential political consequences. A short section explores public opinion on the possibility of an English Parliament and which of these models is the more likely to gain public support. We then turn to the unanswered questions, before concluding.

We find that, despite growing interest among the political class, there remain various major questions about the detail of what an English Parliament might look like and about its likely effects on the political and territorial dynamics of the UK. The key considerations on which there is no consensus among proponents include whether such a body should be directly or indirectly elected, where it should be located, what system it should be elected by and, fundamentally, what the consequences might be for the UK Parliament and Government and for the stability of the Union. While advocates of an English Parliament remain disunited, their proposals may struggle to gain further traction—and thus far there is little sign of growth in public support. Yet the idea deserves to be taken seriously, as the public mood could change and the development of such a body remains quite possible—most likely through incremental steps building on 'English votes for English laws' (EVEL). If this were to occur, its effects could be wide-ranging.

5.2 The History of the English Parliament Idea

On 29 April 1707 the sitting Parliament of England (which also included members representing constituencies in Wales) was, following the Act of Union with Scotland, declared by Royal Proclamation to be the first Parliament of Great Britain (Jones & Farrell 2009: 147). Since then, there has been no English Parliament. This arrangement has largely been accepted with little protest, by both the English public and by political elites. Nonetheless, proposals to re-establish an English Parliament have been made periodically and intensified following devolution to Scotland, Wales

[1] The chapter draws on research conducted for a project funded by the Nuffield Foundation on Options for an English Parliament. The views expressed are those of the authors and not necessarily those of the Foundation.

and Northern Ireland in the late 1990s. In this part of the chapter we briefly trace the history of support for the English Parliament idea among the political class, dividing this into three phases: before the establishment of the devolved legislatures, between their establishment and the 2014 Scottish independence referendum and following that referendum.

5.2.1 Political Support for an English Parliament before 1997

Between 1707 and 1997 proposals for an English Parliament were sometimes made in the context of wider schemes for devolution in the UK. One notable example followed the 1886 defeat of Gladstone's first Irish Home Rule Bill, when 'home rule all round' was widely suggested as an alternative (Kendle 1989: 57–85; Rembold 2000: 201–24). Proposals centred on the establishment of what proponents referred to as a 'federal' system with separate parliaments in Scotland, Wales and England, as well as for Ireland. Some such schemes would have divided England into regions while others would have created an England-wide legislature, with suggestions that this be either separately elected or composed of existing members of the House of Commons sitting for English seats. Objections that are familiar today, particularly relating to England's size and potential dominance relative to Scotland, Wales and Ireland, were raised in this period. 'Home rule all round' was nonetheless seriously considered by a cabinet committee in 1911–12 (Kendle 1989: 137–45). David Lloyd George, then Chancellor of the Exchequer, proposed a version under which equivalent powers would be devolved to an Irish Parliament and to grand committees of MPs representing English, Scottish and Welsh constituencies as a transitional measure. Distinct English, Scottish and Welsh parliaments would be introduced at a later date. Ultimately, however, Prime Minister Herbert Asquith concluded that extending home rule beyond Ireland would introduce 'unnecessary complications for which there seemed no fundamental need', so the legislation eventually introduced was confined to Ireland (Kendle 1989: 145).

Despite this, calls for wider decentralisation did not disappear. In 1919 the House of Commons agreed to establish a Speaker's Conference with a remit to draw up a 'scheme of legislative and administrative devolution within the United Kingdom' (cited in Evans 2017: 367). As Evans has described, arrangements for England were a major area of disagreement between conference members. Initially there was a divide between those proposing an English legislature, notably the Scottish Liberal MP Murray Macdonald, and those advocating England's division into regions, such as the academic and Unionist MP Sir Halford Mackinder. The conference gradually reached the view that devolution to English regions would be too complex and that all-England institutions were preferable. However, major divisions remained over whether devolution should entail the establishment of separate, directly elected legislatures for the nations of the UK or changes inside Parliament to create 'Grand Councils' consisting of parliamentarians from each nation.[2] The conference concluded without agreement on this issue and its report made little impact (ibid.: 10).

When devolution next returned to the political agenda in the 1970s no English institutions were proposed. Reporting in 1973, the Royal Commission on the Constitution (the Kilbrandon Commission) dismissed the possibility of a devolved English Assembly similar to those that it recommended for other parts of the UK, stating that a 'federation consisting of four units—England, Scotland, Wales and Northern Ireland—would be so unbalanced as to be unworkable' (Royal Commission on the Constitution 1973: para. 531). The Labour Government that attempted to introduce Scottish and Welsh devolved assemblies agreed, ruling out both an English legislature and regional assemblies with legislative powers (Office of the Lord President of the Council 1976: 7–8). The passage of the legislation was frustrated by the opposition of some Labour MPs, famously including Tam Dalyell, who raised what became known as the 'West Lothian Question'—the conundrum whereby MPs representing Scottish constituencies would remain free to vote on English matters, while the same matters in Scotland would be devolved. Yet the idea of an equivalent English Assembly was not seriously discussed at this time. Writing later, Dalyell (2016: 74) recalled that he thought a federation featuring England would be 'completely out of balance' and was 'just not workable'—in raising the West Lothian Question he was seeking to make the case against the Scottish and Welsh proposals, not the case for an English legislature.

5.2.2 Political Support for an English Parliament, 1997–2014

The context rapidly changed after the 1997 election, with endorsement through referendums in Scotland and Wales for the new Labour Government's devolution proposals. Among the mainstream parties it was primarily the Conservatives that debated the idea of an English Parliament during this period. The first significant indication of support on the Conservative backbenches came in January 1998, in a private member's bill sponsored by Teresa Gorman MP calling for a referendum on an English Parliament (HC Deb., 16 January 1998: cols 589–661). In debate, Gorman stressed that she would have preferred not to have devolution at all, but argued that since it was happening the English must have 'fair and equal treatment'. Fellow Conservative MPs Peter Luff and David Davis, as well as Liberal Democrat Simon Hughes, also spoke in favour.[3] Gorman later published her proposals as a

[2] Under this proposal, for each nation there would have been a 'Council of the Commons', consisting of the MPs sitting for constituencies in that nation, and a 'Council of Peers', containing a number of peers equal to half the number of MPs from that nation. The proposal was that these arrangements would be trialled for five years, after which a decision would be made on whether to move to directly elected institutions separate from Parliament, continue with these arrangements or return to former arrangements (Evans 2017: 380–1).

[3] The other sponsors of the bill were all Conservatives: David Amess, Christopher Gill, John Hayes, Richard Shepherd, Ann Winterton and Nicholas Winterton. No Labour members spoke in support.

pamphlet, *A Parliament for England*, arguing that the 'harmony which the citizens of the United Kingdom have established over the centuries cannot survive if it is permanently biased against its largest component' (1999: 12).

Shortly after the debate on Gorman's bill, Conservative leader William Hague (1998a: 13–14) announced that an English Parliament was among four options that the party would consider as it searched for the 'least damaging answer to the West Lothian question', which had re-emerged following proposals to establish the new devolved bodies. At that year's Conservative Party Conference, Hague (1998b) again hinted that he could support 'an English Parliament in some form', while a survey carried out by the *Scotland on Sunday* newspaper suggested that more than half of Conservative MPs backed the idea (BBC News 1998). But the party eventually opted for what became known as EVEL (see Chapter 6 by Gover and Kenny), which remained its policy thereafter.

In 1998, in parallel with these events, a Campaign for an English Parliament (CEP) was set up to advocate the idea from outside Westminster. Although launched at the Conservative Party Conference (BBC News 1998), the CEP has included a mix of members from different political backgrounds—one of its most prominent spokespeople, Eddie Bone, being an active trade unionist and former Labour Party supporter. The CEP's central demand has been the establishment of an English Parliament to parallel the arrangements in Scotland. The organisation has always been run on a shoestring budget by volunteers, supported by a relatively small active membership.[4] Nonetheless, the CEP has retained a visible presence in discussions about the English Question through protests, online activity and attendance at public events. It has never contested elections but some of its members have stood as candidates for the English Democrats, a minor party launched in 2002 (Kenny 2014: 194). One of this party's central policy demands is an English Parliament, though it also has a broader agenda. Its electoral success has generally been limited, but the party's candidate Peter Davies was elected Mayor of Doncaster in 2009.[5]

Some party political interest in an English Parliament during this period also came from the United Kingdom Independence Party (UKIP), though this was somewhat patchy. UKIP's manifesto for the 2010 general election included proposals for a significant overhaul of the devolution settlement, whereby the devolved assemblies in Scotland, Wales and Northern Ireland would each be replaced with bodies made up of Westminster MPs for the relevant area, meeting on a part-time basis.[6] An equivalent arrangement would apply to England—creating an 'English Parliament' (UKIP 2010: 13). The party's support for the idea was not consistent (Hayton 2016: 408), but one of the most visible proponents of the idea at this time was its then deputy leader, Paul Nuttall (2011). The extent to which UKIP can be

[4] In an interview in 2016, campaign organisers claimed a few thousand members.

[5] Davies later left the party, citing a migration of former British National Party (BNP) members into the party (Kenny 2014: 194).

[6] The same pledge did not appear in 2001 or 2005.

considered an English nationalist party is the subject of Chapter 8 by Robert Ford and Maria Sobolewska.

Hence, despite support from some relatively fringe groupings and a small number of MPs, calls for an English Parliament never reached the mainstream during the period 1997 to 2014. Labour, the party of government for most of these years, was dismissive, whilst despite William Hague's initial flirtation, the Conservatives chose to focus on EVEL instead. Survey evidence—summarised in Section 5.5—suggested that there was also little public enthusiasm for the idea (Curtice 2006: 122). It was thus reasonable to conclude, as Robert Hazell did, that an English Parliament was 'not seriously on the political agenda' (Hazell 2006a: 9). Subsequently Harding et al. (2008: 84–5) suggested that the idea would only 'really gain credibility if heavyweight politicians in mainstream parties came out in support', or if UKIP started winning substantial numbers of seats.

5.2.3 Political Support for an English Parliament, 2014–

The period since the Scottish independence referendum of September 2014 has for various reasons seen rising interest in the territorial constitution, including a renewed focus on the English Question. This was very visible in the declaration by then Prime Minister David Cameron (2014), in Downing Street the morning after the vote, that having offered the Scottish Parliament increased powers 'the millions of voices of England must also be heard'. Cameron's preferred response was EVEL, and—as described in Chapter 6—a version of this was implemented through changes to House of Commons standing orders after the 2015 general election. The change appeared partisan, securing no support from opposition parties; it clearly benefited the Conservatives, who at that time held only one seat in Scotland. Hence EVEL's introduction was politically controversial and the procedure could prove vulnerable in future. Crucially, the version introduced fell short of that often previously discussed, and desired by some Conservatives, by not actually preventing Scottish, Welsh and Northern Irish MPs from voting on English legislation (Gover & Kenny 2016: 14). Instead, the new system provides for a 'double veto', whereby English bills or clauses are voted on separately by English MPs and by the whole House, with either able to prevent agreement. It therefore remains possible that England-only legislation could be blocked despite having support from a majority of English MPs.

Following the referendum, calls for an English Parliament became more audible. In the immediate aftermath, former Conservative Cabinet Minister John Redwood (2014) was particularly vocal in his support for such a policy. David Davis—who, following his support for Teresa Gorman's bill had been a serious candidate for the party leadership in 2005 and was later appointed to the Cabinet as Brexit Secretary in 2016—also reiterated his support for the policy in an article in the *Sunday Times* (Davis 2014). A Ten Minute Rule Bill proposing a federal structure for the UK, including an English Parliament, was introduced by Conservative backbencher Andrew Rosindell in November 2014, co-sponsored by Redwood, alongside the chair of the Conservative 1922 Committee Graham Brady and several MPs from other parties, including senior Labour backbencher Frank Field (HC Deb., 25 November 2014: cols. 795–7).[7]

Conservative moves to speak for England could be seen as connected to the pressure that the party was under in this period from UKIP, as discussed by Ford and Sobolewska in Chapter 8. In the European Parliament elections of 2014, which preceded the Scottish independence vote by three months, UKIP outpolled all other parties. Cameron's statement was in part a response to this electoral threat. In the subsequent general election UKIP dropped its call for an English Parliament, instead demanding EVEL at Westminster (UKIP 2015: 56). However, the English Parliament proposal reappeared in more detailed form in 2017 (UKIP 2017: 59–60) when key proponent Paul Nuttall was briefly leader of the party (Maddox 2016).

One of the main changes at this time was increased interest in an English Parliament on the Labour side, though proponents undoubtedly remained a minority.[8] Labour was always resistant to EVEL, given the political threat that it posed due to the party's traditional strength at Westminster in Scottish and Welsh constituencies. But with this policy becoming a reality, the party had to consider its response and did so in an environment—following the 2015 general election—where it had just lost all but one of its Scottish seats to the Scottish National Party (SNP). All of this added to a sense among some Labour figures that the party needed to appeal better to patriotic English voters, among whom some polls noted a growth in English, as opposed to British, national identity (Kenny 2014: 83). Manifestations of such interest included an e-book, *Labour's Identity Crisis: England and the Politics of Patriotism* (Hunt 2016a), featuring essays from ten 2015 general election candidates, and calls for an English Labour Party (Cruddas 2015). After leaving Parliament at the 2015 election, former Cabinet Minister John Denham went on to establish a Centre for English Identity and Politics at the University of Winchester. It subsequently hosted a speech by former Shadow Education Secretary Tristram Hunt (2016b), in which he suggested that a referendum should be held on the

[7] The full list of sponsors was: Andrew Rosindell (Con), Frank Field (Lab), Kate Hoey (Lab), Douglas Carswell (UKIP), Greg Mulholland (LD), Elfyn Llwyd (PC), Angus Brendan MacNeil (SNP), Sir William Cash (Con), John Redwood (Con), Jim Shannon (DUP), Martin Vickers (Con) and Graham Brady (Con).

[8] Frank Field had in fact shown interest in this topic since at least 2007, when he sponsored an early day motion noting that 'those polls that have questioned the English report a clear majority in favour of an English parliament; and further notes that it is this issue, and not Scottish independence or even House of Lords reform, that is the issue that voters now put at the top of their priorities for constitutional reform' (EDM 670 of session 2006–7). Long before this, senior Labour MP Tony Benn had proposed a Commonwealth of Britain Bill, comprising a radical package of constitutional reforms, among them 'national Parliaments elected for England, for Scotland and for Wales', each of which would 'enjoy the power to legislate in all matters save only defence, foreign affairs and Commonwealth [UK-level] finance', and each of which would 'elect its own Executive' (Benn & Hood 1993: appendix 1).

establishment of an English Parliament. Former Shadow Business Secretary Chuka Umunna (2015b) likewise indicated support for such a body.

The period following the 2016 EU referendum, which included demands from the SNP for a second Scottish independence vote, saw responses from key Labour figures proposing an explicit move to federalism (Carrell 2017; Gordon 2017). As with debates a century earlier, it was unclear whether this should encompass all-England institutions or a revival of Labour's previously failed proposals for regionalism. Scottish Labour figures have understandably been wary of setting out proposals for England's future, while their English counterparts have yet to promote an agreed vision. But at least some such figures clearly consider an English Parliament to be one of the options worthy of serious consideration.

In its twentieth year, the CEP has continued to press the case for an English Parliament. But it has now been joined by increasingly credible figures in the two main parties willing to contemplate such a move. It is hence no longer possible to dismiss an English Parliament as an entirely fringe idea.

5.3 Drivers of Proposals for an English Parliament

Before turning to the detail of proposals for an English Parliament it is worthwhile to consider what drives proponents to seek such a change. Different political goals may imply the suitability of different models of political institution. Indeed, the different objectives of proponents help to explain the diversity, as well as the relatively underdeveloped nature, of the proposals for an English Parliament that so far exist.

As indicated, the idea of an English Parliament was initially proposed by advocates of devolution as a component of wider schemes for federalism, or 'home rule all round'. But concerns about the disproportionate size of England, compared to the UK's other component parts, helped contribute to the failure of these schemes. Another contributor was the relative disinterest shown by the English, to whom Westminster appeared adequately representative of English needs. Instead, devolution proceeded in a more pragmatic, piecemeal and demand-led manner, with concessions to those geographic areas that sought them—initially Ireland and subsequently Scotland, Wales and (with revived institutions of a more pluralist kind) Northern Ireland. Devolution hence proceeded around England's borders, leaving the English with the existing status quo. Nonetheless, creation of these new bodies could not help but have indirect effects on English representation.

The revival of pressure for an English Parliament was therefore reactive. In the immediate aftermath of Labour's reforms in the 1990s proponents were not necessarily those who had supported devolution but included many who had opposed it—as illustrated by Teresa Gorman. This case was based on demands for fairness and greater symmetry in the devolution settlement. John Redwood, who warned at that time that devolution would lead to *The Death of Britain* (1999), has more recently justified his support for an English Parliament by claiming that 'What is good enough for Scotland is good enough for England' and that 'Labour's one-sided devolution … left unfinished business' (Redwood 2014); his proposed solution is for 'England to get EVEN' (Redwood 2015).[9] Very similar rhetoric is used by the CEP, whose central argument is the need for equality of representation between England and Scotland. As Aughey (2010: 514) says of the CEP, '[t]he substance of its case is equity'. Likewise David Davis (2014) has suggested that 'both logic and justice' demand an English Parliament.

Another reactive response has been that an English Parliament is necessary to defend England against its 'break up' through the establishment of regional structures, which (in line with long-standing dilemmas over English devolution) provide an alternative means of rebalancing following establishment of the new Scottish, Welsh and Northern Irish bodies. The CEP was active in opposing Labour's plans for regional government, particularly during the successful campaign for a 'No' vote in the North East referendum in 2004. The organisation argues that creating regional structures would amount to 'the destruction of England' (CEP 2018b). John Redwood (2014) has also argued strongly against regionalism, emphasising that neither devolution to regions nor cities will provide a suitable forum for the setting of English income tax rates (to mirror the powers now devolved to the Scottish Parliament)—only an English Parliament is suited to do that.

These calls hence appear pragmatic, reactive and, to an extent, driven by grievance. However, a more positive case is also made by many proponents of an English Parliament, based on the benefits of representation and 'voice' for the English, allowing an expression of English identity. Notably 'voice' is one element judged clearly lacking by Gover & Kenny (2016) in their assessment of the EVEL procedures. Introducing his bill in 2014, Andrew Rosindell suggested that such an arrangement would 'provide democratic self-government for all four countries, with autonomy and freedom over their own affairs, and the ability to uphold their own identities, traditions and laws' (HC Deb., 25 November 2014: cols 795–6). This kind of positive vision is also promoted by the CEP. In a lecture at Winchester Eddie Bone (2016) suggested that 'Neither the Union parliament, nor the British government, can or should be encouraged to "speak for England"', pointing out that English MPs face a dilemma—to speak for England and deny their role as representatives in a *British* Parliament, or speak for Britain and deny the English a distinct voice. These concerns were heightened following the Brexit vote, where the voices of the devolved areas (and Scotland in particular) became very audible in the debate, via elected representatives from those areas, but there was no distinct English voice or English representation round the table.

From a left perspective, John Denham (2016: 5) has commented that a progressive and patriotic Englishness cannot develop 'while there are no democratic forums or systems of democratic government to provide the focus and crucible of debate',

[9] The latter of these capitalises 'even' not just for emphasis, but to draw a parallel with EVEL, in order to call for 'English votes for English needs'.

making an English Parliament an 'essential Labour movement demand'. Similar sentiments have been echoed by the singer-songwriter Billy Bragg (2000) and by George Monbiot (2009), who has argued that 'to support an English parliament, you don't have to love England, you only have to love democracy'. For many, the demand for an English Parliament is thus strongly rooted in civic nationalism, though for others this also has undertones of ethnic nationalism.[10]

The relationship between demands for an English Parliament and the preservation of the UK is likewise far from straightforward. A frequently cited claim by proponents is that such a body would help to shore up the Union and avoid the UK's break-up. The logic often presented is that continued failure to establish an English Parliament will feed growing resentment and dissatisfaction towards the Union among the English (e.g. Bayliss 2016; Bone 2016). Nonetheless, both the CEP itself and the English Democrats have flirted increasingly openly with the attractions of English independence (BBC News 2014; Cullen 2016). Such groups show less concern for the effect that establishing such a body would have on Scottish sentiments—where the dominance of an English Parliament in any negotiations with the UK centre could well have a centrifugal effect. SNP politicians such as Alex Salmond have actively encouraged an English Parliament (*The Andrew Marr Show* 2015), arguing in favour of the need for balance, but the likelihood is that they see this as ultimately promoting a separatist cause. Recent interest in federalism—particularly among Labour figures—is intended in part to provide a compact that will be attractive to the Scots, with clearly defined residual responsibilities for UK-level institutions. Nonetheless, this seems more likely to be palatable north of the border if the English partners are smaller regions, rather than a dominant English Parliament (and potentially Government—as discussed in Sections 5.4 and 5.6).

This provides some flavour of the kind of pragmatic political and campaign-focused arguments that exist among those in favour of an English Parliament. Debates are diffused by many other pragmatic political purposes as well. For Conservatives, particularly during the period of Labour dominance at UK level, all-England institutions such as EVEL or an English Parliament offered the potential to establish an arena that their party might hope to control politically. Competition from UKIP to appeal to patriotic English voters offered further electoral encouragement in this direction. Subsequently, Labour's electoral weakness—not only in large swathes of England, but also in Scotland post-2010—created fresh incentives to appeal to voters who identify predominantly with an English national identity and may have a sense of grievance against the 'special treatment' of other parts of the UK. These various factors clearly help to explain why interest in an English Parliament has gradually broadened among the political class.

[10] For discussion of the distinction between civic and ethnic nationalism see Brown (2000).

5.4 Models for an English Parliament

We have seen that the number of proponents of an English Parliament at elite level has grown and that support has expanded across the political spectrum. The drivers of this interest in all-England political institutions are varied and in some cases conflicting. This helps to explain why no consistent blueprint for an English Parliament has yet emerged. Instead, competing models have been suggested, all of which remain underdeveloped.

Many of those who have expressed in-principle support for the English Parliament idea have done so only through short interventions, such as newspaper articles, blog posts or mentions in speeches. The number of longer-form texts devoted to the idea remains very limited and these tend to focus more on the arguments for creation of such an institution than on the precise form that it should take.[11] The most notable absence is of a single, detailed blueprint prepared by the CEP—even twenty years after its formation various key questions about how the organisation's preferred model would work remain unanswered. The reason for this is, again, partly pragmatic. Group leaders have deliberately focused on rallying support for the *principle* of an English Parliament, realising that laying down the detail would risk dividing supporters.[12] Nonetheless, a basic model does exist and can be clearly delineated as distinct from the preferences of some other supporters of an English Parliament.

5.4.1 The Separately Elected Model for an English Parliament

The CEP's vision of an English Parliament sees it as a new political institution, separate from the UK Parliament and subject to its own elections—in the same way as the legislatures in Scotland, Wales and Northern Ireland. This fits the CEP's emphasis on the need for equality of representation, which also leads to a clear demand that England's new Parliament should have 'powers at least as great as those of Scotland's' (CEP 2018a). The CEP is very explicit about some of the consequences of this change—in particular that it would require a separate English Government and First Minister, again paralleling those in the other devolved areas. Nonetheless, the group remains far less decided on other key matters, such as the size of the proposed new body, its location, the most appropriate electoral system and the wider consequences for the territorial nature of the UK state. For example, the CEP says relatively little about the effects on Westminster or Whitehall, or whether the change would require a formal move to federalism. In practice, adherence to the Scottish model of devolved powers would leave fairly limited competencies at the UK level, while an English Parliament with substantially lesser powers

[11] For examples see Gorman (1999), Ormond (1999), Clougherty (2007) and Kempley (2011).

[12] Interview with senior figures in the CEP, 13 December 2016.

than Scotland's would likely frustrate supporters and could create a more complex patchwork of devolved and reserved powers.

This model for an English Parliament is the most instinctively obvious among the alternatives. As no such parliament presently exists, some kind of new body needs to be created and this approach provides the clearest parallel to the arrangement now existent in the other historic nations of the UK. Such a model has attracted various supporters. It was proposed in Teresa Gorman's pamphlet (1999) and was more recently advocated by David Davis (2014), who explicitly suggested that a separate 'English parliament, an English first minister and an English cabinet' had become a constitutional inevitability. The model does, nonetheless, also fall prey to some of the most obvious criticisms. For example, former Conservative and UKIP MP Douglas Carswell (2011) has dismissed the English Parliament idea on the basis of 'More politicians? Another talking shop? Another tier of elected officials with ready-made excuses for not getting things done?', concluding that such a body might not be very different from 'a mega regional assembly'. In evidence to the House of Lords Constitution Committee—which rejected the notion of an English Parliament in its 2016 report on *The Union and Devolution*—Professor Adam Tomkins (now a Conservative MSP) suggested:

> If you had an English First Minister with the powers of the Scottish First Minister, that English First Minister would have a bigger budget than and would be more powerful and important than the United Kingdom Prime Minister. That is a recipe for collapsing the Union rather than strengthening the Union. (Constitution Committee 2016: 94)

The CEP firmly rejects criticisms such as Carswell's, which highlight the added costs of creating a new legislature for England. Eddie Bone (2016) has argued that 'the work of the British parliament would be very substantially reduced and thus a much smaller parliament can represent the constituent parts of the Union'. Nonetheless, there is no blueprint for the future of either of the chambers. Tomkins' criticisms regarding the effect of the size and dominance of England on the stability of the UK are more difficult to counter.

5.4.2 The Dual Mandate Model for an English Parliament

The clearest rival to this vision of an English Parliament as a new and separate body to Westminster is the notion that a new forum might instead evolve more organically from the existing House of Commons, forming a natural next step from EVEL. This model has also existed for some time and one of its most consistent supporters has been John Redwood (2006, 2014, 2015). In some respects his proposal barely differs from a 'strong' application of EVEL, as many Conservatives had originally hoped would be adopted.[13] As discussed at greater length in Chapter 6, several

[13] For example the party's 2005 manifesto proposed that 'exclusively English matters should be decided in Westminster without the votes of MPs sitting for Scottish constituencies' (Conservative Party 2005: 22).

schemes prior to the implementation of EVEL in 2015 had envisaged it as excluding MPs from non-English seats from voting on England-only legislation, while some had also proposed that such legislation should take most of its Commons stages in an England-only forum such as a grand committee. But the version of EVEL implemented in 2015 was significantly weaker, enabling all MPs to retain the right to vote on all bills. The only use so far of an England-only forum has been shortly after the report stage, to ensure that England-only clauses command support among a majority of MPs voting from English seats. Gover & Kenny's research on the first year of operation of EVEL found that this stage typically included no substantive discussion and lasted just a couple of minutes (2016: 25).

The model of English Parliament supported by this second group of proponents would build upon the stronger version of EVEL—restricting consideration and voting on bills to MPs representing the territory concerned—and take it further. However, the detail is generally not elaborated. House of Commons business would be scheduled so that certain days or weeks were restricted to England-only matters, not limited to legislation but likely also including debates and question times. The same logic might be applied to select committees, with some becoming explicitly England only. Such a model not only provides a strong degree of continuity and appears consistent with the piecemeal and pragmatic way in which the British constitution has often developed (particularly regarding Westminster's responses to pressures for devolution), it also addresses head-on some of the criticisms articulated in Section 5.4.1. While supporting the broad principle of the Gorman Bill, Liberal Democrat MP Simon Hughes suggested that 'We the English members, who represent English seats, could conduct English business. There would be no extra expense, no new Chamber and no new bureaucracy would be required' (HC Deb., 16 January 1998: col. 618). The proposal in UKIP's 2010 manifesto was similar—suggesting that 'English MPs would meet in Westminster for English only days as an "English Parliament"' (UKIP 2010: 13). This kind of 'dual mandate' model, whereby the English Parliament is made up of existing MPs representing English seats, was also envisaged in Andrew Rosindell's 2014 bill (HC Deb., 25 November 2014: cols 795–6) and has found support from commentators such as Simon Heffer (2008).

A gradualist solution of this kind has, however, been firmly rejected by some proponents of an English Parliament, who see it as not worthy of the name. The CEP (2018c) dismisses the dual mandate model as 'English Parliament lite'—it clearly sits awkwardly with their aspiration for an institution comparable to those in the other devolved areas of the UK, allowing expression of separate English 'voice' (particularly by the voters, to whom the dual mandate model would give just one vote for two only partially distinct institutions). A key difference to the vision of the CEP and English Democrats is that this model does not envisage creation of a separately accountable English Government or First Minister—instead leaving the UK Government accountable to both the existing House of Commons and the subset of it which forms the English Parliament. Presumably some Whitehall departments (including major spending departments like health and education) would de facto become largely or wholly accountable to the English Parliament, but a significant anomaly arises regarding the confidence relationship (as further discussed in Section 5.6). One of the obvious risks with this model is the one referred to by Bogdanor (2014) in his arguments against EVEL as 'bifurcation'—that is, the possibility of a UK Government that does not enjoy a majority in the English Parliament. Such a scenario is highly unlikely with respect to the Conservatives, but more possible with respect to a future Labour Government. Although this risk may be small based on historic voting figures (Russell & Lodge 2006: 71), it is a problem which cannot occur in the same way with a separately elected English Parliament.

5.4.3 Other Models for an English Parliament

These may be seen as the two primary, competing models of an English Parliament supported by proponents of such a body. However, other variants exist. One is an elaboration of the separate institutions model, which goes further in terms of envisaging impact on existing parliamentary arrangements, while also attempting to tackle the accusations of increased cost and bureaucracy that the idea sometimes attracts. Such a model was spelt out, though not elaborated in detail, by the cross-party Constitution Reform Group chaired by former Conservative Leader of the House of Lords, Lord Salisbury. Under this proposal 'the existing House of Commons could simply become the English Parliament, with the existing House of Lords becoming the Federal Parliament' (Constitution Reform Group 2015: 20). While often presented as incremental (the use of the term 'simply' in this case implies a certain ease of transition), such a proposal would in fact entail the complete reshaping of the Westminster Parliament, with both existing chambers being replaced. The Lords would take on some kind of territorial, representative structure, while Scottish, Welsh and Northern Irish members would all be removed from the Commons. Despite its innate ambition, a number of figures have expressed support for variants of this model, including the Labour MP Frank Field (2014) and left-leaning journalist Will Hutton (2014). It does not have explicit support from the CEP or any of its leading spokespeople, but is nonetheless consistent with the organisation's goals.

More recent suggestions have included the proposal in UKIP's 2017 manifesto (UKIP 2017: 59–60) that the English Parliament should instead sit in the Lords chamber, following abolition of that body, or ideas that an English Parliament could be built upon some kind of indirectly elected representation from local and regional governments. The latter proposal is very embryonic, but has support from some Labour figures.[14] Related suggestions include 'making Westminster a place where strong regional and city authorities meet to discuss and decide on matters affecting the whole country' (Umunna 2015a). Any of these proposals would clearly need significant further development.

[14] Interview with senior Labour figure, 20 December 2016.

5.5 Public Attitudes towards an English Parliament

While there may be growing interest in the idea of an English Parliament among politicians and political activists, it can reasonably be asked whether the English electorate actually want such a body—and whether there is any evidence of rising public support. This could obviously be crucial in determining whether any such change is put into effect.

As John Curtice shows in Chapter 12, evidence from public opinion surveys is not wholly conclusive. The longest time series on this question has run each year from 1999 to 2015 as part of the British Social Attitudes (BSA) survey. This asks respondents their view on how England should be governed, offering three options. It has consistently found majority support for the status quo, in contrast to relatively limited support for either an English Parliament or regional assemblies, with little change over time (see Figure 5.1). But a different BSA question, based on agree/disagree options has found strong support for the principle that 'Scottish MPs should no longer be allowed to vote in the House of Commons on laws that only affect England'. In 2015, 60 per cent agreed or strongly agreed with this statement, while just 11 per cent disagreed or strongly disagreed (Curtice 2016: 12). This option equates to the 'strong' version of EVEL, which was not the one implemented in 2015. A shorter time series has appeared in the Future of England survey, which began in 2011. This includes all four of these options together—EVEL (in its strong variant) alongside the status quo, an English Parliament or regional assemblies. It has consistently found EVEL to be comfortably the most popular option (see Table 5.1), with an English Parliament securing relatively limited support.

One consistent finding from all of these polls it is that voters instinctively prefer solutions that address England as a whole over those proposing English regional institutions. EVEL has generally prevailed over the option explicitly identified as an English Parliament, but the strong form of EVEL set out in these surveys, whereby non-English MPs are excluded from voting on English-only legislation, has not been implemented and could be seen as equating to—or at least a step in the direction of—the dual mandate model. If future England-only legislation supported by a majority of MPs sitting for English seats were vetoed by MPs representing constituencies elsewhere in the UK, public support for this model could grow further.

A few one-off polls have used a different structure, simply asking whether or not an English Parliament should be established. These have demonstrated much greater support for the principle than when it is presented as one of a list of options, as shown in Table 5.2. The peak came in the immediate aftermath of the Scottish independence referendum, when one such poll found 59 per cent expressing support for establishment of an English Parliament and only 11 per cent opposed. Hence, while there is no clear evidence for strong public pressure to create such an institution, political circumstances could see this grow. The likeliest cause might be controversies over voting at Westminster, for instance if a UK majority were to veto a proposal favoured by English MPs. This could create momentum for a strengthened form of EVEL, at least in the first instance, hence generating pressure towards the dual mandate model.

Figure 5.1 Trends in Support for Alternative Options for English Governance (BSA)

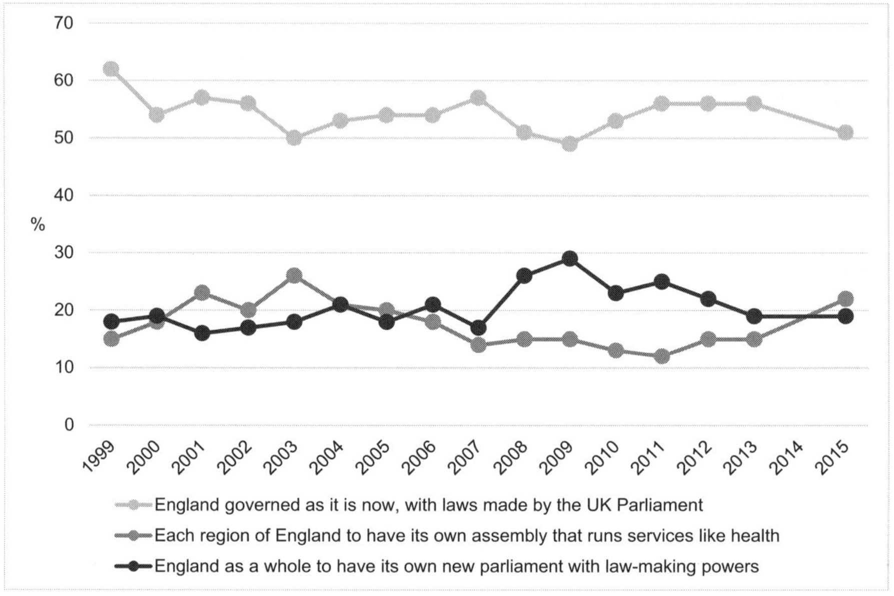

Note: The question asked was: 'With all the changes going on in the way different parts of Great Britain are run, which do you think would be best for England?'

Source: BSA survey, 1999–2015.

Table 5.1 Trends in Support for Alternative Options for English Governance (FoE)

	2011	**2012**	**2014**
For England to be governed as it is now with laws made by all MPs in the UK Parliament	24	21	18
For England to be governed with laws made by English MPs in the UK Parliament	34	36	40
For each region in England to have its own elected assembly	9	8	9
For England as a whole to have its own new English Parliament with law-making powers	20	20	16
Don't know	14	16	17

Note: The question asked was: 'With all the changes going on in the way different parts of the United Kingdom are run, which of the following do you think would be best for England?'

Source: Future of England survey, 2011–14.

Table 5.2 Responses to Yes/No Questions regarding an English Parliament

	Support	Oppose	Don't Know
a) The formation of a new English Parliament, similar to the Welsh and Northern Irish assemblies (May 2015)	48	21	31
b) Setting up an English Parliament for only English MPs (Dec. 2014)	41	29	20
c) Setting up an English Parliament for MPs representing only English constituencies (Oct. 2014)	53	41	6
d) Should there be a new English Parliament? (Sept. 2014)	59	11	20
e) Setting up an English Parliament for only English MPs (Sept. 2014)	40	33	27
f) The establishment of an English Parliament within the UK (Jan. 2012)	49	16	34

Source: (a) YouGov/*Sunday Times*; (b) ComRes/ITV; (c) ComRes/BBC; (d) Survation/*Mail on Sunday*; (e) ComRes/ITV; (f) ICM/*Sunday Telegraph*.

5.6 Unanswered Questions and Constitutional Dilemmas

We have seen that the visions of proponents of an English Parliament differ substantially. Those supporting a separately elected body vehemently reject the dual mandate model on the basis that it does not offer the English, and particularly English voters, a distinct voice, nor equivalence to the devolved institutions created in the other nations of the UK (including with regard to its denial of a separate English Government). Supporters of more incremental approaches reject the more radical step of creating completely new institutions as either politically unrealistic or perhaps even undesirable. The scale of ambition of the CEP, as well as the lack of detail, remain major obstacles to implementation of its scheme. The Salisbury model, as one possible elaboration, helps illustrate the size of the challenge even if seeking implementation in an ostensibly incremental way.

Just as there are two key models for an English Parliament, there are two means by which it might come about. The separately elected model (including its Salisbury elaboration) would require explicit design and active choice. Proponents have suggested either a constitutional convention to deliberate on the detail (Umunna 2015b) and/or a referendum to confirm the support of English voters (Hunt 2016b). Both of these key steps occurred before creation of the Scottish Parliament. Alternatively, public and political pressure might result in an English Parliament on the dual mandate model developing through typical British incrementalism and 'muddling through'. On balance this makes it appear, if anything, more likely—thus examination of its possible consequences is at least as important.

In selecting any model of an English Parliament, there are various key questions which must be answered, many of which have so far been either strategically or accidentally overlooked by proponents of the idea. We have addressed these in more detail elsewhere (Russell & Sheldon 2018), but summarise them here.

First, what powers should an English Parliament have? This is an area on which there is significant agreement among proponents, though the consequences have not been worked through. Most supporters seek an English Parliament with roughly equivalent powers to the Scottish Parliament. This would create a powerful body with oversight of policy in a wide range of areas, such as health, education, the environment and local government, alongside some tax-raising powers and some control of welfare policy. The implications of such a degree of devolution for England on the residual powers of the UK Parliament are considerable and imply a federal arrangement with a relatively weak centre. There are also questions about how to deal with the existing asymmetry in the devolution settlement as the bodies in Northern Ireland and Wales do not all have equivalent powers. Some degree of greater standardisation (for example to create a separate legal jurisdiction in Wales, which would be a significant reform from a Welsh perspective, if less so for England) might become necessary. Greater asymmetry might be accommodated within the dual mandate model, but could nonetheless be difficult to maintain. A related question is how an English Parliament would be financed; the Scottish Parliament is funded primarily through a block grant based on the Barnett formula, which is linked to changes in the UK Government's English spending. The need to fund an English Parliament (particularly with a separate English Government) would nullify these arrangements and some alternative would need to be found.

Secondly, does England require its own government, accountable to an English Parliament? The most obvious problem with the dual mandate model is that it creates a parliament without a government. The UK Government would remain accountable to two bodies, creating significant complexity and an apparent accountability gap. Some departments, or ministers within departments, would in practice be accountable only to the English Parliament. That body would presumably lack the de jure power to remove the Government from office, but might well gain that power de facto, given England's size and political importance. Significant tensions could occur if the political majority differed among MPs sitting for English seats and those across the UK, and this might require 'oversized' coalitions to be formed at UK level in order to guarantee English support. In addition, one of the key grievances of the CEP is that no governmental actors specifically speak for England in negotiations with the UK Government where Scotland, Northern Ireland and Wales are represented—for example most recently over Brexit. This would not be resolved by the dual mandate model.

Thirdly, where should an English Parliament (and its UK equivalent) be located? The dual mandate model would result in two bodies with different jurisdictions being co-located in the same building at Westminster. The same would apply (for different reasons) under the Salisbury model. These arrangements would be highly unusual in international terms—the norm is for federal legislatures to be located separately from legislatures of any component territorial units.[15] Under a separate English Parliament model, either it or the UK equivalent might be located outside London—perhaps in the North of England. The choice of which body retained the Palace of Westminster would be hugely symbolic. Many English Parliament supporters would no doubt like to 'reclaim' Westminster as their own, but this could reinforce the impression (resultant from England's population and the likely powers of such a body) that this was the dominant institution in UK politics. Retention of Westminster by the UK Parliament (however diminished) might in turn help shore up its role.

Fourthly, how should an English Parliament be elected? There has been relatively little debate among proponents over the preferred electoral system for an English Parliament.[16] Different systems clearly have different likely consequences for party representation. Those used for the bodies in Scotland, Wales and Northern Ireland were deliberately chosen to be more proportional than Westminster, boosting minor party representation. In England the main beneficiaries of such a system based on recent voting patterns would be the Liberal Democrats, UKIP and the Greens. The likely outcome of elections would be either coalition or minority governments for England. The dual mandate model would obviously maintain representation using first past the post—whose legitimacy is disputed by all of the aforementioned parties and under which there remains a greater likelihood of single-party majority government.

Fifthly, what should be the consequences of an English Parliament for the current institutions in Whitehall and Westminster? A separate English Parliament holding to account a newly formed English Government would clearly require enormous upheaval in Whitehall, with explicit division of governmental as well as parliamentary responsibilities. The dual mandate model would not immediately require the same, but the degree of interwoven responsibility, as already indicated, could potentially create confusion and weakened accountability. Under any model (short of the break-up of the Union) a UK Parliament would continue to exist; different models place this in the House of Commons, the House of Lords or potentially elsewhere. The implication (which is explicitly stated in the Salisbury model), is often that the UK Parliament should become unicameral. But most federal states instead choose bicameralism, with a first chamber directly elected on a population basis and a second chamber representing territorial units (often unevenly; often not directly elected—see Coakley 2014; Lijphart 1999). The Salisbury model, whereby the UK Parliament would be unicameral and possibly indirectly elected, would be very unusual indeed. But proponents of other models of an English Parliament provide less detail.

[15] Several major federations, including the USA and Australia, have their federal legislatures located in specially administered federal districts. Where the federal legislature is located in the same city as a substate legislature, as for example in Germany, it is not located in the same building.

[16] UKIP's 2017 manifesto proposes use of the additional member system (UKIP 2017: 60). Eddie Bone has also hinted at support for proportional representation (Bone 2012).

Finally, and fundamentally, what are the consequences of an English Parliament for the territorial integrity of the UK? Proponents often claim that creation of such a body would help to hold the Union together; opponents claim the reverse. The size and political importance of England have been seen for more than a century as a barrier to such all-England solutions. In addition, the extent of power devolved in other areas would present challenges to a cohesive Union if extended to England, particularly given the absence of the kind of 'concurrent' or 'shared' powers that exist in many federal systems. Proponents need to have very robust ideas about the structure and functioning of the UK state after the establishment of an English Parliament and whether that implies (some form of) federalism. Such proposals do not exist in any current scheme.

5.7 Conclusions

The idea of an English Parliament has been discussed for well over a century, particularly in the context of other devolution schemes—and most recently in order to rebalance following Labour's devolution in the 1990s, which created the Scottish Parliament, Welsh Assembly and Northern Ireland Assembly. Nonetheless, no agreement on what such a body should look like has yet been reached. In more recent years, support for an English Parliament has become more mainstream, with Harding et al.'s (2008) requirement that the proposal should gather support from senior figures in the two main parties now met. Hence this can no longer be considered an entirely fringe proposal and deserves serious consideration and interrogation. In particular, while some Conservatives have flirted with the proposal since the 1990s, support has grown among political actors following the 2014 Scottish independence referendum, including various Labour figures who have expressed an interest in the idea.

The motivations of these various proponents have differed. Many see establishment of an English Parliament as a necessary rebalancing, following the creation of elected bodies for the other nations of the UK. Some believe it is essential to facilitating English 'voice' and identity. Proponents have argued that a new body speaking for England is required in order to maintain the stability of the Union; others fear (or perhaps hope, in the case of the SNP) that such a body would drive the Union apart. A consistent concern whenever the notion of an English Parliament has been discussed is the dominant size of England within the UK.

It is very notable that twenty years after having been placed more firmly on the political agenda thanks to Labour's devolution settlement, and despite growing elite support, no model of an English Parliament has yet emerged which can unite its proponents. Indeed, some proponents anticipate that getting too far into specifics is liable to fracture support. Two distinct models can be discerned from debate so far—one based on a separately elected English Parliament, and an English Government, and the other resulting from a formal division of responsibilities within Westminster itself. Each leaves major questions unanswered.

Strikingly, the key tensions within debates about the governance of England remain much as they were in Gladstone's day: Should England have its own political institutions, or should its dominance be mitigated through creation of regional bodies? Should English representation come through new assemblies, or can it be accommodated within the Westminster Parliament? Urgent though these questions are in the context of debates about the territorial future of the post-Brexit UK, they appear today to be no closer to being answered. It could prove wise to refer these fundamental conundrums to some kind of deliberative citizen-led convention (see Renwick & Hazell 2017), though even then successful resolution would not be guaranteed. In the absence of such a process, and of agreement between proponents of an English Parliament, the most likely outcomes are either no action or a stealthy and typically British inching, in a relatively unplanned way, towards the dual mandate model. This model in particular thus deserves careful attention, as it appears incremental but could have far-reaching and potentially destabilising effects.

References

The Andrew Marr Show (2015), 'The Andrew Marr Show interview: Alex Salmond, MSP, former First Minister', http://news.bbc.co.uk/1/shared/bsp/hi/pdfs/26071503.pdf, accessed 29 January 2018.

Aughey, A. (2010), 'Anxiety and injustice: the anatomy of contemporary English nationalism', *Nations and Nationalism*, 16(3): 506–24.

Bayliss, C. (2016), '"The UK will COLLAPSE" UKIP leader vows to fight for English Parliament to save Britain', *Daily Express*, 30 November.

BBC News (1998), 'New push for English assembly', http://news.bbc.co.uk/1/hi/uk_politics/186414.stm, accessed 29 January 2018.

BBC News (2014), 'English Democrats seek independence for England', http://www.bbc.co.uk/news/uk-politics-26583314, accessed 29 January 2018.

Benn, T. & Hood, A. (1993), *Common Sense: A New Constitution for Britain* (London, Hutchinson).

Blick, A. (2016), *Federalism: The UK's Future?* (London, The Federal Trust).

Bogdanor, V. (1999), 'Devolution: Decentralisation or disintegration?', *Political Quarterly*, 70(2): 185–94.

Bogdanor, V. (2014), 'Why English votes for English laws is a kneejerk absurdity', *The Guardian*, 24 September.

Bone, E. (2012), 'Counties together—under an English Parliament', Campaign for an English Parliament, https://thecepreview.wordpress.com/counties-together-under-an-english-parliament/, accessed 29 January 2018.

Bone, E. (2016), 'Speech to the Centre for English Identity and Politics, University of Winchester', Campaign for an English Parliament, https://thecepreview.wordpress.com/2016/11/14/the-cep-speech-to-the-center-for-english-identity-and-politics-at-winchester-university-101116/, accessed 29 January 2018.

Bragg, B. (2000), 'Why York should be the capital of England', *The Guardian*, 12 January.

Brown, D. (2000), *Contemporary Nationalism: Civic, Ethnic, and Multicultural Politics* (London, Routledge).

Bryant, C. (2008), 'Devolution, equity and the English Question', *Nations and Nationalism*, 14(4): 664–83.

Cameron, D. (2014), 'Scottish independence referendum: statement by the Prime Minister', HM Government, https://www.gov.uk/government/news/scottish-independence-referendum-statement-by-the-prime-minister, accessed 29 January 2018.

Carrell, S. (2017), 'Gordon Brown pushes "patriotic" third option for Scotland after Brexit', *The Guardian*, 18 March.

Carswell, D. (2011), 'Do we need an English Parliament?', Douglas Carswell's blog, 9 June, https://web.archive.org/web/20121013185814/http://www.talkcarswell.com/home/do-we-need-an-english-parliament/1965, accessed 30 January 2018.

CEP (Campaign for an English Parliament) (2018a), 'Aims, principles and policies', https://thecepreview.wordpress.com/aims-principles-and-policies/, accessed 29 January 2018.

CEP (Campaign for an English Parliament) (2018b), 'Regionalisation: the destruction of England', https://thecepreview.wordpress.com/regionalisation-the-destruction-of-england/, accessed 29 January 2018.

CEP (Campaign for an English Parliament) (2018c), 'Your questions', https://thecepreview.wordpress.com/your-questions/, accessed 29 January 2018.

Clougherty, T. (2007), *A Parliament for England* (London, Adam Smith Institute).

Coakley, J. (2014), 'The strange revival of bicameralism', *Journal of Legislative Studies*, 20(4): 542–72.

Conservative Party (2005), *Are You Thinking What We're Thinking? It's Time for Action: Conservative Election Manifesto 2005* (London, Conservative Party).

Constitution Committee (2016), 'The Union and devolution', Tenth Report of Session 2015–16, HL Paper 149, House of Lords.

Constitution Reform Group (2015), *Towards a New Act of Union: A Discussion Paper* (London, Constitution Reform Group).

Cruddas, J. (2015), 'Labour is lost in England', Labour List, http://labourlist.org/2015/09/jon-cruddas-labour-is-lost-in-england/, accessed 29 January 2018.

Cullen, S. (2016), 'Independence for England?', Campaign for an English Parliament, https://thecepreview.wordpress.com/2016/08/17/independence-for-england/, accessed 29 January 2018.

Curtice, J. (2006), 'What the people say—if anything', in R. Hazell (ed.), *The English Question* (Manchester, Manchester University Press), 119–41.

Curtice, J. (2016), 'Politics: political attitudes and behaviour in the wake of an intense constitutional debate', *British Social Attitudes*, 33: 89–116.

Dalyell, T. (2016), *The Question of Scotland: Devolution and After* (Edinburgh, Birlinn).

Davis, D. (2014), 'Scotland has spoken: let's listen to England', *The Sunday Times*, 21 September.

Denham, J. (2016), 'England: a crisis', *Fabian Review*, 128(2): 4–5.

Evans, A. (2017), '"Too old a country … too long accustomed to regard her life as one and indivisible": England and the Speaker's Conference on Devolution', *Contemporary British History*, 31(3): 366–83.

Field, F. (2014), 'An English Parliament: the only way to save the UK', Frankfield.com, http://www.frankfield.co.uk/latest-news/news.aspx?p=102868, accessed 29 January 2018.

Gordon, T. (2017), 'Kezia Dugdale fleshes out Scottish Labour federalism plan', *The Herald*, 13 February.

Gorman, T. (1999), *A Parliament for England* (Cheltenham, This England).

Gover, D. & Kenny, M. (2016), *Finding the Good in EVEL: An Evaluation of 'English Votes for English Laws' in the House of Commons* (Edinburgh, Centre on Constitutional Change).

Hague, W. (1998a), *Speech to the Centre for Policy Studies by the Rt Hon William Hague MP* (London, Centre for Policy Studies).

Hague, W. (1998b), 'William Hague: 1998 Conservative Party Conference speech', http://www.ukpol.co.uk/william-hague-1998-conservative-party-conference-speech/, accessed 29 January 2018.

Harding, A., Hazell, R., Burch, M. & Rees, J. (2008), 'Answering the English Question', in R. Hazell (ed.), *Constitutional Futures Revisited: Britain's Constitution to 2020* (Basingstoke, Palgrave Macmillan), 73–89.

Hayton, R. (2016), 'The UK Independence Party and the politics of Englishness', *Political Studies Review*, 14(3): 400–10.

Hazell, R. (2006a), *The English Question* (London, Constitution Unit).

Hazell, R. (2006b), 'Introduction: What is the English Question?' in R. Hazell (ed.), *The English Question* (Manchester, Manchester University Press), 1–21.

Heffer, S. (2008), 'England, arise and claim self-determination!', *Daily Telegraph*, 23 April.

Hunt, T. (ed.) (2016a), *Labour's Identity Crisis: England and the Politics of Patriotism* (Winchester: Centre for English Identity and Politics, University of Winchester).

Hunt, T. (2016b), '"We need a solution to the English Question"—Tristram Hunt calls for English referendum', Labour List, http://labourlist.org/2016/02/the-labour-party-has-a-problem-we-need-a-solution-to-the-english-question/, accessed 29 January 2018.

Hutton, W. (2014), 'We have 10 days to find a settlement to save the Union', *The Guardian*, 6 September.

Jeffery, C., Wyn Jones, R., Henderson, A., Scully, R. & Lodge, G. (2014), *Taking England Seriously: The New English Politics* (Edinburgh, Centre on Constitutional Change).

Jones, C. & Farrell, S. (2009), 'The House of Lords, 1707–1800', in C. Jones (ed.), *A Short History of Parliament: England, Great Britain, The United Kingdom, Ireland and Scotland* (Woodbridge, Boydell Press).

Kempley, J. (2011), *A Parliament for England: The Unfinished Project of Devolution in Britain* (Cambridge, Wilberforce Society).

Kendle, J. (1989), *Ireland and the Federal Solution: The Debate over the United Kingdom Constitution, 1870–1921* (Kingston, McGill-Queen's University Press).

Kenny, M. (2014), *The Politics of English Nationhood* (Oxford, Oxford University Press).

Lijphart, A. (1999), *Patterns of Democracy: Government Forms and Performance in Thirty-Six Countries* (New Haven, CT, Yale University Press).

Maddox, D. (2016), '"We need an English Parliament": Nuttall demands Scot MPs be booted out of House of Commons', *Daily Express*, 25 November.

Monbiot, G. (2009), 'Someone else's England', monbiot.com, http://www.monbiot.com/2009/02/17/someone-elses-england/, accessed 29 January 2018.

Nuttall, P. (2011), *A Union for the Future* (Newton Abbot, UKIP).

Office of the Lord President of the Council (1976), *Devolution: The English Dimension. A Consultative Document* (London, The Stationery Office).

Ormond, J. (1999), *An English Parliament: Proposals for Transparency and Fairness in a New Constitutional Settlement for England* (London, Bow Publications).

Redwood, J. (1999), *The Death of Britain?* (Basingstoke, Macmillan).

Redwood, J. (2006), 'Devolution and the West Lothian Question', John Redwood's diary, http://johnredwoodsdiary.com/2006/12/18/devolution-and-the-west-lothian-question/, accessed 29 January 2018.

Redwood, J. (2014), 'If it's good enough for Scotland … let England have its own parliament', *The Guardian*, 19 September.

Redwood, J. (2015), 'England wants to get EVEN: now Hague must ensure that it does', Conservative Home, http://www.conservativehome.com/platform/2015/02/john-red

wood-mp-england-wants-to-get-even-now-hague-must-ensure-that-it-does.html, accessed 29 January 2018.

Rembold, E. (2000), '"Home rule all round": experiments in regionalising Great Britain, 1886–1914', in P. Catterall, W. Kaiser & U. Walton-Jordan (eds), *Reforming the Constitution: Debates in Twentieth-Century Britain* (London, Frank Cass), 201–24.

Royal Commission on the Constitution (1973), *The Report of the Royal Commission on the Constitution* (London, The Stationery Office).

Renwick, A. & Hazell, R. (2017), *Blueprint for a UK Constitutional Convention* (London, Constitution Unit).

Russell, M. & Lodge, G. (2006), 'The government of England by Westminster', in R. Hazell (ed.), *The English Question* (Manchester, Manchester University Press), 64–95.

Russell, M. & Sheldon, J. (2018), *Options for an English Parliament* (London, Constitution Unit).

UKIP (United Kingdom Independence Party) (2010), *UKIP Manifesto: Empowering the People* (Newton Abbot, UKIP).

UKIP (United Kingdom Independence Party) (2015), *UKIP Manifesto 2015: Believe in Britain* (Newton Abbot, UKIP).

UKIP (United Kingdom Independence Party) (2017), *UKIP 2017 Manifesto: Britain Together* (Newton Abbot, UKIP).

Umunna, C. (2015a), 'Britain needs wholesale federalisation—and Labour must lead the way', *The Guardian*, 27 October.

Umunna, C. (2015b), 'These are "perilous times" for the left', *New Statesman*, http://www.newstatesman.com/politics/2015/07/chuka-umunna-these-are-perilous-times-left, accessed 29 January 2018.

Part II

Speaking for England? The Political Parties

6

Interpreting EVEL: Latest Station in the Conservative Party's English Journey?

DANIEL GOVER & MICHAEL KENNY

6.1 Introduction

ON THE MORNING after the Scottish independence referendum, in September 2014, Prime Minister David Cameron gave a speech in which he welcomed Scotland's vote to remain in the UK, and he went on to declare that: 'I have long believed that a crucial part missing from this national discussion is England. We have heard the voice of Scotland—and now the millions of voices of England must also be heard. The question of English votes for English laws—the so-called West Lothian question—requires a decisive answer' (Cameron 2014). This call led—following the election of a single-party Conservative Government in May 2015—to the establishment of a new set of procedures in the House of Commons known as 'English votes for English laws' (hereafter EVEL). The scheme created new mechanisms for MPs representing constituencies in England to vote down legislation that applies only in England.

EVEL has been highly divisive in UK party politics and has been criticised by some for accentuating territorial and national tensions at a moment when the Union had just been saved from the threat posed by Scottish nationalism. In response to Cameron's post-referendum statement, Nick Clegg—then Deputy Prime Minister and leader of the Liberal Democrats, the Conservatives' coalition partners—declared this to be an exercise in 'conventional party political point scoring', warning that the Conservatives 'could jeopardise the Union they purport to defend' (Clegg 2014).

How it is that the political party that has for so long seen itself as the traditional guardian of the Union, and the inveterate opponent of devolution, became the architect of a policy which is seen by its opponents as endangering the Union, remains somewhat mysterious. In this chapter we ask whether this reflects a deeper shift in the nature of the Conservative Party's approach to the Union, explore different

Proceedings of the British Academy, **217**, 117–136, © The British Academy 2018.

ways of understanding the evolution of its territorial statecraft, and emphasise some important differences of perspective within the party's ranks. We consider the introduction of EVEL against this background, drawing on material gathered from a broader investigation which the authors have conducted into this reform.

The chapter is organised into several discrete sections. We start by setting out the broad development of different strands of Conservative thinking about the Union, followed by the various designs that began to emerge for institutionalising English control over Westminster legislation. There follows a close-up focus upon the period 2014–15, when the Conservative-led Coalition Government sought to inject political energy into the English Question. We then focus on the design and operation of the EVEL procedures during the 2015–17 Parliament and identify some important political tensions and inconsistencies affecting them. In the next section we step back from these developments, drawing upon several existing interpretations of the UK's territorial politics to deepen contemporary understanding of Conservative motivations and thought. We conclude with some reflections on how the Tory Party might now be required to approach these issues, given the outcome of the 2017 general election and the imperatives associated with Brexit.

6.2 The Conservatives, the Union and Devolution: A Historical Preamble

Unionism has long been central to the Conservative Party's self-image—an identity that was forged in part during earlier moments when the idea of introducing devolution to different territories of the UK was under consideration. In response to political unrest in the late 19th and early 20th centuries, a succession of Liberal governments sought to implement schemes for 'home rule' to Ireland, under which control over domestic matters would be transferred to a separate Irish legislature and executive. The Conservatives opposed such moves on the basis that home rule would weaken the integrity of the UK and this opposition became a hallmark of the party's approach to the Union during this period. One of the most contentious features of arguments for devolution concerned the consequences of any home rule scheme for Westminster—and in particular how Ireland should be represented in a UK legislature that had only limited responsibility for Irish matters. Gladstone's 'in and out' solution—included in his 1893 bill, under which Irish MPs would continue to sit at Westminster but would only be entitled to vote on certain matters—was ultimately regarded by him as unworkable (Bogdanor 2001). But the political conflicts stirred by debates about a federal settlement ensured a significant political realignment, as a split within the ranks of the Liberal Party resulted in a small group of Liberal Unionists forming an alliance with the Conservatives, a development which led ultimately to the formation of today's 'Conservative and Unionist' Party.

Against this historical backdrop, the Conservative Party's current enthusiasm for the idea of giving new voting rights to English MPs is, at first sight, surprising. Yet the move represents the culmination of a process of argument and deliberation that has been unfolding for several decades. This involved acceptance by many of the party's post-war leaders, most notably Edward Heath, of the case for limited devolution to Scotland in order to stabilise the wider unionist project, followed by the adoption, once more, of a more sceptical position in the wake of Margaret Thatcher's emergence as leader in the 1970s. One of the key episodes in this process was the attempt of the Labour Government in the late 1970s to introduce devolution to Scotland and Wales. Speaking in the debates on the Scotland Bill in 1977, Conservative MP Francis Pym, Shadow Leader of the Commons, expressed fears that 'the consequences of this Bill, if enacted, will in the course of time damage the Union and could conceivably prove fatal to its continuance' (HC Deb., 14 November 1977: col. 74). The same Commons debates also provided the occasion for Labour MP Tam Dalyell to pose his iconic 'West Lothian Question' for the first time:

> For how long will English constituencies and English hon. Members tolerate not just 71 Scots, 36 Welsh and a number of Ulstermen but at least 119 hon. Members from Scotland, Wales and Northern Ireland exercising an important, and probably often decisive, effect on English politics while they themselves have no say in the same matters in Scotland, Wales and Ireland? (HC Deb., 14 November 1977: col. 123)

During the course of the bill's passage, the Conservatives backed a proposal that would have enabled certain votes that were carried by Scottish MPs, but did not apply in Scotland, to be confirmed two weeks later by a second Commons vote. The rationale for this was to give MPs the chance to reconsider their original decision. The party's leadership defended this solution as maintaining the equality of all MPs, thus distinguishing it from Gladstone's earlier 'in and out' proposal (Francis Pym, HC Deb., 17 July 1978: col. 159).

This particular response to the West Lothian Question disappeared from view along with Labour's devolution proposals of that period.[1] But the issue resurfaced, this time more resonantly, in the context of debates triggered by the devolution settlements introduced in Scotland, Wales and Northern Ireland in the late 1990s. For many of its unionist supporters, devolution was, in part, intended to offset concerns about England's dominance within the Union and head off the growing threat of nationalism in different parts of the UK. But in its 1997 manifesto the Conservative Party warned that Labour's devolution proposals would 'create strains which could well pull apart the Union' (Conservative Party 1997: 50).

[1] Both the Scotland Act 1978 and the Wales Act 1978 required devolution to be approved through a referendum in which a majority (comprising at least 40 per cent of eligible electors) voted in support. The subsequent referendum in Wales did not achieve majority support, while in Scotland the slim majority in favour did not pass the 40 per cent threshold.

6.3 Early Designs for EVEL

Following successful campaigns in September 1997, devolution was introduced by Labour in both Scotland and Wales against the objections of the Conservatives. But, having drawn attention to the salience and intractability of the West Lothian Question during these earlier debates, the Conservatives began to entertain new ideas for solving it and linked these to the demand for some kind of counterbalancing reform for England as a response to the asymmetry created by a devolution settlement which did not extend to the largest part of the UK. In a speech delivered in February 1998, Conservative leader William Hague signalled his intention to begin 'a full debate' about further reform (Hague 1998). And, writing in his autobiography in this period, Heath set out his own view that Scottish MPs could be prevented from voting on England-only legislation (Heath 1998: 565). During the course of the next two decades, more detailed proposals were aired in Conservative circles, contributing to a developing body of specialist knowledge on this question and enabling the party to include commitments to introduce a version of EVEL in its general election manifestos from 2001 onwards (Conservative Party 2001, 2005, 2010).

The first major contribution to this debate was the report of the Commission to Strengthen Parliament (2000), a body appointed by Hague and chaired by the Conservative peer (and constitutional expert) Lord (Philip) Norton of Louth. Under its proposals, the Commons Speaker would be required to certify the territorial application of legislation; then any provisions applying exclusively to England (or England and Wales) would pass through a revised Commons legislative process, with second reading, committee and report stages all voted on by English (or English and Welsh) MPs only and reflecting the party balance in that part of the UK. For third reading (the bill's final stage during its initial Commons passage), all MPs would formally be entitled to vote, but the commission anticipated the development of a convention that those representing parts of the UK not affected by the legislation would not do so. In effect, the commission thus envisaged England-only legislation being voted on by English MPs alone, which represented a relatively robust, 'full-strength' version of EVEL.

The salience of this issue was significantly boosted by the contentious passage of legislation that applied primarily to England during Blair's second term in government, on the issues of tuition fees and foundation hospitals (Russell & Lodge 2006). The Government's reliance on Scottish MPs in key parliamentary votes on these bills stirred a loud chorus of complaint, particularly in Conservative circles (e.g. Tim Yeo, HC Deb., 27 January 2004: col. 275). These votes also attracted extensive commentary about the injustices being done to England, from press and politicians alike, and appear to have touched a nerve among some English audiences. Analysis of mainstream national media, for instance, shows that mentions in the UK press of the term 'West Lothian Question'—a useful indicator of interest in this topic—spiked significantly in the few years subsequently, as shown in Figure 6.1.

A new version of EVEL was subsequently elaborated in a report produced by the Conservative Democracy Task Force (2008), set up by party leader David Cameron

Figure 6.1 Newspaper Mentions of West Lothian Question per Year, 1996–2015

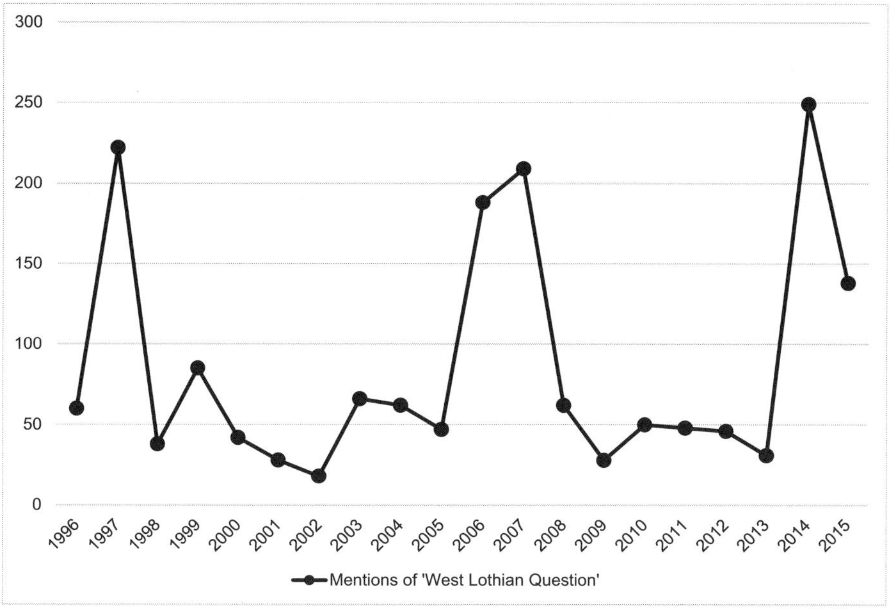

Source: LexisNexis search of UK national newspapers for the term 'West Lothian Question', conducted by the authors, 1 January 1996 to 31 December 2015.

and chaired by Kenneth Clarke MP. This body was an important part of the political attempt to brand the Conservatives as concerned about democratic questions, many of which an increasingly unpopular Labour Government appeared insensitive towards. Clarke's report recommended that legislation certified as English should pass through a Commons legislative process that afforded MPs from England, and also those from across the UK, veto rights at different stages. The second and third reading stages of bills would, on this model, be voted on by the whole House, allowing all MPs the chance to vote against the entire bill at either end of its Commons passage. But English MPs would have control at committee and report stages—the two Commons stages at which a bill is amendable—enabling them to revise or delete any provisions that they disagreed with (and/or to add new ones). In comparison with the Norton model, this represented a 'medium-strength' variant of EVEL—as the passage of England-only legislation would require the assent of both English and UK-wide MPs, but neither would have the power to force through legislation against the wishes of the other.

However, the most influential and important document setting out the arguments for reform emerged from outside the party. It was produced by the McKay Commission (2013), an independent body established by the Government as part of the Conservative–Liberal Democrat coalition agreement (HM Government 2010) and chaired by the highly respected former Clerk of the Commons, Sir William

McKay.[2] The commission concluded that, post-devolution, English voters needed to have their interests more clearly delineated and protected at Westminster—perhaps the first time this hitherto heterodox argument had been so clearly accepted in official quarters (Kenny 2015). Yet these unconventional notes were blended with more constitutionally orthodox ideas. Thus, in contrast with some of the earlier proposals circulating within the Conservative Party, the commission explicitly rejected the establishment of a formal veto right for English representatives, instead preferring mechanisms to enable their preferences, or 'voice', to be more clearly articulated and acknowledged.

These various proposed answers to the West Lothian Question are an important barometer of the growing conviction in different parts of the political world that some kind of balancing reform was required to alleviate the asymmetries bequeathed by devolution. Arguments for such a reform generated some important intellectual and policy tributaries within the Conservative Party. An equally important impact was to help legitimate the notion that the English were entitled to expect a more substantial degree of recognition and protection within the UK Parliament. And the appearance of this idea in such official quarters is one sign that the long-established consensus that the West Lothian Question was insoluble was starting to crack.

6.4 The English Question Emerges, 2014–15

The appearance of the McKay Commission's report caused little stir in 2013, except in specialist constitutional circles. Labour simply ignored it, having already declined to make any submission to it. For the Government, too, the commission was widely understood as a sop to the Conservative Party's base, engendering little interest from either coalition party's leadership. Behind the scenes, the requirement to formulate an official government reply sparked limited discussions between the two parties, with some Liberal Democrat figures willing to explore the possibility of achieving an agreement that it could trade for other policy concessions as part of the bargaining game that had come to define intra-governmental relations by 2013. Accordingly, representatives of the two parties hammered out an agreement on a version of EVEL. But, although this proposal was put before the Prime Minister and Deputy Prime Minister, it was not pursued any further—a telling sign of the lack of interest in this question, at this juncture, among either party's leadership.[3]

Further progress on the agenda was stimulated by the Scottish independence referendum and a growing conviction in Conservative circles that, in its aftermath, the English Question needed to be publicly aired and might also present

[2] The commission's official title was the Commission on the Consequences of Devolution for the House of Commons.

[3] Source: interviews with officials from the Conservative and Liberal Democrat parties.

tactical benefits for the party. Indeed, Conservative interest in this issue was already growing, partly in response to the sharp rise in popularity of the United Kingdom Independence Party (UKIP) in 2012–13 and the appeal of its brand of populist nationalism to disillusioned Conservative voters. While UKIP's primary focus was upon the issues of immigration and Europe, its core support lay in England and some of its senior figures were keen to speak to English grievances in the context of the Scottish referendum. UKIP leader Nigel Farage raised the question of English representation during the weeks leading up to the referendum vote (BBC News 2014), while various opinion surveys from the period reported that a striking number of those to whom the party appealed tended to identify as English rather than British (Jeffery et al. 2014; see also Ford and Sobolewska, Chapter 8). The concern that the Conservatives were being outflanked by a party that spoke more directly to a mood of heightened English irritation weighed heavily on the former's strategists.

But the growing salience of the English constitutional issue also represented a response to a different kind of political incentive: the chance to outmanoeuvre the Conservatives' main opponents on an issue which the Scottish referendum had brought to the fore. Both Labour and the Liberal Democrats had generally favoured schemes for greater regional self-government in England as their preferred response to the English Question, as John Denham discusses in Chapter 7. This preference was bound up with the association many progressives drew between English national identity and right-wing political attitudes. Both parties responded to the Conservatives' interest in the West Lothian anomaly by challenging the latter's unionist credentials and offering a defence of the new status quo—as exemplified by Clegg's response to Cameron's statement in Section 6.1.

Having aired the question of English grievance in September 2014, Cameron moved to establish a cabinet committee chaired by William Hague, the then Leader of the House of Commons, to consider how best to implement EVEL. The outcome of this process was a command paper that, very unusually, set out four different options for reform: three Conservative and one Liberal Democrat (Leader of the House of Commons 2014). The Conservative options were based on earlier proposals, discussed in Section 6.3: Norton's relatively 'full-strength' variant, Clarke's 'medium-strength' model, and an option based on some of the McKay Commission's proposals but strengthened to incorporate a formal veto. The appearance of disagreement within the Government's ranks was accentuated by the publication of the separate Liberal Democrat option.[4]

The Conservative Party's grassroots in this period tended to favour stronger versions of EVEL, of the kind proposed by Norton. A survey of party members for the Conservative Home website found that 78 per cent favoured completely barring

[4] This emphasised devolution of power within England and argued that the party balance on any new England-only parliamentary body should be determined based on the votes cast for each party rather than its number of MPs.

MPs from outside England from voting on English-only matters, while only 33 per cent supported the weaker solution of an English-only committee stage (Goodman 2014).[5] This more robust form of EVEL also attracted significant support among the parliamentary party. Some, such as high-profile backbencher John Redwood (2015), had long advocated such a position, while informal canvassing of parliamentary opinion also led the party leadership to appreciate that this was the preferred option of a substantial section of its own Commons backbenchers.[6] Others favoured a rather different approach, seeking to bridge the party's unionist heritage, its support for the idea of devolution outside England, and the need to adapt the UK Parliament to obviate English concerns. Thus, a pamphlet written by constitutional expert Roger Gough and backbench MP Andrew Tyrie (Gough & Tyrie 2015) argued that, although a formal veto right for the Commons was now necessary—a commitment that went further than the McKay Commission's proposals—a 'full-strength' version of EVEL risked destabilising the Union.

Debates about EVEL were only one manifestation of a much broader shift in territorial thinking within the Conservative Party during these years. In 2014 a review into Scottish governance, commissioned by the Scottish Conservatives and chaired by Tory peer Lord Strathclyde, concluded that Scotland should be granted a significant measure of fiscal devolution, reflecting a wider argument for a looser union which did not make so many demands upon English taxpayers (Scottish Conservatives 2014). Separately, various Conservative commentators were by now openly questioning the rationale for union and the depth of the party's commitment to it. Writing in *The Spectator*, Matthew Parris (2010) expressed surprise at the discovery of his own profound indifference to the fate of the Union. Other pundits sympathetic to the party were more troubled by the divergence between England and the UK, but could not see a way around this trend (Moore 2014). For some English Conservatives, it was increasingly apparent that their commitment to England, and maintaining the traditional sovereign authority of the state, counted for more than maintaining the domestic union; but for many other Tories, the need to preserve the Union and head off further territorial conflicts remained paramount.

EVEL's re-emergence on the political agenda temporarily pushed the Liberal Democrats towards their Labour opponents, given their overlapping outlooks on this issue. In late 2014 the two parties privately discussed supporting an amendment to a government bill to force the establishment of a constitutional convention, whose remit would include options for greater English scrutiny of legislation, but this dialogue came to nothing.[7] Meanwhile the Conservatives plumped for the third model of EVEL set out in Hague's paper (the strengthened version of the McKay proposals) but were unable to secure support from the Liberal Democrats to put the matter to a vote in the Commons. In the 2015 general election campaign

[5] Respondents to this survey were able to register their support for multiple options, or for a single one.

[6] Source: interview with official from the Conservative Party.

[7] Source: interviews with officials from the Liberal Democrat and Labour Parties.

the Conservative Party included the proposals in its manifesto (Conservative Party 2015a), while the pledge was also central to its 'English manifesto'—the first occasion the party had published such a document (Conservative Party 2015b).

6.5 The Operation of EVEL, 2015–17

Having promised in its manifesto to table its proposals within the first 100 days of the general election, the newly elected Conservative Government moved quickly to implement its commitment on this issue. Two months after the election, the incoming Leader of the House, Chris Grayling, published a series of proposed changes to the 'standing orders' of the Commons (the formal rules that govern procedure in that chamber). These were ultimately approved by MPs—following a series of relatively minor revisions—in October 2015.

Under these new procedures, MPs representing constituencies in England (and England and Wales) were accorded the opportunity to veto legislative provisions that applied only in the relevant part of the UK. To achieve this, the Commons Speaker was given a new responsibility to examine legislation for its territorial application and to 'certify' any provision that met specified criteria. Legislation thus certified would then require the consent of MPs from the area concerned for it to be passed by the Commons, achieved primarily through new 'legislative grand committees'. Importantly, this veto right did not override the existing right of the whole House to vote at the main legislative stages, including the ability to reject any bill or to make amendments to it. This constitutive aspect of the reform—labelled the 'double veto' by some commentators—meant that legislation certified as applying only to England required approval by a majority of both English and UK-wide MPs for it to be passed.[8] In broad terms, the Government opted for a medium-strength version of EVEL—avoiding the more robust proposals associated with some of its backbenchers, while also offering a substantive innovation in the form of an unprecedented 'English veto', which proved highly unpopular with its political opponents.

In the final vote to approve the procedures, MPs divided neatly along party lines. All those in favour were Conservatives, while all opposed were from other parties (including one independent).[9] Yet this apparent unanimity masked some unease within the Conservative parliamentary party about the risks that EVEL might pose for the Union, while various figures expressed concern about the implications of a radical redesign of the UK constitution which might unduly complicate the business of the Commons and aggravate territorial tensions. These views were aired, for instance, by backbench MPs Dominic Grieve and Edward Leigh, who

[8] For further explanation and discussion of the procedures, see Gover & Kenny (2016a, 2018).

[9] Division result 312–270. Those voting in favour: Conservative (312). Those voting against: Labour (200), SNP (54), DUP (6), Liberal Democrat (3), Plaid Cymru (3), Social Democratic and Labour Party (3), Independent (1). Figures exclude tellers (HC Deb., 22 October 2015: cols 1253–6).

raised concerns about how EVEL might apply on legislation with so-called 'Barnett consequentials'—referring to the practice by which the block grant to the devolved bodies is adjusted by reference to English spending decisions. Leigh spoke for a small, but not insignificant, minority of Tories when he argued that 'the Union is at stake' (HC Deb., 7 July 2015: col. 197). Such arguments reflected a deeper fear that, while the Conservatives may well have achieved short-term political advantage by tabling this issue, the reform also had the potential to accentuate a long-standing weakness in the party's own territorial position—making even more transparent the predominantly English base of its parliamentary representation. Equally, the Scottish National Party (SNP)'s ascendancy in Scottish politics presented a new dilemma for the Conservative Party, bringing into British politics a powerful Anglo-Scottish tension of the kind that British statecraft has long sought to defuse.

There have also been early signs of a very different pressure among those calling for a more robust form of EVEL, usually on the ground that the English now wanted for themselves what had been offered to other national groups in the UK. And the relative limitations of the new system, from this perspective, were illustrated in 2016 by the Government's attempts to relax Sunday trading laws through its Enterprise Bill. Although the policy would have applied only in England and Wales, and attracted majority support from English and Welsh MPs, it was defeated by UK-wide MPs—with the votes of Scottish MPs proving decisive (Gover & Kenny 2016b). In fact, the way in which the Government drafted this provision (by also including material that would have applied in Scotland) meant that it would not have been certified under EVEL by the Speaker—a situation that throws into relief the potential for future governments to circumnavigate these procedures should they wish to do so. But, even if the clause had related solely to England and Wales, the 'double veto' aspect of EVEL would have meant that all MPs would still have had the power to block the policy. This feature of EVEL also set limits upon Conservative ambitions in other policy areas that pertain only to England (or England and Wales), such as foxhunting and grammar schools. For how long the current procedures will retain the support of those who wish for a more full-throated form of English legislative control remains far from clear.

This new system has been afflicted by other inconsistencies and strains as well. It has, rather notably, been justified through reference to two quite distinct values. These can be associated with the achievement of a degree of 'voice', on the one hand, and the provision of a 'veto', on the other. Whereas arguments for an enhanced English voice in Parliament tend to emphasise opportunities for deliberation and the importance of some degree of recognition for the English interest, the idea of veto refers to the particular right to block legislation from being imposed on England against the wishes of its elected representatives. Cameron, as noted in Section 6.1, responded to the result of the Scottish independence referendum by arguing that it was time for 'the millions of voices of England [to] be heard', while his party's subsequent English manifesto pledged to address 'the need for English MPs to express their voice on matters affecting England only' (Conservative Party 2015b: 8). Yet when it turned to implement EVEL, his Government ended up delivering a comprehensive kind of procedural veto and did little to encourage the enhancement of voice. There is, for instance, little incentive for MPs to view the new 'legislative grand committees' as meaningful deliberative forums. During the 2015–17 Parliament these committees were almost entirely perfunctory, most concluding without any substantive contributions at all (Gover & Kenny 2016a, 2018).

In its presentation of these reforms, the Government also tended to conflate two very different understandings of their purpose. Specifically, it interlaced the kind of conservative case for judicious, incremental adjustment—which defenders of the constitutional order, from Edmund Burke through to today's moderate voices in the party, have favoured—with the language of popular sovereignty and suppressed nationhood, themes which Enoch Powell and Margaret Thatcher brought into the mainstream of party thinking. These different arguments speak to different parts of the British Conservative tradition which have long held differing perspectives on issues of nationhood and constitution. The first of these strands evolved, after the end of the empire, towards a different vision of the United Kingdom, as a flexible polity which could accommodate modest forms of devolution and could pool sovereignty within a wider European arrangement. Its adherents have generally supported reform to the UK's internal constitutional arrangements for prudential reasons—including to protect the Union from the potential disaffection of the largest national population of the UK. Its leading proponents, such as Kenneth Clarke and Andrew Tyrie, tend to be sceptical about the idea that the Union can function if England is accorded some form of devolution in an attempt to achieve 'symmetry'. This traditional view was reflected in the then Leader of the House Chris Grayling's contention that EVEL would serve 'to strengthen the Union' by making it fairer and more balanced (HC Deb., 2 July 2015: col. 1667).

Yet Cameron's rhetoric in September 2014, and much Conservative discourse since, gestured simultaneously at a very different idea—the notion, associated with contemporary figures like MPs John Redwood and David Davis, that England deserves the same democratic rights that have been granted to the other parts of the UK. This perspective has its roots in the vision of parliamentary sovereignty and English heritage which were advanced from the political margins by Powell and were institutionalised in the party's mainstream by Thatcher and her successors. On this—arguably more 'Jacobin'—view, England cannot retain its sovereignty while involved in a legal or political union with other countries, while the domestic union is regarded as viable only when framed and managed on England's terms. Technical adjustments to the legislative rules of the House of Commons are unlikely to measure up to the heady rhetoric of self-government and 'taking back control' which this second discourse invokes.

The disjuncture between reality and some of the rhetoric associated with this reform has created a space which disenchantment, and more radical demands on behalf of the English, may come to fill. Senior backbenchers like Redwood are adamant that the terms of the devolved union place undue constraints upon the English and have demanded to know why the principle of self-government has not been extended to the largest nation of the UK. As he put it to William Hague in a Commons debate in 2014: 'England expects English votes for English issues. We expect simplicity and justice now: no ifs, no buts, no committee limitations, no tricks. Give us what we want. We have waited 15 years for this. Will he now join me in speaking for England?' (HC Deb., 16 December 2014: col. 1270). Such figures are willing to support EVEL in the short term, on the tacit understanding that it works to ensure that English interests are not disregarded in Parliament, but they may turn against the current system should it prove unable to guarantee that the preferences of English MPs are not overridden.

In practical terms, however, the notion of achieving devolution at the English level faces enormous obstacles, not least because there are no extant institutions of English governance, and English affairs are so interwoven into the development of UK-wide policy and legislation. For this reason, too, Cameron's rhetoric sat awkwardly with the tradition, referenced in Section 6.2, of Conservative pragmatism towards the constitutional machinery of the UK. Distinct arrangements for the governance of the non-English territories have long been a hallmark of the British state, as has been the absence of England as a distinct entity within the functionally defined structures of the state, as discussed by Jim Gallagher in Chapter 4. Arguments about the possibility and wisdom of labelling as 'English' those government departments with functions that are now exercised primarily in relation to England have begun to break the surface of British politics in recent years and a number of public bodies—for instance NHS England—have quietly started to announce their territorial jurisdiction. But these developments remain under the political radar and calls for some kind of equivalent devolution arrangement for England remain fundamentally at odds with the territorial character of British governance.

The Conservative Government's presentation of EVEL reflects a tendency to 'over claim' and a desire to appeal simultaneously to different parts of the party, which may come to have significant repercussions for the Union as a whole. But these inconsistencies and tensions are perhaps also an indication that Conservative thinking about England's place within the domestic union is less anchored than it once was. In Section 6.6, we discuss different ways of understanding the much broader shift in party thinking that led to the introduction of EVEL.

6.6 The Decline of Unionist Statecraft?

To gain analytical purchase on this issue, we draw insights from three notable, and broadly complementary, accounts of the historical development and nature of Conservative thinking about the territorial dimensions and constitutional character of the UK state: Andrew Gamble's analysis of the reassertion of the enduring English core of British Conservatism; Jim Bulpitt's account of the kind of territorial statecraft which was integral to the Conservative political outlook and which became increasingly problematic from the 1980s onwards; and Richard Rose's observation of the role played by the party system in providing an underpinning for the Union.

For Gamble (2016), the Anglo-centric vision of the UK that became apparent in Conservative circles in the early 2000s should be seen as the continuation of an older version of Toryism that was partially effaced by the ascendancy of unionism and empire, but never entirely eclipsed by either. While allegiance to the Union has long been key to this lineage, it had always been secondary to the need to protect the sovereignty of the British state, the core of which is England and its traditional institutions. The Conservatives, he suggests, have become increasingly willing and ready to discard the garments that were once so important to Conservative identity. For a growing number of today's Tories, the passion and enthusiasm once elicited by the UK as a multinational state have steadily dissipated over the last few decades. And so, while the Union remains important and valued, it is for many Conservatives glimpsed in increasingly instrumental terms—as a source of Britain's geopolitical standing or as a conduit to economic prosperity. Latterly it has come to be seen increasingly as a constraint and a burden—a potential block upon England's aspirations and sovereignty. For now, the Union subsists in Conservative Party thinking so long as other parts of the UK participate within it on English terms and show that they are willing to share the priorities and outlook associated with the Conservatives. But Gamble detects an underlying, tectonic shift in mentality on the part of many Tories. This position, he suggests, takes the party back to its 'Tory roots, shorn of the Whig trappings of union and empire which have been the framework of Conservative politics for so long' (Gamble 2016: 361).

The appetite among parts of the Conservative Party for maintaining the old union state, and its attendant constitutional order, has, Gamble observes, been waning for some while. Key episodes in this process include the fissure that opened between Ulster Unionism and British Conservatism, the decline of unionism and the Conservative presence in Scotland, and the party's diminished standing in the post-industrial cities of northern England, all of which have in turn consolidated its identity as a party of South East and 'middle' England. On this view, the shift towards a more accommodationist approach to both the European and domestic unions that prevailed in the party from the era of Macmillan to Heath gave way to a reassertion of a unitary understanding of the UK, viewed through the lens of a traditional English constitutionalism. This set in train a rejection of devolution under Thatcher as she sought to rebuild a different 'politics of nationhood' (Lynch 1999) for the party. Thatcher's tenure was, on this account, a vital moment in the journey that Gamble describes. In important respects she laid the foundations for the revival of a political Englishness and the emergence of an Anglo-centric Euroscepticism among many British Conservatives, a force which played a major role in the UK's referendum on EU membership in June 2016. Cameron's talk in September 2014 of protecting England's interests, and enhancing England's hitherto suppressed voice, continued in the trajectory established by Thatcher. And EVEL, on this view, looks like a further step towards the reassertion of England as the more authentic and integral political community for the Conservative Party.

Important and insightful as this interpretation is, whether Gamble's characterisation captures the entirety of the party and its traditions of thinking—or merely an important and increasingly influential, part of it—is a key question. The 'double veto' feature of EVEL is revealing on this score, in that it also reflects a desire by party managers to appease those Conservatives who remain committed to an older, Heathite vision of the UK constitution. Gamble's emphasis on an enduring lineage of English Toryism over the last century or more can be usefully complemented by an appreciation of profound shifts in the instincts and wisdom associated with those charged with territorial management on the part of the British state over the same period. Jim Bulpitt's (1983) suggestive, and much debated, historical sketch of the changing 'territorial statecraft' of previous eras also sheds light on the judgements and calculations of elite actors in relation to the constitutional order. In particular, his characterisation of the demise of the relatively stable territorial system of the middle decades of the 20th century (which he christened the era of the 'dual polity') helps us understand, more generally, the dissolution of the coordinates and governing reflexes associated with Conservative statecraft.

Bulpitt's interpretation stemmed from a 'realist' appreciation of the gap that existed between official rhetoric about the merits of the unitary state, on the one hand, and the complex and variegated manner in which territorial management was undertaken by the centre in Britain, on the other. Put simply, this involved the granting of strategic concessions to local elites to protect the basic autonomy of the central British state. While the English Parliament ceased formally to exist in 1707, in practice it expanded after union with Scotland, absorbing territories from other parts of Britain and becoming the legislature of the whole UK. Securing the hegemony of the state within this expanded territory was premised upon the recognition that special arrangements might be necessary for the governance of its non-English territories. The domestic elite, he intimated, tended to prefer short-term fixes and to avoid systematic reforms, and sought instinctively to avoid foundational and principled solutions to constitutional and territorial problems—a judgement that casts an important shadow over some of the territorial 'fixes' that have been attempted in the last two decades, EVEL included. Crucially, in this narrative, the centre's approach to territorial management was defined in terms of its inclination to stay above territorial politics itself and to keep the latter at some remove, both in terms of its objectives and in the composition and personal relations of its elite.

Bulpitt's characterisation of the period of relative stability in territorial relations, which prevailed from the 1920s to the 1960s, as the era of the 'dual polity', is of particular interest because of his account of the reasons for, and consequences of, its dissolution. In these decades there emerged a relatively stable settlement based upon the attempt of party leaders, especially Tory ones, at the centre to ensure that the realm of 'high politics' was insulated from the demands bubbling up from the localities. To achieve this separation, a considerable degree of autonomy was offered to sympathetic local elites. To this end, a succession of Conservative leaders granted enhanced administrative autonomy and, for the most part, held back from pursuing centralist ambitions or attempting to achieve uniformity across the UK. It was in this period that the Macmillanite ethos merged with a new, modernising current of Conservatism which saw merits in pooling sovereignty with other European countries. This settlement ultimately started to unwind during the late 1970s and, as yet, no stable alternative to it has been located. During the Thatcher era, the Conservatives' avowed appeal to what Bulpitt termed 'provincial England', and attempt to reintroduce a more centralised form of governance and unitary perspective on the UK, made it highly likely that territorial politics would become a major field of conflict once more.

While it is hard to divine how Bulpitt would have responded to events that followed his own death (in 1999), his scepticism about the prospects for a stable future for the UK after devolution merits consideration in the light of subsequent events. The turn towards greater self-government as a way of solving the problem of the growing appeal of nationalism in the peripheral territories was, in his view, mistaken, since it meant creating political structures which might be captured by actors who did not wish to play the role ascribed by the central state to compliant elites and whose appeal would lie in their capacity to mobilise opposition to the state—a judgement that has proved immensely prescient in the case of Scotland. He feared as well that setting the UK's informal and flexible arrangements on a more formal, quasi-legal, footing would create the kinds of institutional obstacle and minority advantage that were likely to inflame the resentments of the English majority and limit the flexibility and room for manoeuvre of those tasked with managing territorial affairs.

Since 2007, there have been various indications that the statecraft paradigm which Bulpitt believed had evolved over successive centuries has entered a period of profound crisis. One sign of its increasingly dysfunctional character is the growing polarisation between the ways in which the two main UK parties have approached constitutional issues, a situation which is a major contributor to current instability and was a crucial backdrop to Cameron's decision to inject political energy into the English Question in 2014. According to Richard Rose (1974), the stability of the British model rested to a considerable degree upon the capacity of the party system to defuse territorial and national tensions and promote functional over national questions in political life. The more recent deepening conflict suggests that, contrary to his analysis of its operation in 1974, the party system became increasingly a source rather than a defuser of tension. Not since the Irish Question raged has such deep doctrinal division over territory and state been so prevalent in high politics in the UK.

In the current period, as discussed by John Denham in Chapter 7, Labour has, for the most part, remained hostile to arguments about devolution for England, offering a tepid case for administrative decentralisation to its regions and largest cities—an approach which has tended to lack popular resonance and was viewed in some quarters as an illegitimate attempt, with Brussels' connivance, to break England apart. The Conservatives, meanwhile, have become the champions of the English interest in UK politics. In this context, issues such as West Lothian have come to be viewed in strongly partisan terms and the prospects for some kind of cross-party consensus on the future shape of the UK constitution appears to have receded. These differences have been overdetermined by the parties' divergent and increasingly fractured territorial bases (a situation that has in turn been accentuated by the retention of one of the features commonly associated with the 'Westminster model': the first past the post voting system for UK general elections). Labour's position (until 2015) as the UK party most likely to win Scottish and Welsh seats has rendered the party more wary of calls for constitutional change that might be disadvantageous to those peripheries and especially suspicious of arguments for devolution to England as a whole. The perception in Labour circles that England is a fundamentally conservative country in electoral terms is—as Iain McLean (2007) has demonstrated—both influential and significantly overplayed in the party's mindset.

For their Conservative counterparts, the mirror image of this pattern of representation has also, over time, exercised an important influence upon the Tory outlook. As Northern Ireland became an electorally distinct entity in the 1970s and the Conservatives subsequently lost their foothold in Scotland, England became ever more important to their parliamentary position and the party tended to win seats overwhelmingly in the South and South East. These are, broadly, places that are the largest net contributors to the public finances, compared to those Labour-represented ones that are the largest net recipients of them. This markedly bifurcated pattern of representation has done much to deepen and accentuate the divergent constitutional thinking of both parties and served to inject political energy and conflict into some of the questions about constitutional order and territorial equity which the party system has, for the last century, been effective at managing and defusing, in Bulpittian terms.

6.7 Conclusions

These different, but overlapping, interpretations offer important insights into the trends and processes that have been integral to the complex evolution of the territorial politics of the British Conservative Party. They bring into view the rich hinterland of Tory thinking about union, constitution and nation which lies behind the party's increasing interest in the seemingly arcane West Lothian Question and the growing belief of many Conservatives that its resolution could be intimately connected to the idea of rebalancing the Union to assuage English anxieties and aspirations. Gamble's interpretation, in particular, points to a gradual and inexorable shift in the Conservative Party's mindset towards the notion that the domestic, as well as European, union may not represent an ideal vehicle for the expression of English sovereignty. And EVEL may well be an important staging-post on the journey that he identifies. In complementary style, Rose's analysis highlights the political contexts and factors that have been integral to the perpetuation of the Union, a number of which are no longer necessarily conducive, we have suggested, to constitutional stability.

Nevertheless, such is the contingent, and often unpredictable, character of political life that what looks, at one moment, like an established trend can at a later point seem like a more contingent and less linear phenomenon. In the volatile circumstances created by recent political events in the UK, the plurality of Conservative ways of thinking about the Union, and England's place within it, have become especially apparent and increasingly important. The key developments here were Theresa May's catastrophic general election campaign in 2017 and its surprising outcome, including the Conservative Party's loss of its Commons majority, a significant upturn of fortunes for the party in Scotland and a stronger-than-expected result for Labour in England.

In contrast to 2015, the Conservative Party opted not to publish an English manifesto in 2017 and made little attempt to evoke English grievances in its broader campaign. Indeed, the return of the party's traditional billing as the 'Conservative and Unionist' Party followed directly upon May's attempt, since assuming the premiership in July 2016, to conciliate those parts of the UK that had voted against Brexit, while seeking also to promote a 'hard' version of the latter as the assumed expression of the will of the people. The election result has thrown much of this strategy into the air, while the 'confidence and supply' arrangement agreed with the Democratic Unionist Party (DUP) means that the territorial dynamics at play within British politics have changed quite considerably. This unexpected development, allied to the party's resurgence in Scotland, means that the Conservatives no longer look so unequivocally English in Parliament, even though they remain by some margin the most popular party within England.

Quite how the party will respond to this change in the territorial composition of its parliamentary strengths, and how also it will deal with Labour's surprising appeal in parts of England where it was widely assumed that it would struggle, are now important and open-ended political questions. And they are made more complicated still by the challenges associated with forging a parliamentary coalition in support of any particular Brexit deal. This shift in the territorial political landscape serves to put the arguments set out here under a new spotlight. It also throws into relief the persistence of some important countervailing forces to the seemingly inexorable drift of the Conservative Party away from the Union. While the party has, over the last few decades, become increasingly southern English in its parliamentary base, its recent electoral successes in Wales, especially in 2015, and Scotland, in 2016 and 2017, may well have a bearing upon how the party comes to approach the Union.

In terms of EVEL more specifically, one of its most important features arises from its quasi-legal character. This complex and rather opaque way of implementing a seemingly straightforward democratic principle means that EVEL is almost invisible to the wider public. Indeed, the procedures associated with it have served to 'depoliticise' the West Lothian Question and have drained political energy from an issue which the party sought to emphasise in late 2014. The inclination of the party's current leadership is to keep things this way, but whether a future leader will follow the same path—especially if the question of additional devolution to other parts of the UK resurfaces, or the party finds itself in opposition but with a majority among English MPs—is uncertain. On the other hand, if EVEL does endure for the course of a full parliamentary term, the likelihood that it will become part of the furniture at Westminster and cease to be the focus for party political debate would increase considerably.

Much is to be gained, we have suggested, from considering this controversial reform through the lens of two distinct historical processes. The first, shorter-term cycle to which we draw attention is the emergence since the late 1990s of the belief among many Conservatives that devolution had generated a degree of asymmetry which necessitated a further set of reforms to protect the position of England within the UK legislature. This emergent stream of thinking was focused primarily, though never entirely, on the West Lothian Question, and it resulted in growing support across the party for the idea of EVEL. But this fairly recent development needs also to be understood in relation to a much longer political cycle—the historically rooted disjuncture in the Conservative psyche between those who believe that the UK can only survive if it continues to adapt to new challenges and attempts to resolve some of its anomalies when required to do so, on the one hand, and those who have come to believe that the UK needs to be reimagined in unitary terms. In the wake of Thatcher, the rise of Euroscepticism in the party and the vote for Brexit, this latter tendency is ascendant in both party and Government. But following the 2017 general election result it is now compelled to operate in a situation which it no longer commands and where it may well need to compromise with other constitutional ideas and visions. In these unforeseen and unprecedented circumstances, it is very likely that the party's English journey may have some surprising, unexpected, twists to come.

Acknowledgements

This work was supported by the Economic and Social Research Council and the Centre on Constitutional Change (Grant no. ES/L003325/1) and by a British Academy/Leverhulme Small Research Grant (Grant no. SG152634). We would also like to thank the party officials, civil servants and politicians who agreed to be interviewed by us, under condition of anonymity, about the emergence of this issue during the life of the Coalition Government. And we are grateful also to Andrew Gamble, Roger Gough, Matthew Hanney and Akash Paun for their comments on an earlier draft of this chapter.

References

BBC News (2014), 'Nick Clegg backs "radical" English devolution plan', *BBC News*, 12 September, http://www.bbc.co.uk/news/uk-politics-29155854, accessed 29 May 2018.

Bogdanor, V. (2001), *Devolution in the United Kingdom* (Oxford, Oxford University Press).

Bulpitt, J. (1983), *Territory and Power in the United Kingdom: An Interpretation* (Manchester, Manchester University Press).

Cameron, D. (2014), 'Scottish independence referendum: statement by the Prime Minister', Gov.uk, 19 September, https://www.gov.uk/government/news/scottish-independence-referendum-statement-by-the-prime-minister, accessed 29 May 2018.

Clegg, N. (2014), 'This opportunity cannot be hijacked', *Liberal Democrats*, 21 September, http://www.libdems.org.uk/nick_clegg_this_opportunity_cannot_be_hijacked, accessed 29 May 2018.

Commission to Strengthen Parliament (2000), *Strengthening Parliament* (London, Conservative Party).

Conservative Democracy Task Force (2008), *Answering the Question: Devolution, The West Lothian Question, and the Future of the Union* (London, Conservative Party).

Conservative Party (1997), *You Can Only Be Sure with the Conservatives: The Conservative Manifesto 1997* (London, Conservative Central Office).

Conservative Party (2001), *Time for Common Sense* (London, Conservative Party).

Conservative Party (2005), *Are You Thinking What We're Thinking? It's Time for Action: Conservative Election Manifesto 2005* (London, Conservative Party).

Conservative Party (2010), *Invitation to Join the Government of Britain: The Conservative Manifesto 2010* (London, Conservative Party).

Conservative Party (2015a), *Strong Leadership, a Clear Economic Plan, a Brighter, More Secure Future: The Conservative Party Manifesto 2015* (London, Conservative Party).

Conservative Party (2015b), *Strong Leadership, a Clear Economic Plan, a Brighter, More Secure Future for England: The Conservative Party English Manifesto 2015* (London, Conservative Party).

Gamble, A. (2016), 'The Conservatives and the union: the "new English Toryism" and the origins of Anglo-Britishness', *Political Studies Review*, 14(3): 359–67.

Goodman, P. (2014), 'Four in five party members want EVEL now', *Conservative Home*, 30 September, http://www.conservativehome.com/thetorydiary/2014/09/four-in-five-party-members-want-evel-now.html, accessed 29 May 2018.

Gough, R. & Tyrie, A. (2015), *Voice and Veto: Answering the West Lothian Question* (London, Centre for Policy Studies).

Gover, D. & Kenny, M. (2016a), *Finding the Good in EVEL: An Evaluation of 'English Votes for English Laws' in the House of Commons* (Edinburgh, Centre on Constitutional Change).

Gover, D. & Kenny, M. (2016b), 'Sunday trading and the limits of EVEL', Constitution Unit blog, 10 March, https://constitution-unit.com/2016/03/10/sunday-trading-and-the-limits-of-evel/, accessed 29 May 2018.

Gover, D. & Kenny, M. (2018), 'Answering the West Lothian Question? A critical assessment of "English votes for English laws" in the UK Parliament', *Parliamentary Affairs*, 17 February, https://academic.oup.com/pa/advance-article/doi/10.1093/pa/gsy003/4868636, accessed 29 May 2018.

Hague, W. (1998), 'Change and tradition: thinking creatively about the constitution', *Centre for Policy Studies*, 24 February, http://www.cps.org.uk/files/reports/original/130308135318-ChangeandTraditionsHague.pdf, accessed 29 May 2018.

Heath, E. (1998), *The Course of My Life: My Autobiography* (London, Hodder & Stoughton).

HM Government (2010), *The Coalition: Our Programme for Government* (London, Cabinet Office).

Jeffery, C., Wyn Jones, R., Henderson, A., Scully, R. & Lodge, G. (2014), *Taking England Seriously: The New English Politics* (Edinburgh, Centre on Constitutional Change).

Kenny, M. (2015), 'Englishness politicised? Unpicking the normative implications of the McKay Commission', *British Journal of Politics & International Relations*, 17(1): 152–70.

Leader of the House of Commons (2014), *The Implications of Devolution for England: Presented to Parliament by the First Secretary of State and Leader of the House of Commons by Command of Her Majesty*, CM 8969 (London, HMSO).

Lynch, P. (1999), *The Politics of Nationhood : Sovereignty, Britishness, and Conservative Politics* (Basingstoke, Macmillan).

McKay Commission (2013), 'Report of the commission on the consequences of devolution for the House of Commons', http://webarchive.nationalarchives.gov.uk/20130403030652/http://tmc.independent.gov.uk/wp-content/uploads/2013/03/The-McKay-Commission_Main-Report_25-March-20131.pdf, accessed 11 February 2016.

McLean, I. (2007), 'Two possible solutions to the West Lothian Question', paper presented at a meeting organised by Open Democracy and the IPPR, 30 May.

Moore, C. (2014), 'Cast caution aside in the fight for the United Kingdom', *The Telegraph*, 3 January, http://www.telegraph.co.uk/news/uknews/scotland/10549241/Cast-caution-aside-in-the-fight-for-the-United-Kingdom.html, accessed 29 May 2018.

Parris, M. (2010), 'With a shrug of the shoulders, England is becoming a nation once again', *The Spectator*, 18 December, https://www.spectator.co.uk/2010/12/with-a-shrug-of-the-shoulders-england-is-becoming-a-nation-once-again/, accessed 29 May 2018.

Redwood, J. (2015), 'England wants to get EVEN: now Hague must ensure that it does', *Conservative Home*, 2 February, http://www.conservativehome.com/platform/2015/02/john-redwood-mp-england-wants-to-get-even-now-hague-must-ensure-that-it-does.html, accessed 29 May 2018.

Rose, R. (1974), *Politics in England Today* (London, Faber & Faber).

Russell, M. & Lodge, G. (2006), 'The government of England by Westminster', in R. Hazell (ed.), *The English Question* (Manchester, Manchester University Press), 64–95.

Scottish Conservatives (2014), *Commission on the Future Governance of Scotland* (Edinburgh, Scottish Conservatives).

7

Labour and the Governance of England

JOHN DENHAM

7.1 Introduction

THE 1997–2010 LABOUR GOVERNMENT introduced wide-ranging constitutional reforms, including devolution to Scotland and Wales, the establishment of the Northern Ireland Assembly, the incorporation of the European Convention on Human Rights into UK law, Freedom of Information, House of Lords reform and the establishment of a Supreme Court. It also created the post of Mayor of London and the Greater London Assembly.

These reforms created new democratically elected bodies, new statutory institutions and new rights for UK citizens. The devolution process also established an expectation that referendums would be used on major reforms to the territorial constitution, meaning statutory changes in the balance of power and responsibility between central and subnational tiers of government.

Noting that Tony Blair was notoriously uninterested in constitutional matters, Vernon Bogdanor argued that:

> It is a paradox that Blair's government will be primarily remembered for the massive and radical constitutional changes … which have permanently altered the way in which Britain is governed. (Cited in Diamond & Kenny 2011: S53)

Despite the breadth and ambition of these reforms, the constitutional governance of England was largely unchanged when Labour left office. This was despite the fact that New Labour had initially presented its proposals for Regional Development Agencies (RDAs) and, ultimately, elected assemblies, as part of a coherent package of constitutional reforms for every part of the UK (Labour Party 1997).

By 2010, however, and with the important exception of London (discussed in Chapter 10 by Tony Travers), no new democratic bodies had been created for England. The only attempt to create a new democratic body outside London was defeated in the North East Assembly referendum in 2004, leading swiftly to the abandonment of plans for similar referendums elsewhere.

Proceedings of the British Academy, **217**, 137–158, © The British Academy 2018.

The Labour Government certainly made changes to the way in which England was administered. It reformed the role and leadership of local authorities, replacing the old committee system with a new 'leader and cabinet' model and introducing directly elected mayors in a small number of places. Labour also created an extensive system of regional administration, building on reforms initiated by the previous Conservative Government. But no significant powers, resources or rights were granted to local authorities or to citizens. The regional structures were swiftly swept away, with little opposition, by the incoming Government in 2010 (Sandford 2010). Unlike the changes in Wales, Scotland and London, Labour's regional reforms had not been entrenched at any level. England was left as the only part of the Union whose domestic policy was permanently managed by the Government of the UK. It can be argued that, relative to voters in other nations, English voters had fewer powers to shape national domestic legislation by 2010 than they had enjoyed in 1997.

This chapter explores the factors shaping New Labour's approach to England. It draws heavily on eight interviews conducted by the author with key ministers, advisors, policy-makers and local government leaders, including three former Cabinet ministers involved in local and regional government policy (John Prescott, Ruth Kelly and Hazel Blears).[1] The chapter also draws upon the first-hand experience of the author, who was a minister for ten years, played a part in policy debates before and after Labour's period in office and had eleven years' service in local government.

The chapter argues that, having initially framed its regional governance policy as part of a coherent package of UK-wide constitutional reforms, the policy as implemented was framed primarily in functional terms as defined by the priorities of central government and its view of economic policy and public service reform. We argue that this outcome had its roots in: conflicting priorities within Labour as it entered government, Labour's traditional commitment to the unitary state, its competing agendas of centralisation and localisation and its reluctance to consider the nature of the English nation and its constitutional position within the Union.

The detailed story of Labour's regional and local government reforms has been set out in several previous studies (for instance Stewart 2014; Wilks-Heeg 2009; Wilson & Game 2011). In Section 7.2, we only provide an outline of key relevant events. Descriptions of the Labour Government often emphasise the roles played by key individuals and the conflicts between them. This chapter argues that these were less significant than Labour's traditions of political thought and practice, and that MPs and the wider party, across the UK and in English local government, all played a role in limiting Labour's constitutional ambitions.

[1] The interviewees were Lord John Prescott, Rt Hon Ruth Kelly, Rt Hon Hazel Blears, Graham Allen MP, Lord Jeremy Beecham, Geoffrey Norris (advisor to Tony Blair), Robert Hill (advisor to Tony Blair), and Mike Ward (advisor on local government and Chief Executive of the London RDA).

These questions are of more than historic interest. In 1997, few in Labour would have expected that the UK would now be leaving the EU, that Labour would be the third party in Scotland and that the Union itself would have nearly been lost. The new political landscape poses challenges for Labour and raises the question of whether its thinking and practice has moved on significantly since the party was last in government.

The UK constitution remains unstable. While the pressure for Scottish independence has lessened somewhat it would be premature to assume it will not return. It is unclear what long-term future will emerge from Brexit for Northern Ireland. Any future constitutional reform agenda may find it hard to ignore England's governance and position in the Union, given evidence of an increase in English political identity (Jeffery et al. 2014; see also Chapters 1, 8 and 13). Survey data reveals a post-1999 rise in the proportion of people preferring to identify as English rather than British, although the rise in Englishness may have subsequently plateaued (see Chapter 12). Englishness also appears to have become more politicised, with a correlation between English identity and policy preferences such as Brexit and the creation of an English Parliament (Chapter 8).

In the 2015 election, fears that a minority Labour Government would not be able to protect English interests from the Scottish National Party (SNP) may well have delivered the Conservative majority. It was the 'English' within England whose votes were most decisive in taking the UK out of the EU, a phenomenon explored in detail by Ford and Sobolewska in Chapter 8. Labour lags behind the Conservatives with regard to support from English-identifying voters and faces a significant electoral challenge in England.

The politics of the four nations of the UK have developed in distinctive ways, with elections contested and won by different parties. This remains true after the 2017 election, despite the swing towards two-party politics on the mainland (the increase in Labour's vote share ranging from 2.8 per cent in Scotland to 10 per cent in England and 13 per cent in Wales).

In Parliament, the 'English votes for English laws' (EVEL) reforms discussed by Gover and Kenny in Chapter 6 have introduced an English veto on English-only legislation. The devolution of some powers and resources to newly created combined local authorities with elected mayors (including in Greater Manchester, the subject of Chapter 11) has also changed the landscape of English local government.

Taken together these changes create a complex challenge for the Labour Party as it approaches the election due in 2022. We draw out the lessons that can be learned from the experience of the last Labour Government and briefly assess the progress made in responding to this challenge.

7.2 The Labour Government and England, 1997–2010

Both before and after the 1997 election Labour presented its English regional policies as part of a coherent package of UK-wide constitutional reform that included devolution to Scotland and Wales and the establishment of the Greater London Assembly (see, for instance, HM Government 1999; Labour Party 1997).

The 1997 manifesto, however, left tensions unresolved. John Prescott had held the regional policy brief since 1983 and was a powerful advocate for RDAs and the establishment, in due course, of elected regional assemblies. Jack Straw, drawing on the work of the author, had highlighted the scale of the regional administrative state established by the Major administration and called for improved scrutiny. Another focus was the aspirations of local government for greater powers and autonomy. While these were acknowledged in party policy documents, many in the leadership also wanted to see the modernisation of local government and were supported by think-tanks such as the New Local Government Network. A further group led by Keith Vaz MP developed discussion papers on city-led economic development.

Labour came to power advocating new RDAs to take a strategic approach to planning, transport, environment and economic development. Labour also proposed the establishment of nominated regional chambers, based on regional local authority networks, to scrutinise the Government Offices for the Regions and the many public services now delivered through quangos. In due course—but only once unitary local government had been introduced and subject to referendums—elected regional assemblies would replace the chambers.

The implications of this policy had not been fully explored. It was not clear if central government departments would need to change their practice to reflect the new regional approach, or whether new assemblies would set their own priorities or simply implement central government priorities. Nor was it clear how greater autonomy for local councils would sit with ensuring that authorities delivered national public service priorities, or whether and when unitary local government would be introduced.

As we show in Section 7.3, different figures within the Labour Government had quite different understandings of what should happen and of their responsibilities to support the agenda. It was quite possible to hold quite different interpretations of party policy and its implementation. Bruised by previous election defeats and anxious to maintain tight public discipline, this lack of clarity was not surprising:

> In the sort of calculus of what you need to win, having a lot of policy looked to have more downsides than it did upsides. (Geoffrey Norris, interview with author, 2017)

In their most ambitious form Labour's plans for regional assemblies and for local government autonomy would have required significant changes in the functioning of central government and in its relationships with regional administration and local councils. The policy process did little to ensure that the party at any level was either fully committed to the proposed reforms or understood the potential contradictions between them:

> People say New Labour was timid but … we actually were hugely, prolifically creative, but … not disciplined; we did not prioritise enough. I still think a lot of that comes down to totally inadequate thinking and work prior to 1997—except in the area of education. (Robert Hill, interview with author, 2017)

Labour's plans for Scotland and London had benefited from extensive work outside the party, for example by the Constitution Unit (Leicester 1996), as well as debate within the party. Scotland had also seen a deep-seated process of civic engagement by the broadly based Constitutional Convention. Nothing equivalent took place in England. Instead, as noted, Labour's English policy consisted of three, largely separate, strands: local government modernisation, regional government and city leadership. Little civic engagement had been undertaken in relation to any of this policy work.

The RDAs were established quickly, though their impact was limited by the extent to which they were obliged to continue significant regeneration commitments from the previous Government. Ministers were reluctant to vest significant powers in the new agencies. There was little agreement in Government on the best models for either the delivery or the accountability of public services.

Regional scrutiny bodies—with members appointed by the Government and local authorities—were established, but moves towards elected assemblies were delayed by disagreements within the Government over their powers and by the failure to introduce a unitary local authority structure. The North East referendum was not held for seven years and then in unpropitious circumstances. By 2004 much of the gloss had been lost from New Labour.

> We lost the referendum because the Government was unpopular. If it had been held in 2000 I guess we would have won it. (Lord Beecham, interview with author, 2017)

Although John Prescott had initially believed that the referendum in the North East would be 'a cert' (Lord Prescott, interview with author, 2017), the offer was thin. The proposed assemblies were an additional tier of government. Both ministers and local councils were reluctant to see any of their powers move to regional level. Plans for any further assemblies were abandoned and, with this, the prospects of any significant English constitutional change involving new democratic bodies or the statutory devolution of power from Whitehall disappeared. After 2004, the broader UK agenda was not mentioned; the emphasis was on local councils and their relationship with their communities. Increasingly the Labour narrative focused on developing the role of city regions centred on major local authorities.

However, the death of elected assemblies did not end the development of Labour's administrative structures in the regions. The Conservative Government had established Government Offices for the Regions in 1994. Indeed, Labour had initially advocated regional chambers and elected assemblies to hold these offices and quangos to account. In government Labour expanded a powerful, complex layer of regional administration, but quite independently of any real progress on democratic scrutiny (Sandford 2006).

Many central initiatives delivered locally created management headaches for Whitehall, with a Cabinet Office report in 2000 calling for stronger regional coordination (Performance and Innovation Unit 2000). The Treasury strengthened the role of RDAs in regional economic policy. Government Offices for the Regions expanded and other departments and quangos were encouraged to give the strengthened regional administration greater power and coherence by developing largely coterminous regional structures (the Department of Health being one of the few to resist). In some policy areas (for example, fire and probation) new structures were explicitly proposed to reflect the new regionalism.

As the regional tier grew, government, council, public service and business leaders became increasingly concerned to coordinate policy delivery and to make best use of flexible and pooled budgets. Labour expanded regional administration primarily to support partnerships with local and regional stakeholders in order to ensure the delivery of central government priorities. As it became clear that policy delivery through departmental silos obstructed effective policy coordination and flexible use of funds, Labour moved, through the Sub-National Review (HM Treasury 2006) to integrate further regional structures and to engage local stakeholders. This aimed to broaden the role of RDAs to bring regional economic, spatial and social development into a single regional strategy for each region. To engage local stakeholders more effectively, scrutiny and oversight would come from a combination of local authority leaders, regional ministers and regional select committees.

From 2005 Labour's public narrative increasingly emphasised the important role of local authorities, reflecting a mix of principled support for greater devolution, a pragmatic recognition of the limits of centrally imposed policy and targets, which had proliferated in the early years of Labour rule, and the need for enhanced leadership in economic growth and 'place-shaping'. However, Labour no longer placed English reform in a UK context (HM Government 2006). Former Communities and Local Government Secretary Ruth Kelly recalls that:

> It [constitutional reform] wasn't at the forefront of my mind … the size of Scotland and Wales meant they could be run, you know, at that level, but England was too big and it needed devolved power. I was thinking more about local government and cities being place shapers. (Ruth Kelly, interview with author, 2017)

The leadership role of major cities had initially been marginalised by regionalism and local government modernisation. City regions had been championed by David Miliband, Kelly's predecessor at the Department for Communities and Local Government (DCLG), after the failure of elected assemblies, and were endorsed in the Sub-National Review (Stephens 2005). Government encouraged new 'combined authorities' and 'local' and 'multi-area' agreements. The 2009 budget promised new devolved resources for Birmingham and Manchester, with Hazel Blears signing a major city deal with Greater Manchester (whose combined authority was approved just before the 2010 election).

Local government ministers reduced the burden of targets on local government during Labour's third term in office. The Total Place project supported pilot pooled budgets across local public services (HM Treasury/DCLG 2010) and local authorities were promised greater powers to scrutinise all local public services, including those provided by the private sector (DCLG 2009). But progress on the ground was limited by the time of the 2010 election.

New leadership models were introduced and councils encouraged to see themselves as 'place-shapers'. Elected mayors were judged a success in London but, without additional powers and resources, had a mixed record elsewhere. Local government became more efficient and extended the Conservative approach of commissioning and managing tendered services. Councils were urged to devolve power to local communities. But participation in local elections continued to fall and aspirations to foster greater local engagement in local decision-making were largely unrealised.

Labour had created the increasingly powerful and influential regional structures its regionalists had wanted, but without creating any legal or democratic mechanisms to embed them in the governance of England. The new structures only engaged a narrow cadre of local authorities, business and other civic leaders. When the incoming Coalition Government quickly abolished RDAs and Government Offices in 2010 few powerful voices were raised in opposition. Only in London, where the legal powers and democratic election of the mayor and the Greater London Authority (GLA) had created popular support for the institutions, did Labour's regional reforms survive.

Otherwise England's governance was left little changed. By 2010 English local government had not gained any new powers nor been granted any further autonomy or resources as of right. The creation of new local institutions outside local council influence including academy schools and NHS foundation trusts had further reduced the responsibility of elected local authorities. Whitehall held the whip hand over England as it had in 1997. Local government had been reformed but it had gained no entrenched rights, enhanced resources or powers and, as a result, Labour's reforms outside London cannot be considered as representing a constitutional change in the governance of England.

7.3 The Forces Shaping Labour Policy and Practice

This chapter now examines the major influences that shaped these events. Drawing on interviews with some of the leading policy-makers and advisers from these years, it is argued that the decisions taken by Labour in government reflected its deep-seated understanding of the state and its roles; its competing cultures of centralisation and localisation; its vision of England as a nation in the context of devolution to Scotland and Wales; and its attitude to questions of national identity. We discuss these four factors in turn.

7.3.1 Labour's Commitment to the Unitary State

Despite the radicalism of Labour's commitment to establish the Scottish Parliament and Welsh Assembly with significant legislative and executive powers, for many in England and in the Westminster leadership this did not indicate a profound rethinking of previous approaches to government.

The incoming government was ‘driven by political necessity’ (Geoffrey Norris, interview with author, 2017) to deliver change in Scotland and in Wales (and, because of Thatcher’s symbolic abolition of the GLC, to London). It is not clear that English Labour ministers believed that devolution would lead, per se, to better government in Scotland and Wales, or indeed, to London. Few saw the change as pursuing a principled constitutional reform for the UK as a whole:

> We were pragmatic constitutionalists, I mean we weren’t like the Liberal Democrats, it wasn’t a positive part of our programme to sort of paint a picture of a federal Britain. (Geoffrey Norris, interview with author, 2017)

Like previous Labour governments, New Labour was committed to the idea of the parliamentary unitary state as the vehicle for delivering progressive economic and social change. That constitutional tradition also rests upon the notion that the very idea of England was embedded in the continuity of Parliament, the monarchy and other institutions (as discussed in Chapters 2 and 3). England did not need its own political identity because the institutions of the state embodied England. In this regard, Labour largely conformed to the British constitutional tradition, discussed in Part I, of regarding the structures that were appropriate for the governance of Britain to be appropriate for England too. From this perspective, it was not England that was in an anomalous position after devolution but Wales and Scotland. Labour’s outlook did not require reconsidering the governance of England as a whole.

At the most senior level, there was little support for devolution to or within England. John Smith (party leader from 1992 to 1994) had long championed Scottish and Welsh devolution, but had opposed change for England, as Labour MP Graham Allen recalls:

> I remember trying to convince John Smith about devolution in England and beyond the regions to local government; he used some swear words that even I hadn’t heard as his way of dismissing these opinions of mine. (Graham Allen, interview with author, 2017)

Tony Blair inherited Smith’s devolution commitments but had little interest in developing them further:

> Tony Blair certainly seemed a very pragmatic constitutionalist; he wasn’t particularly interested per se in constitutional reform. I think he had a view that England is a unitary state, which I basically think is true. He didn’t get terribly excited by the notion of regions; that you needed to have a regional equivalent in England of the assemblies or parliaments that you were establishing in Wales and Scotland. (Geoffrey Norris, interview with author, 2017)

In the run-up to the 2004 North East referendum, Blair was, at best, lukewarm about the campaign. He was a North East MP who supported a focused effort on regional economic growth, but his scepticism about assemblies had been reinforced by the slim majority for Welsh devolution:

> You shouldn’t underestimate the impact of the Wales vote. If Wales didn’t want it, what appetite would there be for something in parts of England? (Robert Hill, interview with author, 2017)

Former Deputy Prime Minister John Prescott also noted that Labour's commitment to radical devolution was constrained by the party's embrace of the unitary state:

> We are a naturally centralised party; we believe in capturing power and then to use it; and that, to use it, is by central government ministers doing it. Most of our people were centralisers when we came in. (Lord Prescott, interview with author, 2017)

Even in local government, the demand for radical devolution of elected power was much more muted than the desire for effective means of developing a regional economic strategy. The Labour Party in England was as accepting of Welsh and Scottish devolution as English MPs had been. It supported active regional policy but was far from deeply committed to elected regional assemblies:

> There was always a tension between powers and funds for regional economic development, and political devolution. The demand for political devolution would always be sidestepped and confused by a promise of funding or competence for economic development. The real interest in the Labour Party is much more in regional economic imbalances than it is in constitutional change. (Mike Ward, interview with author, 2017)

The political practice of Labour in England also worked against the promotion of radical constitutional change:

> It goes quite deep in English Labour Party culture that we did not seek to work with civil society. [In Scotland] they worked with the trade unions and the churches and other bodies and the voluntary sector in a way that we have never done … We are as an organisation very wary of sitting down in a room where we don't have a majority, we don't like coalitions, we don't like minority governments. (Mike Ward, interview with author, 2017)

The focus of council leaders on the development of their own authorities was eventually rewarded by the Government's acceptance of city regions as the focus of growth. But, despite routine calls for additional power and resources, there was no great pressure from Labour in the country for more radical change:

> Why weren't Labour local authority leaders banging the drum and having a coherent view of what they wanted? … Why hasn't there been that drive from English local government? … Those people in local government and local parties who should have been articulating this case weren't—or at least not in any particularly coherent and effective ways. (Graham Allen MP, interview with author, 2017)

There were many issues on which the Labour Party found itself at odds with the Labour Government, but on constitutional reform the party and Government were both uncertain about radical change and more concerned with the exercise of power where it already lay.

7.3.2 Ideas of Regional and Local Government

Despite the imminent introduction of Scottish and Welsh devolution, John Prescott had based much of his argument for RDAs on the need to have a broadly comparable and consistent approach to economic development within England, Wales and Scotland:

> I was arguing for all of them—it should be for London as well; I argued that unemployment in London was just as bad as it was in some parts of the North East … It had to be an overall solution whether you were a nation state or whether you were … an English local area. (Lord Prescott, interview with author, 2017)

Powerful English lobbies had also to be satisfied, including the northern MPs whose predecessors had derailed Labour's 1970s devolution plans by defeating the timetable motion for the Scotland and Wales Bill in 1977. That had opened the road to further backbench rebellions on the 1978 devolution legislation, when Labour MPs voted to enforce an ultimately fatal requirement that 40 per cent of all registered voters had to back the proposals in the 1979 referendums (see McLean 2016):

> People like Jack Cunningham … would say 'the Scots have got the Scottish Development Agency; I can't get my MPs in the North East to troop through the lobby to vote for Scottish devolution if they are not going to have a development agency of their own'. (Mike Ward, interview with author, 2017)

However, with much of the policy poorly defined and with lukewarm support from the Labour leadership, it was relatively easy for other parts of the Government and wider Labour movement to resist John Prescott's aspirations for powerful regional devolution. Government ministers were reluctant to cede powers to the new RDAs, or later, to the elected assemblies:

> When the Department [of Transport, Environment and the Regions] came knocking on the door saying hand over responsibility to RDAs, none of the colleagues greeted the Deputy Prime Minister's proposal warmly; they were all resisting. (Geoffrey Norris, interview with author, 2017)

As a health minister charged with delivering waiting time targets, the author saw regional structures as an unnecessary diversion, a view shared by senior advisors:

> From my perspective as the PM's advisor for the NHS, [we were] mostly interested about keeping health out of all this stuff, and letting the health service get on with delivering its own huge agenda. (Robert Hill, interview with author, 2017)

Resistance to the regional agenda also reflected unresolved differences in Labour's approach to accountability. Some parts of the Government were keen to work through local government (albeit to deliver centrally set objectives). In others, new institutions outside local or regional structures were being fostered:

> People like David Blunkett, who was taking over training, wanted to make it local authority structures; they wanted to keep the power, they didn't want to break it up. We didn't want regional hospital boards, we wanted them more local, so the conflict really within Labour was 'what was the accountability structure?' (Lord Prescott, interview with author, 2017)

Labour local authorities wanted greater autonomy, but their priorities centred on their own institutions. Labour local government was generally reluctant to see any of their powers move to the regional level, and resistance to unitary authorities—a key part of party policy—ran deep. It was for this reason that Prescott initially prioritised RDAs:

> If you just said I'm going to change local government and then do devolution, you would just have a bloody big argument about local government structure … what I wanted to do was get on with the economic structure, get on with dealing with unemployment. (Lord Prescott, interview with author, 2017)

The North East Assembly was eventually put forward as an additional tier of government without unitary councils, albeit only after the failure to change had been used by some government ministers to delay the enabling legislation.

Many in local councils looked for greater powers and autonomy and a revival of local democracy. A 1995 party policy document, *Renewing Democracy*, had promised increased powers, greater flexibility over the use of local taxes and a more flexible approach to partnerships with other organisations (Labour Party 1995).

However, local authorities were regarded by the Labour leadership (if not by most councillors) as often poorly led, inefficient and provider-dominated. The initial focus of modernisation was the improvement of local authority services:

> We were trying to come to terms with the quality of local authority services … to develop more user-orientated ways of being responsive to quality and service; the image of Labour and Labour [local] government was pretty dire. (Robert Hill, interview with author, 2017)

Few connections were made between the agenda for modernising local government and the regionalisation agenda. Prime Minister Blair's own 1998 pamphlet on local government in England makes no mention of the regional chambers or assemblies (Blair 1998). The central role of councils in local economic and social leadership was ultimately recognised by Labour's Sub-National Review (HM Treasury 2006). Their ability to resist and survive devolution proposals from central government worked, in the end, to their advantage (John 2014).

However, the expanded structures of regional administration also supported New Labour's more radical policies and not always to the benefit of local government. These included the promotion of diversity, contestability and choice in public service delivery, and Labour's support for hospital trusts, academy schools and other independent local institutions placed outside local democratic structures:

> The model of decentralization, decision-making reform we alighted upon was basically 'let's hand over decisions to the individual unit, the hospital, the school'. If anything, we wanted to delay a local government [role]. It was essentially within the unitary state; it was the citizen, the immediate institution and then the central government, with the Government Office within the region helping us. (Geoffrey Norris, interview with author, 2017)

While some had reservations about the regional structures—'that's only the civil service seeking to control the regions by their own people' (Lord Prescott, interview with author, 2017)—the regional tier was also important for those ministers who were keen to push a level of decentralisation and policy-making:

> I thought they [the Government Offices] were a very good thing; you would get some chance of some integration. I particularly liked the economic agenda where you had

> planners and economic development and housing and community and crime. (Hazel Blears, interview with author, 2017)

The commitment to a new localism was also constrained by arguments within Government. Ruth Kelly recalls tension between city-led growth and regional policy:

> Gordon [Brown] was worried about the town that was outside the city region … he thought if city regions attracted more resources, it might be at the expense of those satellite towns. (Ruth Kelly, interview with author, 2017)

Many departmental ministers were concerned about increasing the 'postcode lottery' if too many powers were devolved; much time was spent trying to devise minimum core national standards. Even decentralising ministers recognised limits to the transfer of powers to localities:

> I also think it's legitimate that when you are taxing people at the centre as well as locally, then the centre has a legitimate interest in what's done with that money. So there always needed to be some accountability and there will still be accountability in devolution, you know, it won't be simply, here's the whole lot of the central government spend. (Hazel Blears, interview with author, 2017)

Labour's practice evolved over its time in office. Initially characterised both by a high degree of centralisation and an unfulfilled rhetorical commitment to radical devolution, it moved towards a more sophisticated system of regional governance and a greater if limited level of localism. As Mark Sandford (2005) has suggested of the growth of regional administration: 'Prior to 1997, New Labour's emphasis had been on the democratisation, rather than the extension, of regional administration. In government, it [regional administration] came to represent an integral feature of Labour's approach to governance even though it never formed an explicit part of New Labour's narrative or politics' (Sandford 2005: 4).

Nonetheless, outside London the structures were swiftly dismantled in 2010, leaving only the legacy of combined authorities and the idea of city-regional economic leadership on which the incoming Government would build in its plans for a 'Northern Powerhouse' and city and county devolution deals. However, rather than marking a radical devolutionary break with Labour, this agenda continues to be guided by central government's concern to deliver its own priorities (Sandford 2016).

7.3.3 Labour and England

Whatever the aspirations of the party in Wales and Scotland, Labour in England saw devolution to the other nations as essentially a political response to the potential challenge of nationalist parties. Reassured by Shadow Scottish Secretary George Robertson's 1995 claim that 'devolution would kill nationalism stone dead' (reported in Taylor 2015), English Labour MPs assumed the Scots knew what they were doing:

> People like [former Scottish Labour leader Donald] Dewar and all felt, 'right we've got to defeat nationalism by going to a Scottish Parliament'. He felt that by going for a Scottish Parliament, the Scottish solution, they would eliminate the nationalists in Scotland. It didn't happen that way, but that's what they thought. (Lord Prescott, interview with author, 2017)

Scottish Secretary Donald Dewar told the Commons why the Prime Minister was not introducing the second reading of the Scotland Bill in 1998:

> The Prime Minister trusts Scots to do this. It would seem odd in a devolution measure if that were not so. (HC Deb., 12 January 1998: col 20)

No English Labour MP spoke in this debate. As Dewar implied, Labour regarded devolution as a matter of concern only for the Scots (and the Welsh). This reflected Labour's resistance to addressing England as a nation as part of its ambitions for constitutional change across the UK. The Scottish Labour MP for West Lothian Tam Dalyell once again questioned why Welsh and Scottish MPs should vote on English legislation on otherwise devolved matters, but the reputed comment of Lord Chancellor Derry Irvine that 'the best thing to do about the West Lothian question is to stop asking it' reflected the mood of Labour north and south of the border. Labour MPs, including the author, who acknowledged the strength of Dalyell's argument, nonetheless saw it as a manageable anomaly (within a constitution with many anomalies) that would fade as the new elected assemblies gained new powers.

English legislation had always been determined by the full UK Parliament with ministers drawn from across the Union. English Labour MPs did not envisage that the devolution settlement would have any serious implications for the governance of England. The creation of the Scottish Parliament and Welsh Assembly were described as devolution from a sovereign Westminster; the implication that powers could be taken back by Westminster was used to understate the constitutional radicalism of the change. Few anticipated that, within a few years, a Labour Government would have to plead the sovereignty of the Union Parliament to overrule its own recalcitrant English backbenchers.

Initially Labour could govern England as it wished. The party enjoyed sustained a healthy English majority until 2010 (although it fell behind the Conservatives in the popular vote in England in 2005). However, despite its large majority, the Labour Government relied on Welsh and Scottish MPs to deliver two pieces of controversial legislation opposed by many English Labour MPs. The creation of NHS foundation trusts in 2003 required the support of every Scottish Labour MP (and an English Health Secretary from a Scottish constituency). The introduction of £3,000 per annum university tuition fees likewise passed only—as Dalyell had warned—as a result of the votes of MPs whose own constituents would not have to pay them.

It was now impossible to acknowledge concerns about the devolution settlement without undermining the Government's own legitimacy. Senior figures publicly opposed any argument for a system of English decision-making on English issues. In 2006, in reference to the proposal to create an English Parliament, Lord Chancellor Charlie Falconer was emphatic that this was not on the agenda: 'Not today, not tomorrow, not in any kind of future we can see now' (cited in Morris 2006; see also House of Commons Justice Committee 2009: 55).

Although, as Bogdanor observed (cited in Diamond & Kenny 2011), Labour had created an 'English Parliament' that decided English issues albeit without an exclusively English membership, the priority for English Labour MPs throughout the 1997–2010 period was to deliver Labour policy in England, rather than to pursue a distinctly English set of policies. Despite having unpopular policies like tuition fees imposed on their constituents, few Labour MPs demanded any change. In 2009 only 4 per cent of Labour MPs supported EVEL (IPPR 2009).

The Labour Party was more likely to identify different interests within England than a common English national interest. As Lord Beecham, former head of the Local Government Association, put it:

> It is easy enough to talk about England as if it is a coherent identity and it isn't … all regions have their sub-regions and the affinity diminishes the further up you go … Part of this plays itself negatively. It's what we are not, rather than what we are potentially. It can start with the national level—'we are not London and we feel neglected'—and then it seeps in to differences at the regional level. (Lord Beecham, interview with author, 2017)

To many English MPs, England was also too likely to be dominated by prosperous southern conservatism. Constant references to the 'north–south divide' before, during and after the Labour Government reflected the idea that England was fundamentally divided by different political, economic and social interests. Believing that Labour could not represent large areas of the South (despite the gains made in 1997 and London emerging as one of Labour's strongest areas), many Labour MPs from the North and the Midlands saw their interests in policies that championed regional interests against those of 'the South'.

The Scottish and Welsh parties shared this mistrust of 'conservative England'. (The Conservative Government had piloted the poll tax in Scotland as recently as the 1980s.) Scottish and Welsh Labour politicians such as Peter Hain and Gordon Brown have argued, with Kilbrandon, that England would be too dominant in a federal United Kingdom. They resisted the idea of England as a political nation, instead preferring to speak of 'the nations and regions' of the United Kingdom and to advocate administrative regionalisation of England under the authority of the UK Government and Parliament.

However, the vision of Labour as the unifying champion of the more deprived regions and nations against the prosperity and conservatism of southern England was undermined by the devolution of domestic policy to Wales and Scotland. Labour has yet to come to terms with its own paradox.

The failure to consider the governance of England as a nation has contributed to Labour's inability to reach an intellectual consensus on the role of local government, regional structures and the relationship of these tiers to Whitehall and

Westminster. Faced with competing local and regional English agendas, and the self-interest of Scotland and Wales, the default option has always been to revert to centralism under the UK Government.

England itself was never considered an important level of government, in the context of either UK devolution or the governance of England. Overall, this study supports Graham Allen's observation that:

> It just wasn't that we were 'ready to go' and then a few people at the top stopped it. In a real sense the party itself wasn't really geared for a radical devolution to England. (Graham Allen MP, interview with author, 2017)

7.3.4 England and Englishness

Nor did Labour engage with English cultural identity. Indeed, there were two phases in which Labour tried to develop a new sense of British identity. In the early years, New Labour wanted to be associated with 'cool Britannia', a passing phase of British cultural influence in music, fashion and art. But despite Blair's description of Britain as 'a young country', too much of Labour's narrative of the United Kingdom was rooted in shared experiences from the past.

After becoming Prime Minister in 2007, Gordon Brown made a concerted effort to define a historically rooted story of enduring British values (Brown 2006). But, at a time of growing emphasis on individual national identities across the UK, Brown's Britishness had nothing to say about England.

As a government, Labour made no attempt to engage with English identity and politics and individual interventions by senior figures were few and far between. In a BBC interview in 2000, Home Secretary Jack Straw anticipated a rise in English identity in response to devolution and the EU and captured the ambivalence that many felt about Englishness. Arguing that they should stop apologising for being English and celebrate English achievement, he nonetheless warned that:

> We should recognise the downside of being English—this aggressive, jingoistic streak—and try to eliminate it … the English are potentially very aggressive, very violent. (Cited in Esler 2015)

Liam Byrne and Ruth Kelly argued for the recognition of England's culture and political identity in 2007 (Byrne & Kelly 2007), while the author of this chapter spoke about the importance of English identity in 2010 (Denham 2010) but these were isolated individual initiatives. Graham Allen concludes that the culture of Labour in power works against recognising English identity:

> We [Labour in government] know who we are; we run the place and we don't need to be from a place. People who were a bit dispossessed never had the self-confidence to say I don't need an identity. (Graham Allen MP, interview with author, 2017)

The 'English Question' had been the subject of academic and media interest in the early years of devolution (Hazell 2006). English public opinion relatively quickly came to the view that English MPs should decide English legislation and that the

Barnett formula was unfair to England (Jeffery et al. 2014). The Campaign for an English Parliament (CEP) was founded in 1998. EVEL first appeared in the Conservative manifesto of 2005. However, these debates did not translate into popular pressure on MPs or their activists.

Labour's traditions, experience and political geography all worked together to make it unlikely that the party would want to foster a sense of English political identity. Nor did it feel significant pressure to do so from outside the party, either from other parties or the public.

7.4 Labour in 2017: Engaging with England at Last?

The political landscape at the election due in 2022 will be very different to 1997. Around the millennium a profound shift took place in national identities in England. Those who identified as British dropped sharply. A settled picture emerged in which 'equally English and British' remains the most popular at around 40 per cent and those who are 'predominantly English' now outweigh the 'predominantly British' (Jeffery et al. 2014).

Labour last won the popular vote in England in 2001 when there was little difference in vote share by national identity. By 2015, Labour was third to the Conservatives and the United Kingdom Independence Party (UKIP) amongst the 'predominantly English'. Recovering somewhat in 2017, Labour was still behind the Conservatives amongst the 'predominantly English' and the 'equally English and British' (Denham & Devine 2017). The Brexit vote revealed a similar polarisation by identity (Henderson et al. 2016; see also Chapter 8).

In 2015, fear that a minority Labour Government would not defend English interests against the SNP may have delivered the Conservative majority (Cowley & Kavanagh 2016). The vast majority of English residents support either the principle behind EVEL or an English Parliament (see Chapter 5), while English identifiers are most dissatisfied with the current devolution settlement.

Polarisation by identity may also be mirrored in a growing division of England between the 'cosmopolitan liberals' and the 'socially conservative', according to recent research (Jennings & Stoker 2016). Since losing power in 2010, Labour has advanced significantly amongst middle-class, highly educated and British-identifying voters but lost ground relative to the Conservatives amongst working-class and English-identifying voters. Labour's collapse in Scotland in 2015 and only limited recovery in 2017 means that, in crude terms, Labour's hopes at the next election rest on winning in England and amongst 'English' voters without losing their current supporters.

The governance of England has also changed, with the development—which in some ways extends the architecture set down by Labour—of more powerful combined local authorities with elected mayors mainly in large city regions such as Greater Manchester (see Chapter 11). The infrastructure of local and regional economic development has, however, become more fragmented, with Local

Enterprise Partnerships gaining influence and competence. The gap between the economic performance of English regions and the London conurbation is now wider than when John Prescott was introducing RDAs in the late 1990s. The need for massive fiscal transfers from London and the South East to the rest of England (and the UK) remains (see Chapter 9).

The evidence that Labour's past thinking has been reassessed in the light of old and new political challenges is mixed. More figures from all wings of the party have highlighted the growing importance of English identity. As Russell and Sheldon in Chapter 5 note, a number of senior Labour figures, including Tristram Hunt (when an MP) and Chuka Umunna MP, have recently advocated an English Parliament. Liam Byrne, Shabana Mahmood and the Red Shift group of MPs have called for an 'English socialism'. The English Labour Network, set up to be 'for Labour in England and for England in Labour' has support amongst MPs, Labour council leaders and activists. Further, during the 2015 Labour leadership campaign, twenty council leaders and MPs called for an English Labour Party as part of a federal UK Labour, warning that:

> In England and in Wales we are in danger of repeating Labour's recent story from Scotland. A hope that things will turn out ok, the party in some places being the conservative establishment, not responding to people's wishes but appearing to be centrally designed and above all a failure to really believe with a passion in devolution such that electors will look elsewhere. (Allen 2015)

There are other recent signs of changing Labour attitudes towards English national identity. For instance, the St George Cross was used as branding on official Labour literature in the Stoke by-election in 2017. Sion Simon's unsuccessful mayoral campaign directly criticised the Barnett formula as unfair to the West Midlands. In a symbolic step, London Mayor Sadiq Khan declared himself both a Londoner and English on St George's Day 2017.

Even before 2015 one could perceive the beginnings of a shift in Labour's English narrative. As Labour leader, Ed Miliband had argued that:

> We in the Labour Party have been too reluctant to talk about England in recent years … for too long people have believed that to express English identity is to undermine the United Kingdom. This does not make sense. (Miliband 2012)

Ed Miliband also advocated making the Lords 'a Senate of the nations and regions'. This idea, together with Labour's broader call for a constitutional convention, was, however, not developed in any detail. The 2017 manifesto gave greater recognition of England's political identity than any other in the period considered here. It promised a 'Minister for England', repeated the 2015 call for a 'constitutional convention', offered the possibility of a 'federal UK' and promised a 'relationship of equals' between England, Wales and Scotland (Labour Party 2017: 103).

The language of this document reflects a growing recognition of England's political and constitutional importance. However, there is little detail behind these proposals. It is not clear what powers the 'Minister for England' would have or what their relationship would be with Cabinet ministers with English responsibilities.

The timing and working of the Constitutional Convention, including whether it is a political or civic process, is ill-defined. And the wording of the relationship between England and the rest of the UK is sufficiently ambiguous to allow both for an England with its own democratic mandate and a return to administrative devolution from the UK Government. The party's 2017 manifesto also promised a return to regional government offices. Although the manifesto described Labour as 'the party of devolution', little was said about the powers of local government or of combined authorities (Labour Party 2017).

And some senior voices, including former Prime Minister Gordon Brown, continue to argue that England must be divided into regions within a federal UK, a proposal that resists the recognition of English political identity. A 'devolution summit' in March 2017, attended by Labour's leaders in Wales and Scotland, Gordon Brown and members of the Shadow Cabinet, was reported as advocating non-legislative devolution to English regions but with enhanced powers to Scotland, including the right to sign international treaties. In the Commons, Labour continues to oppose EVEL, effectively rejecting any future democratic equivalence between England and the other parts of the UK.

The party's instinct to resist or deny a political identity for England while advocating enhanced powers for the other nations of the UK remains strong. Labour's centralising traditions also remain deeply entrenched. It is not clear whether its 2017 manifesto proposals to establish a National Education Service and a National Care Service ('National' here meaning English, as a result of the devolution of these functions to the other nations) would involve local authorities or whether they would be delivered under central control.

In 2014 Ed Miliband and Ed Balls reacted angrily when the Labour-led Manchester local authorities agreed a devolution deal with Conservative Chancellor George Osborne. The deal was a logical development of the city-led growth and combined authorities agenda initiated by Labour, but the Westminster leadership did not want Labour councils giving Conservative policy legitimacy. Labour local authorities were keen to take powers they had not gained under Labour. Since 2015, Labour-led councils in many parts of England have continued to engage with the Government on devolution deals and the creation of new elected 'metro mayors'.

The development of the new combined authorities and the willingness of Labour local authorities to engage with Conservative ministers suggest a growing self-confidence amongst Labour's local leadership. As city region and county deals take shape, leaders are beginning to develop new ideas, as reflected in the call by the Mayor of Greater Manchester, Andy Burnham, for a 'Council of the North' to tackle region-wide issues and to 'speak with one voice for the North' (GMCA 2017). Local authorities successfully resisted elected regional assemblies under New Labour. It looks even less likely that a top-down imposition of democratic regional government could take place today.

7.5 Conclusion

Labour failed to embed any lasting constitutional change in the governance of England outside London. This chapter has argued that this was due less to the role of individual Labour politicians and more to deeply held traditions in Labour's thinking at all levels of the party. Even after devolution to Scotland and Wales, Labour clung to the idea of the UK and its institutions as a unitary state. It was comfortable with, and eventually dependent on, a Union parliament legislating for England. It was deeply attached to centralist practice in government. At national level, it lacked confidence in local government; at local level, there was little consensus about whether or how power and resources should be devolved. Labour did not acknowledge England as political entity, seeing the nation as divided and inherently conservative and believing that some regions of England shared stronger interests with Wales and Scotland than with the rest of England. This view was reinforced by Welsh and Scottish Labour who feared the potential influence of a more coherent English political voice. Whether a future Labour Government will deliver more profound change will depend on the extent to which Labour's thinking evolves. The party will also have to adapt to the significant social and economic changes, including to the local governance of England, that have taken place since 2010.

The picture is mixed. There is now more recognition of both England and of English identity at all levels of the party. Labour's promise of a constitutional convention and its rhetorical commitment to devolution opens the possibility of change for England. The electoral need to win support amongst English-identifying voters may encourage Labour to acknowledge the importance of identity in gaining an audience for its policies. On the other hand, the 1997 manifesto also opened the possibility of change without delivering it. The party's policy had not been adequately thought through, contained multiple competing strands and did not have sufficient support amongst the membership, local authorities or MPs. Radical change was blocked.

Labour's centralists, and those who oppose an English political identity, remain strong, although they are more broadly challenged than twenty years ago. The creation of regional structures appears much more difficult with the growth of more powerful combined local authorities, but there is no consensus on the alternative. It remains to be seen whether progress can be made before the next election. A historical perspective suggests that issues that are unresolved before an election are likely to remain unresolved afterwards.

References

Allen, G. (2015), 'Letter to Labour leadership candidates', http://grahamallenmp.co.uk/campaigns/constitutional_convention, accessed 28 November 2017.

Blair, T. (1998), *Leading the Way* (London, IPPR).

Brown, G. (2006), 'Speech to the Fabian New Year Conference, London 2006', *British Political Speech*, http://www.britishpoliticalspeech.org/speech-archive.htm?speech=316, accessed 20 November 2017.

Byrne, L. & Kelly, R. (2007), *A Common Place* (London, Fabian Society).

Cowley, P. & Kavanagh, D. (2016), *The British General Election of 2015* (London, Palgrave Macmillan).

DCLG (Department for Communities and Local Government) (2009), 'Strengthening local democracy', http://webarchive.nationalarchives.gov.uk/20120919181816/http://www.communities.gov.uk/publications/localgovernment/localdemocracyconsultation, accessed 20 November 2010.

Denham, J. (2010), 'The case for celebrating Englishness and St George's Day', *Optimistic Patriot*, http://www.theoptimisticpatriot.co.uk/post/103719538803/the-case-for-celebrating-englishness-and-st, accessed 20 November 2017.

Denham, J. & Devine, D. (2017), 'English identity and the governance of England', British Academy, https://www.britac.ac.uk/sites/default/files/English%20Identity%20and%20the%20governance%20of%20England.pdf, accessed 20 November 2017.

Diamond, P. & Kenny, M. (2011), *Reassessing New Labour* (London, Wiley Blackwell).

Esler, G. (2015), 'University of Kent address: is it UK rest in peace', caltonjock.com, https://caltonjock.com/2015/04/29/gavin-esler-university-of-kent-address-is-it-uk-rest-in-peace-jack-straw-you-have-within-the-uk-three-small-nations-under-the-cosh-of-the-english/comment-page-1/, accessed 29 November 2017.

GMCA (Greater Manchester Combined Authority) (2017), 'Mayor backs new body to speak for the North', GMCA News, 23 August, https://www.greatermanchester-ca.gov.uk/news/article/181/mayor_backs_new_body_to_speak_for_the_north, accessed 1 January 2018.

Hazell, R. (ed.) (2006), *The English Question* (Manchester, Manchester University Press).

Henderson, A., Jeffery, C., Lineira, R., Scully, R., Wincott, D. & Wyn Jones, R. (2016), 'England, Englishness and Brexit', *Political Quarterly*, 87(2): 187–99.

HM Government (1999), *Your Region, Your Choice* (London, Stationery Office), https://publications.parliament.uk/pa/cm200809/cmselect/cmjust/529/529i.pdf, accessed 28 November 2017.

HM Government (2006), *Strong and Prosperous Communities* (London, Department of Communities and Local Government), https://www.gov.uk/government/publications/strong-and-prosperous-communities-the-local-government-white-paper, accessed 20 November 2017.

HM Treasury (2006), 'Sub-national economic development and regeneration review', http://webarchive.nationalarchives.gov.uk/+/http://www.hm-treasury.gov.uk/sub-national_economic_development_regeneration_review.htm, accessed 20 November 2017.

HM Treasury/DCLG (Department for Communities and Local Government) (2010), 'Total place: a whole government approach to local services', http://webarchive.nationalarchives.gov.uk/20130125093102/http://www.hm-treasury.gov.uk/d/total_place_report.pdf, accessed 20 November 2010.

House of Commons Justice Committee (2009), *Devolution Ten Years On*, Fifth Report of Session 2008–9, vol. 1 (London, House of Commons).

IPPR (Institute for Public Policy Research) (2009), 'The English Question: the view from Westminster', https://www.ippr.org/public/research/publications/the-english-question-the-view-from-westminster, accessed 20 November 2017.

Jackson, B. (2016), 'Labour and the nation' *Fabian Review*, 128(3): 8–11.

Jennings, W. & Stoker, G. (2016), 'The bifurcation of politics: two Englands', *Political* Quarterly, 87(3): 372–82.

John, P. (2014), 'The great survivor: the persistence and resilience of English local government', *Local Government Studies*, 40(5): 687–704.

Labour Party (1995), *Renewing Democracy, Rebuilding Communities* (London, Labour Party).

Labour Party (1997), *New Labour: Because Britain Deserves Better*, http://labourmanifesto.com/1997/1997-labour-manifesto.shtml, accessed 28 November 2017.

Labour Party (2017), *For the Many Not the Few* (London, Labour Party), https://labour.org.uk/wp-content/uploads/2017/10/labour-manifesto-2017.pdf, accessed 30 May 2018.

Leicester, G. (1996), *Scotland's Parliament: Fundamentals for a New Scotland Act* (London, Constitution Unit), http://www.ucl.ac.uk/political-science/publications/unit-publications/3.pdf, accessed 28 November 2017.

McLean, I. (2016), 'The No-men of England: the Geordie revolt that defeated the Scotland and Wales Bill in 1977', *Political Quarterly*, 87(4): 601–8.

Miliband, E. (2012), 'Full transcript: Ed Miliband's speech on Englishness', *New Statesman*, 7 June, https://www.newstatesman.com/blogs/politics/2012/06/full-transcript-ed-milibands-speech-englishness, accessed 6 December 2017.

Morris, N. (2006), 'English Parliament would "wreck UK"', 11 March, http://www.independent.co.uk/news/uk/politics/english-parliament-would-wreck-uk-6106903.html, accessed 29 November 2017.

Performance and Innovation Unit (2000), *Reaching Out: The Role of Central Government at Regional and Local Level* (London, Cabinet Office).

Sandford, M. (2005), *The New Governance of the English Regions* (New York, Palgrave Macmillan).

Sandford, M. (2010), 'The abolition of regional government', House of Commons Library, http://researchbriefings.parliament.uk/ResearchBriefing/Summary/SN05842, accessed 20 November 2017.

Sandford, M. (2016), 'Signing up to devolution: the prevalence of contract over governance in English devolution policy', *Regional & Federal Studies*, 27(1): 63–82, https://doi.org/10.1080/13597566.2016.1254625, accessed 30 May 2018.

Stephens, A. (2005), 'UK Government studies the case for city regions', CityMayors.com, 15 December, http://www.citymayors.com/government/cityregions_uk.html, accessed 20 November 2017.

Stewart, J. (2014), 'An era of continuing change: reflections on local government in England 1974–2014', *Local Government Studies*, 40(6): 835–50.

Taylor, B. (2015), 'Killing it stone dead', BBC News, 4 February, http://www.bbc.co.uk/news/uk-scotland-31129382, accessed 20 November 2017.

Wilks-Heeg, S. (2009), 'New Labour and the reform of local government', *Planning Practice and Research*, 24(1): 23–39.

Wilson, D. & Game, C. (2011), *Local Government in the United Kingdom* (Basingstoke, Palgrave Macmillan).

8

UKIP, Brexit and the Disruptive Political Potential of English National Identity

ROBERT FORD & MARIA SOBOLEWSKA

8.1 Introduction

The defining feature of English national identity in post-war British politics for many decades was its absence. While nationalist political organisations arose in all three of the other constituent parts of the United Kingdom, none appeared in England. There seemed to be no great desire to define or defend a separate political identity among a people who continued to use the terms 'English' and 'British' interchangeably.

That picture has changed over the past decade or so, with the political mobilisation of a particular strain of English national identity—one which is particularly appealing to culturally conservative and politically disaffected English voters. This form of Englishness is concentrated among the minority of English voters who identify primarily or exclusively as English and has proved to be the most politically potent expression of English identity in many years. The emergence of a more politicised Englishness than in the past reflects growing political and social division in England over the meaning of English identity and its relationship to British identity. Britishness was and is the preferred political and cultural identity of England's political and social elites. It was from the outset a political project designed to build a unified citizenry out of diverse national cultures (Colley 1992), which later bled into a second project to accommodate and incorporate the ethnic and religious diversity associated with mass migration (Brown 2007; Parekh 2000). Englishness was marginalised and downplayed in both of these projects—reflecting the sustained desire of Anglo-British elites to build a broader and more inclusive political identity. However, this may have served to increase the attractiveness of Englishness for those in England who rejected these elite projects and the values they reflected, thus creating a politically dissatisfied subset of English voters ready to be swayed by the appeal of a distinct 'radical right' brand of nationalism (Mudde 2007; see also Chapter 13).

Proceedings of the British Academy, **217**, 159–186, © The British Academy 2018.

Preferences for English or British identity show a clear social structure. White working-class English citizens with low education levels, who feel politically marginalised and threatened by social change (Ford & Goodwin 2014a, 2014b), are most prone to see themselves as primarily or exclusively 'English', while graduates, ethnic minorities and migrants are most attracted to a British identity. Three changes begun under New Labour helped to politicise this divide between the 'English English' and the 'British English': devolution, the emergence of a socially liberal elite political consensus and (above all) immigration. All three of these developments increased the attraction to 'left behind' voters of an ethnically exclusive, culturally conservative and chauvinistic sense of politicised Englishness, defined in opposition to the expansive British identity they increasingly associated with immigration, diversity and political marginalisation. The radical right nationalism that such voters now associated with English identity tends to exclude ethnic, religious and cultural outsiders and sets itself against the UK and EU political institutions which oblige the English to share power with other nations (Jeffery et al. 2014; Wyn Jones et al. 2012, 2013).

Social divides in English national identity attachments have been visible in survey data for many years (Curtice & Heath 2000; Heath & Tilley 2005; Tilley, Exley & Heath 2004), but have only recently become mobilised into party competition with the sudden success of a relatively new party, the United Kingdom Independence Party (UKIP), from 2013 onwards.[1] Although the party's founders and early activists avoided explicit appeals to an exclusive English identity, UKIP's radical right nationalist agenda—focused on opposition to the European Union and, since around 2006, also to immigration—resonated strongly with English identifiers, and the party soon began to turn this to their advantage (Jeffery et al. 2014: ch. 5). In a sense, then, while UKIP is both formally and consciously a British party, it is one whose radical right nationalism resonates most strongly with the 'English English'.

UKIP's electoral success forced a response from the Conservatives, who saw the party as a growing electoral threat and whose many Eurosceptic backbench MPs were sympathetic to the party's stance on Europe. The eventual result was a referendum vote on EU membership—which further mobilised English identity and radical right nationalism—forces which contributed to the UK's vote to leave Europe. The Conservative Government sought to take back control of the newly mobilised ethnic English electorate in the aftermath of the EU referendum by embracing UKIP's twin causes of Brexit and immigration. This succeeded to an extent in 2017—the Conservatives achieved their highest share of the vote since 1979 in large part by attracting UKIP supporters and Brexit backers (Curtice et al. 2018)—but the strategy came with unexpected political costs. The embrace of the radical right nationalist agenda attractive to the 'English English' minority produced a counter-mobilisation from the larger segments of the electorate who

[1] Ironically, UKIP began by imitating earlier British nationalist political projects in attempting to subsume Englishness in a broader political identity, as reflected in its name.

reject this agenda, in particular the socially liberal, ethnically diverse segments who favour British over English identity.

The emergence and mobilisation of a politicised English identity allied with a radical right nationalist outlook has destabilised the political system. The polarising effects of Brexit will make it very hard to put this genie back into the bottle, yet the party that first mobilised and politicised divisions over English identity and nationalism—UKIP—has collapsed electorally, at least for the time being. Further destabilising political conflicts are likely in coming years as the Brexit process unfolds, and many of these will have the potential to generate new tensions between 'English' and 'British' English identifiers and their conflicting visions for a post-Brexit Britain.

8.2 England's Identity Divide: The 'English' English and the 'British' English

The project of building a British identity required, from the outset, the political marginalisation of Englishness as a distinct political identity. England is so numerically and economically dominant within the larger United Kingdom political unit that expressions of a distinct English identity and interests always have destabilising potential. Mainstream politicians of both traditional governing parties have had, alongside a shared interest in political stability, particular ideological and electoral incentives to downplay political Englishness in favour of a broader British identity. The Conservatives have usually emphasised Britishness due both to their ideological commitment to maintaining Britain's constitutional structure and their belief that the promotion of British patriotic sentiment serves their political interests (Lynch 2000). Labour have long had an incentive to downplay the outsized role played by Scotland and Wales in their electoral coalition—and combat electoral threats from the 'Celtic' nationalist parties—by emphasising a commitment to an overarching British identity binding the nations together.

When political debates about how to reconstruct national identity in the wake of mass post-Second World War migration got underway, Britishness—a national identity which already incorporated the notion of unity in diversity—was settled upon as the vehicle for integrating new, racially and culturally distinct minorities (Parekh 2000). English identity was largely neglected, even though the overwhelming majority of migrants settled in England, which is, as a result, much more ethnically diverse than any of the other constituent nations in Britain. This produced a curious paradox—although the change wrought by mass migration occurred mainly in England, debates over the consequences of this change seldom mentioned English identity. Perhaps reflecting the political focus on Britishness as a vehicle for integration, England's immigrants and ethnic minorities are much more likely than white voters to volunteer a British identity (Wyn Jones et al. 2012: 24–5) and to reject Englishness as an identity which they often perceive as excluding them.

Two features have thus characterised the evolution of English identity in relation to British identity. First, British identity has been embraced by the political mainstream, while Englishness has been marginalised and downplayed. Secondly, British identity has become the vehicle for the integration of new immigrant minorities, while English identity has barely featured in debates over integration and multiculturalism—or has been regarded as an obstacle to these (Barnett 2016; Hunt 2016). English identity has evolved in reaction to both of these trends—as Britishness has become associated with the political mainstream, so a particular sense of ethnically exclusive Englishness has become attractive to more marginalised and disaffected English voters. As Britishness has become the vehicle for progressive ideas such as diversity, multiculturalism and openness, so those who are more sceptical of such ideas have gravitated towards this form of Englishness, which they have come to associate with the rejection of such ideas. The substantial and politically significant minority of the English who regard Englishness as a rejection of a wider Britishness are those we will call the 'English English'. They are distinct from the 'British English' who gravitate to a cosmopolitan British identity and are from the largest segment of the English public—those who remain happy to blur together their English and British identities.

Table 8.1 illustrates the distribution of national identity attachments among the English. Blurred and overlapping national identities remain the norm. When asked by British Social Attitudes (BSA) survey interviewers to choose between English and British identity, the most popular answer is to reject the choice by declaring oneself 'equally English and British'. Around 30–40 per cent of the English public do that. Another tenth reject the choice in a different way, by refusing both identities and/or declaring another allegiance. Around half of the English public thus remain happy with the traditional messy compromise, either because they blur together their English and British identities or because they regard neither as significant. Of the half who take a side, those who emphasise English identity are the larger group, with around a third of English respondents in most years expressing a closer allegiance to England than Britain—but only around half of this group call themselves 'English only'. The core 'English English' thus represent around one in six of the English public, with another one in six sympathetic to their stance. Their political mobilisation by UKIP and Brexit form the focus of much of this chapter. On the 'British English' side, around a quarter of respondents in most years favour British identity over English—and a majority of this group describe themselves as 'British only'. The counter-mobilisation of this group against a Conservative-embraced 'hard Brexit' was in part responsible for the surprise surge in Labour support in the 2017 election.

The 'English English' and their sympathisers are thus a minority in England. This contrasts with the situation in Scotland, where the majority favour Scottish over British identity, though most Scots do not reject British identity entirely either (Curtice, Devine & Ormston 2013). The minority who emphasise Englishness is, however, a large and stable one—around a third or more of the population in all the surveys conducted from 1999 to 2013 (though the group who reject British identity altogether is much smaller). A group this size could pack a considerable political

Table 8.1 English and British Identity Attachments in England, 1999–2013

	English Only, Not British	More English than British	Equally English and British	More British than English	British Only, Not English	Other/ None/ Don't know
National ID—English or British?						
1999	17	14	37	11	14	7
2000	18	14	34	14	12	9
2001	17	13	42	9	11	8
2003	17	19	31	13	10	9
2007	19	14	31	14	12	10
2009	17	16	33	10	13	11
2013	14	12	42	8	13	11
2015	17	10	42	8	13	11

Source: BSA surveys.

punch if mobilised and, as we shall see, the 'English English' are a quite distinct group in other respects.

The relative popularity of Englishness and Britishness varies a lot between social groups, as shown in Table 8.2. English identity is more popular with older respondents, the working class, those with no formal qualifications and those in the lowest income quartile. By contrast, a preference for Britishness is most common among the professional middle classes, university graduates and—particularly—immigrants and ethnic minorities. Taken together, this suggests Englishness is a more attractive identity for the 'left behind' (Ford & Goodwin 2014a)—economically insecure and socially conservative sections of the white electorate, who tend to express higher levels of political disaffection and opposition to rising diversity and liberal social values. This pattern is consistent with Jennings & Stoker's (2016) observation of a growing bifurcation of political identity and economic experience into 'two Englands'. However, in between the extremes of 'English' England and 'British' England there remains a broad middle ground: identification as equally English and British remains the most popular choice for all social groups apart from (very narrowly) ethnic minorities and those with no qualifications.

The social distribution and disruptive potential of English identity stem from its association with a distinctive political outlook: radical right nationalism. The populist radical right political parties that have sprung up across Europe in recent decades (Mudde 2007) have a common core ideology, emphasising an ethnic sense of national identity, focused on birth and descent, and a chauvinistic form of nationalism, presenting the national in-group as superior and foreigners as hostile and threatening. This radical right nationalism is much more prevalent among those who emphasise English over British identity, as Table 8.3 illustrates. This sets out the prevalence of various ethnic and chauvinistic nationalist ideas among those preferring English identity, those preferring British identity and those equally

Table 8.2 Social Distribution of English and British Identities

	More English or Only English	Equally English and British	More British or Only British
Age			
18–34	25	54	21
35–49	23	51	26
50–64	31	42	26
65 and over	40	41	20
Class (NS–SEC scheme)			
Professionals and managers	25	47	28
Intermediate	25	50	24
Employers in small orgs/self-employed	33	45	22
Lower supervisory & technical	36	49	15
Semi-routine and routine	34	47	19
Education			
No qualifications	42	38	20
GCSEs or equivalent	32	52	16
A-levels or higher education below degree	23	55	22
University graduate	23	41	36
Ethnicity			
White	32	48	20
Ethnic minority	12	43	46
Migrant status			
Native born, native parents	32	49	19
Native born, at least one migrant parent	22	46	32
Born abroad	17	30	54
Income quartile			
First	23	47	29
Second	30	48	22
Third	29	52	19
Fourth	34	45	22

Source: BSA survey, 2013.

Note: NS-SEC: National Statistics Socio-Economic Classification

Table 8.3 English Identity National Attachments and Views about Radical Right Nationalism

	More English or Only English	Equally English and British	More British or Only British
Ethnic nationalism			
Being born in Britain very important to being British	54	41	28
Having British ancestry very important to being British	39	27	16
Those who do not share British customs and traditions can never be fully British	65	48	41
Chauvinistic nationalism			
Rather be a citizen of Britain than any other country (strongly agree)	43	29	28
World would be better if other countries were more like Britain	38	31	24
Government should limit the imports of foreign products to protect its economy	52	48	43
Britain should follow its own interests, even if this leads to conflicts with other countries	60	40	42
Foreigners should not be allowed to buy land in Britain	36	24	21
British television should give preference to British films and programmes	35	25	23

Source: BSA survey, 2013.

attached to both. Unfortunately, we must make use of questions which ask about the nature of *British* rather than *English* nationalism, as questions about the latter are as yet unavailable in survey data. Despite this limitation, the questions do give us an insight into how support for radical right ideas about the nature of nationhood varies between those who emphasise the 'English' and 'British' aspects of their national identities.

We find a consistent pattern running through these data. Support for radical right nationalism is consistently higher among those who place greater emphasis on English over British identity. English identifiers place greater emphasis on birth, descent and culture as markers of national membership; they are more likely to regard their nation as superior to others and to favour pursuing national interests even when this brings conflict. English identifiers also favour various actions to limit foreign economic and cultural influence. While all of these radical right nationalist ideas find some support across the identity spectrum, a greater emphasis on Englishness goes consistently with stronger expressions of radical right nationalism.

8.3 The Political Agenda of the English English: Europe, Immigration, Political Reform

English national identifiers are thus both socially and politically distinct from the majority of English voters who either emphasise Britishness or blur both identities together. Until recently, though, English national identity has had little political relevance (Curtice & Heath 2000). Three developments during the New Labour governments of 1997–2010 played key roles in changing that by mobilising English identity and radical right nationalism into the heart of party competition. The first was devolution (Jeffery et al. 2014; Wyn Jones et al. 2013). Scotland, Wales and Northern Ireland gained new political institutions, while most of England did not. The main exception was London—the ethnically diverse, socially progressive and economically dominant capital city, discussed in Chapter 10 by Tony Travers. The presence and growing influence of these new institutions highlighted the inequality inherent in New Labour's asymmetric devolution process—an inequality that left the 'English English' with the shortest straw. In the past decade (i.e. since 2008) of economic crisis and more constrained budgets, growing proportions of the English have come to see the fiscal and political settlement of devolution as unfair and as favouring the devolved nations over England (Curtice, Devine & Ormston 2013; Wyn Jones et al. 2013), although it remains unclear how important any of these attitudes are on their own to the 'English English', who tend to place greater emphasis on immigration control and EU membership.

Secondly, the socially liberal consensus politics of the Blair, Brown and Cameron governments—with a focus on middle-class voters and multicultural, progressive social values—served to intensify the sense of political marginalisation among the radical right nationalist electorate who found English identity most attractive (Ford & Goodwin 2014a, 2014b; Jennings & Stoker 2016). This may in turn increase both the attraction of a more politically assertive English nationalism as a vehicle for the 'English English' to express their rejection of this socially and economically liberal consensus (Harris 2016; Marguiles 2016) and their desire for distinct political institutions and organisations as outlets for their conception of English identity.

The third and perhaps most important development has been the rise of immigration to the top of the political agenda (Duffy & Frere-Smith 2014; Ford, Jennings & Somerville 2015). Mass migration has become a powerful symbol of rapid and disruptive social and cultural change and of the celebration of diversity, developments that English-identifying voters often find threatening and alienating (Gest 2016). Labour under Tony Blair liberalised immigration policies from its arrival in office (Somerville 2007) and in 2004 was one of only three EU members to grant unrestricted access to migrants from the new, poorer 'A8' member countries from the former Eastern Bloc.[2] The surge in migration

[2] The A8 countries are the Czech Republic, Estonia, Hungary, Latvia, Lithuania, Poland, Slovakia and Slovenia.

from Europe which followed had three critical effects: the salience of immigration as a political issue rose, voters came to see high immigration as bound up with Britain's EU membership for the first time (Evans & Mellon 2016) and public confidence in Labour's ability to manage the issue collapsed. The failure of the Conservatives under David Cameron to deliver on a rash election pledge to dramatically cut immigration—driven in part by the Government's inability to control migration from the EU—reinforced these dynamics, this time with voters focusing their anger on the centre right.

A distinct radical right nationalist political agenda, with a distinct political constituency among English identifiers, was thus in place by the time UKIP's surge in support began (Wyn Jones et al. 2013; Henderson et al. 2016), as illustrated in Table 8.4. Opposition to immigration is highest among English identifiers. Large majorities of the 'English English' believed in 2013 that immigration should be reduced 'a lot', regarded it as bad for the economy and saw it as undermining national culture. British identifiers, by contrast, are much more comfortable with immigration. English identifiers also express more concerns about the shift to a more multicultural society which New Labour celebrated and which immigration accelerated. Some 70–80 per cent saw national identity as threatened by the increased migration of Muslims, Eastern Europeans and black and Asian people.

English national identity and Euroscepticism are also closely bound together in the public mind (Wellings 2012). More than half of English identifiers in 2013 said there was little or no benefit to the UK from EU membership—the only group where a majority felt this. Over eight in ten believed that Britain should not follow EU decisions it disagreed with, while less than half of the more outward-looking British identifiers would reject EU rulings in this way. English identifiers were also already visible as the core of the future EU referendum 'Leave' vote. Three years before Britain voted on Brexit, more than half of English identifiers were committed to voting Leave if given the chance to do so, the only one of the three national identity segments where 'Leave' had majority support at this point.

While English identity has a strong and early association with Euroscepticism, English identifiers had less clear early views about political reform within England itself. Just over a quarter supported an English Parliament in 2013, as discussed in Chapter 5 by Russell and Sheldon, hardly a ringing endorsement for devolution within the Union from its natural constituency. Indeed, support for the far more drastic option of seceding from the UK altogether is only a little lower. Nor is resentment towards the next largest actor in the Union concentrated among English identifiers. True, more than seven in ten English identifiers express support for withdrawing Scottish MPs' rights to vote on English matters (see Chapter 6) and nearly half also believe Scotland gets more than its fair share of public spending. However, similar attitudes are found among British identifiers, suggesting such concerns are not peculiar to the 'English English' but may instead reflect broader 'common-sense' notions of political fairness in a devolved system.

Table 8.4 Political Divides between English and British Nationalists in England

	More English or Only English	Equally English and British	More British or Only British
Immigration			
Immigration should be reduced a lot	71	57	48
Migration bad for the British economy	58	49	37
Migration undermines British culture	56	48	36
Identity—threat from minorities			
Britain would begin to lose its identity if more Muslims came to live here	80	64	53
Britain would begin to lose its identity if more Eastern Europeans came to live here	76	62	52
Britain would begin to lose its identity if more black and Asian people came to live here	70	59	43
European Union			
Little or no benefit to UK from EU membership	51	36	28
Britain should follow EU decisions even if it disagrees with them (share disagreeing with statement)	83	58	49
The EU should have less powers than member states	69	58	53
Would vote to leave EU if there was a referendum	54	35	30
Devolution			
Support for English Parliament	28	19	16
Support for English independence from UK	24	12	15
Scotland gets more than its fair share of public spending	45	29	43
Scottish MPs should not be able to vote on English policies	71	60	64

Source: BSA survey, 2013.

8.4 UKIP, Brexit and the Political Mobilisation of English Identity

UKIP have, from their foundation, presented themselves as a UK-wide political movement focused on opposition to the European Union, and the party has campaigned in all parts of the United Kingdom. However, from the outset their message has resonated most strongly in England,[3] and their electoral performance has been consistently stronger in England than in the other UK nations—for example, the party's six strongest regions in the 2014 European Parliament elections were all in England and all of the party's strongest constituency performances in both 2010 and 2015 came in English seats (Ford & Goodwin 2014b; Goodwin & Milazzo 2015). UKIP success in England has come by mobilising radical right nationalism among English identifiers, as Table 8.6 illustrates.

UKIP politically mobilised this more exclusionary and chauvinistic form of English identity because the party's core issues of Europe and immigration both resonated with the long-standing concerns of English identifiers (Jeffery et al. 2014). The 'English English' are more prone to see the EU as a suspect foreign institution with no legitimate right to interfere in British life and to see mass immigration as a threat to national identity and cultural heritage. Unfortunately, the BSA surveys did not ask detailed questions on English or British nationalist beliefs during UKIP's 2014–16 surge, but their most recent 2013 data on this issue does coincide with the beginning of UKIP's rise. As Table 8.5 illustrates, UKIP's 'early adopters' are very distinct in the strength of their English identity and in their support for ethnically exclusive and chauvinistic radical right nationalism.

While English identity and radical right nationalism were already widespread among UKIP supporters in 2013, the party was far less popular then than subsequently. Did UKIP grow by further mobilising support from the 'English English' minority or did it diversify beyond this initial core? To answer this question, we turn to the British Election Study (BES) internet panel, which began collecting data in early 2014, at the beginning of the UKIP surge in support. The BES panel has less detailed questions on national identity, but does include a regular question on the strength of respondents' English and British identity attachments. Respondents are asked to rate the strength of their feelings of Englishness and Britishness on seven-point scales, with a rating of one meaning 'not at all English/British' and a rating of seven meaning 'very strongly English/British'. The levels of English identity reported on this measure are rather more intense than in the somewhat different BSA questions, with nearly half of respondents scoring themselves at the highest point on the scale.

Figure 8.1 tracks UKIP support in the BES panel by the strength of respondents' stated attachment to English identity. UKIP is two to three times higher among

[3] Along with 'Anglo-Wales'—the parts of Wales most geographically and culturally proximate to England.

Table 8.5 English Identity and Radical Right Nationalism among Different Party Identifiers, 2013

	All	Labour Identifiers	Conservative Identifiers	UKIP Identifiers
English vs British identity				
English only or more English than British	26	23	31	41
Ethnic nationalism				
Being born in Britain very important	40	34	44	61
Having British ancestry very important	27	19	31	54
Those who do not share British customs and traditions can never be fully British	51	43	51	73
Chauvinistic nationalism				
Rather be a citizen of Britain than any other country (strongly agree)	31	28	37	47
World would be better if other countries were more like Britain	31	29	37	44
People should support their country even if it is wrong	19	15	23	32
Government should limit the imports of foreign products to protect its economy	48	50	45	62
Britain should follow its own interests, even if this leads to conflicts with other countries	46	40	53	76
Foreigners should not be allowed to buy land in Britain	26	24	24	50
British television should give preference to British films and programmes	27	28	27	44

Source: BSA survey, 2013.

the very strong English identifiers as among those with weaker commitment to Englishness throughout the panel. In addition, nearly all the variation in support comes among the strongest English identifiers. Support peaked among this group at over 20 per cent around the time of the European Parliament elections (June 2014) and again around the time of the EU referendum (June 2016). By contrast, UKIP support among those expressing more moderate identity attachments was nearly flat at around 6–9 per cent in all panel waves. UKIP's ebbs and flows thus appear driven mainly by their success or failure in mobilising the most strongly committed English identifiers.

We can examine the relationship between English identity and UKIP support further by using regression analysis to test the impact of both English identity and the radical right nationalist agenda associated with it on willingness to support UKIP. In Table 8.6, we present four models of English support for UKIP in two different elections—the European Parliament elections of 2014 and the general

Figure 8.1 Support for UKIP by Level of English Identity

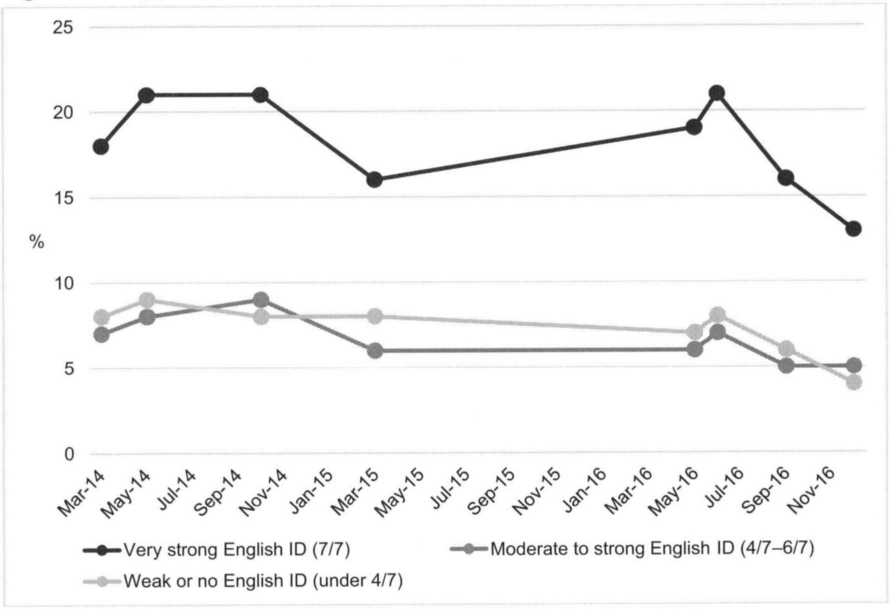

Source: BES internet panel, 2014–16.

election of 2015.[4] All variables are coded on a zero to one scale, to enable more effective comparison of their relationship with UKIP support.

Model 1 looks solely at the impact of attachment to English and British identity. The second adds in the two radical right nationalist political issues most associated with English identity—the European Union, which, as we saw in Table 8.4, English identifiers reject, and immigration, which exclusively English identifiers find more threatening.[5]

Model 3 adds in measures capturing two other potential sources of attraction to UKIP among English identifiers: discontent with existing political arrangements. Discontent is measured as (dis)satisfaction with UK democracy, and respondents' perceptions of politicians' responsiveness to 'people like them'. The specific political tensions of devolution are captured as perceptions of an unfair share for England from the Union and support for distinct English institutions, either via 'English votes for English laws' (EVEL) or via a separate English Parliament. The final model adds in two measures of the socially conservative values often associated

[4] We also tested alternative measures of UKIP support, including respondents' reported propensity to ever cast a vote for the party (on a 0–10 scale) and measures of vote switching from the Conservatives and Labour to UKIP during each election campaign period. These results are presented in Table 8.9.

[5] The BES included two similar measures capturing views of European integration, each asked to half of their sample. We combined the two measures. Immigration is measured with two items capturing respondents' views of the economic and cultural impact of migration

with radical right nationalism: opposition to the equal opportunities agenda and authoritarianism. The equal opportunities measure combines three items asking whether respondents think equal opportunities for women, ethnic minorities and gay and lesbian people have gone 'too far' or 'not far enough'. The authoritarian values scale incorporates support for law and order, traditional values and traditional authority.[6]

The top half of Table 8.6 looks at English support for UKIP in the 2014 European Parliament elections. This was the party's greatest electoral triumph—they topped the poll overall, winning 27 per cent of the overall vote and becoming the first new party to win any UK-wide election since Labour in the 1920s. UKIP won over 30 per cent of the vote in six UK regions—all in England, outside of London. English identity strongly predicts UKIP support when entered into the regression model on its own—while British identity shows a weak negative relationship.

When we introduce Euroscepticism and opposition to immigration, the effect of identity is sharply reduced, suggesting that the relationship between Englishness and UKIP support may be mediated by these two issues. In other words, it is UKIP's distinctive stances on the issues of Europe and immigration in particular which account for much of the party's popularity with English identifiers (Jeffery et al. 2014), though it is worth nothing that a stronger attachment to Englishness is still associated with higher UKIP support even after controlling for attitudes on immigration and Europe.

The results from Model 3 suggest UKIP have also mobilised both general and specific political resentments. English voters who are dissatisfied with UK democracy, and those who believe politicians have little interest in what they think, were more likely to back UKIP in 2014. So too were English voters who favoured a stronger institutional voice for England, via EVEL or a separate English Parliament, and those who felt England did not get a fair share of UK government spending. Socially conservative values, introduced in Model 4, also predict UKIP support. English voters who believe the equalities agenda has gone too far were much more likely to back the party, while those who hold authoritarian social values were also somewhat more likely to vote UKIP.

The overall pattern of support for UKIP in the 2015 general election, shown in the second half of Table 8.6, paints a similar picture. Stronger English identity once against strongly predicts UKIP support when examined on its own, while those with stronger attachments to Britishness are more likely to reject the party. The direct effect of English identity once again falls sharply when we add in attitudes to immigration and the EU, once again suggesting these issues are the primary channels through which English identity has been politically mobilised by UKIP. General dissatisfaction with democracy and politicians was an even stronger predictor of

[6] All of these measures are taken from earlier waves to the UKIP vote choice outcome variable, to avoid the possibility of reverse causation—for example, voters switching to UKIP, then subsequently adopting the more nationalistic and socially conservative stances held by the party.

Table 8.6 National Identity, the Radical Right Political Agenda and Support for UKIP, 2014–15

	Model 1: English and British Identity	**Model 2: Add Views of Immigration and the EU**	**Model 3: Add Political Views**	**Model 4: Add Social Conservatism**
2014 European Parliament elections				
Intercept	**–2.46*****	**–2.10*****	**–2.59*****	**–3.73*****
Englishness (0–1 scale; 1 = most English)	**2.40*****	**0.57****	**0.51****	**0.39***
Britishness (0–1 scale; 1 = most English)	**–0.40***	**–0.43***	–0.15	–0.21
Views on EU integration (0–1 scale, 1 = most Eurosceptic)		**2.87*****	**2.71*****	**2.51*****
Economic impact of immigration (0–1 scale, 1 = most positive)		**–1.07*****	**–0.97*****	**–0.86*****
Cultural impact of immigration (0–1 scale, 1 = most positive)		**–1.89*****	**–1.77*****	**–1.44*****
Satisfaction with UK democracy (0–1 scale, 1 = most satisfied)			**–0.52****	**–0.59*****
Politicians don't care what people like me think (0–1 scale, 1 = strongest agreement)			**0.84*****	**0.79*****
Does England get fair share from Union? (0–1 scale, 1 = strongest agreement)			**–0.55****	**–0.44***
Governing England (ref: UK Parliament, all MPs vote)				
UK Parliament, only English MPs vote on English laws (1 = respondent favours this option)			**0.28****	**0.24***
Separate English Parliament (1 = respondent favours this option)			**0.36****	**0.36****
Opposition to equal opportunities (0–1 scale, 1 = highest opposition)				**1.40*****
Authoritarian values (0–1 scale, 1 = most authoritarian)				**0.76***
Model fit (pseudo-R square)	*0.04*	*0.26*	*0.27*	*0.28*
N	*8130*	*8130*	*8130*	*8130*

	Model 1: English and British Identity	Model 2: Add Views of Immigration and the EU	Model 3: Add Political Views	Model 4: Add Social Conservatism
2015 Westminster elections				
Intercept	**–3.60*****	**–3.40*****	**–4.56*****	**–5.16*****
Englishness (0–1 scale; 1 = most English)	**2.49*****	**0.49****	**0.59****	**0.55****
Britishness (0–1 scale; 1 = most English)	**–0.69*****	**–0.42****	–0.14	–0.10
Views on EU integration (0–1 scale, 1 = most Eurosceptic)		**2.78*****	**2.55*****	**2.44*****
Economic impact of immigration (0–1 scale, 1 = most positive)		**–1.37*****	**–1.17*****	**–1.10*****
Cultural impact of immigration (0–1 scale, 1 = most positive)		**–1.45*****	**–1.27*****	**–1.12*****
Satisfaction with UK democracy (0–1 scale, 1 = most satisfied)			**–0.96*****	**–0.97*****
Politicians don't care what people like me think (0–1 scale, 1 = strongest agreement)			**1.55*****	**1.56*****
Does England get fair share from Union? (0–1 scale, 1 = strongest agreement)			–0.06	0.05
Governing England (ref: UK Parliament, all MPs vote)				
UK Parliament, only English MPs vote on English laws (1 = respondent favours this option)			**0.30***	**0.26***
Separate English Parliament (1 = respondent favours this option)			**0.36***	**0.34***
Opposition to equal opportunities (0–1 scale, 1 = highest opposition)				**0.86*****
Authoritarian values (0–1 scale, 1 = most authoritarian)				0.18
Model fit (pseudo-R square)	*0.03*	*0.19*	*0.22*	*0.22*
N	*12442*	*12442*	*12442*	*12442*

Note: Asterisks denote the statistical significance of the correlations: * = p<0.05; ** = p<0.01; ***=p<0.001.

Source: BES internet panel, 2014–15.

UKIP support in 2015 than in 2014, which fits with earlier research showing that the party attracts a more politically disaffected electorate in domestic elections than European Parliament votes (Ford, Goodwin & Cutts 2012). Social conservatism in the form of opposition to the equal opportunities agenda also continues to predict UKIP support in 2015, but authoritarian values do not.

UKIP was most successful in its two strongest election performances among voters expressing the strongest attachment to English identity and the most support for the radical right nationalist political agenda associated with it—Euroscepticism, opposition to immigration, social conservatism and demands for political reform. UKIP's sharp rise to political prominence was thus a powerful demonstration of the disruptive political potential of a distinct sense of English identity allied to a radical right nationalist political agenda. UKIP's surge destabilised both of the traditional political parties, who found themselves losing support from English identifiers and under intensified electoral pressure to address this group's political concerns. The central plank of the Conservatives' response to this new electoral threat—David Cameron's pledge of a referendum on EU membership—set the stage for an even bigger political disruption: Brexit.

Table 8.7 takes a look at English identity, the radical right nationalist political agenda and support for Brexit in June 2016.[7] We use the same set of models as in Table 8.6, with one exception. We do not include views of the EU as a predictor of Brexit support, as the relationship is close to tautological: it is hard to see how a voter could support leaving the EU without a negative view of the EU's influence and powers. We find that both English identity and the wider political outlook bound up with it are strongly associated with support for Brexit. Voters expressing a stronger attachment to Englishness were a great deal more likely to support Brexit, as shown in Model 1. As before, much of this relationship is mediated through English identifiers' opposition to immigration, though on this occasion economic concerns about immigration mattered as much as cultural concerns.

General political disaffection also predicts support for Brexit, though less consistently. English voters who felt ignored by politicians were more likely to back Brexit, while those who were dissatisfied with UK democracy showed a weaker tendency in the same direction. Specifically English political resentments also predicted Brexit support—those favouring a stronger institutional voice for the English, via EVEL or a separate English Parliament, were more supportive of Brexit. The values associated with radical right nationalism also strongly predicted support for Brexit—voters opposed to the equal opportunities agenda or who held more authoritarian social values were much more likely to back Brexit.

Support for Brexit was stronger in England than in any other constituent nation in the Union, and both the size of the English electorate and the strength of the

[7] We also examined the links between English nationalism and support for Brexit at earlier time points in the BES panel and found the patterns discussed here to be remarkably stable over time. These analysis tables are presented in Tables 8.9 and 8.10.

Table 8.7 National Identity, the Radical Right Nationalist Agenda and Support for Brexit in England

	Model 1: English and British Identity	**Model 2: Add Immigration Views**	**Model 3: Add Political Views**	**Model 4: Add Social Conservatism**
Intercept	**–1.91*** **	**1.03*** **	–0.19	**–1.94*** **
Englishness (0–1 scale; 1 = most English)	**2.50*** **	**1.17*** **	**1.06*** **	**0.88*** **
Britishness (0–1 scale; 1 = most English)	0.01	0.15	0.35	0.17
Economic impact of immigration (0–1 scale, 1 = most positive)		**–2.25*** **	**–2.22*** **	**–1.82*** **
Cultural impact of immigration (0–1 scale, 1 = most positive)		**–2.33*** **	**–2.13*** **	**–1.76*** **
Satisfaction with UK democracy (0–1 scale, 1 = most satisfied)			–0.08	**–0.33***
Politicians don't care what people like me think (0–1 scale, 1 = strongest agreement)			**0.93*** **	**0.75*** **
Does England get fair share from Union? (0–1 scale, 1 = strongest agreement)			–0.31	–0.22
Governing England (ref: UK Parliament, all MPs vote)				
UK Parliament, only English MPs vote on English laws (1 = respondent favours this option)			**0.65*** **	**0.63*** **
Separate English Parliament (1 = respondent favours this option)			**0.90*** **	**0.85*** **
Opposition to equal opportunities (0–1 scale, 1 = highest opposition)				**1.11*** **
Authoritarian values (0–1 scale, 1 = most authoritarian)				**2.06*** **
Model fit (R square/pseudo-R square)	*0.06*	*0.27*	*0.29*	*0.31*
N	*8071*	*8071*	*8071*	*8071*

Note: Asterisks denote statistical significance of the correlations: * = p<0.05; ** = p<0.01; ***=p<0.001.

Source: BES internet panel, wave 9 (post-referendum wave, June–July 2016).

Leave vote in England's more Eurosceptic regions helped carry the day on 23 June 2016, despite the reservations of voters in Scotland, Northern Ireland (and London). The evidence we have reviewed suggests that exclusively English identity and the radical right nationalism associated with it played a central role in this decision (see also Henderson et al. 2016 who arrive at similar conclusions). Brexit mobilised English identifiers, who saw it as an outlet for their radical right nationalism: the strongest English support for 'Leave' came from English voters most strongly attached to traditional social values and most strongly opposed to immigration and the 'equalities' agenda. Brexit was also a politically radical choice—the choice to leave the EU being the biggest change to Britain's political and economic relations with other countries for over forty years. It is thus logical that support for this radical change was highest among English voters most unhappy with the status quo. Brexit was thus a powerful demonstration of the disruptive potential of Englishness: the cultural and political anxieties of English identifiers proved more powerful in the final analysis than the economic uncertainties of leaving the EU or the chorus of elite political and business voices urging caution.

8.5 English Identity and the Radical Right Nationalist Agenda after Brexit: Unstable Alliances, Unresolved Questions and More Disruption to Come?

The shock Brexit result brought about a swift realignment in the governing parties. David Cameron's socially liberal and pragmatically pro-EU conservatism departed, along with the Prime Minister and his Chancellor George Osborne. Cameron's successor Theresa May embraced not only Brexit but the broader radical right nationalist political outlook underlying the 'Leave' victory. May announced that immigration control would be a top priority in negotiating the terms of Britain's exit from the EU and made it clear that she was prepared to sacrifice Britain's membership of the single market to achieve this control—positions clearly aligned with the preferences of the 'English English'. May underlined her sympathy for the radical right nationalism which had motivated many 'Leave' voters in her first speech to the Conservative conference as party leader, when she called for a 'spirit of citizenship' which 'respect[s] the bonds and obligations that make our society work' and attacked cosmopolitan liberal 'citizens of the world' as 'citizens of nowhere' who 'don't understand what the very word "citizenship" means' (May 2016).

Much of the political agenda which attracted English identifiers to UKIP and 'Vote Leave' was quickly adopted by May's Conservatives in the aftermath of the 'Leave' victory. When Theresa May persuaded the House of Commons to vote for an early election in April 2017, the Conservatives' strategy in England was to expand their support by embracing Brexit and thus recruiting Eurosceptic English nationalists from UKIP and elsewhere. The Conservatives' Brexit-focused strategy produced the largest rise in their overall British vote share since 1979, yet Theresa May's party still lost their majority. The Conservatives' adoption of a heavily UKIP-tinted agenda produced a major reaction at the opposite end of the political spectrum—among the socially liberal, cosmopolitan and pro-EU 'British English'—who swung heavily behind the Labour Party. Initial estimates suggest that turnout among the under forties increased sharply in 2017 and that political divides by age and education rose to all-time highs (Curtice et al. 2018; Curtis 2017; Skinner 2017). The Conservatives expected strong support from the pro-Brexit 'English English' to deliver an increased majority in 2017. Instead, the result revealed an England now deeply and evenly divided over identity and values, with the radical right nationalism of the 'English' English at one pole and the liberal multiculturalism of the 'British' English at the other. While most English voters still reject both extremes of the identity and values divides, the polarising campaigns of 2016 and 2017 have mobilised these divides into politics to an unprecedented extent.

Yet while the English electorate is polarised on national identity and social values as never before, the election campaign and result did not provide any clear path for politicians looking to bridge these new divides. The Conservatives and Labour won their largest combined share of the vote since 1970, with over 80 per cent of voters backing one of the two largest parties, yet both have none the less been destabilised by the mobilisation of English identity and radical right nationalism, and the difficult questions it raises remain unresolved. The Conservatives discovered that an uncompromising radical right nationalist agenda of hard Brexit, immigration control and socially conservative values is not the recipe for electoral dominance they assumed. Yet the party now faces a dilemma. If it waters down its approach to Brexit and immigration, it risks alienating the English identifiers it has attracted from UKIP and elsewhere—voters with low levels of trust in politics and only a weak attachment to the Conservatives. But if the party ploughs ahead with its uncompromising approach, it could lose even more ground among the younger, socially liberal and multicultural 'British English'.

Labour also faces unresolved questions. The party artfully fudged its approach to Brexit in the 2017 election—accepting the result, but arguing for a 'softer' implementation. This helped Labour to retain support from enough English identifiers who backed Brexit, while also registering major gains from the more 'British English' multicultural liberals who opposed leaving the EU. Yet it will be hard for the party to blur its approach on these issues indefinitely. Labour will at some point have to take clearer positions on issues such as immigration rules, Britain's relationship with Europe and the value of diversity and globalisation. Whatever position they take is bound to antagonise one side of the identity divide.

Beyond Brexit there are also unresolved questions about the governance of England itself. Both UKIP and the 'Leave' campaign attracted support from English voters dissatisfied with the existing political arrangements in the Union and keen for a stronger, more institutionalised voice for England. The Conservative governments of 2010–17 took some steps to address these demands, via EVEL rules in the House of Commons (see Chapter 6) and the introduction of additional devolved 'city region' government structures (see Chapter 9). Yet such steps remain at best a partial response to the desire of English identifiers for a clearer political voice. EVEL is complicated and poorly understood. The newly devolved city regions have limited powers and cover only a minority of England's territory and population. At the same time, the devolved governments of Scotland and Wales have continued to strengthen, while the reliance of the Conservative minority government on support from the Democratic Unionist Party (DUP) has increased the symbolic and substantive influence of one Northern Irish community (at the same time as the collapse of devolution marginalised the other Northern Irish community, whose chief political representatives, Sinn Fein, refuse to take their seats at Westminster). The current constitutional settlement and delicate balance of power in Parliament are unlikely to address English identifiers' suspicion that 'outsiders' have too much power. A stable and comprehensive reform to UK and English governance structures that might more effectively respond to such concerns remains a long way off—and with Brexit set to dominate the political agenda for the next few years, further progress looks unlikely in the short run.

Could UKIP exploit these internal tensions and unresolved questions to stage a political comeback? At first glance, the party's prospects look bleak at the time of writing (March 2018). UKIP has been in a state of perpetual crisis since the Brexit vote. It has lost four leaders—Nigel Farage, Diane James, Paul Nuttall and Henry Bolton—in little more than a year. The party's membership is falling and its financial backing has dried up. UKIP's vote in 2017 fell to its lowest level since 2001, losing five in six of the voters won in 2015. In large part, this reflects the current belief on the part of the English identifiers and radical right nationalists who formed UKIP's core support that Brexit will address their political concerns. Yet such a belief seems unlikely to last. The process of disentangling Britain from Europe is likely to take far longer, and require far more compromises, than these voters expect. The Brexit process will not produce control of EU immigration for a number of years (if at all) and whatever new migration regime is agreed is unlikely to be as draconian as English identifiers would like it to be. Likewise, whatever policy Britain develops for immigration after Brexit will not reverse England's long-running drift towards greater diversity, multiculturalism and social liberalism. Indeed, the 2017 election results suggest it could even accelerate such changes, as the voters who most strongly support such values have now politically mobilised in reaction to the threats they perceive from Brexit. So the implementation of Brexit is likely to produce renewed disaffection which UKIP could exploit, while a halt or reversal to the withdrawal process, which cannot be ruled out entirely, could also produce a major political backlash among the 'English English'.

If and when feelings of 'Brexit betrayal' rise, UKIP remains the most plausible outlet for their expression. As Table 8.8 illustrates, those most attached to English identity and to radical right nationalism remain sympathetic to UKIP.[8] If UKIP

[8] The question of whether England gets a fair share from the Union has not been asked since wave 6 of the BES panel so is dropped from this analysis.

Table 8.8 Englishness, the Radical Right Nationalist Agenda and Willingness to Ever Vote UKIP

Probability of Ever Voting UKIP (0–1 Scale, 0 = "Very Unlikely" 1 = "Very Likely")	**Model 1: English and British Identity**	**Model 2: Add Immigration and EU Views**	**Model 3: Add Political Views**	**Model 4: Add Social Conservatism**
Intercept	0.02	**0.12*****	0.01	**–0.20*****
Englishness (0–1 scale; 1 = most English)	**0.40*****	**0.11*****	**0.10*****	**0.08****
Britishness (0–1 scale; 1 = most English)	0.01	0.02	0.03	0.01
Views on EU integration (0–1 scale, 1 = most Eurosceptic)		**0.39*****	**0.36*****	**0.33*****
Economic impact of immigration (0–1 scale, 1 = most positive)		**–0.09***	**–0.08***	**–0.04**
Cultural impact of immigration (0–1 scale, 1 = most positive)		**–0.23*****	**–0.21*****	**–0.15*****
Satisfaction with UK democracy (0–1 scale, 1 = most satisfied)			0.02	0.00
Politicians don't care what people like me think (0–1 scale, 1 = strongest agreement)			**0.09****	**0.08****
Governing England (ref: UK Parliament, all MPs vote)				
UK Parliament, only English MPs vote on English laws (1 = respondent favours this option)			**0.07*****	**0.06*****
Separate English Parliament (1 = respondent favours this option)			**0.06****	**0.05***
Opposition to equal opportunities (0–1 scale, 1 = highest opposition)				**0.22*****
Authoritarian values (0–1 scale, 1 = most authoritarian)				**0.19*****
Model fit (R square)	*0.10*	*0.32*	*0.33*	*0.35*
N	*3643*	*3643*	*3643*	*3643*

Source: BES internet panel, wave 10 (December 2016). Predictor variables taken from previous waves.

manages to hold itself together financially and organisationally a natural constituency remains for the party to mobilise if and when the political mood among English identifiers shifts against the Conservatives. If, on the other hand, UKIP's collapse proves terminal, then there will be an opening in the political system for a potential new entrant to exploit. English identifiers and radical right nationalism have already upended British politics twice in the past five years, propelling a fringe party to unprecedented electoral heights and then helping to pull the UK out of a 40-year-old political relationship with Europe. The voters who drove these changes are more aware than ever of their electoral power. It is quite possible that they will wield it again to disrupt British politics in the years to come.

8.6. Conclusion: Divided Identities for a Divided Nation

The stability of the United Kingdom has long depended on the willingness of citizens in its largest constituent nation to subsume their distinct identity into the broader, constructed political unit. Scottish or Welsh nationalist demands can be, and have been, accommodated via asymmetric devolution processes, but the sheer size of England makes English nationalist demands inherently more destabilising and their accommodation more difficult. For a long time, the quiescence of the English was taken for granted, and indeed the complaint of academics as recently as the mid-1990s was that the English needed to stop infusing 'everything that is English into the common property of Britishness' (Crick 1991) and develop 'a self-confident and explicit national feeling' (Crick 1995). Twenty years later, the political mobilisation of a distinct form of English identity has destabilised the British party system and constitutional settlement and looks set to pull the whole of the UK out of the European Union. Be careful what you wish for.

The roots of this politically mobilised English identity run deep. Surveys conducted since the 1990s have revealed a long-running divide in how the English see themselves. On the one hand, a socially conservative, ethnically exclusive English identity has long attracted a substantial minority with an emphasis is on ancestry and descent, a suspicion of outsiders and foreigners and a reluctance to cooperate or share power with them. This outlook is itself in part a reaction to the more socially liberal, culturally cosmopolitan and outward-looking British identity long favoured by England's political and social elites, which has its own mass following in the English electorate. This divide, evident between some of the more exclusively 'English' and 'British' identifiers in the English electorate, also reflects and articulates many of the other social and value divides which have been growing in political prominence over recent decades (Ford & Goodwin 2014b, 2017; see also Chapter 13). Yet the divides it maps on to—between young and old, university graduates and school leavers, ethnic minorities and culturally conservative white voters—are very different to the divides of class, region and income which have traditionally structured English party politics. As a result, the recent mobilisation of national identity in England has proved to be just as politically disruptive as the mobilisation of distinct national identities has proved elsewhere in the United Kingdom and beyond it.

The emergence of a distinct political agenda associated with English identity has reflected the growing salience of a new set of political conflicts, in particular over immigration and the European Union, where English identifiers have distinct views, as well as the emergence of a new political party—UKIP—which has mobilised them. UKIP's political priorities—strong opposition to immigration, traditional social values and staunch hostility to the European Union—closely reflect the views of English voters who express the strongest attachment to English identity. UKIP is, in its values and political priorities, a typical radical right nationalist party, and it has attracted its strongest support from English identifiers and in English constituencies and regions. It is thus a radical right English nationalist party in all but name and, in its brief moment in the political spotlight from 2013 to 2017, it fundamentally reshaped British politics by giving voice to the agenda and priorities of the 'English English'.

UKIP achieved this despite only ever getting one MP elected to Parliament, by forcing a reaction from the larger parties threatened by its rise. UKIP's mobilisation of English identifiers forced the Conservatives to commit to a referendum on EU membership. The referendum, in turn, provided a much bigger stage for the conflict between the more insular, socially conservative outlook of English identifiers and the more liberal, cosmopolitan outlook typical of the 'British' English to play out. English identity politics was not the only factor influencing choices in the 2016 referendum, but it was most likely an important one. All of the concerns that are most intensely expressed by English identifiers—opposition to immigration, social and cultural conservatism, political disaffection and support for separate English political institutions—were associated with higher support for Brexit.

Brexit, however, has not proved to be the end of the story. The referendum campaign provoked intense political mobilisation by the 'English' English, but the post-EU referendum election of June 2017 seems to have sparked a similarly intense reaction from the 'British' English, helping Labour achieve its largest vote share increase in over seventy years. The two votes just a year apart have highlighted how deep the identity divides in England have become and how powerfully they have disrupted English party politics. While the majority of the population remains in the 'equally English and British' middle, the two extremes of 'English not British' and 'British not English' have been able to mobilise more effectively and have played a crucial role in two successive national votes. While predicting what comes next is hazardous in such uncertain times, one thing looks likely: English divides over national identity will continue to play a major role in the disruptions to come.

Table 8.9 Alternative Measures of UKIP Support, 2014–15

	Voting UKIP	**Probability of Ever Voting UKIP (0–10 scale)**	**Switching Con to UKIP**	**Switching Lab to UKIP**
2014 European Parliament election				
Intercept	**–2.17****	**0.70**	**–3.21****	**–3.21****
Englishness	**0.10****	**0.14****	0.10	0.11
Views on EU integration				
Economic impact of immigration	**0.18****	**0.14****	0.08	0.03
Cultural impact of immigration	**0.29****	**0.35****	**0.17****	**0.36****
Satisfaction with UK democracy	**–0.20****	**–0.22***	–0.13	–0.13
Politicians don't care what people like me think	**0.20****	0.11	**0.19****	0.05
Does England get fair share from Union?	**–0.15****	–0.19*	**–0.25****	0.03
Governing England (ref: UK Parliament, all MPs vote)				
UK Parliament, only English MPs vote on English laws	**0.42****	**0.54****	0.33*	0.16
Separate English Parliament	**0.46****	**0.41***	0.34	0.34
Opposition to equal opportunities (scale)	**0.42****	**0.70****	**0.30****	**0.44****
Authoritarian values (scale)	**0.14****	**0.25****	0.07	0.11
Model fit (R square/pseudo-R square)	*0.24*	*0.25*	*0.09*	*0.13*
2015 Westminster election				
Intercept	**–3.83****	**1.39****	**–4.95****	**–4.56****
Englishness	**0.12****	**0.11****	**0.37****	**0.13***
Views on EU integration				
Economic impact of immigration	**0.23****	**0.28****	0.07	0.13
Cultural impact of immigration	**0.24****	**0.37****	**0.21***	**0.21****
Satisfaction with UK democracy	**–0.35****	**–0.21****	**–0.42***	–0.16
Politicians don't care what people like me think	**0.40****	**0.21****	0.14	**0.28****
Does England get fair share from Union?	–0.04	**–0.20****	0.09	–0.07
Governing England (ref: UK Parliament, all MPs vote)				
UK Parliament, only English MPs vote on English laws	**0.47****	**0.78****	–0.35	**0.44***
Separate English Parliament	**0.55****	**0.79****	–0.39	0.27
Opposition to equal opportunities (scale)	**0.29****	**0.65****	0.05	**0.27***
Authoritarian values	**0.06****	**0.17****	0.07	**0.10***
Model fit (R square/pseudo-R square)	*0.30*	*0.30*	*0.06*	*0.16*

Table 8.10 English Nationalism and Support for Brexit over Time

	Support for Brexit March 2014	Support for Brexit June 2015	'Leave' Vote June 2016
Intercept	**–1.83****	**–1.66****	**–1.71****
Englishness	**0.10****	**0.11****	**0.16****
Economic impact of immigration	**0.23****	**0.30****	**0.30****
Cultural impact of immigration	**0.22****	**0.19****	**0.29****
Satisfaction with UK democracy	–0.05	**–0.09***	–0.11
Politicians don't care what people like me think	**0.13****	**0.11****	**0.19****
Does England get fair share from Union?	**–0.15****	**–0.15****	–0.06
Governing England (ref: UK Parliament, all MPs vote)			
UK Parliament, only English MPs vote on English laws	**0.26****	**0.40****	**0.62****
Separate English Parliament	**0.37****	**0.53****	**0.83****
Opposition to equal opportunities scale	**0.26****	**0.20****	**0.28****
Authoritarian social values scale	**0.22****	**0.21****	**0.21****
Model fit (R square/pseudo-R square)			

References

Barnett, A. (2016), 'It's England's Brexit', openDemocracyUK, 4 June, https://www.opendemocracy.net/uk/anthony-barnett/it-s-england-s-brexit, accessed 29 June 2017.

Brown, G. (2006), 'Britishness', speech at Fabian New Year Conference, 14 January.

Colley, L. (1992), *Britons: Forging the Nation 1707–1837* (New Haven, CT, Yale University Press).

Crick, B. (ed) (1991), *National Identities and the Constitution* (Oxford, Blackwell).

Crick, B. (1995), 'The sense of identity of the indigenous British', *Journal of Ethnic and Migration Studies*, 21(2): 167–82.

Curtice, J. & Heath, A. (2000), 'Is the English lion about to roar? National identity after devolution', in R. Jowell, J. Curtice, A. Park, K. Thomson, L. Jarvis, C. Bromley & N. Stratford (eds), *British Social Attitudes: The 17th Report* (London, National Centre for Social Research), 155–74.

Curtice, J., Devine, P. & Ormston, R. (2013), 'Devolution', in A. Park, C. Bryson, L. Clery, J. Curtice & M. Phillips (eds), *British Social Attitudes: The 30th Report*, http://www.bsa.natcen.ac.uk/media/38458/bsa30_devolution_final.pdf, accessed 29 June 2017.

Curtice, J., Fisher, S., Ford, R. & English, P. (2018), 'Appendix 1: an analysis of the results', in P. Cowley & D. Kavanagh, *The British General Election of 2017* (Basingstoke, Palgrave Macmillan).

Curtis, C. (2017), 'How Britain voted at the 2017 election', https://yougov.co.uk/news/2017/06/13/how-britain-voted-2017-general-election/, accessed 30 May 2018.

Duffy, B. & Frere-Smith, T. (2014), 'Perceptions and reality: public attitudes to immigration', IPSOS-MORI Social Research Institute, https://www.ipsos.com/ipsos-mori/en-uk/perceptions-and-reality-public-attitudes-immigration, accessed 30 May 2018.

Evans, G. & Mellon, J. (2016), 'How immigration became a Eurosceptic issue', LSE Brexit blog, 5 January, http://blogs.lse.ac.uk/brexit/2016/01/05/how-immigration-became-a-eurosceptic-issue/, accessed 14 September 2017.

Ford, R. & Goodwin, M. (2014a), *Revolt on the Right: Explaining Support for the Radical Right in Britain* (Abingdon, Routledge).

Ford, R. & Goodwin, M. (2014b), 'Understanding UKIP: identity, social change and the left behind', *Political Quarterly*, 85(3): 277–84.

Ford, R. & Goodwin, M. (2017), 'Britain after Brexit: a nation divided', *Journal of Democracy*, 28(1): 17–30.

Ford, R., Goodwin, M. & Cutts, D. (2012), 'Strategic Eurosceptics and polite xenophobes: support for UKIP in the 2009 European Parliament elections', *European Journal of Political Research*, 51(2): 202–34.

Ford, R., Jennings, W. & Somerville, W. (2015), 'Public opinion, responsiveness and constraint: Britain's three immigration policy regimes', *Journal of Ethnic and Migration Studies*, 41(9): 1391–1411.

Gest, J. (2016), *The New Minority: White Working Class Politics in an Age of Immigration and Inequality* (Oxford, Oxford University Press).

Goodwin, M. & Milazzo, C. (2015), UKIP: Inside the Campaign to Redraw the Map of British Politics (Oxford, Oxford University Press).

Harris, J. (2016), 'Britain is in the midst of a working class revolt', *Guardian Comment is Free*, https://www.theguardian.com/commentisfree/2016/jun/17/britain-working-class-revolt-eu-referendum, accessed 29 June 2017.

Heath, A. & Tilley, J. (2005), 'British national identity and attitudes towards immigration', *International Journal on Multicultural Societies*, 7(2): 119–32.

Henderson, A., Jeffrey, C., Lineira, R., Scully, R., Wincott, D. & Wyn Jones, R. (2016), 'England, Englishness and Brexit', *Political Quarterly*, 87(2): 187–99.

Hunt, T. (ed.) (2016), 'Labour's Identity Crisis: England and the Politics of Patriotism', Centre for English Identity and Politics, http://repository.winchester.ac.uk/281/1/Denham_book_Labour%27s%20Identity%20Crisis.pdf, accessed 30 May 2018.

Jeffery, C., Wyn Jones, R., Henderson, A., Scully, R. & Lodge, G. (2014), *Taking England Seriously: The New English Politics* (Edinburgh, Centre on Constitutional Change).

Jennings, W. & Stoker, G. (2016), 'The bifurcation of politics: two Englands', *Political Quarterly*, 87(3): 372–82.

Lynch, P. (2000), 'The Conservative Party and nationhood', *Political Quarterly*, 71(1): 59–66.

Marguiles, B. (2016), 'English nationalism and its role in the referendum', OpenDemocracy.net, https://www.opendemocracy.net/uk/ben-margulies/english-nationalism-and-its-role-in-referendum, accessed 29 June 2017.

May, T. (2016), 'The New Centre Ground', Speech to the Conservative Party Conference, Birmingham, http://press.conservatives.com/post/151378268295/prime-minister-the-good-that-government-can-do, accessed 27 June 2018.

Mudde, C. (2007), *Populist Radical Right Parties in Europe* (Cambridge, Cambridge University Press).

Parekh, B. (2000), *The Future of Multi-Ethnic Britain* (London, Runnymede Trust).

Skinner, G. (2017), 'How Britain voted in the 2017 election', Ipsos MORI, https://www.ipsos.com/ipsos-mori/en-uk/how-britain-voted-2017-election, accessed 3 January 2018.

Somerville, W. (2007), *Immigration under New Labour* (London, Policy Press).

Tilley, J., Exley, S. & Heath, A. (2004), 'Dimensions of British identity', in A. Park, J. Curtice, K. Thomson, C. Bromley & M. Phillips (eds), *British Social Attitudes: The 21st Report* (London, NatCen Social Research), 147–67.

Wellings, B. (2012), *English Nationalism and Euroscepticism: Losing the Peace* (Bern, Peter Lang AG).

Wyn Jones, R., Lodge, G., Henderson, A. & Wincott, D. (2012), 'The dog that finally barked: England as an emerging political community', IPPR, https://www.ippr.org/files/images/media/files/publication/2012/02/dog-that-finally-barked_englishness_Jan2012_8542.pdf, accessed 30 May 2018.

Wyn Jones, R., Lodge, G., Jeffery, C., Gottfried, G., Scully, R., Henderson, A. & Wincott, D. (2013), *England and its Two Unions: The Anatomy of a Nation and its Discontents* (London, IPPR).

Part III

An England of Cities and Regions

9

Territory and Power in England: The Political Economy of Manchester and Beyond

MICK MORAN, JOHN TOMANEY & KAREL WILLIAMS

9.1 Governing England after the Destruction of the Dual Polity

> Territorial politics … that arena of political activity concerned with the relations between the central political institutions in the capital city and those interests, communities, political organisations and governmental bodies outside the central institutional complex, but within the accepted boundaries of the state, which possess, or are commonly perceived to possess, a significant geographical or local/regional character. (Bulpitt 2008: 59)

MANY FORCES SHAPED the bargain usually summarised as 'Devo Manc'. Some were specific to Manchester. The local political coalition that was critical to negotiating the deal, for instance, in part involved the attempted creation of a city region out of the ashes of the old metropolitan county that was destroyed in the 1980s. But this is a book about governing *England* and it is therefore important to recognise how Devo Manc is a response to two sets of problems: the problems that the centre now has in governing a polity whose coherence is uncertain in the age of national systems of devolution and the problems faced by local political leaders in an era of industrial decline and fiscal austerity.

An analytically creative attempt to understand the governing consequences of the interaction between local and central problems can be found in the work of James Bulpitt, author of *Territory and Power in the United Kingdom*. We use the 2008 edition, but it is over thirty years since he developed the idea of the 'dual polity' to try to understand an earlier momentous change. Mrs Thatcher had destroyed a tacit understanding about the spheres of local and central government: destroyed, in other words, 'the structure of territorial politics in which the Centre and periphery has relatively little to do with each other'. Bulpitt's old pre-1980s dual polity consigned low politics—the grinding labour of administration—to the locality and reserved high politics—the domain of strategic choice and of congenial activities like diplomacy—to the centre (Bulpitt 2008: 139). His framework remains relevant to Devo Manc and city deals in two ways. First, the city and devolution deals can be seen as an attempt to create a new dual polity. We argue that this attempt is inherently unstable because it is driven by economic pressures and fiscal stresses which both arise from the failure of the great Thatcher experiment and undermine the possibility of a stable new settlement. The contortions of the Manchester deal—the way it simultaneously announces great changes but preserves central powers—arise precisely from the difficulty of recreating a stable dual polity. Secondly, Bulpitt's concept of (high) politics as a 'court system' helps us understand, we will show, the way Greater Manchester's devolution deal can be seen as an accommodation between two interlocked elites in London's Whitehall and Manchester's town hall. At first sight, Devo Manc exhibits features of what Bulpitt terms a 'capital city bargaining model', 'in which peripheral groups and governments articulate, defend and satisfy their interests within the institutional complex of the Centre, especially the legislature and executive' (Bulpitt 2008: 68). But the bargain, we show, is riddled with tensions and limitations.

The background is well known and is summarised and anticipated in Bulpitt's classic. The age of Thatcherism destroyed the institutionalised division of spheres between centre and periphery, high politics and low politics, strategy and administration. The destruction involved central displacement of key local functions (for instance in housing and education) and growing central control over tax and spending decisions. It also involved the abolition of the metropolitan counties because they were centres of political resistance. New Labour in power introduced devolution reforms in Scotland and Wales that radically modified duality in those jurisdictions, but it made little attempt to alter that balance of power in England itself. Thus Greater Manchester had no city region government for two decades after 1986. Post-'dual polity' politics were then increasingly economically troubled after the great financial crisis as the centre shifted the burden of austerity measures onto local authorities. By the mid-2010s, the central state was increasingly unable to fund foundational services in health, care and education from tax revenue; while the central and local state's preferred mix of regional and industrial policies manifestly did not diffuse the benefits of growth to 'left behind' regions and localities.

Bulpitt's dual polity defended the locality against the centre—but it also protected the centre from invasion by the periphery. At the heart of 'the centre', in the Treasury and 10 Downing Street, elite decision-making works through court politics. This revolves around a small number of powerful office holders; it places great importance on the management of reputation by a politics of presentation; it is ill-equipped to grapple with tedious administrative detail or the grinding labour of policy delivery, or to manage conflicts about resource choice when there is widely agreed solution. The breakdown of duality sucked the centre into the low politics of resource allocation, an unattractive prospect in the era of permanent austerity after 2010; while persisting concern about regional economic imbalances dramatised issues about the ineffectuality of central strategy and policies. By the mid-2010s, devolution was thus attractive for the Whitehall court: it could delegate the uncongenial work of managing austerity cuts and intractable problems about responsibility for economic imbalances.

Why then was a devolution deal enthusiastically accepted by Greater Manchester if the centre wanted to give local decision-makers extra responsibilities within a Whitehall-defined framework where they gained very few extra powers? We show, especially in Section 9.3, how the atrophy of local democratic institutions had empowered a local elite in the City of Manchester's town hall; other borough leaders bought in to the devolution deal on the grounds that it was an unrepeatable offer from the centre and that any benefits could be divided up later through local intra-elite arguments. The city, in other words, was marked by a *coterie politics*: control of decisions by a small group of key actors, a kind of mirror image of the court arrangement which typified the Whitehall elite. Manchester, of course, was not all unusual in this respect. Popular participation in local politics (indicated, for instance, by electoral turnout) is, across the country, low by European standards. But the longevity of single-party rule in Manchester was a distinctive feature. This town hall coterie rested its case on a new economic orthodoxy that emphasises the importance of urban agglomerations as the source of economic growth, an argument elaborated in the 2009 Manchester Independent Economic Review (MIER 2009; see also Emmerich 2017). At the same time, Manchester was characterised by a relatively cohesive 'urban growth coalition' which linked political and property interests. This coalition had already transformed the urban core through residential and commercial development and now stood to gain from any deal which increased city region prerogatives in relation to planning and infrastructure (Harding 1991). The political weight of the Manchester town hall leadership, coupled with the ideological constraints that hem in urban development, created powerful contingent forces that pushed the deal through and made it difficult for the other Greater Manchester boroughs to oppose the deal, despite there being no guarantee of harmony between the ten boroughs in the long run.

The Manchester urban growth coalition is mostly a property development project. But the maintenance of adult care services or the regeneration of the northern boroughs of Greater Manchester are not property projects; and we will argue that the property-led transformation of the centre has worked in practice to marginalise the outer boroughs. From this point of view, the crucial issue is that the Osborne devolution offer was not to Manchester City Council but to the Greater Manchester city region of ten boroughs. Sharp internal differences both within and between boroughs would inevitably create division between winner and loser boroughs and groups when hard choices had to be made further down the line. Devolution to Scotland, Wales and Northern Ireland in the late 1990s had supported, or even reinforced, central control within their devolved systems. Devolution in the Manchester case was a deal made by the Whitehall court and the city coterie; but it had to be implemented in very different institutional circumstances. Without the centralisation of decision-making, coterie control over dissent and management of internal differences across the ten boroughs is much more problematic in Greater

Manchester. Conflicts over land-use planning between the new metro mayor and borough leaders are an early indication of the tensions (Williams 2017a, 2017b).

To emphasise what will be argued in this chapter: we are not suggesting that conditions in Manchester are unique to the city or the city region. On the contrary, the withering of local political participation has had similar effects across the whole kingdom. Nor are we suggesting some conspiracy by an oligarchy. The civic leaders of Manchester have for decades—and especially since the catastrophe of the IRA attack in the city in 1996—been moved by a public interest vision of urban regeneration. The key points are that the political condition of local government created a town hall coterie, a small cohesive elite of politicians and property developers, and that this coterie has relied heavily on property-led regeneration in the central boroughs and on cultivating relations with parts of the Whitehall elite.

9.2 The Centre's English Devolution Agenda

The landmark New Labour constitutional reforms at the end of the 1990s created one obvious gap: apart from the arrangements for London (discussed in Chapter 10) they left the territorial government of England untouched. As discussed by John Denham in Chapter 7, Labour inherited the commitment to strong state centralisation and its commitment to the Westminster model of territorial politics from its Conservative predecessor—an inheritance that stretched back to the 1920s. The devolution reforms for Scotland and Wales marked the partial abandonment of this tradition of constitutional conservatism. But abandoning or modifying it in the case of England faced obvious difficulties.

It involved a search for defensible boundaries and spatial foundations of devolved government in a territory where over a century of economic and cultural change had drained provincial England of resources and of the distinct identity which undoubtedly existed in the devolved territories. The English regions are nothing like Anderson's (1993) 'imagined communities'. Earlier attempts to nibble at the problem—such as the proposal in the minority report of the Royal Commission on the Constitution (1973) for five regional assemblies in England—came to nothing. Hence the 'cartographic anxiety' that afflicts regional geographers when drawing a map of any system of devolved English government (Harrison 2013; Painter 2008). This burdens any attempt at territorial reform with an irreducible tension. On the one hand, there is no intellectually satisfactory way of drawing a map. But on the other, there is a pragmatic need to define the boundaries of any governing system: without it, everyone is lost about how to answer primary questions of government, such as who is to be commanded and who is to provide services.

New Labour's first attempted answer involved placing a bet on imagined (regional) communities. It singled out the one 'region' beyond London which conventional wisdom suggested did have something approaching a distinct sense of identity, the North East, organised a referendum on a proposed system of regional government for the area with few credible powers and hoped to create an institutional leader capable of hauling laggards in its wake. The resulting referendum defeat in 2004 is well documented: in a postal ballot (chosen to maximise participation) 48 per cent voted and of those 78 per cent rejected the proposals for regional government. Planned ballots in other regions (the North West and Yorkshire and the Humber) were first postponed and then abandoned.

After this episode, more technocratic regional institutions and identities continued to live a precarious life. New Labour did create eight Regional Development Agencies (RDAs) in 1999 as planning mechanisms to deal with English regional problems that were larger than local. They were abolished by the incoming coalition administration, which in 2012 replaced the RDAs with Local Enterprise Partnerships (LEPs) between local authorities and business. The LEPs met the political objective of empowering local business but were smaller scale, poorly funded and lacking in powers. But by then an alternative boundary definition derived from economics was gaining influence. If English politicians could not define regions, economists could identify city regions by population density in the core and travel to work flows from hinterlands to form functional urban regions. This had some political support because the core cities alliance, coordinated from Manchester, had been established as long ago as 1995, although the political task of building city regions remains unfinished at best.

Understanding how city regions came to be central to the problem of English devolution after New Labour under the Cameron Coalition Government turns on three things: economic crisis, electoral strategy and the political culture of the metropolitan court.

The great financial crisis of 2007–9, and the ensuing recession, wrecked the public finances and produced a new era of budgetary austerity. After 2010 the centre tried to solve the politically toxic problem of how to make these cuts by loading the burden on localities and local government dutifully took a disproportionate share of the burden of austerity. Delegating austerity made political sense for the centre, but the strategy threatened to suck the central state further into the unpleasant details of resource choice in localities, especially on adult care. This intervention actually strengthened the burgeoning 'national world of local government' (Rhodes 1986). Well-organised networks of nationally organised local government associations give localities a voice, allowing them to intervene in central debates about resource allocation—precisely the kind of invasion by the periphery that the dual polity was designed to prevent. Structural biases in the territorial allocation of resources further threatened 'imbalance': funding formulas meant that cuts fell disproportionately on authorities in the most deprived communities, which particularly meant Labour authorities, especially in the North of England.

George Osborne was not only Chancellor but chief political strategist to Prime Minister Cameron. An electorally acute Chancellor could not fail to notice the political dangers in all of this; the unequal distribution of austerity could strengthen Labour as party of choice outside the South of England. A Conservative Party, at that point virtually extinguished as a Westminster parliamentary force in Scotland, was also experiencing a long-term decline in the North of England. In 2014, when the 'Northern Powerhouse' initiative was launched, only three Conservative Cabinet Ministers (Osborne, Hague and McLoughlin) could credibly claim to represent northern constituencies; most represented constituencies in the suburban South East and its extension along the Thames Valley. The Chancellor's talk in 2010 of rebalancing of the economy through a 'march of the makers' had come to nothing; another initiative would distract from all that and could offer a political dividend. (A subsidiary tactical advantage for the centre was that the Devo Manc deal, announced in 2014, would wrong-foot the metropolitan Labour leadership in the Westminster Parliament.)

Fiscal pressures and electoral tactics thus begin to make sense of the emergence of a 'Northern Powerhouse' strategy and the proposed devolution deals with city regions. It gave the centre a solution to the problem of how to devolve austerity without being sucked into the noxious and tedious details of resource allocation, and it offered some chance of stemming long electoral decline for the dominant Conservative partner in the coalition. But these factors only explain why the Powerhouse initiative happened; they do not explain why it took a particular institutional form. One partial solution to this conundrum is obvious: after the failure of regional devolution there was a policy hole. To understand how it was filled we need to look at the political culture in the centre. (And at the political culture of Manchester City Council, the subject of Section 9.3.)

What Bulpitt wrote in his classic still applies: 'whatever the location, a court ethos has always dominated the Centre's activities' (2008: 20). The idea of a court brings with it associations of kings, courtiers and clientism. So, we prefer the more neutral term coterie politics to describe policy-making by a small elite group with shared interests. Coterie politics precisely describes the state of affairs in the core executive, notably after 2010 when an unusually powerful Chancellor dominated. We can speak of coterie politics when three conditions exist: there is a tiny decision-making community around powerful office holders (or better still one office holder); influence is personalised because the role and power of individuals in the coterie cannot be inferred from organisation charts; and limited day-by-day accountability is counterbalanced by a concern with reputation and how things appear. All this is unstable insofar as coteries must struggle with intractable policy problems for which there is no intellectually coercive or socially mandated solution. The resulting uncertainty about solutions means that skills in advocacy and the manipulation of symbols are important to influence and manage reputation.

Coterie politics is intensely personal because the entire system revolves around formal and informal meetings with key office holders and subsequent announcements which have consequences for individual reputation as much as for policy. But it is also underpinned by ideas and competition for influence within the coterie that produce economic assumptions, social narrative and political calculation about which interests need to be accommodated—the 'official mind' in Bulpitt's designation. From this point of view, by the early 2010s the city region was an idea whose time had come for the coterie around Chancellor Osborne, which established the What Works Centre on Local Growth and drew on think tanks like the Centre for

Cities to inform its approach to policy. A new 'territorial code', to use Bulpitt's term, emerged which drew on new urban economics and agglomeration theory to claim that large cities are unique sources of economic productivity and dynamism, with the capacity, given the right institutional levers such as elected mayoralties, to transform regional economic fortunes. This narrative simply overrode disputes about whether larger cities did indeed perform better economically, while regular assertions of the strength of the US mayoral model ignored the inconvenient truth that electoral turnout in such mayoral elections is routinely below 30 per cent.

It is well known that the city region devolution formula which the Treasury offered to Manchester as part of 'Northern Powerhouse' was consistent with the agglomeration narrative and the highly centralised arrangement that has shredded the dual polity. It was 'an offer you can't refuse' which ignored, for instance, the result of the 2012 Manchester referendum rejecting an elected mayoralty, and it obliged the different boroughs (who had fallen out over the proposed introduction of congestion charging) to agree to act under a common institutional umbrella of the elected mayoralty and the combined Greater Manchester Combined Authority (GMCA). It was a bargain announced without any previous public consultation or even much discussion with local councillors (Jenkins 2015). And that was perfectly understandable, because it was the product of the intertwining of two systems of coterie politics, in Whitehall and in Manchester town hall respectively. Coupled with the ideological constraints shaping forms of urban development, which meant there was no obvious alternative model to follow, this created powerful contingent forces which produced the deal and helped to ensure the support of all the Greater Manchester boroughs.

We examine Manchester's politics in Section 9.3 before turning to consider the economic contradictions of the city's transformation.

9.3 Manchester Politics: The Town Hall and the Growth Coalition

Journalistic reports of the political process which produced the 'deal' of 2014 paint a consistent picture. Locally, it was driven from Manchester town hall by two top city council office holders, who had cultivated and built their reputation with the Whitehall core executive over several years (Jenkins 2015; Wigmore 2016). For nearly twenty years there had been an enduring axis between a long-established chief executive and leader of the council: Howard Bernstein was chief executive 1998–2016; Richard Leese leader of the council 1996–. That city council in turn was dominated by a single party; even in 2017 there was only a solitary non-Labour (Liberal Democrat) councillor. This domination in turn rested—as has been characteristic of the whole local government system—on narrow popular foundations. The council electoral results for 2012—at the start of the cycle which led to the devolution deal—are characteristic. In those elections, which returned Sir Richard Leese as councillor for Crumpsall, city-wide turnout was 25.3 per cent, the range varying from 13.6 (City Centre ward) to Didsbury West 37.6. Leese won by a large majority (2,499 against the next closest, 225) on a turnout of 29.2 per cent.

This constrained popular electoral base (for English local government) was matched by a narrow base of activists in the political class. Although reliable figures of membership for the constituent parts of Manchester are not available, the picture painted in Pemberton & Wickham Jones' (2013) analysis (based on returns in the 2010 leadership ballot) shows a 'relentless and persistent collapse' of Labour's membership across the UK, with the single exception of London, after a period of recruitment success in the 1990s. That collapse was accentuated by the exodus after the invasion of Iraq in 2003. Separate figures do not exist for Manchester but by 2010 the average size of membership in constituencies in the North West where Labour held the Westminster seat was 307; Pemberton & Wickham Jones (2013) calculate that that figure has fallen 54 per cent since the climactic year of 1997. Lately, of course, the Corbyn membership surge, for the moment, has transformed local party memberships, especially in the cities.

This is not to suggest that the party in Manchester was doing unusually badly by national standards. Low electoral turnouts and a declining membership are part of the national picture, and in terms of its membership Labour in the region was not performing particularly badly by national standards. The essential point can be put simply: domination of the council by Labour, the party's withered grassroots, low turnout in elections and the long reign of two powerful office holders meant that decisions were taken by a town hall coterie where Howard Bernstein was the key fixer. Many members of the political class, including ordinary councillors, had little influence or knowledge of what was going on, while citizens who were not Labour Party members were inactive and uninformed. There was thus symmetry between the coterie politics of Whitehall and Manchester town hall. The metro mayor model, which was George Osborne's requirement for a devolution deal, has its origins in these conditions. A single authoritative leader able to do deals with central government and local business was seen as suited to the prevailing political and economic circumstances described in Sections 9.3 to 9.5.

The distinguishing feature of the 'Manchester' governing system was the alliance of the town hall coterie with property developers. It created a very British version of the 'urban growth machine' (Harding 1991). It was the product of attempts by public-spirited civic leaders to try to find a model of economic regeneration in a world where the historical foundations of the industrial economy had rotted away. The strategy was the opposite of the conspiratorial: the Manchester miracle was endlessly celebrated by civic leaders. If the leading property developers were not part of the decision-making political coterie they certainly had privileged access to all the office holders and enjoyed the status of a protégé interest group which merited political protection and sponsorship. The property sector had much the same status in Manchester as financial services in London.

The status of property in Manchester came from its role in reinventing an economically depressed post-industrial economy. Major industrial interests had disappeared or relocated. The period of industrial decline in the 1970s and 1980s saw the virtual disappearance of industrial big business or finance as major actors in the local political system. The 'reinvention' from the early 1990s centred on the key resource of land, whose development and allocation could be both a source of huge private wealth and, crucially, was mediated by (local) public authority planning permissions. From the mid-1990s, there were large-scale property projects in or near the city centre: the first and largest was the Spinningfields development, which, in effect created a new central business district. The significant corporate political actors were all property based: the regionally based family firms included John Whittaker's Peel Holdings and the Oglesby family's Bruntwood; more corporate inward investors included Allied London and the Abu Dhabi Group, owners of Manchester City Football Club (Blakely & Evans 2013). In alliance with their professional helpers, these are Manchester's 'place entrepreneurs' (Rodgers 2009) who use their networked position in the local decision-making system to get things built and earn returns on investment.

A town hall political coterie dominated by a small number of powerful office holders is therefore integrated with a property-based post-industrial business elite. And through the 1990s and 2000s much of this was informal. Some of the mechanisms of integration were ad hoc: both Leese and his deputy leader of the city council, for instance, have served as directors of the Ship Canal Company, the enterprise which makes Peel Holdings the North West's leading property developer. But the Coalition Government's LEP has, since 2010, played some part in institutionalising network relations, bringing together figures like Leese, the leader of Trafford Council, the founder and chair of Bruntwood, the regional director of BT (who chairs the LEP) and the president of the area's largest university. The presence of Manchester University's president also alerts us to another feature of Manchester's urban growth coalition; it depends heavily on 'boosterism' and enlists all those concerned to propagate local strengths in the face of competition from rival centres. Andy Burnham joined the board following his election as Mayor of Greater Manchester (Greater Manchester LEP 2017).

Occasionally, boosterism comes from staging 'mega events' and putting up iconic buildings that supposedly raise city profiles globally. In the case of Manchester, the obvious instances are the Commonwealth Games in 2002, the Manchester International Festival since 2007 and the construction of the Bridgewater Hall. But more everyday boosterism depends on enlisting city institutions. In the American version, local media interests are key 'boosters' because of the connection between local economic development and advertising revenue. The regional media system in Greater Manchester lacks this significance, but the universities, notably the University of Manchester, have bought into boosterism. This is partly because the university is itself a major property owner, which is, for example, redeveloping its Business School site in partnership with Bruntwood. But, more important, the university has interests in boosting the profile of the city, since it operates in highly competitive fields nationally and internationally for the recruitment of students and staff and for research funding.

The strategy of building a coalition of civic leaders and property developers to create property-based regeneration has been pursued consistently and openly. It is an instance of the 'urban entrepreneurialism' identified by David Harvey (1989). But the problem with all this can be simply stated: it does not work. In other words, it is not creating an economy with the infrastructure and skills to match globally successful centres and it is creating an economy characterised by great inequality and a low-skilled, low-reward labour force, as we show in Section 9.4.

9.4 Manchester Economy: Agglomeration and Planning Permissions

The intellectual rationale for a Manchester City Deal was established in 2009 by the final report of the MIER. Framed by the new urban economics, the argument was that Greater Manchester, with 3.2 million people, was the city region 'best placed to take advantage of the benefits of agglomeration and increase its growth' (MIER 2009). The review argued the precondition was the devolution of more powers to an upgraded version of the Association of Greater Manchester Authorities (AGMA) through which the ten boroughs had, since 1986, managed emergency services, public transport and waste. The review then recommended the new authority should adopt economic policies which were entirely orthodox within a city-region core/periphery framing of Greater Manchester's problems: investment in transport and skills would make the labour market work better as upskilled workers could commute to central sites and this would be backed by house building on greenfield sites 'in the places people wanted to live' (MIER 2009).

All this seemed urgent because the problem of Greater Manchester's under-performance was real enough (see Folkman et al. 2016). Using the standard gross value added (GVA) measure, London GVA per capita is twice that of Greater Manchester; the latter's GVA per capita is, in turn, twice that of northern boroughs like Oldham, while the City of Manchester itself has many deprived districts. Over time, Greater Manchester has done no more than hold its position against other British core cities, while the large internal inequalities between the central city and the northern boroughs have become entrenched since deindustrialisation engulfed the area in the 1980s. The GVA relativities had not changed in three decades on the standard metrics, but the central city had been physically transformed by rebuilding and enabled by planning permissions.

The leading role of the City of Manchester was itself the unintended consequence of the way in which the Thatcher Government abolished the Greater Manchester County Council in 1986. The AGMA survived as the residuary legatee whose limited role was to manage collective services. Pragmatic councillors and officers in the adjacent boroughs of Manchester and Salford then concluded that they would have to get things done at borough level through alliances with the private sector. From the late 1980s, in a deindustrialised city that meant getting things built by giving private developers planning permission to put up whatever was most profitable. The social consequences were then determined by the imbalance between limited job creation in the outer boroughs and large-scale building in the centre.

Since deindustrialisation, Greater Manchester has had a limited capacity to create (net) new private jobs and the public and private jobs which have been created are not in the outer suburbs. In the pre-2008 period, under New Labour before austerity, Greater Manchester job creation was heavily dependent on the public sector where health and education spending was creating jobs in the centre. The public sector accounted for over half of the 46,000 extra jobs created in the ten Greater Manchester boroughs between 1998 and 2008. Because of the concentration of hospital, university and administrative functions in central Manchester, Manchester City with 20 per cent of the population claimed 16,000 of these jobs, accounting for 40 per cent of Greater Manchester's total job creation. The post-2008 story is dismal. The outer northern boroughs of Oldham, Rochdale and Tameside are in a dire plight because they are now net losers of both private and public sector jobs. Once again, the net gains are concentrated in the central city and the inner south-west quadrant. From 2008–14 Manchester City gained 30,000 net new jobs while four of the ten Greater Manchester boroughs saw job loss (Folkman et al. 2016).

What the City of Manchester and adjacent Salford borough could do was give planning permission for rebuilding on central brownfield sites that lay derelict after deindustrialisation. However, the construction of offices and adjacent flats in the centre undermined any possibility of distributing prosperity through commuting from dormitory suburbs to central offices. From the mid-1990s, the central city and the inner south-west around Salford Quays were rebuilt on a high-rise logic of profit as private developers turned square footage into cubed rental value. The transformation of office space began at Barbirolli Square in 1997, with the Spinningfields development subsequently providing a new central business district. Private developers also built adjacent lift-served blocks of one- and two-bedroom flats, typically sold to buy-to-let landlords—often foreign—who rented them to junior white-collar workers. Large-scale development since the late 1990s has created a kind of parallel new town of work spaces and flats in the centre. Manchester City centre (excluding Salford and Trafford) has, since 1997, added 5.38 million square feet of office space, which creates around 50,000 new work spaces. In parallel, there was large-scale building of one- and two-bedroom flats, with Manchester and Salford together adding 44,000 flats between 1991 and 2011.

This physical reformatting in a city region with a limited capacity to create new jobs hampered the growth of long-distance radial commuting within the city region and encouraged migration to rented flats in the city centre. The flats encourage in-migration to Manchester and Salford of 25–34-year-olds who are generally too old to be students but young enough to be mobile and unencumbered. Between 2001 and 2014, this population increased by 46,000 in Manchester City and Salford and declined in all other boroughs; 34 per cent of these inner-city 25–34-year-olds are born outside the UK (Folkman et al. 2016: 28–9). This undermined the rationale for policies which would remake Manchester in the image of a city region like London, which is substantially dependent on large volumes of radial commuting by public transport from outer boroughs. In Greater Manchester, long-distance commuting is discouraged because the Manchester City region combines relatively cheap central flats and inner residential suburbs with low wages and high fares from the outer boroughs. There is not the imbalance between a small number of central residents and a large number of commuters from dormitory suburbs. In 2011, 109,000 residents lived and worked in the City of Manchester and this almost exactly equalled the net inflow of 108,000 commuters from outside the borough. Most commuting is done by car so that (excluding movements from Salford to Manchester) 60–70 per cent of the commutes in to Manchester City from the nine other boroughs are by car. Lower public transport fares would help but the primary limit on commuting into the centre is increasingly not access to cheap public transport but the ready availability of one- and two-bedroom inner-city rented flats.

Greater Manchester is thus a city region which has been formatted for growth that excludes outer boroughs by the monoculture of flat building in the centre. But, rather than face this fact and the need to restrict flat building, policy-makers preferred the soft vision of the 2009 Independent Economic Review, which advocated adding infrastructure and skills to build a city region where public transport could take people to the jobs. This quickly became the unchallenged framework for official policy. In response to the Independent Economic Review, in August 2009 AGMA published an economic strategy which endorsed the skills and infrastructure agenda which has been carried through into all the subsequent policy documents of the GMCA (which replaced AGMA in 2011).

City centre development paused in the downturn after the financial crisis, but planners and developers soon resumed in a more frenetic way as Manchester's property-based business elites ignored the risks of overbuilding and property price crash in buy-to-let flats, mimicking experiences elsewhere (Weber 2016). Officials were no less bullish about a property-based future. In late 2016, the GMCA published a draft Greater Manchester Spatial Framework (GMSF) which envisaged by 2035 a near doubling in the number of flats in the new town in the centre, plus over 175,000 homes on new edge city estates for houses and warehouses, often on greenfield sites off the orbital M60 and other major roads. Edge city was a new concept necessary for the property developers when they had built on the prime inner-city brownfield sites; it was not clear that edge city would do anything other than add congestion for most of the city's residents who live between the centre and the edge.

9.5 The Devolution Deal

Under the conditions described in the previous sections, the devolution deal of November 2014 between Westminster and town hall coteries was not a hard bargain struck after adversary elites had struggled for advantage with each side finally making painful concessions, along the lines of Bulpitt's capital city bargaining model. Conflict was limited because both coteries had a shared belief in agglomeration economics as the driver of growth and this provided the framework in which each side got what it wanted within a framework of orthodox Treasury objectives and controls which neither side thought was onerous or unfair; as for the social side, this could be added later and be presented as Manchester's opportunity to gain from pioneering the integration of health and care. But, if we step outside the local elite's calculative framework of ex ante advantage, the ex post outcome is unlikely to benefit the mass of Greater Manchester citizens. The aim of raising the secular rate of growth through local action was a fantasy because local policymakers did not gain significant new policy levers or powers to do this and their established policy preference for boosting skills and infrastructure did not engage local specifics; while Greater Manchester was now taking local responsibility for social administration of health and care under conditions of austerity.

All this is complicated because the Greater Manchester devolution deal was unrolled in five stages. The first deal of November 2014 was publicly signed by the Chancellor and the ten borough heads in Manchester town hall to attract maximum public attention. It covered a consolidated transport budget, a housing investment fund and strategic planning. It agreed the institutional framework of the reformed system, notably the creation of an elected mayor and a 'cabinet' of leaders of the ten separate boroughs to form a GMCA, and it made plans to transfer the roles of the Police and Crime Commissioner to the new mayor, to be elected in 2017.

Three subsequent expansions were announced in 2015. First, in the March budget the Chancellor announced a pilot scheme to allow retention by the authority of 100 per cent of any additional business rate growth. Secondly, in July, Greater Manchester and NHS England announced a consolidation of health and social care budgets to allow joint planning at the Greater Manchester level. Thirdly, initiatives announced in conjunction with the Spending Review later that year involved tying the institutions of the new authority to national bodies: for instance, involving the Infrastructure Commission in providing advice on investment priorities for the North. They also envisaged (subject to legislation) giving the newly elected metro mayor power to introduce a business rates supplement. Finally, the expansion of the bargain announced in March 2016 mostly continued this theme of collaboration between the new institutions, planning, for instance, on joint commissioning of offender management services, youth justice and services for youth offenders, the courts and prisons estates, 'sobriety tagging' and custody budgets.

As the King's Fund concluded after examining the plan to integrate the health and social care budgets, the bargain involved not devolution but delegation (McKenna & Dunn 2015). By way of contrast, the Scots had got something altogether more radical in 1999 which could be termed devolution: Scotland gained control of a total budget (a block grant from Whitehall) with autonomy to allocate resources according to priorities determined by the devolved administration and the capacity to make laws independent of the Westminster legislature. (The original devolution settlement also gave the Scottish Government power to vary the standard rate of income tax by three pence in the pound up or down, though the power was never used before being replaced in 2016 by a more extensive form of income tax devolution.)

The devolved budgetary arrangements for Scotland (and the other devolved nations) opened the way to striking differences between Scotland and England in policy choices (for instance, in the funding of residential care and in the funding of higher education) as the Scottish Government began to make choices about the allocation of resources that differed from those made for England (and mostly Wales) in the Westminster system. And the transfer of legislative authority has further widened the divide: for instance, over the extent to which foundational services (like housing and water) are privatised and over the way key public services such as school education are regulated.

None of this is possible under Devo Manc. As the summary of the evolving deals shows, the bulk of the new institutional arrangements are about four things: first, improving coordination between what the central policy-making institutions aim to do and what the new Manchester institutions wish to do (for instance, liaising with the National Infrastructure Commission (NIC)); secondly, creating an incentive system for the new institutions to encourage them to access centrally created resources (creating a Life Chances Investment Fund from the Troubled Families Programme, Working Well pilot and the Cabinet Office Life Chances Fund); thirdly, tweaking the local taxation system to create some locally available extra resource via the promise of a supplementary business rate; and fourthly, managing newly combined budgets, mainly health and care, whose size will be decided centrally.

Delegation instead of devolution leaves the freshly created institutions (especially the directly elected metro mayor) very little room for manoeuvre. That point is made more pertinent still by what we know about social care and health. Integrating the two services was always going to be a challenge because health is free at point of use and care is not and the two systems are organised in separate ways. Matters were not helped by naive expectations about how this one structural reform of integration could deliver cost savings plus better outcomes for patients plus reduced hospital activity. In early 2017, a National Audit Office report warned that the national Better Care Fund was not delivering these objectives (National Audit Office 2017). And by November 2016, Greater Manchester had already accepted that integration of health and care was desirable but would not save money; it then calculated that Greater Manchester faced a cumulative £2 billion deficit on health and care by 2021 and asked for an interim £214 million from the Treasury because 'financial pressures in social care pose a real threat' to Manchester's ability to deliver devolution (Bounds 2016).

Thus, the changes in Greater Manchester, though the most extensive of all those negotiated by English city regions, were still limited and conservative. Their immediate effect was back to the future because they recreated something like Bulpitt's old dual polity in the new context of an austerity state. Under the Manchester deals, the centre reserves control over large strategic choices about how resources are to be raised and the global level of resource raising while it places at the local level the awkward choices involving the allocation of those resources between the claims of different services and different groups. Furthermore, the deals made no provision for legislative powers and for the ensuing scope for policy variation that accompanies the legislative power which has been a central feature of the Scottish devolution experience, facilitated by the fact that Scotland had retained its separate legal system ever since the Union of 1707.

London and Wales may give us some indications of possibilities. London's mayoralty and authority (discussed by Tony Travers in Chapter 10) has made a success of delegation. It has equipped the capital with a powerful lobbying voice in the struggle both for access to centrally created resources, as the territorial balance of spending on infrastructure projects makes abundantly clear; it has also given London a voice in the global competition for the allocation of resources by corporate capital. As the success in attracting and mounting the 2012 Olympics shows it has also given the capital an unexampled set of institutions for the parallel activity of boosterism, although its costs and benefits remain contentious. We also know from the case of Wales that the limited original system of devolution—amounting to not much more than delegation—created political dynamics that pushed the system towards the Scottish model. In delegation or in devolution in the present UK polity, 'settlements' settle nothing.

But to state the obvious, Manchester is neither Wales nor London. Will the new city region arrangements have the potential to expand into devolution, or at least to function as an effective competitor for central resources on the London model? That is something that can only be definitively answered by time—and by examining the wider English context of the Manchester reforms, the theme of Section 9.6.

9.6 Beyond Manchester

The Manchester model of devolution, which has developed over several decades, has been shaped by elite bargaining and informed by a distinctive territorial code that is founded on a model of urban economics, enduring austerity and the alleged benefits of metro mayors (Tomaney 2016). The Manchester experience has informed a framework promoted by the centre for the limited rollout of devolution deals with other groups of local authorities so that Greater Manchester becomes the model. The prize for the centre is a new dual polity in which the periphery is left to manage its own economic growth.

We have already questioned the long-term viability and durability of the dominant economic model in Greater Manchester. The forms of urban development and their enabling policies have produced high levels of socio-economic and geographical inequality, which emerged as issues in the 2017 metro mayor election. Despite growing discussion about 'inclusive growth', it is unclear how an economic model based on financialised residential and commercial property development can provide widely distributed social benefits.

A feature of the previous dual polity which dominated the middle of the 20th century, according to Bulpitt, was the supporting role played by Keynesian economics, which helped guarantee domestic social peace through fiscal redistribution. Bulpitt errs, however, when he claims that Keynesianism 'possessed no regional or territorial dimension' (Bulpitt 2008: 138). Keynesianism had significant territorial distributional impacts both through the automatic stabilisers identified by Kaldor and via an extensive panoply of regional policies, including regional investment incentives, development area designations, new towns and other large-scale infrastructure investments. This 'spatial Keynesianism', established by the 1945 Labour Government and only finally undone by the Thatcher Government after 1979, limited the growth of geographical inequalities (Kaldor 1970; Pike, Rodríguez-Pose & Tomaney 2017). The new urban economics pays no attention to matters of redistribution and instead largely accepts the case for enhanced territorial competition. A kind of neoliberal governmentality operates in the periphery whereby localities accept they must help themselves and have no rightful claims on resources from the centre: 'growth is seen as a good in itself: it is only by the state, that the living standards of the underprivileged can improve. With such a conception, the issue of redistribution as a key consideration of economic strategy is lost' (Harding 1991: 312). On the contrary, the uneven geography of austerity has seen its severest impacts on services in the northern cities, suggesting that devolution is currently configured, to use Bulpitt's language, more as 'indirect rule' (where local elites administer the priorities of the centre) rather than a 'capital city bargaining model' (where the interests of the periphery invade the centre).

Few other northern cities, in any event, possess the coterie and urban growth coalition that is visible in Manchester and which has produced the residential property boom in the urban core, which is in turn in part the result of the relative scale, density and morphology of the conurbation. The emerging fiscal model that underpins devolution—such as business rate retention, land value capture mechanisms—relies heavily on further concentrated commercial and residential property development rather than growth in the real economy. Although the Manchester model has been adopted in Liverpool and Teesside, advancing it in Sheffield, Leeds and Newcastle proved more problematic because the economic and political conditions are less propitious. In Birmingham, Cambridge and Bristol, with faster-growing property values, a version of the Manchester model has been implanted. Manchester is in competition with other English cities for investment in the built environment and for additional deals with the centre. The highly asymmetrical, deal-based nature of devolution in England is tacit admission of this. For these reasons, it is difficult to envisage how devolution in its present form can provide a stable framework for the management of territorial politics in England. This partly explains the limited appeal of the metro mayor model in other parts of England and the problems in implementing it, notably in the North East, Sheffield, East Anglia and Lincolnshire, which initially were slated to be in the first-wave mayoral elections. Given changes in personnel at the centre—notably the departure in 2017 from the political scene of Manchester's chief interlocutor, George Osborne—the outlook for devolution is uncertain. Systems of coterie politics are highly vulnerable to changes in membership.

9.7 Conclusion

> The crisis consists precisely in the fact that the old is dying and the new cannot be born; in this interregnum a great variety of morbid symptoms appear. (Gramsci 1971: 276)

Gramsci's well-known aphorism seems especially appropriate to our case. Growing spatial and political inequalities in England, most graphically evidenced in the geography of the Brexit vote, make the case for a new territorial settlement in the UK. But we have demonstrated the striking contradictions in the current episode. We have highlighted how devolution deals rest on underlying economic ideas that help to explain why the metro mayor model has emerged as the preference of the official mind. We have identified the leading role of Manchester in these developments, but have emphasised the contingent forces and the social limits of this model of development and the great difficulty of replicating it in places which lack its configuration. This is likely to preclude the possibility of a stable territorial code. Indeed, the emerging model seems more likely to exacerbate the political and economic tensions which it is intended to address. Bulpitt's analytical categories developed over thirty years ago to describe the distinctive dual polity in the UK remain remarkably prescient, albeit that they require adaptation to a shifting context.

References

Anderson, B. (1993), *Imagined Communities* (London, Verso).

Blakely, G. & Evans, B. (2013), *The Regeneration of East Manchester: A Political Analysis* (Manchester, Manchester University Press).

Bounds, A. (2016), 'Manchester asks for extra £214m to cover social care costs', *Financial Times*, 29 November, https://www.ft.com/content/683356dc-b647-11e6-ba85-95d1533d9a62, accessed 31 May 2018.

Bulpitt, J. (2008), *Territory and Power in the United Kingdom* (Colchester, ECPR Classics).

Emmerich, M. (2017), *Britain's Cities, Britain's Future* (London, London Publishing Partnership).

Folkman, F., Froud, J., Johal, S., Tomaney, J. & Williams, K. (2016), 'Manchester transformed: why we need a reset of city region policy', CRESC Research Report, http://hummedia.manchester.ac.uk/institutes/cresc/research/ManchesterTransformed.pdf, accessed 31 May 2018.

Gramsci, A. (1971), *Prison Notebooks* (London, Lawrence & Wishart).

Greater Manchester LEP (Local Enterprise Partnerships) (2017), 'Board members', http://gmlep.com/board/, accessed 9 October 2017.

Harding, A. (1991), 'The rise of urban growth coalitions', *Environment and Planning C: Government and Policy*, 9: 295–317.

Harrison, J. (2013), 'Configuring the new "regional world": on being caught between territory and networks', *Regional Studies*, 47(1): 55–74.

Harvey, D. (1989), 'From managerialism to entrepreneurialism: the transformation in urban governance in late capitalism', *Geografiska Annaler. Series B, Human Geography*, 71(1): 3–17.

Jenkins, S. (2015), 'The secret negotiations to restore Manchester to greatness', *The Guardian*, 12 January, https://www.theguardian.com/uk-news/2015/feb/12/secret-negotiations-restore-manchester-greatness, accessed 31 May 2018.

Kaldor, N. (1970), 'The case for regional policies', *Scottish Journal of Political Economy*, 18: 337–48.

McKenna, H. & Dunn, P. (2015), 'Devolution: what it means for health and social care in England', Kings Fund, https://www.kingsfund.org.uk/sites/files/kf/field/field_publication_file/devolution-briefing-nov15.pdf, accessed 31 May 2018.

MIER (Manchester Independent Economic Review) (2009), *Manchester Independent Economic Review: Reviewers' Report*, https://www.greatermanchester-ca.gov.uk/download/meetings/id/1386/manchester_independent_economic_review, accessed 26 June 2018.

National Audit Office (2017), 'Health and social care integration', https://www.nao.org.uk/wp-content/uploads/2017/02/Health-and-social-care-integration.pdf, accessed 31 May 2018.

Painter, J. (2008), 'Cartographic anxiety and the search for regionality', *Environment and Planning A*, 40: 340–61.

Pemberton, J. & Wickham-Jones, M. (2013), 'Labour's lost grassroots: the rise and fall of party membership', *British Politics*, 8(2): 181–206.

Pike, A., Rodríguez-Pose, A. & Tomaney, J. (2017), *Local and Regional Development* (London, Routledge).

Rhodes, R. A. W. (1986), *The National World of Local Government*, New Local Government Series, 26 (London, Routledge).

Rodgers, S. (2009), 'Urban geography: urban growth machine', in R. Kitchin & N. Thrift (eds), *International Encyclopedia of Human Geography* (Oxford, Elsevier), 40–5.

Royal Commission on the Constitution (1973), *Memorandum of Dissent by Lord Crowther Hunt and AT Peacock*, Cmnd 5460 (London, HMSO).

Tomaney, J. (2016), 'Limits of devolution: localism, economics and post-democracy', *Political Quarterly*, 87(4): 546–52.

Weber, R. (2016), *From Boom to Bubble: How Finance Built the New Chicago* (Chicago, Chicago University Press).

Wigmore, T. (2016), 'Can local government save Labour', *New Statesman*, 28 January, http://www.newstatesman.com/politics/staggers/2016/01/can-local-government-save-labour, accessed 31 May 2018.

Williams, J. (2017a), 'Greater Manchester's controversial housing masterplan could be delayed', *Manchester Evening News*, 6 July, http://www.manchestereveningnews.co.uk/news/greater-manchester-news/greater-manchesters-controversial-housing-masterplan-13288112, accessed 31 May 2018.

Williams, J. (2017b), 'The growing Labour rift over housing and homelessness', *Manchester Evening News*, 20 September, http://www.manchestereveningnews.co.uk/news/greater-manchester-news/growing-labour-rift-over-housing-13651019, accessed 31 May 2018.

10

London within England: A City State?

TONY TRAVERS

10.1 Introduction: London as a Civic Entity

THIS CHAPTER CONSIDERS London's development as a major city and civic entity and reforms which have taken place to its government, including the changes made alongside devolution to Scotland and Wales. It also analyses the way the capital is perceived externally and internally within the UK. Finally it considers whether further devolution to London or more radical reform to its constitutional status might take place.

London is by far the largest city in the United Kingdom and is different in many ways from the countries of which it is capital. Because the UK is a union of four nations, London is capital both of England and of the UK, mirroring the dual role of the Westminster Parliament as it governs these two geographical entities in different ways. But there is much more to London than its role as the capital of a complex quasi-federal state.

The metropolis is epic in scale and was famously described by an 1854 Royal Commission as a 'province covered with houses' (Davis 1988: 5). Unlike Birmingham, Manchester, Leeds and other major cities, it did not benefit from the creation of a single unitary council following the passage of the Municipal Corporations Act 1835. London struggled on with a patchwork of parishes and ad hoc boards. Even the creation of the Metropolitan Board of Works (MBW) in 1855 did not bring directly elected government to the metropolis. The MBW was merely a joint committee designed to preserve the sovereignty of the parishes and boards whose members controlled it. It was only with the coming of the London County Council (LCC) in 1888–9 that the word 'London' was applied to a geographically defined government area other than the ancient City of London. It was the latter's unwillingness to expand or reform that generated London's patchwork of governance.

Thus, historically it has been the case that London existed more as a geographical description than as a civic reality. Of course, there had been a 'Metropolitan'

Proceedings of the British Academy, **217**, 207–226, © The British Academy 2018.

Police Service since 1829 and the 'Metropolitan' Board of Works from 1855. But the word 'London' was avoided as an official description of the wider built-up area of the capital until the creation of the LCC: 'Ministers … were not subjected to the pressure for the resolution of London's problems that we might expect today. London was not an entity, hardly even a concept' (Port 1999: 103). Moreover, even after the Great Reform Act 1832, it had only 18 Members of Parliament out of a national total of 658, though the City of London had great influence over as many as 100 MPs (Port 1999: 104).

The growth of the British Empire made London the capital not only of the United Kingdom, but also home of the Imperial Parliament. This fact, and the global trade that centred on the City of London and London Docks, ensured that the vast city became a seething entrepot of money, trade and people. Piccadilly Circus was seen as the 'hub of the Empire'. Soho and Whitechapel were filled with exotic, foreign businesses which could not be found elsewhere in the country.

This history is important. The City of London's territorial conservatism and the metropolis's size together conspired against a proper civic identity of the kind enjoyed by cities such as Sheffield or Liverpool. Writing in 1828, Fenimore Cooper wrote of London that 'Many think the place already too large for the kingdom' and recorded that the great road contractor John McAdam 'considers the size of London an evil' (cited in Gomme 1898: 6). The emotions aroused by the city's economic power, population and sprawl are considered in more detail in Section 10.5.

The LCC undoubtedly gave London a civic identity. The council became one of the most powerful municipal authorities in the world, providing schools, colleges, hospitals, housing, tramways and many other services. Its best-known leader, Herbert Morrison (1934–40), was a figure of national stature. But by 1939, the LCC's area represented only a quarter of the sprawling metropolis. Calls emerged for a 'Greater' London government.

London School of Economics (LSE) academic William Robson, originally writing in the 1930s, described the consequences of the lack of effective civic government for the wider area of Greater London thus:

> This lack of municipal status in the region is a matter of the utmost importance from the point of view of civic consciousness. It explains more than any other single cause both the absence of a strong and effective regional patriotism and also the indifference of Londoners to the monstrous growth and misdevelopment of the region. 'Common government' it is truly said, 'is itself a powerful unifying force, setting a common stamp upon an area and its inhabitants to sentiment which attaches to the community so governed. Common government, if it is to be democratic and successful, presupposes a degree of community, but also strengthens community.' (Robson 1948: 324)

It took until 1965 for the Greater London Council (GLC) to become the directly elected city-regional authority for virtually the whole of the continuously built-up area centred on the LCC area. But even when this reform occurred, the GLC was created as a 'strategic', relatively weak, authority, with most municipal power vested in thirty-two boroughs and the City of London. Vernon Bogdanor, writing in 1978 in the context of the then proposed devolution to Scotland and Wales, dismissed any notion of London 'nationalism' or even much of a civic identity:

> Thus the Greater London Council, although administering the affairs of a larger population than that of Scotland, constitutes no challenge to Parliamentary authority, both because its powers are more limited than those proposed for Scotland and Wales and because the Assemblies will derive their prestige from the idea of nationality. It is for these reasons that the G.L.C. is not thought by the vast majority of electors—one may reasonably conjecture—to represent London as the Assemblies would represent Scotland and Wales. (Bogdanor 1978: 252)

As if to make Bogdanor's point about the GLC's lack of challenge to parliamentary authority, the GLC was abolished within twenty-one years of its inception. Between 1986 and 2000, the city once again had no elected metropolitan government. In 2000, a Greater London Authority (GLA), consisting of a mayor and assembly, was created following a legislative process which involved a referendum about whether or not the new institution should be introduced. The civic identity of the London city region was restored, this time with the support of a majority of those who voted in each borough.

The purpose of recalling this history is to stress the relative newness and historic weakness of the London identity. Unlike Scotland or Wales, London is not a nation or, arguably, a region as such. It is a 1,500 square-kilometre mega-city which is very much bigger than any other in the UK, but also a place where the characteristics of the population are substantially different from those of the country as a whole. The things that make London radically unusual are its wealth, ethnic diversity, economic power, public transport dependency, housing need and internationalism. It also has a number of differences relating to design and institutions.

When considering the future of London within the quasi-federal UK, it is important to take account of both its distinctness from and connectedness to the rest of the country. The border between London and the rest of the country is similar in length to that between England and Wales, though the economic connectedness is vastly greater between London and the rest of the 'greater' South East. Hundreds of millions of journeys a year cross the London border. Economically, the city is intensely interconnected with the wider UK.

But the urban form and demographics of London are unique within the UK and, indeed, Europe. Almost 40 per cent of Londoners were born overseas, with a similar proportion being from minority ethnic communities. Some London boroughs have a 'white British' population of under 20 per cent. The diverseness of the ethnic diversity in some parts of the capital is unusual compared to other global cities. The word 'Londoner' is all-embracing and generously bestowed. The capital is so big and so variegated that its residents appear to welcome all comers to the great melting pot. The fact that London voted by 60 per cent to 40 per cent to remain in the European Union and it was the only region in England and Wales to do so is up-to-date proof of its different outlook and views.

This chapter examines whether, contrary to Bogdanor's assessment of the GLC, the 2000 creation of the GLA was a change of a constitutional nature. The post-2000

Mayor of London can be argued to have been sufficiently powerful to challenge governmental, if not parliamentary, authority. Also, the mayor's powers are greater than those of the GLC. 'Greater' London identity is now far-longer established than in the 1970s and, importantly, the rapid demographic and ethnic changes to its population can be argued to have strengthened London identity. The 2016 EU referendum vote strongly suggested a significant difference between London and English sentiment.

The importance of identity as a driver of nationalism and/or devolution is self-evident. Much research in recent years has pointed to the rise of different identities at the national and subnational level and their impact on voting in Scotland in particular. Northern Ireland, for different reasons, also has a political system influenced by identity. Within England, London identity is real. Issues of identity are considered further in Sections 10.3 to 10.7.

10.2 Devolution to London

The brief discussion in Section 10.1 mentions a number of metropolitan governance institutions. Each of these: the MBW, the LCC, the GLC and now the GLA has given London a form of city-wide government. The LCC was formed as part of a wider reform of county government throughout England and Wales, while the MBW, the GLC and GLA were each unique to the capital. It would be hard to argue that the creation of the first three were 'devolution' as such. The MBW was simply a joint committee empowered to deliver better infrastructure. The LCC was a county similar in kind to, say, Lancashire or Middlesex, though without a cricket team. The GLC was created in such a way as to be London's first city-regional authority and thus paved the way for the GLA, which was created in 2000 as part of the Blair Government's programme of devolution within the UK. The Government intended the GLA to be the first of a series of regional governments within England.

But it is important to note that while the creation of the GLC in 1965 had the effect of defining 'London' as a geographical area with an administrative purpose, it was part of a local government reorganisation rather than devolution as such. The Royal Commission on Local Government in Greater London 1957–60 (the Herbert Commission) had been appointed to consider the need to reform the structure of local government in the capital. The Royal Warrant stated that the commission should:

> examine the present system and working of local government in the Greater London area; to recommend whether and, and if so what, changes in local government structure and the distribution of local authority functions in the area, or any part of it, would better secure effective and convenient local government; and to regard, for these purposes local government as not including the administration of police, or of water. (Herbert 1960: i)

The Herbert Commission was required to look at local government as it was, excluding police and water, and propose possible structural reforms. There was no remit to propose, for example, that powers held by Whitehall departments or even nationalised industries should be transferred to the London government.

Once created, the GLC did benefit from a substantial devolution of power in 1969. Labour Transport Minister Barbara Castle negotiated a deal with Conservative GLC leader Desmond Plummer to transfer London Transport (LT) from central government control to the GLC. The capital's Underground railway and buses thus became the responsibility of London's city-regional government for the first time. However, in 1984, Margaret Thatcher's Government renationalised LT, reversing the devolution of the late 1960s. The GLC was then abolished in 1986, with a number of further transfers of power from the London government to Whitehall, including city-wide planning, transport, major roads and the South Bank arts complex (Hebbert & Travers 1988: 24–55).

Paradoxically, the Thatcher Government's abolition of the GLC paved the way for the beginnings of devolution to London. The vacuum left by GLC abolition became the subject of much interest among Opposition politicians, think tanks and academics. Surely a city as large and important as London could not be left without proper city government? In 1994, the Major Government created a number of 'government regional offices', including a Government Office for London (GOL). As if to stress the importance of London, the civil servant appointed to head GOL was more senior than those in the other eight English regions. Doubtless this appointment also allowed the Government to keep a close eye on the ever-powerful capital.

Labour, in Opposition, developed policies for devolution to Scotland and Wales. The abolition of the GLC had, separately, created an impetus for the re-creation of London-wide government. By chance, Labour's devolution policy and the reform of London government met in the party's 1997 manifesto. Once in office, devolution was implemented for Scotland, Wales and Northern Ireland, while in London, city-wide government was restored.

Importantly, the creation of the new GLA (consisting of a directly elected mayor and assembly) involved devolving a number of powers which had been nationalised in 1986, plus some that had never been devolved before. Thus, strategic planning, fire and emergency services and economic development were to be mayoral responsibilities. London Transport was to be handed back to London, and new powers in relation to roads, taxi and minicab regulation, river services and even commuter rail were to be devolved. Most significantly, the Metropolitan Police, which had been the Home Secretary's responsibility since its creation in 1829, was to some extent to become a GLA responsibility. The mayor would set the police budget and have a role in appointing the commissioner (DETR 1998).

While the creation of the new London government could be seen as re-creating a county-type municipal entity, in reality it was very different. London was intended to be the vanguard of regional devolution within England: a parallel to the Scottish and Welsh reforms. Although the GLA was elected for the first time in 2000 (a year after the Scottish Parliament and Welsh Assembly) it shared with these new institutions a transfer of powers which had previously been the responsibility of central government. In addition, the fact the executive functions of the GLA were in the hands of a directly elected mayor meant the reform was radical in an entirely different way. For the first time, voters in part of the UK were to elect an American-style mayor, fusing executive and representative functions. The coming together of devolution of powers and this new form of office made the reform of London's government appear even more important than the simple creation of a new metropolitan government.

10.3 London and Constitutional Reform

London can be seen as a city, a city region or a region. It is part of a wider 'Greater South East' region (London plus the South East and the East), which, in terms of the balance between urban and rural areas resembles, say, the North West rather more than the built-up area of Greater London alone. London may be classified as a standard administrative region, but it is more correctly seen as a city region.

The reform of London government in 2000, as outlined, transferred responsibilities from central government departments to the new GLA. But this transfer would not alone make the reform 'constitutional'. A constitutional reform would imply a greater degree of permanence and also an institution that reflected a distinct London identity. The decision to hold a confirmatory referendum was a step towards permanence. Indeed, voters in all thirty-two boroughs and the City voted to introduce the GLA. London's identity had long been different to the rest of the UK (densely urban, cosmopolitan and rootless). The introduction of a mayor to represent the vast city (with a single voting district) could be seen as a step towards a unique London identity. At the time the Greater London Authority Bill was going through Parliament there was some discussion of the extent to which the London reform was indeed constitutional.

The Greater London Authority Act 1999 was one of the largest pieces of legislation in British history. It attempted to create an institution which was distinctly different from the GLC. Ministers, notably Nick Raynsford, wanted the mayor and assembly to be strategic and to operate with a small administration. As is true with more recent attempts to devolve power to Greater Manchester and other English cities, the Government in the late 1990s was uncertain about how far it wished to go in devolving power. Devolution in the UK (particularly England) has always to begin with a centralised decentralisation process:

> The creature spawned by this mammoth piece of legislation [the GLA Act] bears all the hallmarks of New Labour—and more generally, the deep markings of an era of extraordinary confusion between a desire to devolve and a desire to retain central control. (Travers 2004: 66)

Having said this, the GLA was different from traditional local government in a number of ways. First, innovative and more proportional voting systems were to be used for the first time in England, apart from in European Parliament elections. The

GOL commissioned research from academics which proposed adopting particular forms of election for the mayor and assembly (Dunleavy & Margetts 1998). Their proposals were adopted. The mayor was to be elected using a 'supplementary vote', where voters could vote twice on a single ballot paper, thus expressing first and second preferences. The assembly used the 'additional member' system which was also in operation for Scottish Parliament and Welsh Assembly elections, ensuring minor party representation in City Hall. While a change in voting systems did not of itself indicate a constitutional reform, it certainly made the new London government resemble the Scottish and Welsh reforms and thus implied a parallel with their devolutionary intent.

Secondly, the creation of the role of Mayor of London aggrandised the political leadership of the new London government. In a lecture to the Constitution Unit at University College London (UCL), the Lord Chancellor, Lord Irvine of Lairg, stated:

> We decided on the supplementary vote system: that is, in effect, a system of improved first past the post. We did this because the Mayor will be in a unique position. Never before has so large an electorate voted for a single individual ... The Mayor's authority will be enhanced by the fact that he will enjoy a broader base of support than might be achieved by first past the post alone. (Irvine 1998)

There is no evidence that the mayoral model was adopted in London as a political response to the city's particular identity and demographics. But the creation of a single jurisdiction with over 7 million residents has created pressure on those standing for mayor to reflect the complex identities and differences found in the capital. Identity has influenced mayoral policies and actions.

Thirdly, the London government arrangement would be unlike those elsewhere in the UK. Another member of the Government, Lord Whitty, speaking late in 1998, explained why:

> London is unique. It is neither regional nor local in the same sense as the rest of the country. The metropolis requires—and will get—special treatment ... The new greater London authority will be a new type of government, tailored specifically to London's needs. (HL Deb., 30 November 1998: cols 345–6)

So, the new London city-regional government arrangement was different from other forms of local government and operated at a 'subnational' scale. In the late 1990s, the city's population was just over 7 million, making it second only to the neighbouring South East in terms of regional population, albeit occupying just 8 per cent of the latter's land mass. As a city, its nearest UK rival was Birmingham, with a population of about 1 million. In the 2002 White Paper 'Your region, your choice', the Blair Government explicitly linked devolution to Scotland and Wales with the re-creation of London-wide government:

> [The Government] ... has given the people of the UK a greater say in the way they are governed and in the delivery of policies. We have devolved decision-making from UK Ministers and Whitehall to Scotland, Wales, and Northern Ireland—each with different arrangements to match its circumstances—and we have created a city-wide strategic authority for London. (DTLR 2002: 9)

Moreover, at the time the Government was enacting the GLA legislation, it was intended that London's government would be the first step towards wider elected regional government for England (discussed in Chapter 7 by John Denham). It was proposed that regions could opt for 'greater devolution of power' but only after the idea had been put to a referendum within the region.

Because the UK does not have a written constitution, it is impossible to state definitively that the London reform of 2000 was part of a wider move to a quasi-federal structure for the UK. The GLA, as a form of government, differs from those in Scotland, Wales and Northern Ireland. But the UK can probably be argued to be 'quasi-federal' in the sense that Scotland (at least) has a form of devolved law-making, government and tax-raising, which are, in effect, permanent, and were explicitly described as such in the Scotland Act 2016 (discussed by Akash Paun in Chapter 3).

Having considered this issue, Oonagh Gay, writing for the House of Commons Library, cautiously concluded:

> [M]ajor changes to the very structure or mix of the local government system, or its relationship with central government … may be regarded, to some degree at least as 'constitutional'.
>
> London (metropolitan) government can be regarded as distinct from the generality of English or British local government for a number of reasons. Its place as the historic seat of government is one example, as it the sheer size, in population and geographical terms. In a political context, the debate about London governance in the last decade or so has been about 'restoration' of an existing form of democratic government … rather than simply the creation of a totally new governmental tier, as with devolution or regionalism, or the restructuring of existing counties/districts. As such it can be portrayed as a constitutional issue by some. (Gay 1998)

London was not a nation like Scotland or Wales. Its new metropolitan government would not have legislative or many supervisory powers. The thirty-two London boroughs and the City of London were not subsidiary to the GLA in the way local government in Scotland, Wales and Northern Ireland would be to devolved governments there.

Yet the mayor and assembly were responsible for major services for a population and economy far larger than Scotland. The possibility that London was in the vanguard of a wider programme of regional devolution in England meant that, in 2000, it was possible to imagine that much or all of England would be governed by devolved assemblies by 2010. As it turned out, London alone within England benefited from any form of regional devolution. In this sense, the capital's post-2000 Government resembled Scotland, Wales and Northern Ireland more than any other part of England, at least until the city-regional mayoral elections of 2017. London's form of devolved government sits on the boundary between the entrenched, 'quasi-federal' systems in Scotland, Wales and Northern Ireland, and England's more traditional system of local government, which remains clearly subordinate to Westminster. The other city regions may, as their new governments evolve, join London on this boundary.

10.4 London Government, 2000–2018

There have been five GLA elections, with three mayors elected in the years since 2000. The Mayor of London has become established as one of the most visible elected officials in the UK. Ken Livingstone, Boris Johnson and Sadiq Khan, while mayor, have received consistent national media coverage and have been able to achieve prominence well beyond London. In June 2021, the GLA will have survived longer than the GLC, while city-regional mayors will be in operation not only in London, but also in (at least) Greater Manchester, Liverpool, Birmingham/West Midlands, Tees Valley, Bristol/West of England, Cambridge–Peterborough and Sheffield/South Yorkshire. Not only has the London model of city-regional government been accepted, but it has been adopted in a modified form in other parts of England.

The turnout at the first five GLA elections was in the 34–45 per cent range. It exceeded 45 per cent in 2008 and 2016. Welsh Assembly elections have seen similar levels of turnout at between 38 and 46 per cent, though Scottish Parliament elections have enjoyed higher figures.

The Mayor of London has responsibility for transport, strategic planning, policing, fire and emergencies and, increasingly, housing. Transport has by far the largest budget and is, with the Metropolitan Police, a visible and politically salient element of London's day-to-day governance. On several occasions, the power of the mayor's mandate has been seen to go well beyond the formal powers given to the office holder. For example, Sadiq Khan's leadership role following the 2016 EU referendum vote represented a direct alternative response to the UK Government's position on Brexit. The mayor has subsequently developed policy on the economy, migration and trade which go well beyond his formal powers. More generally, the mayor and assembly have become the accepted voice of the city and its people. There have been further transfers of power from central government to the GLA since 2000, including greater responsibilities for housing, health and finance.

Successive mayors have appointed senior staff and deputy mayors to create a 'Mayor's Office' of the kind found in larger American cities, notably New York and Chicago. Although Ken Livingstone, Boris Johnson and Sadiq Khan have approached the management of City Hall in different ways, the underlying need for a machine to enact the mayor's policies has been common to the three of them. Livingstone operated through a small team (located inside the mayor's office) of ideological, trusted subordinates. Johnson appointed a number of deputies who worked with significant independence, delivering on broadly stated policy. Khan has evolved a mixture of the previous two approaches, with a tight team in his private office and a number of deputies who operate as agents in the achievement of policy objectives.

Transport for London (TfL) and other agencies whose policies, budgets and boards are subject to direct or indirect mayoral control operate as separate units, with non-political chief officers. The mayor and assembly's bureaucracy is relatively small, as intended by the Government when the GLA was created. There are about 800 staff at City Hall, whereas the former GLC used to employ well over

10,000 at County Hall, home of the GLC until its abolition. But the scale of the Mayor of London's mandate has proved an important democratic ingredient in the development of the power of the office. Other factors have also contributed to the mayor's power:

> In London, a 'strong mayor' executive model was adopted, though without an effective 'legislative' branch to provide oversight. There are no term limits. The London Assembly has relatively few members and only a single opportunity each year to check the executive—it can overturn the Mayor's budget, providing it can pass an alternative one with a two-thirds majority. There is no requirement for the Assembly to vote on mayoral policy. It can scrutinize the Mayor's strategies, but it cannot veto them. Moreover, there is no power of recall over the Mayor. (Travers 2008: 15)

The scale of the mayor's mandate and the limited checks offered either by the assembly or other institutions has ensured the first three mayors have operated with significant autonomy to build up the importance of the role. Despite concerns about central government's willingness to let go of power, the mayors of London have been able to use their mandate and powers to go further than ministerial expectations of devolution.

Another factor that has helped to embed the GLA into the evolving UK political system has been its successful operation of public services. TfL, whose chief officer was given the new title 'commissioner' by Ken Livingstone, has managed the operation of the city's massive urban rail and bus systems, the introduction of congestion charging, the Oyster card, cashless payments, delivering a bike hire scheme, the creation of the Overground, a series of major station improvements and the construction of Crossrail. Compared with many parts of the national rail system, official statistics suggest TfL has been significantly more effective at service and infrastructure delivery than the national rail operating companies (ORR 2017). Arguments for extending TfL's reach to commuter railways immediately outside London have been made from time to time.

The governance of the police has changed since 2000, giving the mayor additional powers while changing the nature of the London Assembly's oversight. The Mayor's Office for Policing and Crime (MOPAC) was created in 2012 to replace the Metropolitan Police Authority and to provide the mayor with power to set the budget and oversee non-operational policing policy. The decision to create MOPAC was in part a response to the creation of elected police commissioners in the rest of England and Wales but it also recognised the need to make police accountability more comprehensible.

The London Fire and Emergency Planning Authority (LFEPA) was originally composed of members of London borough councils and the London Assembly, with all members formally appointed by the mayor. The mayor also set the fire authority's budget and appointed its chair. As with transport, the name of the chief officer was changed to 'commissioner'. Legislation in 2007 allowed the mayor to give policy directions to the fire authority. In 2016, the Government announced its decision to abolish LFEPA and make the mayor directly responsible for fire and rescue services. The Policing and Crime Act 2017 replaced LFEPA with a statutory

London Fire Commissioner and a Deputy Mayor for Fire, both of whom are to be appointed by the mayor (Sandford 2017). Thus, the mayor will have significantly strengthened powers over the fire and emergency services, analogous to those for transport and police.

The mayor has also been able to achieve authority using a number of planning-related powers. In particular the London Plan, which has statutory force, has allowed successive mayors to create a framework within which the city can develop. Matters such as the number of homes to be built within each borough, policy about tall buildings, transport infrastructure, the central activities zone, environmental standards and the protection of green space are all covered by the London Plan. Although Boris Johnson amended Ken Livingstone's plan, many of the underlying principles were similar. It appears that Sadiq Khan is likely to sustain the underlying expansionary and pro-business tone of his predecessors (Mayor of London 2016).

Beyond these formal service-delivery and budgeting activities, the office of the Mayor of London has allowed the GLA to push through change for the capital which central government was either unwilling or incapable of achieving without the intervention of the mayor. It is inconceivable that Whitehall could have introduced road pricing: it has proved incapable of doing so elsewhere in England. Neighbourhood policing would have been far less likely to survive without a mayor to champion it.

On a number of occasions, the Mayor of London has, in effect, forced ministers and Whitehall to concede to the will of London government, suggesting that London's scale and post-2000 institutional set-up has given it some autonomy in its relationship with the UK Government. The mayor has been able to act as a 'check and balance' in relation to Westminster and Whitehall. One of the earliest occasions when the mayor was able to force a policy change on central government was in relation to the London Underground public–private partnership (PPP), which had been put in place by Chancellor of the Exchequer Gordon Brown. The PPP meant private companies delivered upgrades to the Tube on long-term contracts. The mayor had been cut out of the process. Ken Livingstone and his Transport Commissioner Bob Kiley fought the PPP and, in the end, the policy collapsed. While its complexity and contradictions would have almost certainly destroyed it anyway, Livingstone's opposition was fatal and hastened the PPP's demise. Certainly, the UK Government was not powerful enough to save it after the Mayor of London's assault (Wolmar 2002: 185; 2009).

Even more striking was Boris Johnson's de facto removal of Sir Ian Blair as Metropolitan Police Commissioner. Although the Home Secretary had retained the right to appoint the commissioner, it became clear that Johnson had lost confidence in Blair. Blair resigned (Edwards 2008). No one could function effectively as leader of the Met without the Mayor of London's support. The mayor is now as almost as powerful as the Home Secretary in terms of this appointment.

A third, less contentious sphere of policy in which London-wide government has shown its power is housing. Section 31 of the Greater London Authority Act 1999 expressly ruled out any mayoral involvement in housing, education, social services and health. There was concern that dabbling in spheres where the boroughs were primarily responsible would risk a throwback to the difficult relationship between the GLC and the boroughs, notably over housing policy. But Ken Livingstone used the 2004 London Plan to set targets for boroughs to deliver housing. City Hall lobbied for more powers and in 2007 legislation required the mayor to prepare a housing strategy and also to have advisory powers in relation to housing resources. The Localism Act 2011 went further and empowered the mayor to undertake housing investment. As housing has become more politically salient, successive governments have proved willing to extend the GLA's powers to secure provision.

There have been other occasions where the mayor has been able to use the authority of office either to change or enhance government policy. The 2012 Olympics were won for London because of an effective alliance between central and London government, with Ken Livingstone's (and later Boris Johnson's) support and resources being crucial to winning and then delivering the Games. Since the EU referendum vote, Sadiq Khan has given London voice and visibility in relation to the UK Government's response to the Brexit negotiations. He also attended COBRA meetings after terrorist attacks in the capital (Mayor of London 2017). Apart from Scotland, Wales and Northern Ireland, other parts of the UK have not had their needs articulated in this way.

The mayor has also, as have the Scottish and Welsh governments, commissioned studies and reports intended to further the case for devolution. The London Finance Commission (LFC) was first appointed by Boris Johnson, reporting in 2013. Sadiq Khan reconvened the LFC, which reported again in 2017. The LFC has argued for additional tax devolution and, in the 2017 report, made the case for assigned income tax and VAT so as to facilitate the possibility of significant further devolution of services (LFC 2017). Other reports have considered, among other topics, the need for longer-term capital investment. Of course, the mayor cannot force the Government to deliver fiscal devolution or additional resources. But such initiatives do create a longer-term dynamic towards a continuing process of devolution. Strengthening identity or any sense of threat to London's economic position might increase a sense that London should seek more independence. If this were to happen, the UK Government would be under greater pressure, as has been the case in Scotland, to deliver radical change.

Policy commissions and research are important in that they are evidence of the capacity the GLA has to articulate policy needs and possible solutions. Although London Councils, the boroughs' representative body, also has the capacity to act on behalf of London as a whole, it generally acts as a collective voice for its thirty-three members rather than as a 'voice for London'. The mayor is almost always seen as such a voice.

The restoration of London's metropolitan government between 1997 and 2000 coincided with another change that has profoundly affected the city. Net international in-migration to the UK increased rapidly from 1997 onwards, with London absorbing a large share of the total. There have been pulses of migration to the capital from time to time since 1948. In 1995, the overseas-born population of London was about 1.6 million. By 2015, this number had risen to 3.2 million (Migration Observatory 2017). The 'non-white' proportion of the city's population also increased in this period. At the time of the 2011 Census, London's 'white British' population was down to 45 per cent, while in all the other nations and regions of the UK except the West Midlands (where the figure was 79 per cent), the share was over 85 per cent.

The first three mayors of London have presided over an evolving institution in a city that has changed rapidly in many ways. As the city has become more and more populated by those born overseas, it appears that the concept of 'Londoner' may have strengthened. New residents who are not instantly 'British' or 'English' can immediately be Londoners. Intriguingly, this permeable identity is likely to have been strengthened by immigration and, indeed, by the Brexit vote. This issue will be considered further in Section 10.6.

10.5 London: Alien and Separate, the Wrecker of Britain?

London has for centuries been seen as being 'removed' from the rest of both England and the UK. New York, Paris and other mega-cities are sometimes viewed in a similar way. Such places are seen by people elsewhere in their respective countries as anonymous, transient and parasitic. The rapid growth of the capital's population since the mid-1980s after almost fifty years of decline (up from 6.6 million in 1985 to 8.9 million in 2018) has emphasised the golden success of London compared to many less prosperous parts of the country. London is more heterogeneous than any other nation or region in Britain. While this diversity has been seen by successive mayors as an advantage, in many other parts of the UK it is viewed with suspicion, but it is worth noting that London is by far the largest city of UK-born people (over 5 million) in the country.

The EU referendum vote underlined this difference between so-called metropolitan values and those of almost everywhere else in England and Wales, though, in fairness, Manchester, Liverpool, Leeds, Newcastle, Bristol, Brighton, Leicester, Edinburgh, Glasgow, Cardiff and Belfast (among others) also voted 'Remain'. Perhaps London can now be seen part of a wider, 'urban elite' club of cities across the UK.

There is another problem. Because the government of England (and previously the whole of the UK) is hypercentralised and happens to be located in London, it is easy to conflate London as the seat of government with London the place. The use of the word 'London' as a shorthand for central government leads to significant blurring of separate concepts. Research undertaken by YouGov in 2014 for the Centre for Cities and Centre for London suggested:

> There is a clear feeling that our national politics and policymaking does not respond to local needs. A majority also believe that the location of Whitehall and Parliament within London leads to national decisions that are too focused on the needs of the capital, rather than other UK cities. (Centre for Cities 2014)

It is possible that the location of central government may privilege the city in which it has its home. That would be the case for anywhere government happened to be headquartered. The observation that central government does not respond to local needs, similarly, is not about London, but about the competence of ministers and civil servants. The fact that London and its region have been more economically successful than much of the rest of the UK in recent decades could easily be attributed by non-Londoners to the fact that central government operates from there. It would not, of course, explain why, for example, Bristol has a significantly higher level of economic output per head than most other English cities.

The presence of powerful components of the state in London has created another problem for the city and its people. Politicians and commentators have in recent years had to come to terms with the allegation there is a growing chasm between government and the governed. A number of clichés have been developed to describe the cause of the apparent gap. The concept of a 'Westminster bubble' has been joined by criticisms of a 'liberal metropolitan elite'. Both of these jibes imply criticism of London power. The values of the Islington dinner party have, so the argument goes, been imposed by politicians, government and the media on an unwilling population throughout the UK.

Anthony Sampson, as far back as 1962, had analysed what he called the Establishment in his book *The Anatomy of Britain*. Revisiting his theme in 2004, Sampson made the following helpful observation: 'The Establishment which caused such excitement and indignation 40 years ago was always a hazy concept. It often meant no more than "they"—the mysterious people who ruled our lives, or the scapegoats for anything that went wrong' (Sampson 2004). The 'liberal metropolitan elite' are probably similar.

Also, the sense that London is an alien, problematic and separate place is not new. Writing in the reign of Charles I, historian Peter Heylin claimed that London 'is grown at last too big for the Kingdom' and that 'Great Towns in the body of a State are like the Spleen or Melt in the body natural; the monstrous growth of which impoverisheth all the rest of the Members' (Porter 2000: 82).

Critics in Georgian England believed London tainted all it touched, 'sucking in the healthy from the countryside and … devouring far more than it bred'. 'The Capital is become an overgrown monster … which will in time leave the body and extremities without nourishment and support' complained one of Tobias Smollett's characters (Porter 2000: 195). London has long been seen as damaging to the rest of the country, with Josiah Tucker observing in 1783: 'London the Metropolis of Great Britain, has been complained of, for Ages past, as a kind of Monster, with a Head enormously large, and out of all proportion to its Body' (Joyce 2003: 25).

To many critics, London was a place of iniquity: 'the poisoned spring of fashion, the nursery of vice, crime, riot and all other deformities and enormities …' (Porter 2000: 196). By the 20th century, the planner Patrick Geddes was able to describe London's huge outward sprawl as 'perhaps likest to the spreading of a great coral reef' (Porter 2000: 372). More recently, some observers have criticised the difference between government investment in London and the rest of the country (IPPR North 2017).

In his book *The Road to Somewhere*, David Goodhart has a section entitled 'The London conceit'. He argues:

> It is a city that has partially outgrown its country and sometimes feels more attached to the rest of the world than to its national hinterland. The idea that 'city-states' like London are going to replace nation states does not bear close scrutiny but London is an empire-sized city attached to a medium-sized country that no longer has an empire.

And,

> It has, instead, become the apotheosis of the transactional, market society—a wonderful place to have a bolt-hole if you are a rich foreigner, a good place to live and work for a few years if you are an ambitious young incomer from provincial Britain or another country. (Goodhart 2017: 134–5)

Writing of the same issue in a more positive fashion immediately after the EU referendum vote, James Kirkup, a *Daily Telegraph* columnist, delivered a related observation, but with the implication that the city's separate identity put it in a category with devolved nations:

> It is now clear that we can no longer speak of London as being part of England. The UK capital may sit geographically in England, but its political outlook, like its economy, is so widely different as to justify a different constitutional status. This is now the United Kingdom of England, Scotland, Wales, Northern Ireland and London. (Kirkup 2016)

This possibility will be considered in Section 10.7.

10.6 London's Own Sense of Difference

Moralist critics and non-Londoners may wish to cast London as a problematic place, but its own leaders have developed a rather different picture. Successive mayors of London have purposefully promoted a globalised, international and diverse image of the city—very much the one criticised in Section 10.5. Immediately after the 2016 EU referendum, Sadiq Khan launched a #LondonisOpen campaign which carried the potential implication that 'The Rest of the UK is now closed'. The extent to which London is increasingly different from other parts of the country is perhaps suggestive of a possible willingness to be governed in a way that reflects greater separation from the rest of the UK.

Khan's *City for all Londoners* document includes sections that represent a direct rejoinder to those who oppose London's cosmopolitanism:

> London attracts and integrates people from all over the world. It is a magnet for talent and a melting pot of different faiths, ethnicities and nationalities. Its extraordinary

> diversity, entrepreneurial spirit and cosmopolitan culture sets it apart and means our capital is viewed across the globe as a beacon of progress, tolerance and acceptance. (Mayor of London 2016:5)

Whilst it is likely the leaderships of cities such as Manchester, Birmingham and Leeds would see their cities in a similar way, the London mayor definitely has a 'global metropolis' mindset.

London's powerful business sector has been a leader in driving forward the same optimistic, global and open view of the city. A 2014 report about the city's need for investment explained:

> London's success is of benefit to the UK at large. As a global business hub, London serves the country as the principal location for corporate headquarters. It is the UK's international gateway for talent, tourists and investment. Construction and infrastructure spend on London projects directly benefits many parts of the rest of the country. London also makes a significant net contribution to the UK's overall tax revenues: £34 billion in 2013/14 alone. (London First 2014: 2).

London First is here both attempting to convince the rest of the UK that London is good for them, while also pointing out that the capital exports tax to fund services beyond its boundaries. As with Sadiq Khan's quoted remarks, there is little doubt that London's leadership sees the city as separate from the rest of the country.

The residents of the capital also see themselves differently from others in England and Wales. A key element in this difference within the UK can be seen in the extent to which London's population identifies itself as 'British' and 'English' compared to those who live in other parts of England or Wales. The 2011 Census allowed people to choose their identity in relation to being British, English, Welsh, Scottish or Other. They could not, however, identify separately as a 'Londoner'. Nevertheless, Londoners were far more likely than any others in England and Wales to identify as British and were far less likely than those in other regions to see themselves as English. Seventy-five per cent or more of people in the North East, North West, Yorkshire and the Humber, and the East Midlands identified themselves as English, compared to little over 40 per cent in London. On the other hand, over 30 per cent of Londoners identified as British, well above any other part of the country (ONS 2012: figure 4).

Londoners also have different attitudes to migration, a key driver of pro-Brexit votes in the 2016 referendum. Research published in 2014 suggests that in Britain as a whole 51 per cent of the population had negative views about immigration, while only 28 per cent had positive ones. But in London the respective figures were 22 per cent and 54 per cent (Ford & Heath 2014: 5). London is strongly positive about immigration, though the 22 per cent who were negative is suggestive of concerns about the scale of change even in London. The issue of the impact of immigration on Londoners was explored in some detail in the book *This is London* by Ben Judah.

London's mayor, major businesses and, to some extent, its people see themselves as separate from the rest of their country. It would be important, of course, to recognise that a number of parts of the city inevitably feel strongly English and that most people outside London would probably not want to choose a replacement for London as England's capital. However, it would be important to note that London itself is plural. Five boroughs voted to leave the EU, even though there was a 60:40 'Remain' majority across the city as a whole. Parts of London have much in common with surrounding counties such as Essex, Kent and Surrey. Nevertheless, this outer borough difference is insufficient to overwhelm the broader London identity and attitudes.

10.7 London: A City State in the Making?

Sections 10.5 and 10.6 have outlined the extent to which London is seen as separate and different from the rest of the UK. The EU referendum vote significantly reinforced that perception. At the start of this chapter, the evolution of a London civic identity was described. From having little or no such identity, one has been forged since the invention of 'Greater London' in 1964–5. As observed, commentators such as William Robson wished to see this forging of identity, though there is no evidence the creation of a wider London identity was an official purpose of the 1965 reform. Notwithstanding the abolition of the GLC, this wider London has existed for over half a century: the post-2000 GLA adopted the same boundaries as the GLC. The office of Mayor has reinforced the sense of a place with a single political identity. The mayor is elected from an electorate of over 5 million voters across the 1,500 sq. km of the city.

Sadiq Khan's *City for all Londoners* document observed:

> This year [2016] the GLA marked its 16th anniversary. It is unthinkable now that, before the turn of the millennium, London had no elected city-wide representation. It is my strong view now that London needs more powers if it is to continue to prosper. (Mayor of London 2016)

The London Finance Commission proposed significant fiscal devolution to the capital (LFC 2017). A memorandum promising further devolution of powers over skills, health and criminal justice was signed at the time of the 2017 Budget between the mayor, the boroughs, the Chancellor and Sajid Javid, the Communities Secretary. While modest in scale, the direction of change was clear. With new mayors elected in other city regions in May 2017, it is inevitable that there will be wider political pressure for devolution within England.

London's 'Remain' vote in the EU referendum is clear democratic evidence that the capital has a separate demography and political outlook. In other countries, a city of almost 9 million people would almost always have far more devolved power than is currently the case for London within the UK. The need for different policies in relation to trade, migration and investment will be reinforced in the coming years.

Future devolution to Scotland, Wales and Northern Ireland and, indeed, other English cities, may depend on voters' responses to the capacity of the UK Government to handle the many challenges that face it from now to 2020 and beyond. If Westminster and Whitehall are seen to falter, or to fail to produce effective management of Brexit or taxation and spending, the question of the future integrity of the British state is likely move to centre stage.

The key issue now is whether the existence of a mayor and assembly for almost twenty years has, as in Scotland and Wales, created powerful home-grown demands for greater devolution of power. Successive mayors (and the boroughs) have lobbied for new responsibilities and a number have been given. There is little discernible 'Clapham omnibus' public pressure for reform. However, an issue such as Brexit could yet, if it produced serious adverse consequences, create circumstances where a popular demand for greater independence was generated. The contemporary weakness of national politics might make such a demand harder to resist than in the past.

London could easily handle significantly greater devolution. It has a city-wide and borough system of government which has proved effective for many years. It has an established civic identity. It is seen as separate and different by people inside and outside its boundaries. Similar cities overseas benefit from far greater devolved power. London surely will not become an independent city-state within the next few years, but it could take steps towards far greater autonomy. Tim Oliver has published a neat summary of the options for possible increased political separation of London from the rest of the UK, including greater autonomy for its existing government, the possible removal of the UK Parliament/Government from London and even London becoming an independent 'city state' (Oliver 2017).

Brexit, if it impacted badly on London, could generate resentment that might lead to calls for greater separation from the rest of the UK. Studies have produced different projections about the impact that quitting the EU might have on London's economy (Dhingra, Machin & Overman 2017; also Chen et al. 2017). Ironically, it is yet possible that anti-Brexit London might benefit from leaving the EU, at least relative to the rest of the country. The key determinant of any drive for increased separation or independence will be perceptions within the city of how fairly it is treated by the Government. If London voters feel they are being neglected or wrongly treated, 'London nationalism' could emerge.

England and the UK need London to succeed, for cultural and economic reasons. Devolution could allow for greater governmental difference without threatening the Union. Londoners themselves may in future feel they need to be more demanding about devolution and start a popular lobby for change. Given the 'anything can happen' nature of contemporary UK politics, London independence is less unthinkable than it would have been even five years ago.

References

Bogdanor, V. (1978), 'Devolution and the constitution', *Parliamentary Affairs*, 31(3): 252–67.

Centre for Cities (2014), *City Views: How Do Britain's Cities See London?* (London, Centre for Cities).

Chen, W., Los, B., McCann, P., Ortega-Argilés, R., Thissen, M. & van Oort, F. (2017), 'The continental divide? Economic exposure to Brexit in regions and countries on both sides of the Channel', *Regional Science*, Wiley, http://onlinelibrary.wiley.com/journal/10.1111/(ISSN)1435-5957/earlyview, accessed 8 January 2018.

Davis, J. (1988), *Reforming London: The London Government Problem 1855–1900* (Oxford, Oxford University Press).

DETR (Department for the Environment, Transport and the Regions) (1998), *A Mayor and Assembly for London*, Cm 3897 (London, HMSO).

Dhingra, S., Machin, S. & Overman, H. G. (2017), *The Local Economic Effects of Brexit*, CEP Brexit Analysis No. 10 (London, Centre for Economic Performance).

DTLR (Department for Transport, Local Government and the Regions) (2002), *Your Region Your Choice: Revitalising the English Regions*, Cm5511 (London, HMSO).

Dunleavy, P. & Margetts, H. (1998), *Report to the Government Office for London: Electing the London Mayor and the London Assembly* (London, LSE Public Policy Group).

Edwards, R. (2008), 'Met Police Chief Sir Ian Blair forced out by Mayor Boris Johnson', *Daily Telegraph*, 2 October.

Gay, O. (1998), 'The Greater London Authority Bill: Electoral and Constitutional Aspects Bill 7 of 1998–99', Commons Briefing papers RP98-118, 11 December, House of Commons Library.

Gomme, G. L. (1898), *London in the Reign of Victoria (1837–1897)* (London, Blackie & Son).

Goodhart, D. (2017), *The Road to Somewhere: The Populist Revolt and the Future of Politics* (London, Hurst Publishers).

Ford, R. & Heath, A. (2014), 'Immigration: a nation divided?', *British Social Attitudes 31*, NatCen, http://www.bsa.natcen.ac.uk/latest-report/british-social-attitudes-31/immigration/introduction.aspx, accessed 17 January 2018.

Hebbert, M. & Travers, T. (1988), *The London Government Handbook* (London, Cassell).

Herbert, E. (1960), *Royal Commission on Local Government in Greater London 1957–60 Report* (London, HMSO).

IPPR North (Institute for Public Policy Research North) (2017), 'New transport figures reveal London gets £1,500 per head more than the North—but North West Powerhouse "catching-up"', https://www.ippr.org/news-and-media/press-releases/new-transport-figures-reveal-london-gets-1-500-per-head-more-than-the-north-but-north-west-powerhouse-catching-up, accessed 13 October 2017.

Irvine, Lord (1998), 'Government's Programme of Constitutional Reform', speech at Constitution Unit, 8 December.

Joyce, S. (2003), *Capital Offenses: Geographies of Class and Crime in Victorian London* (Charlottesville, VA, University of Virginia Press).

Kirkup, J. (2016), 'David Cameron is finished: his failure over Europe will define his place in history', *Daily Telegraph*, 24 June.

LFC (London Finance Commission) (2017), *Devolution: A Capital Idea* (London, Greater London Authority).

London First (2014), *London's Infrastructure Investing for Growth* (London, London First).

Mayor of London (2016), *A City for all Londoners* (London, Greater London Authority).

Mayor of London (2017), 'London's global and European future: Mayor of London's response to the Government White Paper: the United Kingdom's exit from and new partnership with the European Union', Greater London Authority, https://www.london.gov.uk/sites/default/files/londons_global_and_european_future.pdf, accessed 31 May 2018.

Migration Observatory (2017), *Migrants in the UK: An Overview* (Oxford, Migration Observatory).

Oliver, T. (2017), 'We need to talk about the London Question', Constitution Unit blog, 10 May, https://constitution-unit.com/2017/05/10/we-need-to-talk-about-the-london-question/, accessed 1 June 2018.

ONS (Office for National Statistics) (2012), *Ethnicity and National Identity in England and Wales: 2011* (London, ONS).

ORR (Office of Rail and Road) (2017), 'Cancelled and significantly late by TOC—Table 3.7', *Passenger and Rail Freight Performance*, Office of Rail and Road, https://dataportal.orr.gov.uk/browsereports/3, accessed 19 March 2017.

Port, M. H. (1999), 'Government and the metropolitan image: ministers, parliament and the concept of a capital city, 1984–1915', in D. Arnold (ed.), *The Metropolis and its Image Constructing Identities for London c.1750–1950* (Oxford, Blackwell), 101–26.

Porter, R. (2000), *London: A Social History* (London, Penguin).

Robson, W. (1948), *The Government and Misgovernment of London* (London, George Allen & Unwin).

Sampson, A. (2004), 'The new elite', *The Observer*, 28 March.

Sandford, M. (2017), 'The Greater London Authority', Commons Briefing Paper SN05817, House of Commons Library.

Travers, T. (2004), *The Politics of London Governing an Ungovernable City* (Basingstoke, Palgrave).

Travers, T. (2008), 'Reforming London Government', in J. Morris & N. Evans (eds), *The Million Vote Mandate* (London, Policy Exchange/Localis), 14–21.

Wolmar, C. (2002), *Down the Tube: The Battle for London's Underground* (London, Aurum Press).

Wolmar, C. (2009), 'Tube PPP reaches the end of the line', *The Guardian*, 18 December.

11

England in a Changing Fiscal Union

IAIN McLEAN

11.1 Introduction

THE UNITED KINGDOM is a fiscal union, but a strange one by international standards. Tax is collected, for the most part, uniformly throughout the kingdom. The individual nations have had little autonomy on tax rates or the tax base (though this is changing, especially in Scotland). To finance locally determined expenditure, transfers of block grants are made to Scotland, Wales and Northern Ireland, but these follow neither efficiency nor equity principles. England is the default within this system. What the others get depends on what the UK decides to spend in its capacity as the Government of England. It is not clear whether this arrangement is good or bad for England from a (re)distributive point of view. There is no coherent regime for transfers within England.

Any reform proposal involves understanding fiscal federalism, that is, the principles of tax decentralisation (Musgrave 1959; Oates 1999). The first principle of fiscal federalism is that:

> [T]he provision of public services should be located at the lowest level of government encompassing, in a spatial sense, the relevant benefits and costs. (Oates 1999: 1122)

However, for two important public services, the lowest effective level of government is the national level:

> [T]he central government should have the basic responsibility for the macroeconomic stabilization function and for income redistribution in the form of assistance to the poor. In both cases, the basic argument stems from some fundamental constraints on lower level governments … An aggressive program for the support of low-income households, for example, is likely to induce an influx of the poor and encourage an exodus of those with higher income who must bear the tax burden. (Oates 1999: 1121)

Traditionally in the UK, local taxes, especially property rates, paid for local services such as street cleaning and policing. The picture was complicated by two things. First, policy-makers realised, long ago, that areas with the greatest need had the

Proceedings of the British Academy, **217**, 227–244, © The British Academy 2018.

least tax capacity. Secondly, the demand for devolution—'home rule' for Ireland in the 19th century and devolution to Scotland and Wales in the 20th.

The giant of early urban policy in the UK was Edwin Chadwick (1800–1890; cf. Finer 1952; Mandler 2008), the principal architect of the new Poor Law of 1834 and of sanitary reform in the 1840s. Chadwick was a ruthless centralist. Oates' 'assistance to the poor' is part of what is now classed in national accounts as 'social protection'. Traditionally, this was offered by churches, almshouse charities and local property taxes. But rich areas could make good provision and poor areas could not; yet poor people often lived in poor areas. Therefore, as Oates says, they tried to move to rich areas, where they were likely to be classed as 'sturdy beggars'. For instance, the Statute of Cambridge 1388 (12 Rich. II, ch. 7) prohibited any labourer from leaving the hundred, rape, wapentake, city or borough where he was living, without a testimonial, showing reasonable cause for his departure, issued under the authority of the Justices of the Peace.

The Poor Law Amendment Act 1834 (4 & 5 Will. IV, ch. 76), driven by Chadwick, nationalised and toughened the eligibility conditions for poor relief and made it available only in workhouses. It failed to nationalise the revenue side, however. Parishes were grouped into Poor Law Unions, but these units were too small to ensure effective tax redistribution from rich to poor areas—that can only come from a regime where social protection is financed out of general taxation and distributed on a basis of need. The UK moved towards such a system haltingly: in 1908 for state pensions, in 1911 for some sickness and unemployment insurance and from 1945 to 1951 to fund the Welfare State on roughly its present basis. Not all UK taxes are progressive (i.e. levied at a higher rate on rich taxpayers than on poor ones), but income tax and national insurance contributions are, albeit with strange dips in their combined progressivity. Hence social protection, which accounts for some 40 per cent of public expenditure, is both delivered and paid for at national level. Social protection is redistributive, both from rich to poor and from those currently working to the retired.

At this point, we need to introduce the non-identical twins AME and DEL. In the current jargon of the UK Treasury, the first denotes annually managed expenditure and the second departmental expenditure limits. AME mostly comprises benefit and occupational pension expenditure, which is not immediately under the control of government: people who are entitled to a benefit may claim it and those who are not, cannot. AME involves both stabilisation and redistribution. The biggest component is state pension payments, which redistribute from the young to the old. But another major component is sickness and unemployment benefit. Unemployment benefit in particular is an 'automatic stabiliser' in economic jargon. When unemployment goes up in a region, so do benefit payments, which cushion the blow. AME is an important component of a social union (see, e.g., McLean, Gallagher & Lodge 2014: ch. 5). In a social union, entitlement criteria should be identical throughout the Union (but benefit rates need not be, as the cost of living is different in different areas). Scottish nationalists do not believe in a social union of the UK. Full fiscal autonomy for Scotland would involve breaking the social union.

The Scotland Act 2016 transfers responsibility for some social protection spending to the Scottish Parliament, although not the benefits which act as automatic stabilisers. Nevertheless, to that extent it weakens the social union.

What, if anything, does a weakened social union imply for tax and spend in England? As Scotland becomes more autonomous, the regime for the rest of the UK becomes, even more than previously, the regime for England. This has limited policy implications for AME in England, because it depends on entitlements. It has more implications for discretionary expenditure. The part of public expenditure that governments can control in the short run is that which the Treasury labels as DEL. Successive budgets and spending reviews set this for each department, which decides how to allocate its budget around the country. DEL block grants to the Scottish, Welsh and Northern Irish governments are allocated by the Barnett formula, to be described in a moment. There is no government-wide distribution formula for England, but some departments have their own formulae. In health, this dates back to a Resource Allocation Working Party established by David Owen, then Minister of State for Health, in 1976. In local government, it is traditionally called 'rate support grant' and has a long history, but is currently changing rapidly. In education, the policy of recent governments to withdraw schools and colleges from local authority control has killed off any spatial or needs-based formula.

In the 19th century, poverty and destitution were far worse in Ireland than in Great Britain. The whole of Ireland was part of the UK from 1800 to 1921. The first movement for Irish autonomy died out, almost literally, after the Great Famine of 1845–8. It revived, at a party political level, in 1874. From 1880 to 1918 the devolutionist Irish Party, or its factions, controlled every parliamentary seat in Ireland except Dublin University and the Protestant north east. Liberal Prime Minister W. E. Gladstone's conversion to Irish Home Rule led to his party splitting up in 1886 and to twenty years of unionist (Conservative) hegemony. The unionists bitterly resisted political autonomy for Ireland, but knew that they needed to do *something*. They hit on a policy of 'killing Home Rule with kindness' (Gailey 1984: 52). They took local government from the landed classes and gave it to elected county councils, with powers over local social services and social protection, by an Act of 1898. On the revenue side, the Unionist Chancellor George Goschen introduced a formula in the 1888 Budget that came to bear his name. The 'Goschen proportion' assigned some tax receipts in the proportions 80:11:9 for England and Wales, Scotland and Ireland respectively.

However, Goschen failed to introduce fiscal federalism. The tax revenues he assigned were nowhere near the level required to pay for local services in Ireland. They never could have been, as Ireland was relatively poor. When, in a greatly changed world, Northern Ireland was created in 1921, it had the appearance of revenue-driven fiscal decentralisation. In a revenue-driven system, the subnational government raises the costs of local services from local taxation. At the margin, it decides whether to tax more (and hence spend more), or to spend less (and hence tax less). It cannot both spend more and tax less. But in fact, Northern Ireland has always had a wholly expenditure-driven system. For decades, its Government decided what to spend, assessed what it could raise and simply billed the UK for the substantial difference. The UK always paid up without cavilling (Mitchell 2006). Therefore, among other consequences, the Government of Northern Ireland had no incentive to make a serious tax effort over the tax it did control, namely property rates. Although the system has changed to make the Northern Ireland Assembly take the consequences of increases or decreases in its rate revenue, this fails to provide an incentive when there is no Northern Ireland Assembly, as has been the case for much of 2017.

Meanwhile in Scotland, politicians and civil servants always treated the Goschen proportion as a floor rather than a ceiling. They demanded that the Scottish budget for any public service must be at least 11/80ths of the budget for England and Wales. Where specific Scottish conditions such as cold weather or sparse population could be argued as justification for going above Goschen, it was in the interests of the Scots to argue for that. Usually, the UK Government conceded, for the sake of not causing trouble in Scotland (Levitt 2014; Mitchell 2003). This argument was not available to regional lobbies in either Wales or England.

For ninety years after Goschen, HM Treasury, as the monitor of public expenditure, chafed at its relative lack of control over spending in Northern Ireland and Scotland. (Wales was, as in most devolution matters, a lesser concern.) In 1978 a mandarin minuted:

> [T]he Scots and Welsh—and for that matter the Northern Irish—were indeed able to 'have it both ways' in the sense of automatically receiving extra according to the traditional formula [i.e. Goschen] whenever English Departments got more and further additions for special problems peculiar to their own countries. The Scots, over a long period of time (and the Northern Irish in the early 1970s), played this game skilfully and effectively; the Welsh much less so. The result was to build up public expenditure per head on Scottish Office (and NIO) programmes to something of the order of 25% more than England; and in Wales to something like 5% more … [W]e should at least stop the rot by preventing further increases in the differential. (P. Cousins, HMT, 25 September 1978, cited in Levitt 2014: 237)

The device to 'stop the rot' was the Barnett formula, named after (but not created by) Joel Barnett, who was Chief Secretary to the Treasury from 1974 to 1979. It aimed precisely to 'prevent further increases in the differential'. The functions of government are split into those which are devolved and those which are not. (The list of devolved functions is different for each territory—Scotland, Wales and Northern Ireland.) Most devolved functions come within DEL, not AME. Devolved functions are mostly financed out of block grants to each devolved government, which may choose how to spend it on its functions entirely as it wishes. The block grant in year t is the grant in year t-1 plus an increment, which is the territory's population share of the increment from year t-1 to year t being paid to UK departments to carry out in England the functions that are devolved elsewhere. Periodically, the Treasury publishes a list of government functions with their 'Barnett consequentials': that is, the proportion of that policy area that is devolved to each territory (HM Treasury 2015). This 'Statement of Funding Policy' also contains a worked example which may help the reader to understand how Barnett consequentials are calculated (HM Treasury 2015: Annex A).

The details may be mind-stretching, but for England it is important to understand a central paradox. The whole system centres on decisions taken by the UK Government about spending need in England. But it cannot be used to modify spending in England. Barnett was supposed to work by adding equal-per-head supplements to the 'over-generous' baseline for the three territories, so that in due course the baseline would become trivial and spend per head would tend to equality, whereupon the Treasury intended to introduce a needs-based substitute for Barnett (cf. HM Treasury 1979). That never happened. Barnett is still in place and it doesn't work. This is true, whatever meaning one attaches to the word 'work'. It doesn't work politically, because every politician who thinks she understands it believes that it does down her part of the country to the benefit of somewhere else. It doesn't work fiscally, because it is unrelated to relative need, nor does it encourage Scotland, Wales or Northern Ireland to improve their tax efforts. (It does encourage them to reduce spending, but that encouragement does not seem to have had any effect for the first forty years of Barnett.) As a convergence formula, it was always unfair to Wales, where expenditure per head was already below relative need in 1978, according to the Treasury's own estimate (HM Treasury 1979). If it *had* converged, that would have further worsened Wales' position. However, it has not achieved Cousins' stated purpose of preventing further increases in the differential, at least in relation to Scotland.

11.2 The Current Situation

The focus of this chapter is England, for which we need to look at the spatial distribution of income and government spending around the UK. In an ideal world, there would be official figures for:

1. regional income per head (gross domestic product (GDP) or gross value added—GVA);
2. regional tax receipts per head;
3. regional public expenditure per head.

Unfortunately, series (2) does not exist, except for Scotland where it is estimated annually in *Government Expenditure and Revenue Scotland* (*GERS*: see Scottish Government 2016). The *GERS* numbers are very revealing for how Scotland might need to balance its books under full fiscal autonomy or independence, because public expenditure in Scotland greatly exceeds tax revenue raised in Scotland. But they do not make up for the lack of English data.

Table 11.1 shows the latest official estimates of series (1) and (3). Comparisons between them can only be made cautiously, as they are collected by different government departments at different times of year and using different methodologies. But both series carry the badge 'National Statistics', which is the UK Statistics Authority (UKSA)'s warranty that the statistics have been collected impartially using the best available methodology to ensure their reliability and validity (UKSA 2009).

Table 11.1 Public Expenditure and GVA per Head, Regions of the UK, 2015

	Pub Exp./ Head 2014–15, £	Index	GVA/Head (Income Approach), 2015, £	Index	Pub Exp. as % of GVA	Chadwick Index
North East	9347	105	18927	74.7	49.38	78.44
North West	9197	103	21867	86.3	42.06	88.89
Yorkshire and the Humber	8660	97	20351	80.3	42.55	77.89
East Midlands	8159	92	20929	82.6	38.98	75.99
West Midlands	8683	97	20826	82.1	41.69	79.64
East	7881	88	23970	94.6	32.88	83.25
London	9840	110	43629	172.1	22.55	189.31
South East	7756	87	27847	109.8	27.85	95.53
South West	8295	93	23031	90.8	36.02	84.44
England	8638	97	26159	103.2	33.02	100.10
Scotland	10374	116	23685	93.4	43.80	108.34
Wales	9904	111	18002	71.0	55.02	78.81
Northern Ireland	11106	125	18584	73.3	59.76	91.63
UK	8913	100	25601	100	34.82	100

Source: Columns 1 & 2, HM Treasury, 'Public expenditure statistical analyses 2016', table 9.2. Columns 3 & 4, ONS: regional GVA (income approach), tables 2 and 3. Subsequent columns: author's calculations. All official data are National Statistics.

Both sets of official data report at the level of the three non-English parts of the UK and England's nine standard regions. The nine regions are no longer administrative entities, being now purely the top-level statistical reporting entities (NUTS 1 in Eurojargon). Income and public expenditure data become less reliable the smaller the subdivision for which they are reported. Nothing worthwhile can be said about expenditure or revenue below NUTS 1 level.

The first two columns of Table 11.1 report public expenditure per head for the benefit of each of the twelve regions. Expenditure on such items as defence and debt interest, which cannot be apportioned, is simply assigned to the regions on an equal-per-head basis. The source for these columns is HM Treasury's 'Public expenditure statistical analyses', which has reported the regional numbers for many years. A data-cleaning exercise led by the present author on behalf of the Treasury and (what subsequently became the) Department of Communities and Local Government (DCLG) (McLean 2003) improved the accuracy of the English regional numbers. The index column (column 2) shows that the regions where per-head expenditure is highest are, in descending order, Northern Ireland, Scotland, Wales and London.

The next two columns are from the Office for National Statistics (ONS)'s calculations of GVA per head. GVA is a version of what is more commonly called GDP. There are various ways of calculating it and these columns show the calculations based on income. GVA is harder to calculate at subnational level than is public expenditure and the figures should be regarded as fuzzier. The relativities between regions change slowly. London is far the richest region and the gap has widened since we last collated these figures (McLean & McMillan 2003: table 5). The index numbers in column 4 show the mountain that fiscal federalism for England, or the UK, must climb. Income is distributed so unequally that there must be some redistribution. But another way of looking at the index is: What would it take for (say) Wales or the North East of England to reach, or even approach, the astonishing relative productivity of London? This question has troubled many governments and lies behind the efforts of UK governments to promote northern cities as catalysts for growth.

The fifth column shows public expenditure as a proportion of GVA. As it is a ratio of two numbers, each of which contains some uncertainty, the ratio has to be handled with even more care. But it shows the opportunities and the challenge for fiscal federalism in the UK. If local governments in poor parts of the country could grow their local economy, perhaps by altering their tax base and rates, this would make a large contribution to UK growth. However, some support to poor areas will always, foreseeably, have to come from taxpayers in rich areas. So long as Northern Ireland has public expenditure per head approaching 60 per cent of its GVA per head, it is not a candidate for full-on fiscal federalism.

The final column has the tongue-in-cheek heading of 'Chadwick index'. It imagines an omnipotent policy-maker as ruthlessly centralist as Edwin Chadwick, but also ruthlessly egalitarian. This policy-maker would ensure that public expenditure was used only to relieve poverty and would go to regions in inverse proportion to their GVA. Therefore, the poorest region (Wales) would get the most expenditure per head and the richest region (London) would get the least. Expenditure per head would have an index that was just the reciprocal of the index GVA per head. Wales would get (100/71.0) of the average per head and London would get (100/172.1) of the average per head. The column labelled 'Chadwick index' compares the actual out-turn to this hypothetical standard of reciprocity.

My Chadwick index is more a rhetorical device than a serious contribution to tax reform. But it is designed to convey a serious point. Some parts of the country seem to do worryingly well out of public expenditure (notably London and Scotland); some seem to do worryingly badly (notably the North East, Yorkshire and the Midlands).

For what it is worth, the fact that the 'Chadwick index' for England is 100.10 suggests that England *as a whole* neither gains nor loses from being used as the base for Barnett and other territorial devices. The issue is regional (in)equity within England, which none of the current devices addresses.

Of course, not all public expenditure is to relieve poverty. Some is to promote growth (consider capital spending on infrastructure, or spending on higher education and research). It may make sense to concentrate that expenditure on places where it would promote that growth most quickly: which might happen to include transport in London and higher education and research in Oxfordshire. (Or it might not.) Much of DEL spending is to cure the sick, educate the young and so on. It costs roughly the same, per patient and per scholar, to do that in every region. But a partial explanation for the very high public expenditure per head in London is the high cost of land and development there.

11.3 Rival (and Possibly Incompatible) English Devolution Agendas

Options for the governance of England are discussed in other chapters. The subject has a long history. It is convenient, however, to start with the Local Government Act 1972 c.70. This created six metropolitan county councils for the main conurbations, namely, Tyne & Wear, West Yorkshire, South Yorkshire, Merseyside, Greater Manchester and the West Midlands. London already had a metropolitan council, the Greater London Council (GLC) created by the London Government Act 1963 c.63. The idea behind these Acts was that some functions, especially transport and planning, were best managed at the level of the conurbation, whereas others, including (most) education and social services, were best managed at the lower level of the metropolitan or London borough.

The system created by these Acts was abolished by Margaret Thatcher's Conservative Government in 1986, at a time when all seven top-tier authorities were controlled by the Labour Party and one of them was led by Ken Livingstone (then a Labour politician). Current moves to create 'Northern Powerhouses' and 'devolution deals' for city-regional combined authorities look from some perspectives like an attempt to recreate the metropolitan councils (Curtice et al. 2017).

But this begs the question: What is subnational government *for*? One answer is: to deliver services for which UK local government boundaries are too tight. Transport and land-use planning are examples. When Tyne & Wear Council came into existence, the former Newcastle and County Durham had both decided to build an urban motorway to replace the historic A1 through the centre of Gateshead and Newcastle. Unfortunately, Newcastle's part ended at the Tyne Bridge in the centre; Durham's at the Scotswood Bridge, three miles upstream (McLean 2016). As to planning for housing, cities with tight boundaries, which include both Oxford and Cambridge, find it impossible to meet housing demand within their boundaries. 'The ratio of median house prices to earnings is 13:1 in Cambridge and 12:1 in Oxford making them two of the least affordable cities in the UK' (NIC 2017: 8). Yet cities such as these are girded by green belts, which are popular with people who already have houses. They can both sit on a big capital gain and roam freely in the neighbouring fields. An efficient housing policy needs units bigger than these.

The larger a subnational government, the more effectively it can lobby. This may be a mixed blessing. But in the 1970s, it was Tyne & Wear Council that first drew national attention to the disparity between GDP per head and public spending per head between the northern English conurbations on one hand and Scotland on the other. The data pattern revealed in Table 11.1 was already there in 1976. For pointing this out, the council's leaders were labelled 'The No-men of England' (McLean 2016). Likewise, the (re)creation of a Mayor of London and London Assembly in 2000 has meant that there is once again an elected politician who can speak for London and its distinct interests and problems, as discussed in Chapter 10 by Tony Travers.

But regional lobbies have the obvious limitation that they may fight one another for shares of a cake of fixed size. In aggregate, that is wasteful. In a mature system, fiscal federalism must encompass tax powers as well as spending powers. The revival of interest in English devolution since 2010 has made some progress on the spending powers side but very little on the tax devolution side.

It began with a false start: the 2004 referendum in the North East of England to create an elected assembly. The Labour minister driving this agenda, John Prescott, believed that the North East was the region with the strongest sense of local identity (and grievance). He was wrong to believe that this would convert to support for an elected assembly. In a referendum, the proposal was defeated by 78 to 22 per cent. No further moves for political English devolution were made by the Labour Government, as John Denham discusses in Chapter 7, and on coming to power in 2010 the Coalition Government took a step in the opposite direction by abolishing the Regional Development Agencies (RDAs) and Government Offices for the eight English NUTS 1 regions outside London.

However, at the initiative of Chancellor George Osborne, MP for a North West constituency, policy switched. Osborne promoted the idea of a 'Northern Powerhouse', whose boundaries were initially vague. It was clear that it embraced at least the Manchester city region, but was later expanded to cover the territory of the three northern NUTS 1 regions (North East, North West and Yorkshire & Humberside) whose Government Offices and RDAs had only recently been abolished (HM Government 2017). Osborne's agenda was clearly focused on the economic growth potential of core cities in the region, identified as Manchester, Leeds, Sheffield and Newcastle; joined a little more uncertainly by Liverpool and Hull. Not Sunderland (which used to be slightly bigger than Newcastle and is now slightly smaller); not, surprisingly, Bradford (population 528,000), nor any of the other urban centres in the northern conurbation (Department for Transport 2015: 5). For a while, the junior minister for the Northern Powerhouse was Jim (Lord) O'Neill, a well-known investment banker interested in cities as growth points, but he resigned from Government in September 2016, reportedly out of frustration at the downgrading of Northern Powerhouse after the accession of Theresa May to the office of Prime Minister in July.

All recent governments have attempted to meet the objection that by creating larger elected authorities they were simply creating more politicians. Prescott's 2004 proposal required that the district councils in rural Durham and Northumberland be abolished. On its defeat, the districts were reprieved, but they have subsequently been abolished in favour of two unitary councils covering the whole counties. The Coalition and Conservative governments' efforts to create combined authorities insisted that the each new authority should have an elected mayor. Elected mayors were originally a separate idea, which Government thought, wrongly as it turned out, the people would embrace. Most towns and cities that held referendums on the question defeated the proposal for a mayor. Bristol and Liverpool were the only big cities to vote for one. These two cities, and Middlesbrough, which has had one since 2002, now each sits rather anomalously inside a metro region with its own metro mayor.

Policy-makers approached governance in England with both an efficiency agenda and a growth agenda. They overlapped but were not the same and their consequences have stymied one another. The efficiency agenda held that (at least for some functions) bigger was better and also that an executive mayor was the way to deliver services more efficiently and with more accountability. The growth agenda shared with the efficiency agenda an understanding that housing unaffordability impeded economic growth in otherwise successful cities. But its focus was on these successful cities. It was driven, ultimately, by an economic theory of aggregation. Specialised, rapid growth activities bloom when they are clustered together. Governments like to give examples such as motorsport in Oxfordshire; material science in Manchester; genomics in Cambridge and Newcastle.

Although the latter agenda was linked to George Osborne's Northern Powerhouse, it is not inherently northern. Many of the most vibrant English local economies are not in the North. Hence the 'devolution deals' promoted by the 2015–17 Government have been a very mixed bag. Greater Manchester is going ahead, so are, for instance, Greater Liverpool, the West Midlands, Cambridge–Peterborough and Tees Valley (DCLG 2015, 2017). Others have fallen by the wayside: for instance Norfolk and Suffolk and (at the time of writing) the Sheffield city region.

The mixed bag of successes share local council leaders who had an interest beyond turf-protecting NIMBYism (not in my back yard). This is not a point about party politics. The precursor of the 2017 Cambridge–Peterborough deal was a Greater Cambridge deal, based on then-Conservative South Cambridgeshire and anti-Tory (sometimes Labour, sometimes Liberal Democrat) Cambridge City. The leaders of both councils saw that the growth of Cambridge was inhibited by the tight city boundary, which made housing unaffordable and had no space for industry. A quirk of administrative geography may have helped: Cambridge is completely surrounded by South Cambridgeshire, the two forming a doughnut.

Oxford has identical problems and opportunities to Cambridge, but there the local authorities have been totally unable to agree a devolution deal in spite of the financial incentives it offered or the obvious gains from trade from allowing more housing and industry in the Oxford green belt, which mostly lies in neighbouring authorities. The administrative boundaries in Oxfordshire comprise a hub and spokes, not a Cambridge doughnut. The chosen vehicle for the growth and efficiency agendas (which in this case coincide) is therefore a report from the National

Infrastructure Commission (NIC) proposing new infrastructure for the Oxford–Cambridge corridor, which is drawn widely enough to include Milton Keynes and Northampton (NIC 2017). Elected bodies neither wrote nor seriously feature in this document.

11.4 The Missing Tax Dimension: Business Rates and Council Tax

The patchwork of devolution deals agreed up to the time of writing in 2017 does not amount to a policy for the governance of England. The economic geography of England includes conurbations (and within those, 'core cities'), non-core conurbation fringes, medium and small towns and rural areas. The administrative geography is less coherent than at any time since the creation of English county councils in 1888. There are unitary areas, where one local authority carries out all functions; two-tier areas, where two councils simultaneously run services; areas with devolution deals and combined authorities; areas without; a Northern Powerhouse apparently comprising the whole of three former standard regions; and areas administratively defined but with no elected body, such as the 'Oxford–Cambridge corridor'. Add in the various administrative geographies for health, policing and fire and it gets even messier. A more coherent administrative geography is clearly needed.

On the spending side, devolution deals come with offers of extra ability to spend capital on infrastructure, perhaps via more generous borrowing limits. For example, Tees Valley (a re-creation of the abolished county of Cleveland, plus Darlington) was offered 'Control of a new £15 million a year funding allocation over 30 years, to be included in the Tees Valley Investment Fund and invested to boost growth' (DCLG 2015: 3). The population of Tees Valley is about 700,000. This new funding allocation is therefore of the order of £20 per inhabitant per year. It might pay for some better bus stops.

The powers of local government to tax in England are extremely limited. According to the Organisation for Economic Co-operation and Development (OECD) Fiscal Decentralisation Database, the taxes controlled by subnational governments in the UK in 2011 amounted to 4.8 per cent of tax revenue (OECD 2017: table 1). In most federal countries that ratio is between 30 and 40 per cent, reaching 49 per cent in Canada. OECD's data predate the extension of tax powers under the Scotland Acts 2012 and 2016 and the expansion proposed for Wales. They describe a country where only one tax is under local control, namely council tax. The easiest extension towards fiscal federalism would be the relocalisation of business rates. Business rates raise about the same in aggregate as does council tax—some 4 to 5 per cent of tax receipts. They are the descendant of the oldest local tax of all, property rates, which were the sole tax base for local government before 1834.

Business rates date back to the Local Government Finance Act 1988 c.41. This Act introduced the poll tax ('community charge') and a national non-domestic rate ('business rates'). The former was soon repealed to be replaced by council tax; the latter remains. The business rates part of the 1988 Act did not provoke riots in the streets. But it marked a change almost as radical as the poll tax. While keeping the traditional legal structure of property rating, it nationalised it. A UK Government agency (the Valuation Office Agency, VOA) assesses the rateable value of each business premises (and the council-tax band of each house). It covers the whole of Great Britain, but not Northern Ireland. Local authorities collect the uniform business rate, but until 2012–13 the entire English proceeds were pooled and redistributed to authorities on a relative needs basis. This improved equity but at the expense of efficiency. Authorities had no incentive to collect the tax more efficiently. Much more important, they had no incentive to encourage development in their area.

The UK's planning regime dates back to the Town and County Planning Act 1947 (10 & 11 Geo. VI c.51). That made most development subject to planning permission, granted or refused by the local authority. It protected green belts. And it recognised that making planning permission scarce gave it a value, which it attempted to vest in the state. There was to be a tax on the difference between the value of land without planning permission and land with it.

The 1947 Act, and its Scottish counterpart, are the foundations of the regime in Great Britain today. Of its three main limbs, the first thrives. The second is under some threat: from greens on one side and from economists on the other. The latter point out that an unintended effect of green belts is to make land in cities even more scarce and expensive than it would otherwise be, leading to, for instance, the problems around Oxford and Cambridge identified by the NIC (2017). The third limb withered at birth. Hated by landowners, it had not been made effective by the time of the change of government from Labour to Conservative in 1951. Subsequent Labour governments have tried to introduce some form of betterment levy. They have always been knocked back by the succeeding Conservative Government. The remaining stump of this limb is what are now called Community Infrastructure Levies. In these, a developer promises to contribute to some local facilities such as roads or schools, in exchange for planning permission. These disguised taxes are indirect and very expensive to administer.

The planning regime is asymmetric. There are visible costs from granting a permission—physical costs in infrastructure and extra demands for services, but also political costs if the development is unpopular. Almost every development is unpopular with its immediate neighbours, who have votes. There are fewer visible benefits. There may be meagre and administratively expensive benefits from an infrastructure levy. But the main benefits are an improvement in the rateable value and/or council tax base of the authority and whatever future employment and/or income the development would bring if permitted. Under the 1988 regime for business rates, the revenue gain was immediately equalised away into the national pool. So authorities had a built-in incentive to lean towards refusing permission. There must be a better way.

Recognising this, the Coalition Government introduced a Business Rates Retention Scheme (BRRS) in 2013. Under BRRS, councils retain between 25 and

50 per cent of the increment in business rate income that comes from new developments (Amin-Smith & Phillips 2017: figure 4). That changes the incentive structure mentioned, though it is too early to see whether it will lead to big changes in behaviour. It will also increase the proportion of UK tax that is raised subnationally and raise the UK slightly from its low position in the OECD Fiscal Decentralisation Database.

That number was planned to increase further, when the Government announced plans to move to 100 per cent retention of increments in business rates by 2020 (Amin-Smith et al. 2016: 30). Both the 50 per cent and the 100 per cent move have to be accompanied by an array of damping mechanisms to prevent rapid shocks in any one area and by a regime of 'tariffs' and 'top-ups' among authorities. Authorities which would otherwise do very well from the change face a 'tariff', which is redistributed as a 'top-up' to authorities that would otherwise do poorly from the scheme. At the same time, Government would insulate planning authorities from the risk that occupiers successfully appeal their rateable value.

One slightly odd feature of all this is that business rates retention was offered as a carrot to areas contemplating devolution deals. Now this has been watered down to an offer to Liverpool and Greater Manchester to shift to the system three years early (Northern Powerhouse 2016: 19). If both the spending advantages (see the Tees Valley example earlier in this section) and the tax advantages of opting to be a powerhouse are trivial, one wonders why anybody would bother. The entire scheme now seems to be in some doubt.

The other support of local spending in England is council tax. This was introduced in a great hurry after the poll tax fiasco of 1989–91 (Butler, Adonis & Travers 1994). It is levied in eight bands lettered A to H (in Wales, in nine lettered A to I). The headline rate for each council is the amount payable on a house in Band D. The ratios of that number payable in Bands A to C and E upwards are fixed in legislation and councils cannot alter them. They are regressive. The rate for Band A is 2/3 of the Band D rate; the rate for Band H, which has no upper limit, is only double the Band D rate. The ratios are slightly less regressive in both Wales and Scotland.

Council tax is a highly visible tax, like income tax, not a relatively hidden one like VAT or National Insurance contributions. Its visibility leads politicians to make popular promises to freeze rates (Scotland) or to impose penalties on councils which increase the local rate by more than a centrally prescribed amount (England).

The end result is that council tax is one of the worst in the whole quiver of UK taxes (Mirrlees 2011: ch. 16). It is still based on 1991 valuations because no politician except in Wales has dared to revalue. Wales revalued in 2005, intending to revalue at five-yearly intervals, but the 2010 revaluation was cancelled by the UK Secretary of State for Communities and Local Government, Eric Pickles, who liked to boast of his 'muscular localism' (Game 2015). This action was at any rate muscular. Responsibility for a 2015 revaluation transferred to the Welsh Government, which has not decided to hold another valuation, but has created an expert working party on options for local finance (DCLG 2010; Welsh Government 2017).

The consequence of the long failure to revalue is that owners of properties whose relative value has declined since 1991 pay too much, those whose properties' relative value has increased since 1991 pay too little and properties built since 1991 are billed at a pretty arbitrary level.

This failure has a spatial aspect, which makes a bad design worse. Council tax is not only regressive between individuals (people living in expensive houses, who are almost all rich, pay a lower proportion of their income in council tax than people living in cheap houses, many of them poor). It is also regressive between rich and poor parts of the country, for the same reason as the one Chadwick failed to cure in 1834. Poor areas have a lower tax *base*, therefore they must charge a higher *rate* in the pound to their citizens than rich areas. Tax base and tax rate are complements. Traditionally, policy aimed to equalise for this via the funding formula for calculating grants. This system never worked well, and it broke down from about 2010 as the UK Government implemented much bigger cuts to local government spending in areas that were poor and grant-dependent.

11.5 Conclusion: A Possible Move towards Fiscal Federalism in England

So far, this chapter has shown that:

- The Barnett formula for distributing block grants to Scotland, Wales and Northern Ireland does not achieve the convergence that the Treasury planned; that full convergence is the wrong target in any case because Wales and Northern Ireland are relatively poor; and that it gives the governments of these territories no incentive to consider the balance between their taxing and their spending.
- As Barnett is neither efficient nor equitable, it cannot be the basis for formula funding within England.
- Some departments of central government have their own distributive formulae, but the pattern of public expenditure per head around the English regions remains very puzzling.
- By international standards, the proportion of tax controlled locally in the UK is very low.
- The two taxes under local control (council tax and business rates) are very badly designed.

Where might a reforming government go from there?

Adam Smith recognised that land and property are the best tax rate for subnational government. They don't move; so landowners cannot play off one authority against another. Nor can they hide the asset (unless they can hide its ownership in a tax haven, which is a serious policy issue, but out of scope for this chapter).

As Smith wrote in one of the most radical sections of the *Wealth of Nations*:

> Ground-rents are a still more proper subject of taxation than the rent of houses. A tax upon ground-rents would not raise the rents of houses. It would fall altogether upon the owner of the ground-rent, who acts always as a monopolist, and exacts the greatest rent which can be got for the use of his ground …
>
> Ground-rents and the ordinary rent of land are, therefore, perhaps, the species of revenue which can best bear to have a peculiar tax imposed upon them. Ground-rents seem, in this respect, a more proper subject of peculiar taxation than even the ordinary rent of land. (Smith 1776: V.2.74–6; for fuller discussion see McLean 2006: 69–76, 141)

So the basis for fiscal federalism in England is a reformed property tax. Scotland and Wales have taken some tentative steps. Northern Ireland has not. Wales has gone furthest, where the relevant minister has stated: 'I have already indicated my willingness to look at options such as land value tax as an alternative way of raising tax revenue in the longer term' (Welsh Government 2017; cf. also Commission on Local Tax Reform 2015). A land value tax that replaced both business rates and council tax would be proportional to the value of the land. Much of its value lies in its scarcity, which is in part conferred by planning permissions in the 1947 system. This scarcity value means that the income from urban land (excluding the structures on it) is that 'ground-rent' which Smith rightly saw as the most appropriate of all tax bases (Mirrlees 2011: ch. 16).

Whereas council tax is regressive, land value tax would be neutral, or, if a zero rate applied to low value land, progressive. It would correct the incentives facing local authorities far more than would a modest relocalisation of business rates which may not even happen. The authority will bear the revenue from granting a permission and the cost of refusing it. Because the tax would be neutral or progressive, for any given required yield most taxpayers would pay less than under the current regimes because more of the burden would fall on those best able to bear it.

Land value tax would help to solve the efficiency and growth problems of the current system. It would not of itself solve the equity problem. Land values are highest in the places where people most want to live and work: currently, overwhelmingly, in London, with boom cities including Oxford, Bristol and Cambridge not far behind. At least if London boroughs levied realistic land value taxes, the surprising lumping of English public expenditure on London (Table 11.1) could be mitigated, because formula funding for health and education could be adjusted to allow for London's more robust local tax base.

Nevertheless, an equalisation regime will be needed. It cannot be an extension of Barnett to England, for reasons explained in Section 11.2. Nor can it simply depend on the hidden and complex formulae used by central departments to allocate money around England, which produce the strange results shown in Table 11.1. In past work I have pointed to the Australian Commonwealth Grants Commission (CGC) as a model (e.g. McLean 2004, 2005). The CGC's trick is to combine egalitarianism with incentive compatibility. It equalises between the Australian states for their relative needs and relative tax bases. But if a state widens its tax base or increases its tax take, the proceeds are not immediately equalised away from it. UK schemes like the relocalisation of business rates are designed for the same end. But they could be much more radical. Perhaps the way to a robust fiscal union lies under the Southern Cross.

But is there any political demand for fiscal federalism? There is certainly disquiet throughout England, where voters in many parts of the country feel neglected. This has fuelled the rise of English nationalism and (perhaps) the demand for an English Parliament, described in other chapters. It may be that people, nevertheless, don't know even what fiscal federalism is, let alone that it could be a solution to present discontents. Time may tell.

References

Amin-Smith, N. & Phillips, D. (2017), 'The business rates revaluation, appeals and local revenue retention: IFS briefing note BN 193', Institute for Fiscal Studies, https://www.ifs.org.uk/uploads/publications/bns/BN193%20-%20Business%20Rates%20Revaluation.pdf, accessed 13 April 2017.

Amin-Smith, N., Phillips, D., Simpson, P., Eiser, D. & Trickey, M. (2016), 'A time of revolution? British local government finance in the 2010s', Institute for Fiscal Studies, https://www.ifs.org.uk/uploads/publications/comms/R121.pdf, accessed 13 April 2017.

Butler, D., Adonis, A. & Travers, T. (1994), *Failure in British Government: The Politics of the Poll Tax* (Oxford, Oxford University Press).

Commission on Local Tax Reform (2015), 'Just change: a new approach to local taxation', http://localtaxcommission.scot/download-our-final-report/, accessed 20 April 2017.

Curtice, J., McLean, I., Campbell, L., Paun, A., Rogers, M. & Thimont Jack, M. (2017), 'Governing England: devolution and mayors in England', British Academy, http://www.britac.ac.uk/sites/default/files/Devolution%20and%20mayors%20in%20England.pdf, accessed 31 July 2017.

DCLG (Department for Communities and Local Government) (2010), 'Standing up for local taxpayers: Welsh council tax revaluation cancelled', press release, 3 December, https://www.gov.uk/government/news/standing-up-for-local-taxpayers-welsh-council-tax-revaluation-cancelled, accessed 20 April 2017.

DCLG (Department for Communities and Local Government) (2015), 'Tees Valley Devolution Agreement', https://www.gov.uk/government/uploads/system/uploads/attachment_data/file/470127/Tees_Valley_Devo_Deal_FINAL_formatted_v3.pdf, accessed 13 April 2017.

DCLG (Department for Communities and Local Government) (2017), 'Cambridgeshire and Peterborough Devolution Deal', https://www.gov.uk/government/uploads/system/uploads/attachment_data/file/600239/Cambridgeshire_and_Peterborough_Devolution_Deal.pdf, accessed 13 April 2017.

Department for Transport (2015), 'The Northern Powerhouse: one agenda, one economy, one north', https://www.gov.uk/government/uploads/system/uploads/attachment_data/file/427339/the-northern-powerhouse-tagged.pdf, accessed 12 April 2017.

Finer, S. E. (1952), *The Life and Times of Sir Edwin Chadwick* (London, Methuen).

Gailey, A. (1984), 'Unionist rhetoric and Irish Local Government reform, 1895–9', *Irish Historical Studies*, 24: 52–68.

Game, C. (2015), 'Council tax support: Pickles' muscular localism in action', *Public Finance*, 10 April, http://www.publicfinance.co.uk/opinion/2015/04/council-tax-support-pickles%E2%80%99-muscular-localism-action, accessed 14 August 2017.

HM Government (2017), Northern Powerhouse website, http://northernpowerhouse.gov.uk/, accessed 12 April 2017.

HM Treasury (1979), *Needs Assessment Study* (London, HMT).

HM Treasury (2015), 'Statement of funding policy: funding the Scottish Parliament, National Assembly for Wales and Northern Ireland Assembly', https://www.gov.uk/government/uploads/system/uploads/attachment_data/file/479717/statement_of_funding_2015_print.pdf, accessed 6 April 2017.

Levitt, I. (2014), *Treasury Control and Public Expenditure in Scotland 1885–1979: Records of Social and Economic History: New Series 54* (Oxford, British Academy and Oxford University Press).

McLean, I. (ed.) (2003), *Identifying the Flow of Domestic and European Expenditure into the English Regions: Report of a Research Project to the Office of the Deputy Prime Minister* (Oxford and London, Nuffield College and Office of the Deputy Prime Minister).

McLean, I. (2004), 'Fiscal federalism in Australia', *Public Administration*, 82: 21–38.

McLean, I. (2005), *The Fiscal Crisis of the United Kingdom* (Basingstoke, Palgrave Macmillan).

McLean, I. (2006), *Adam Smith, Radical and Egalitarian: An Interpretation for the 21st Century* (Edinburgh, Edinburgh University Press).

McLean, I. (2016), 'The No-men of England: the Geordie revolt that defeated the Scotland and Wales Bill in 1977', *Political Quarterly*, 87: 601–8.

McLean, I. & McMillan, A. (2003), 'The distribution of public expenditure across the UK regions', *Fiscal Studies*, 24(1): 45–71.

McLean, I., Gallagher, J. & Lodge, G. (2014), *Scotland's Choices: The Referendum and What Happens Afterwards*, 2nd edn (Edinburgh, Edinburgh University Press).

Mandler, P. (2008), 'Chadwick, Sir Edwin (1800–1890)', in *Oxford Dictionary of National Biography* (Oxford, Oxford University Press), online edn, January 2008, http://www.oxforddnb.com/view/article/5013, accessed 20 April 2017.

Mirrlees, J. (chair) (2011), *Tax by Design: The Mirrlees Review* (Oxford, Oxford University Press).

Mitchell, J. (2003), *Governing Scotland: The Invention of Administrative Devolution* (Basingstoke, Macmillan).

Mitchell, J. (2006), 'Undignified and inefficient: financial relations between London and Stormont', *Contemporary British History*, 20: 57–73.

Musgrave, R. (1959), *The Theory of Public Finance* (New York, McGraw-Hill).

NIC (National Infrastructure Commission) (2017), 'Cambridge–Milton Keynes–Oxford Corridor: Interim Report', https://www.gov.uk/government/uploads/system/uploads/attachment_data/file/569867/Cambridge-Milton_Keynes-Oxford_interim_report.pdf, accessed 12 April 2017.

Northern Powerhouse (2016), 'Northern Powerhouse strategy', HM Treasury, https://www.gov.uk/government/uploads/system/uploads/attachment_data/file/571562/NPH_strategy_web.pdf, accessed 12 April 2017.

Oates, W. E. (1999), 'An essay on fiscal federalism', *Journal of Economic Literature*, 37: 1120–49.

OECD (Organisation for Economic Co-operation and Development) (2017), Fiscal Decentralisation Database, http://www.oecd.org/tax/federalism/fiscal-decentralisation-database.htm, accessed 20 June 2018.

Scottish Government (2016), *Government Expenditure and Revenue Scotland 2015–16* (Edinburgh, Scottish Government).

Smith, A. (1776), *An Inquiry into the Nature and Causes of the Wealth of Nations* (London, William Strahan), http://www.econlib.org/library/Smith/smWN21.html#B.V, accessed 20 April 2017.

UKSA (UK Statistics Authority) (2009), 'Code of practice for official statistics', https://www.statisticsauthority.gov.uk/wp-content/uploads/2012/11/images-codeofpractice-forofficialstatisticsjanuary2009_tcm97-25306.pdf, accessed 11 April 2017.

Welsh Government (2017), 'Written statement: reforming the finance system for local government', http://gov.wales/about/cabinet/cabinetstatements/2017/financelgreform/?lang=en, accessed 20 April 2017.

Part IV

English Identity and Attitudes

12

How Do People in England Want to Be Governed?

JOHN CURTICE

12.1 Introduction

THE ADVENT OF DEVOLUTION in Scotland and Wales in 1999 (together with the restoration of devolution in Northern Ireland the previous year) created a substantial asymmetry in the constitutional structure of the UK. Three of the country's territories now enjoyed some measure of 'home rule', whereby decisions about many aspects of their domestic affairs were made by elected political institutions whose remit was confined to that territory. But decisions about the domestic affairs of the fourth, and by far the largest, territory—England—were still taken by a UK-wide government and parliament.

That seemed like a potentially unstable position. At its simplest, it clearly created the potential for cries of 'unfair', a cry that perhaps was most vividly articulated by Tam Dalyell in posing the so-called West Lothian Question (Dalyell 1977). Why should Scottish MPs be able to vote on laws that (now) only apply to England when English MPs can no longer have a say in equivalent decisions for Scotland? Indeed, if the purpose of devolution was to enable Scotland and Wales to reflect in public policy the distinct values and culture of voters in their respective parts of the UK, and thereby make their governance more 'democratic', then presumably England could legitimately claim this privilege too?

Meanwhile, a little more subtle development might perhaps also be anticipated. Now that the nationhood of Scotland and Wales was recognised in the form of distinct political institutions, people in England might be expected to become more aware of the fact that, large though England is, it is not synonymous with Britain. As a result, they might become more aware of their English identity and—even more importantly—come to feel that perhaps England's distinct national identity should now be accorded similar recognition to that which has been afforded to Scotland and Wales.

There is a third thread to the debate about devolution. The case for devolution has also been made on functional grounds (Curtice & Seyd 2009). Devolved government, it is argued, means better government, especially so in a globalised world where the role of the state is increasingly focused on 'supply'-side measures such as the provision of a suitably skilled workforce and of an economically and environmentally supportive infrastructure. Effective decision-making on these subjects must, it is argued, reflect the particular needs and opportunities of each region rather than be a one-size-fits-all approach directed from a capital, London, that socially and economically can seem a world apart from the rest of the UK. And if devolution means better government for Scotland and Wales, then presumably this is something that the voters of England might seek to enjoy too?

However, at this point, we can identify an important difference between the debate about devolution in England and that in the rest of the UK. The three territories in the rest of the UK are relatively small and, as a result, the three different arguments in favour of devolution can all be made to point towards the same solution—the creation of distinct institutions for Scotland, Wales and Northern Ireland. However, this is not the position in England. If the aim of devolution is to reflect England's distinct sense of identity, then a case can be made for creating England-wide political institutions. But if the case for devolution is meant to be functional effectiveness, this would seem to point to some form of 'regional' devolution, albeit perhaps across a more limited range of responsibilities. After all, any England-wide institutions would still be serving as much as 85 per cent of the UK's population and would seem just as much at risk of being 'London dominated' as existing UK-wide political institutions. Meanwhile, it is not immediately obvious whether a more 'democratic' system of government demands a constitutional settlement that is identical across the whole of England or one that differs between the various 'regions' of England, assuming it can be agreed what those are.

As will be evident from many of the contributions to this book, thanks to this tension there have been many different schemes and proposals for 'devolution' for England. Some organisations, such as the United Kingdom Independence Party (UKIP), the English Democrats and the Campaign for an English Parliament (CEP), have argued for a devolved English Parliament with powers similar to those of the devolved Scottish Parliament and Welsh Assembly (discussed in Chapter 5 by Russell and Sheldon). The idea has, however, never attracted the support of either the Conservatives or Labour. The only move of any significance that has made been made so far to introduce an England-wide dimension to the elected governance of the UK has consisted of changes to the procedural provisions of the House of Commons. Since 2015 some stages of the consideration of laws that only affect England have been confined to MPs representing English constituencies (Gover & Kenny 2016; see also Chapter 6). This change in effect gives English MPs a veto over the passage of English-only legislation, but given that such legislation still also requires majority support from all MPs, it represents considerably less than the 'English votes for English laws' (EVEL) for which some have argued.

In contrast, both the Conservatives and Labour have at various stages pursued some form of 'devolution' to elected regional institutions in England. The last Labour Government anticipated introducing a system of elected regional assemblies throughout England, but this foundered when, in 2004, voters in the North East of England voted heavily against the Government's plans to introduce such an assembly (with relatively limited powers) in the region (Sandford 2009). Ironically, only Labour's plans for the capital, in the form of an elected mayor and assembly with responsibility above all for public transport in London, came to fruition, following an endorsement of the idea in an earlier referendum held in 2000. However, since 2010 Conservative-led governments have pursued the creation of 'city regions' in which the transport and infrastructure requirements of a city together with its immediate hinterland are taken over collectively by the relevant combined local authorities (Harrison 2012). Covering a substantially smaller area than Labour's regions, to date six such combined authorities have now been established—without seeking voters' approval in a referendum—with each one headed by a directly elected mayor (Sandford 2016).

Our aim in this chapter is to evaluate, using relevant survey data, how people's sense of national identity and their attitudes towards the various forms of devolution proposed for England have evolved in the light of these developments. We begin by assessing whether there is any evidence that the advent of devolution has stimulated the flowering of a sense of English (rather than British) national identity. Thereafter, we assess the incidence and character of the support for devolution for England, including examining how far the different regions of England vary in their attitudes. We then consider what link, if any, there is between people's sense of identity and their attitudes towards devolution and, in particular, whether there is any evidence that support for devolution has increasingly come to be a reflection of people's sense of identity. Finally, we consider the implications of our findings for the future governance of England.

12.2 National Identity

The advent of efforts at systematically and regularly measuring people's sense of national identity in England is a relatively recent development, beginning only shortly before the advent of devolution in Scotland and Wales. This means the body of evidence on the pattern of national identity in England prior to 1999 is relatively limited, making it difficult to come to any strong conclusions about the impact of Scottish and Welsh devolution on the pattern of identity in England. That said, we do have the luxury of more than one measure of identity for the period since then—and, more recently, of more than one survey source for those measures too.

We do, however, have one measure that was first obtained as long ago as 1992 and thereafter on three further occasions prior to 1999. Provided by the British Social Attitudes (BSA) survey, an annual high-quality survey conducted face to face with a random sample of respondents (Clery et al. 2017), the full set of readings is displayed in Table 12.1. The measure is obtained by presenting respondents with a list of all of the identities associated with one or more parts of the islands of Great Britain and Ireland and inviting them to pick which one or ones describe themselves. In the event that they choose more than one, they are then asked to state which one best describes themselves. This procedure provides us with a simple if unsubtle indication of the identity that matters most to people. If people's sense of English identity has come to matter more to them, it should show that the proportion choosing English has increased since the advent of devolution. To simplify matters we show in the table only the proportions choosing 'English' or 'British', as these are by far the two most common choices that respondents make.

Table 12.1 Forced Choice National Identity, England, 1992–2017

	1992	**1996**	**1997**	**1998**	**1999**	**2000**	**2001**	**2002**	**2003**	**2004**	**2005**	
	%	%	%	%	%	%	%	%	%	%	%	
English	31	34	33	37	44	41	43	37	38	38	40	
British	63	58	55	51	44	47	44	51	48	51	48	
Base	*2125*	*1019*	*3150*	*2695*	*2718*	*2887*	*2761*	*2897*	*3709*	*2684*	*3643*	
	2006	**2007**	**2008**	**2009**	**2010**	**2011**	**2012**	**2013**	**2014**	**2015**	**2016**	**2017**
English	47	39	41	41	34	42	43	41	41	38	37	34
British	39	47	45	46	52	43	43	47	47	47	46	48
Base	*3666*	*3517*	*3880*	*2917*	*2795*	*2859*	*2800*	*2799*	*2448*	*3773*	*2525*	*3445*

Note: Respondents living in England only. Those naming any other identity not shown.

Source: 1992: British Election Study (BSE); 1996–2017 BSA survey.

It would appear that there may have been some increase in the prevalence of English identity in the early years of devolution. In 1992, less than one in three (31 per cent) chose English as their main identity, while nearly two in three (63 per cent) said they were British. By 1999 the proportion claiming above all to be English had increased to over two in five (44 per cent) and now equalled the proportion who said they were British. However, if there was an immediate reaction to the advent of devolution elsewhere in the UK, there is no evidence of any continuing trend thereafter. Only on one occasion (2006) have over 44 per cent said they were, above all, English. The figure has, otherwise simply hovered at around the two-fifths mark, while, at 34 per cent, the most recent reading (in 2017) is, in fact, lower than at any point in the previous twenty years. As a result, it still seems to be the case that, when forced to choose, rather more people in England are still inclined to say that they are British rather than English.

Still, we might feel uneasy about relying solely on such a relatively unsubtle measure. A more nuanced portrayal is provided by the so-called 'Moreno' Question (Moreno 2006), which invites people to choose which of five possible combinations of feeling 'British' and feeling 'English', as detailed in Table 12.2, best

Table 12.2 Moreno National Identity in England (BSA), 1997–2017

	1997	1999	2000	2001	2003	2007	2008
	%	%	%	%	%	%	%
English, not British	7	17	18	17	17	19	16
More English than British	17	14	14	13	19	14	14
Equally English and British	45	37	34	42	31	31	41
More British than English	14	11	14	9	13	14	9
British, not English	9	4	12	11	10	12	9
Base	*3150*	*2718*	*1928*	*2761*	*1917*	*859*	*982*
	2009	**2012**	**2013**	**2014**	**2015**	**2016**	**2017**
English, not British	17	17	14	17	17	14	13
More English than British	16	12	12	13	10	11	10
Equally English and British	33	44	42	41	42	42	41
More British than English	10	8	8	8	8	8	10
British, not English	13	10	13	12	13	13	13
Base	*1940*	*2729*	*2799*	*2383*	*3778*	*2525*	*3478*

Note: Respondents living in England only. In 2012 and 2014 the question was not asked of those born in Scotland or Wales.

Source: BSA survey.

describes how they see themselves. Here, though, our time series only begins in 1997 and so gives us just two readings taken before 1999. In practice, the picture we obtain is much the same. There is some sign of an increase between 1997 and 1999 in the proportion who prioritise an English over a British identity—only 24 per cent did so in 1997, but two years later the figure had reached 31 per cent. But for the next decade or so the figure simply oscillated at around 33 per cent or so, while more recently it has typically been below 30 per cent. Indeed, at 23 per cent, the most recent reading is very similar to that in 1997. Meanwhile, the most common single response by far throughout the last twenty years has been 'equally British and English', with more recently at least two in five answering that way. This suggests that for many the two identities are still regarded as largely interchangeable, a pattern that is less apparent when the equivalent Moreno Question is asked in either Scotland (especially) or Wales (Curtice 2013).

More recently, national identity has also been asked on a regular basis by an important academic project known as the Future of England (FoE) survey (Jeffery et al. 2014), which aims to understand how England wishes to be governed and how those wishes have evolved over time. In each case the fieldwork for what has become an annual exercise has been conducted amongst members of the online panel of potential respondents maintained by the polling company, YouGov. Table 12.3 reports the readings of the Moreno Question obtained by this survey. It shows that, when compared with the readings that had been obtained up to that point

Table 12.3 Moreno National Identity in England (FoE), 2011–17

	2011	2012	2014	2015	2016	2017
	%	%	%	%	%	%
English, not British	17	15	11	12	12	10
More English than British	23	20	20	24	21	22
Equally English and British	34	39	41	37	37	33
More British than English	9	10	12	13	14	17
British, not English	7	7	6	6	6	7
Base	*1507*	*3600*	*3705*	*3451*	*5103*	*3168*

Source: FoE survey.

by the BSA survey (see Table 12.2), the initial survey, conducted in 2011, gave the impression that there had been an increase in the proportion who prioritised an English over a British sense of identity. As many as two in five did so, well above the proportion ever recorded by the BSA survey (Wyn Jones et al. 2012). However, subsequently, the relevant figure in the FoE survey has simply oscillated at around a third or so, and the survey does not give any reason to believe that there has been any increase in recent years in the proportion who feel wholly or mostly English rather than British. All that seems to be true is that the proportion in the FoE survey who prioritise a sense of English identity has always been somewhat higher than that obtained at the same point in time by the BSA survey. This is mostly likely a reflection of the very different way that the two exercises are conducted.[1] Meanwhile, this survey too consistently finds that the single most popular response is 'equally English and British'.[2]

It appears then that in the late 1990s there may well have been an increase in the proportion of people in England who prioritised a sense of English identity over a British one, though, in truth, we have too few survey readings of national identity in England prior to the advent of devolution in Scotland and Wales in 1999 for

[1] As noted in the main text, the BSA survey is conducted face to face on a randomly selected sample of the adult population, while the FoE survey is administered over the Internet to members of YouGov's panel of potential respondents. The former is more successful at securing the participation of those with less interest in politics (as, for example, measured by the proportion who say they did not vote at the last election) and is thus, perhaps, more likely to interview those with less firm and structured views about political issues.

[2] Five further readings of the Moreno Question have also been taken recently by YouGov for other clients—in November 2015, December 2016, October 2017, March 2018 and July 2018. At 33 per cent, 35 per cent, 35 per cent, 34 per cent and 36 per cent respectively, the proportions prioritising an English identity were very similar to the figures obtained by the FoE survey. Meanwhile, in most years this survey has also asked its respondents to choose a single identity, thus producing data analogous to those reported in Table 12.1. In the 2011 survey, 49 per cent said they were English and only 42 per cent that they were British, again an imbalance in favour of English that would not be anticipated from previous BSA surveys). But in subsequent years, the proportion choosing British has at least matched (and usually exceeded) the proportion choosing English. In the most recent (2017) survey, for example, 44 per cent opted for British and 41 per cent for English.

us to be entirely sure that this is indeed the case. However, there is no consistent evidence that since then more people in England have come to regard themselves as primarily English rather than British. True, one survey series suggests that the proportion who do so is a little higher than that stated by another, but neither series shows any trend over time towards more people doing so. Meanwhile, both report that the single most common response is 'equally English and British'. In so far as the existence of a distinctive sense of national identity might be regarded as likely to facilitate support for some form of self-government for England, it is not apparent that the environment is any more conducive towards English devolution now than it was in the late 1990s.

12.3 Does England Want Devolution?

At first glance, the answer to this question is a straightforward 'Yes'. For example, when in October 2014, shortly after the Scottish independence referendum, ComRes asked a sample of respondents in England, on behalf of the BBC, whether they supported or opposed 'giving more decision making powers on issues such as tax, education, policing powers to local areas', no less than 82 per cent said that they supported the idea, while only 15 per cent indicated they were opposed. Equally, albeit rather less dramatically, when Ipsos MORI asked in September 2015, 'Thinking overall, to what extent, if at all, do you support or oppose giving more decision-making powers (on issues such as economic development, transport, housing, planning and policing) to local areas?', 49 per cent said that they supported the idea while only 17 per cent said that they were opposed.

But, of course, the propositions put forward in these two polls are rather vague. They perhaps do little more than capture a sentiment in favour of local rather than centralised decision-making, while the questions are not ones that indicate that there might be any downside or alternative foregone. Even then, the Ipsos MORI poll suggests this sentiment is not a particularly strong one. Just 8 per cent said that they 'strongly' supported more local decision-making (while, equally, just 4 per cent were 'strongly opposed'). Meanwhile, as many as 35 per cent either said they neither supported nor opposed more local decision-making, or that they did not know whether or not they did. All in all, it seems that Ipsos MORI's proposition was met with something of a lukewarm reaction. Moreover, when the company repeated their question in another poll twelve months later, only 40 per cent supported more local decision-making, down 9 points, while 20 per cent were opposed. Support for the sentiment may not only not be strong but also not particularly stable.

The impression that support for devolution is relatively lukewarm was reinforced by the results of another poll conducted by ComRes for the Institute for Civil Engineers in February 2016, which focused a little more on the nuts and bolts of—and thus some of the functional claims made for—devolution. When the poll asked, 'Overall, do you think that devolution of powers from central government in Westminster to local areas is likely to have a positive or negative impact on local services?' only 38 per cent answered 'positive' and 17 per cent 'negative'. As many as 45 per cent either said 'neutral' or that they did not know. Meanwhile, when the poll invited people to indicate who should have the authority to make various decisions about transport and infrastructure, 'local areas' or 'central government', as Table 12.4 shows, the set of decisions thought to be best made by local government was relatively limited. Only the franchising of bus services was widely seen as the responsibility of local government. Even in the case of decisions that might be thought to have a particular impact on a local area, such as wind farms and fracking, opinion was more or less divided between those who felt the decision should be made locally and those who felt that it was a decision for central government.

Table 12.4 Attitudes towards Who Should Take Decisions about Infrastructure

Some people say that decisions on major projects should be devolved to local areas to make decision-making more efficient. Others say that decisions should be made by central government in Westminster to make sure that major projects are better coordinated across the country. For each of the following types of project, please indicate whether you think decisions should be made by central government or by local government.

	Local Government	**Central Government**
	%	%
Bus franchising	76	14
New renewable energy facilities (e.g. wind farms)	46	42
New fracking wells	41	41
New train lines/stations	35	55
New power stations	23	66
New motorways	19	71

Note: Base=1724.

Source: ComRes/Institute of Civil Engineers poll, February 2016.

Indeed, the potential limits to the public's appetite for devolution are also underlined by findings reported by the 2014 FoE survey when it asked its respondents whether the policy for a range of public services currently delivered primarily by local councils should be uniform across the whole of England or whether it should be a matter for each council to decide (see Table 12.5). Only in the case of refuse collection and planning was there a majority in favour of local autonomy. Perhaps the level of support for uniformity would have been lower if the alternative was specified as decisions being made by a regional government rather than a local council, but, even so, it appears that in practice there is limited enthusiasm in England for the kinds of policy variation that a strong devolution settlement would bring—and might well be thought necessary if the functional benefits claimed for devolution are to be realised.

Table 12.5 Attitudes towards Uniformity of Policy Areas

Below is a list of policies. Can you say whether you think each policy should be uniform across the whole of England, or whether it should be a matter for each local council to decide?

	Uniform	Up to Local Councils to Decide
	%	%
Refuse collection and recycling	39	54
Planning approvals	39	53
Housing	48	44
Public transport	50	43
Nurseries and child care	64	28
Social services	69	24
Primary school education	74	19
Secondary school education	76	17

Note: Base = 3705.

Source: FoE survey 2014.

What, though, do we find if a specific set of proposals for devolution is put to voters? In each of its the last four exercises, the FoE survey has asked its respondents whether they agreed or disagreed with a number of institutional 'changes to the how England is governed' (see Table 12.6). These ranged from simply giving England its own Secretary of State in the UK Cabinet, just as the other three parts of the UK have their own Cabinet minister, to the creation of a separate English Parliament, thereby perhaps giving England its own devolved institutions too. What emerges is a picture of minority support, but even less opposition, including in respect of the idea of 'city regions' that the UK Government has recently been pursuing (see Chapters 9 and 11). Moreover, there is no sign that support is growing over time—indeed, if anything, what seems to have become more common is the proportion saying 'don't know', a consequence, perhaps, of YouGov's attempt in the wake of the 2015 election to increase the number of people in its panel of potential respondents who are relatively uninterested in politics (Rivers & Wells 2016).

Against this backdrop, it would seem more sensible to assess attitudes towards devolution by looking instead at responses to questions that invite respondents to choose between different options, including, above all, the status quo. It would seem likely that such an approach will give us a better handle on whether voters do want to see a change in how England is governed. In Table 12.7, we show how respondents to BSA have replied when, during the course of the last two decades, they have been presented with three different options for running England—the status quo whereby its laws are made by the UK Parliament, regional assemblies with powers and responsibilities not dissimilar to those of the Welsh Assembly when it was first created and an English Parliament.

Table 12.6 Attitudes towards Specific Proposals for Creating New Institutions in England, 2014–17

	2014	2015	2016	2017
	%	%	%	%
A Secretary of State in the UK Cabinet*				
Strongly agree	22	17	13	11
Tend to agree	31	30	29	29
Neither agree nor disagree	23	24	25	23
Tend to disagree	7	9	9	9
Strongly disagree	4	5	6	6
Don't know	12	14	19	21
UK Government ministers for each of the regions of England				
Strongly agree	18	11	9	8
Tend to agree	33	33	32	33
Neither agree nor disagree	22	25	26	22
Tend to disagree	10	11	11	12
Strongly disagree	6	7	6	6
Don't know	11	12	15	18
An English Parliament				
Strongly agree	26	22	19	17
Tend to agree	28	27	27	25
Neither agree nor disagree	20	21	22	20
Tend to disagree	9	12	12	14
Strongly disagree	6	8	7	9
Don't know	10	10	13	18
City regions**				
Strongly agree	N/A	8	7	6
Tend to agree	N/A	27	27	29
Neither agree nor disagree	N/A	29	29	27
Tend to disagree	N/A	16	14	12
Strongly disagree	N/A	8	7	6
Don't know	N/A	13	16	20
Base	*3705*	*3451*	*5103*	*3168*

Note: * in 2017, 'A UK government minister for England'; ** full wording 'New regional authorities based around the major cities in England (sometimes called city-regions)'; N/A not asked.

Source: FoE survey.

Table 12.7 Attitudes towards How England Should Be Governed, 1999–2015

	1999	2000	2001	2002	2003	2004	2005	2006
	%	%	%	%	%	%	%	%
England governed as it is now, with laws made by the UK Parliament	62	54	57	56	50	53	54	54
Each region of England to have its own assembly that runs services like health*	15	18	23	20	26	21	20	18
England as a whole to have its own new parliament with law-making powers	18	19	16	17	18	21	18	21
Base	*2718*	*1928*	*2761*	*2897*	*3709*	*2684*	*1794*	*928*
	2007	**2008**	**2009**	**2010**	**2011**	**2012**	**2013**	**2015**
England governed as it is now, with laws made by the UK Parliament	57	51	49	53	56	56	56	50
Each region of England to have its own assembly that runs services like health*	14	15	15	13	12	15	15	23
England as a whole to have its own new parliament with law-making powers	17	26	29	23	25	22	19	20
Base	*859*	*982*	*980*	*913*	*967*	*939*	*925*	*1865*

Note: * In 2004–6 the second option read 'that makes decisions about the region's economy, planning and housing'. The 2003 survey carried both versions of this option and demonstrated that the difference of wording did not make a material difference to the pattern of response. The figures quoted for 2003 are those for the two versions combined. Results for respondents living in England only.

Source: BSA survey.

Three key points emerge. First, in most years, just over half—but equally only just over half—have backed the status quo, suggesting that there is far from widespread support for major institutional change in England, but equally that there is a substantial current of discontent with existing arrangements. Secondly, there is no consistent evidence of a decline (or increase) in support for the status quo, at least not since the very early years of the advent of devolution in the rest of the UK. The sight of devolution elsewhere in the UK seems not to have whetted English appetites for a similar arrangement. Thirdly, support for regional assemblies and an English Parliament have seemingly oscillated in response to the changing public policy agenda. Regional assemblies became relatively popular in the run-up to the referendum on creating a devolved assembly in the North East of England in 2004, but following the rejection of the Government's proposals in that referendum, thereafter it was the idea of an English Parliament that was the more popular. Now, however, it seems that regional assemblies may have become more popular again in the wake of the moves towards creating 'city regions' (albeit covering much smaller areas than the official government regions that the last Labour Government envisaged would each have their own assembly), though as yet there is little sign that Conservative supporters have been particularly persuaded of the merits of an idea that is now being pursued by their own Government (Curtice 2016). In any event, even though it might be the case that well over two-fifths of voters in England would like to see the introduction of some form of devolution, there is nothing like a consensus about what form it should take.

Still, as we might anticipate, even in the case of questions that invite people to choose between the status quo and various alternatives, the pattern of answers obtained does depend on how the issue is addressed. For example, in 2015 Opinium asked a question that began as follows:

> *At the moment in England there is no form of devolved government similar to the Scottish Parliament, Welsh Assembly or Northern Ireland Assembly. This means that for areas like health, decisions for England are made by the UK government while for Scotland they are made by the Scottish government. There have been many suggestions for how, if at all, this should change. Of the following please tell us which you would find acceptable.*
>
> *And which of the following would you most prefer to happen?*

The wording might be regarded as encouraging people to express support for devolution. Indeed, as Table 12.8 shows, only just over one in five said in response that the status quo would be 'acceptable', though nearly all of these also went on to say that this was their first preference. Rather, what emerged as the single most popular option was an English Parliament. Nevertheless, even here we can see once again that support for devolution is fragmented across a range of different options.

However, we have not so far addressed the one change to the governance of England that has been made, that is, the introduction of an extra parliamentary stage

Table 12.8 Attitudes towards How England Should Be Governed: An Alternative View

	Acceptable	First Preference
	%	%
English Parliament	31	28
Status quo	23	22
Regional assemblies	20	15
City regions	15	12
Other	3	3
Don't know	21	21

Note: Respondents living in England only. Base = 1800.

Source: Opinium Power and the People Poll, August 2015.

when only MPs representing English constituencies are able to vote, a provision that has come to be known as EVEL. This, of course, does not involve any devolution of power or responsibility from existing central government structures, but simply a change to the way in which English legislation is handled in the House of Commons.

This has long been a relatively popular notion. In Table 12.9, for example, we show how respondents to BSA living in England have reacted to the suggestion that Scottish MPs should not be able to vote at all on English laws, a stronger proposition than that actually enshrined in the new procedure. On almost every occasion at least three-fifths have agreed with the proposition, while little more than a handful have been opposed. Moreover, here there is some sign that attitudes have changed somewhat, in that the proportion who 'strongly agree' as opposed to 'agree' has increased from just under one in five in the years immediately after the advent of devolution, to, more recently, around three in ten.

Table 12.9 Attitudes towards Barring Scottish MPs from Voting on English Laws (BSA), 2000–15

Now that Scotland has its own parliament, Scottish MPs should no longer be allowed to vote in the House of Commons on laws that only affect England.

	2000	2001	2003	2007	2010	2012	2013	2015
	%	%	%	%	%	%	%	%
Agree strongly	18	19	22	25	31	29	30	30
Agree	45	38	38	36	35	36	34	33
Neither agree nor disagree	19	18	18	17	17	15	25	19
Disagree	8	12	10	9	6	7	7	9
Disagree strongly	1	2	1	1	1	1	1	2
Base	*1695*	*2341*	*1530*	*739*	*773*	*802*	*925*	*1865*

Note: In 2013 respondents were not offered the option of saying 'Can't choose', the figures for which are not shown. Results for respondents living in England only.

Source: BSA survey.

The relative popularity of EVEL has been affirmed by the FoE survey. As Table 12.10 shows, this survey has also asked its respondents how they feel about banning Scottish MPs from voting on English laws. As we might by now anticipate, FoE has typically reported rather higher levels of support for the proposition than BSA (and especially so in 2012), oscillating around something close to two-thirds. However, there is no evidence that support for the proposition has increased in the wake of the introduction of the new procedure in 2015.

More recently FoE has asked not about the negative proposition that Scottish MPs should not be able to vote on English laws, but about the positive principle behind EVEL, that is, that only English MPs should be able to vote for English laws (see Table 12.11). Presented in this way, around two-thirds have again typically agreed with the proposition, while only around one in eight express opposition. However, here too there is no sign that support has been increasing in the wake of EVEL's introduction—indeed, if anything, the opposite seems to have happened; only 30 per cent strongly agreed with the idea in the most recent FoE survey in 2017, as opposed to 40 per cent three years previously.

Table 12.10 Attitudes towards Barring Scottish MPs from Voting on English Laws (FoE), 2012–16

*Scottish MPs should be prevented from voting on laws that apply only to England.**

	2012	2014	2015	2016
	%	%	%	%
Strongly agree	55	35	43	37
Tend to agree	26	27	25	27
Neither agree nor disagree	8	15	12	13
Tend to disagree	4	9	7	7
Strongly disagree	2	3	4	3
Base	*1775*	*3705*	*3451*	*5103*

Note: In 2012 the statement read, 'Now that Scotland has its own parliament, Scottish MPs should no longer be allowed to vote in the House of Commons on laws that only affect England.' Responses to this statement were also gathered in 2011, but without giving respondents the option of saying 'Neither agree nor disagree' and consequently the results are not shown here.

Source: FoE survey.

Table 12.11 Attitudes towards Allowing Only English MPs to Vote on English Laws, 2014–17

Changing the rules in parliament, so that only English MPs can vote on laws that would apply only in England (sometimes called English votes for English laws).

	2014	2015	2016	2017
	%	%	%	%
Strongly agree	40	39	34	30
Tend to agree	29	26	29	32
Neither agree nor	14	13	14	14
Tend to disagree	5	7	7	6
Strongly disagree	3	5	4	4
Base	*3705*	*3451*	*5103*	*3168*

Source: FoE survey.

The popularity of EVEL is also evident in the pattern of responses that FoE has obtained when its respondents have been invited to choose between an English Parliament, regional assemblies and English laws being made by the UK Parliament, but in the case of the last of these including an option that only English MPs should be allowed to vote on English laws (see Table 12.12). Every time EVEL has proven to be the single most popular option, with around two-fifths in favour, while now only around one in five back the status quo. But, conversely, it would seem that for many people in England EVEL is the limit of their ambition for devolution—only between a fifth and a quarter choose either an English Parliament or regional assemblies.[3]

Table 12.12 Attitudes towards How England Should Be Governed (FoE), 2011–17

	2011	**2012**	**2014**	**2015**	**2016**	**2017**
	%	**%**	**%**	**%**	**%**	**%**
For England to be governed with laws made by English MPs in the UK Parliament	34	36	40	41	40	38
For England to be governed with laws made by all MPs in the UK Parliament	24	21	18	18	16	19
For England as a whole to have its own new English Parliament with law-making powers	20	20	16	12	16	14
For each region of England to have its own assembly	9	8	9	9	9	5
Base	*1507*	*1774*	*1204*	*1113*	*1739*	*1064*

Source: FoE survey.

But if EVEL appears to be the one reform for which there is widespread public support, support that on some measures at least may well now be rather firmer than when devolution was first introduced in the rest of the UK, we should bear in mind that the issue was not addressed by any survey conducted before 1999. We thus cannot be sure that support for EVEL has been occasioned by the advent of devolution elsewhere, or whether many people in England might always have felt that laws that only apply to England should only be voted on by MPs representing English constituencies. After all, the proposition might be thought to have an 'obvious' democratic logic to it irrespective of whatever arrangements are in place in the rest of the UK.

We have already suggested that there is relatively little enthusiasm for the idea of city regions, though perhaps we should bear in mind that, at present at least, these are only in place or envisaged for some parts of England rather than

[3] We should also note that the FoE survey has on three occasions asked respondents to choose between EVEL, an English Parliament, laws being made by all UK MPs and independence (either within or outside the EU); only between 12 per cent and 17 per cent have backed independence. Meanwhile, recent BSA surveys have found that only between a fifth and a quarter are in favour of independence for Scotland (Curtice & Montagu 2018). There thus seems to be relatively little appetite for ending the Union with the rest of the UK.

for the country as a whole and that this might serve to depress interest amongst voters living where the idea has not been put forward. In any event, one important feature of the Government's proposals for city regions is that they should be headed by a directly elected mayor, even though voters have often rejected the idea of such mayors when local referendums have been held proposing their introduction (Rallings & Thrasher 2014). It is argued that such mayors are essential to the success of such regions, both because they make for more efficient and effective decision-making and because they provide a strong voice that can articulate the interests of their region (Stoker & Wolman 1992). Indeed, previous research by BSA (see Table 12.13) has found that the public accepts some of these arguments. Thus, on three occasions when the issue has been addressed a clear majority have agreed that having a mayor means there is always someone who can speak up for the area, while more agree than disagree that having an elected mayor makes it easier to get things done. At the same time, however, more voters agree than disagree that having a directly elected mayor gives too much power to one person.

Table 12.13 Attitudes towards Directly Elected Mayors

How much do you agree or disagree that having an elected mayor means …

	1998	**2000**	**2011**
	%	%	%
… that there is always someone who can speak up for the whole area			
Agree	59	69	59
Neither agree nor disagree	22	15	22
Disagree	16	14	15
… makes it easier to get things done			
Agree	38	45	38
Neither agree nor disagree	33	26	37
Disagree	25	26	20
… gives too much power to one person			
Agree	44	45	35
Neither agree nor disagree	28	21	34
Disagree	25	32	27
Base	*1767*	*1928*	*1913*

Note: Respondents living in England only.

Source: BSA survey.

In any event, it seems that while voters may not be entirely unsympathetic to the idea of a directly elected mayor, they do not necessarily share the Government's view that they should be a precondition for the introduction of devolution. In the poll on devolution that it carried out in September 2015, Ipsos MORI asked their respondents whether they were more or less likely to support devolution if it came with a directly elected mayor. Only 19 per cent said that they were more likely to do so, almost matched by the 15 per cent who stated that they were less likely to do so. Meanwhile, although in the poll that ComRes conducted on behalf of the Institute of Civil Engineers, 32 per cent agreed that 'Devolution should only take place in an area if it introduces a directly elected Mayor', they were more than matched by the 35 per cent who disagreed. Directly elected mayors do not seem to be an essential part of any devolution project, at least as far as voters are concerned.

12.4 Regional Differences

However, this summary is based on the evidence about attitudes across England as a whole. But perhaps the picture is not the same everywhere. After all, one of the options for devolution in England is the introduction of regional assemblies or city regions and perhaps this idea is more popular in some regions than others. We might anticipate, for example, that those living further away from London are inclined to the view that the capital's interests predominate in the formulation of central government policy and thus for them some of the functionalist arguments in favour of regional government hold more sway in their minds. At the same time, perhaps those living in some regions are more likely than others to have a sense of regional pride or identity that they think should be reflected in how they are governed.

In truth, however, what is more notable about the geographical distribution of attitudes towards devolution in England is their similarity across the country. In Table 12.14, for example, we show the distribution of responses to the Ipsos MORI question on the principle of devolution that we introduced in Section 12.3. This particular poll had a very large overall sample size (3,831) and thus in most regions contains sufficient respondents to give us a reasonably reliable indication of the pattern of attitudes. There is some sign that support for local decision-making is a little higher in Yorkshire, the North West and the South West, all of which are regions where it might be thought that some voters feel that government from a relatively remote London was not necessarily the most effective way of governing their part of the country. However, in none of these regions is the level of support much more than 10 points higher than it is in London itself.

This pattern also predominates in survey research undertaken by Kenealy et al. in February 2015 (Kenealy et al. 2017). In order to ensure that their survey contained a reasonable sample size for every government region irrespective of the size of their population, Kenealy and his colleagues interviewed at least 400 people in every region. However, the survey uncovered very few differences between them. For example, when they asked their respondents whether they agreed with the proposition that 'Some political decision making for England should take place at a regional level rather than centrally in the UK Parliament. For this purpose elected regional assemblies should be created', the level of support only varied

Table 12.14 Regional Distribution of Attitudes in England towards the Principle of Devolution

Thinking overall, to what extent, if at all, do you support or oppose giving more decision-making powers (on issues such as economic development, transport, housing, planning and policing) to local areas?

Government Region		**Support**	**Neither Support nor Oppose**	**Oppose**	**Base**
North East	%	44	27	20	*188*
North West	%	54	25	16	*489*
Yorkshire and the Humber	%	57	22	14	*381*
West Midlands	%	46	29	15	*397*
East Midlands	%	48	30	14	*327*
East of England	%	42	32	18	*413*
South West	%	53	24	19	*426*
South East	%	46	27	18	*678*
Greater London	%	46	28	17	*532*

Source: Ipsos MORI Northern Powerhouse survey, September 2015.

between 50 per cent (in all but one of the six regions south of a line from the Humber to the Mersey) and 56 per cent (in Yorkshire). Much the same was true of the pattern of response to a similar question about city regions that read 'Large city regions in England should have more autonomy to take decisions on certain matters affecting their respective city region. To achieve this more powers should be given to councils in city regions.' Support only ranged between 49 per cent (in East Anglia) and 60 per cent (again in Yorkshire). At the same time, nowhere did the idea of regional assemblies prove particularly popular when pitted against the status quo, EVEL and an English Parliament—even in Yorkshire the proposal was chosen by no more than 29 per cent. Meanwhile, in their presentation of the findings of the 2014 FoE survey, Jeffery et al. report that, across a wide range of questions about the governance of England, the distribution of attitudes looks much the same in every region (Jeffery et al. 2014).

There is, then, perhaps a slight hint that support for some form of regional government may be a little higher in the North of England—but that is the most that can be said. As it happens, these are also the parts of England, London apart, where people are more likely to say that they are 'very proud' 'of being someone who lives in [their particular government region]'. According to the 2003 BSA survey (which administered the question to 3,709 people and thus contained a reasonable sample size in most regions) as many as 49 per cent said that they were very proud of living in the North East, while 39 per cent said the same in Yorkshire and Humberside and 34 per cent in the North East. Nowhere else, apart from the South West (27 per cent), was the figure more than around a fifth. Indeed, outside the North of England the most popular response was that respondents did not think of themselves in that way. However, even in the North of England it can hardly be said that a strong sense of regional pride is a widespread commodity. Moreover, as Curtice & Sandford (2004) show using the same BSA survey, even those with a strong sense of regional pride are only marginally more supportive than other voters of having a regional assembly; they do not necessarily expect such pride to be given institutional recognition.

12.5 Attitudes and Identity

What, though, of people's sense of national identity? We noted at the beginning of this chapter that one of the three sets of arguments in favour of devolution was rooted in identity and in particular recognising England's distinct sense of identity. If this, indeed, is a key motivation for the support that devolution enjoys in England, we should find that those who feel primarily English are more likely to support devolution than those who feel primarily British. Indeed, given that, as Ford and Sobolewska show in Chapter 8, those with a strong sense of English identity have a distinctive demographic profile and are particularly sceptical about the EU and concerned about immigration, we might think it quite likely that they have very different views about how England should be governed too.

Previous research has produced somewhat divergent interpretations as to whether or not attitudes to how England should be governed reflect people's sense of national identity. Writing after devolution in the rest of the UK was no more than a decade old and using data collected by the BSA survey as their evidence, Curtice & Heath (2009: 50) wrote that 'There is some link between national identity and support for an English parliament, but it can hardly be described as a strong one' and that, therefore, 'one could hardly conclude that such support for an English parliament as does exist is based on English nationalist sentiment.' However, somewhat later, after having undertaken their first two surveys (in 2011 and 2012), the authors of the FoE survey argued that 'strength of English identity is clearly associated both with dissatisfaction with the post-devolution settlement and with support for establishing distinct governing arrangements for England', and that their analysis indicated 'the English have begun to form a *political* community seeking some form of self-government' (Wyn Jones et al. 2013: 15).

The differences of outlook in the early FoE surveys between those who said they were primarily or wholly English and those who said they were mostly or wholly British, were certainly rather larger than those identified by Curtice & Heath. For example, the 2012 FoE survey found a 40-point difference between those who said they were 'English, not British', and those who claimed they were 'British, not English', in the proportion who strongly agreed that 'Scottish MPs should no longer be allowed to vote on English laws' (Wyn Jones et al. 2013: 15). Curtice & Heath, in contrast, reported only a 12-point difference in the 2007 BSA survey that they analysed (Curtice & Heath 2009: 55). At the same time, the 2011 FOE found a 22-point difference between the two groups in their level of support

Table 12.15 Attitudes towards How England Should Be Run by Moreno National Identity, 1999, 2007 and 2015

	English, Not British	More English than British	Equally English and British	More British than English	British, Not English
1999	%	%	%	%	%
England governed as it is now, with laws made by the UK Parliament	59	63	61	71	65
Each region of England to have its own assembly that runs services like health	14	16	17	13	14
England as a whole to have its own new parliament with law-making powers	23	19	18	11	17
Base	*491*	*389*	*999*	*298*	*354*
2007					
England governed as it is now, with laws made by the UK Parliament	54	52	61	66	64
Each region of England to have its own assembly that runs services like health*	11	17	15	12	19
England as a whole to have its own new parliament with law-making powers	28	23	14	20	9
Base	*165*	*129*	*267*	*116*	*102*
2015					
England governed as it is now, with laws made by the UK Parliament	46	49	54	48	50
Each region of England to have its own assembly that runs services like health*	26	20	21	26	23
England as a whole to have its own new parliament with law-making powers	24	25	17	20	21
Base	*329*	*194*	*780*	*154*	*222*

Note: Respondents living in England only.

Source: BSA survey.

for the status quo when respondents were presented with the question detailed in Table 12.10 (though subsequent analysis of the 2014 survey did not seem to replicate this result, see Jeffery et al. 2014: 19).

Given the divergence between the earlier BSA findings and that of the more recent FoE surveys, a key question is whether there is any evidence in more recent BSA surveys that those who feel wholly or primarily English have diverged from those who feel wholly or primarily British in their attitude towards devolution. After all, we have already seen that the FoE survey tends to record somewhat higher levels of support for devolution than BSA, so perhaps it is inclined to identify greater differences of outlook between British and English identifiers too. If so, then rather than evidence of an emerging English political community (at least so far as attitudes towards the governance of England are concerned), the more recent findings of the FoE may simply reflect the difference between how it and the BSA surveys are conducted.

Table 12.15 shows the analysis originally undertaken by Curtice & Heath, but with the addition of the most recent BSA reading, taken in 2015, of attitudes towards how England should be run. We can see that, if anything, the 2015 BSA survey found people's attitudes varied according to their sense of national identity, as measured by the Moreno Question, to an even lesser extent than they had done in either 1999 or 2007—though this change may reflect little more than sampling variation. But even if we leave that possibility to one side, what seems more remarkable is the similarity of outlook of those reporting different national identities. There is little evidence in this table to suggest that people's views about how England should be governed are heavily influenced by their sense of national identity.

There is, though, some difference in attitudes towards what we have seen is the most popular proposal for changing the way England is governed, that is, banning Scottish MPs from voting on English laws (and thus EVEL). As Table 12.16 shows, there is often as much as a 20-point difference between one of the pairs of identity categories in their level of support (that is, they either 'strongly agree' or 'agree') for this proposition—though it is not necessarily those who say they are 'English, not British' who are always the most supportive. So, there is some indication that on this subject at least, national identity makes some difference. However, there is not any evidence in the table that the difference has become bigger over time. Moreover, it would clearly be a mistake to suggest that support for EVEL is simply a reflection of an English nationalist sentiment. For even amongst those who say they are 'British, not English' between a half and three-fifths favour banning Scottish MPs from voting on English laws. Perhaps the proposition is simply seen by many voters as just 'obviously' a more 'democratic' arrangement.[4]

[4] We might note that there is also little evidence in the BSA surveys that dislike of the higher level of public spending enjoyed by Scotland is markedly more common amongst those who profess an English rather than a British identity. Amongst those in the 2015 BSA survey who, when asked to state a single identity, said that they were English, 38% felt that Scotland gets more than its fair share of public spending, little different from the 39% figure amongst those that chose British. This contrasts with the

Table 12.16 Percentage Agreeing that Scottish MPs Should Not Be Allowed to Vote on English Laws by Moreno National Identity, 2000–15

	English, Not British	More English than British	Equally English and British	More British than English	British, Not English
	%	%	%	%	%
2000	69	70	63	68	63
2003	73	64	59	57	53
2007	72	71	57	66	53
2013	68	79	62	67	60
2015	70	77	60	62	58
Bases					
2000	*316*	*236*	*571*	*239*	*200*
2003	*255*	*302*	*484*	*209*	*152*
2007	*141*	*112*	*240*	*108*	*80*
2013	*125*	*105*	*356*	*67*	*99*
2015	*279*	*169*	*675*	*123*	*184*

Note: Respondents living in England only.

Source: BSA survey.

12.6 Conclusion

There is one proposal for changing the way in which England is governed that is undoubtedly popular—EVEL. Its popularity, however, rests not so much on any growing English national sentiment as perhaps a perception that even those without a strong sense of English identity share, that EVEL is a more democratic arrangement. Still, in so far as some steps have been taken to introduce EVEL, the UK Government has shown some sensitivity towards public attitudes towards how England should be governed. However, the reform only represents a change in the way in which the existing UK governmental structure operates rather than the introduction of new institutions that take some decisions instead of the UK Government and Parliament. Consequently, we might even wonder whether it is fair to describe it as 'devolution' at all.

In any event, beyond EVEL, no particular proposal for devolution in England secures widespread public approval, including the idea of 'city regions' (with directly elected mayors) that is currently being pursued in a piecemeal fashion by the UK Government. Even the more peripheral regions of England are muted in

finding of the 2014 FoE survey which, in response to the same question, found that 45 per cent of those called themselves English said that Scotland received more than its fair share, while only 31 per cent of those who regard themselves as British did so. Once again, it appears that the difference in the methodology of the two surveys produces rather different findings.

their enthusiasm for regional devolution, not least perhaps because voters are not necessarily ready to embrace the functional arguments in favour of devolution. Equally, there is no clear evidence that support for devolution has grown during the course of the last twenty years, following its introduction in the rest of the UK, or of a growing English nationalist sentiment that, however distinctive its views may be about Europe and immigration (Curtice 2017), is demanding more devolution for England.

In short, although there is an apparent recognition of a democratic argument in favour of EVEL, neither the functionalist nor the 'nationalist' arguments in favour of English devolution have as yet at least taken firm root in the minds of voters in England. Perhaps if either the Conservatives or Labour were to show interest in the introduction of a more radical form of devolution than either has contemplated so far, this might change—yet it is also evident that there is relatively little public pressure on them to do so. As a result, although the current arrangements whereby England is governed via the UK Government structure rather than any institutions of its own are clearly not without their critics, the fragmentation of support for any of the alternatives and the apparently low level of public engagement in much of the devolution debate means that those arrangements may yet survive in more or less their current form for some considerable time to come.

References

Clery, E., Curtice, J. & Harding, R. (eds) (2017), *British Social Attitudes: The 34th Report* (London, NatCen Social Research), http://www.bsa.natcen.ac.uk/latest-report/british-social-attitudes-34/key-findings/context.aspx, accessed 19 January 2018.

Curtice, J. (2013), 'Future identities: changing identities in the UK—the next 10 years', Government Office for Science, https://www.gov.uk/government/uploads/system/uploads/attachment_data/file/275762/13-510-national-identity-and-constitutional-change.pdf, accessed 19 January 2018.

Curtice, J. (2016), 'Political behaviour and attitudes in the wake of an intense constitutional debate', in E. Clery, J. Curtice & M. Phillips (eds), *British Social Attitudes: The 33rd Report* (London, NatCen Social Research), http://www.bsa.natcen.ac.uk/latest-report/british-social-attitudes-33/politics.aspx, accessed 19 January 2018.

Curtice, J. (2017), 'Brexit: litmus test or lightning rod?', in E. Clery, J. Curtice & R. Harding (eds), *British Social Attitudes: The 34th Report*, NatCen Social Research, 157–80.

Curtice, J. & Heath, A. (2009), 'England awakes? Trends in national identity in England', in F. Bechhofer & D. McCrone (eds), *National Identity, Nationalism and Constitutional Change* (Basingstoke, Palgrave Macmillan), 41–63.

Curtice, J. & Montagu, I. (2018), 'Scotland: How Brexit has created a new divide in the nationalist movement', in D. Phillips, J. Curtice, M. Phillips and J. Perry (eds), *British Social Attitudes: The 35th Report* (London, NatCen Social Research), http://bsa.natcen.ac.uk/latest-report/british-social-attitudes-35/scotland.aspx, accessed 27 July 2018.

Curtice, J. & Sandford, M. (2004), 'Does England want devolution too?', in A. Park, J. Curtice, K. Thomson, C. Bromley & M. Phillips (eds), *British Social Attitudes: The 21st Report* (London, Sage), 201–19.

Curtice, J. & Seyd, B. (2009), 'Introduction', in J. Curtice & B. Seyd (eds), *Has Devolution Worked?* (Manchester, Manchester University Press), 1–16.

Dalyell, T. (1977), *Devolution: The End of Britain?* (London: Jonathan Cape).

Gover, D. & Kenny, M. (2016), *Finding the Good in EVEL: An Evaluation of 'English Votes for English Laws' in the House of Commons* (Edinburgh, Centre on Constitutional Change).

Harrison, J. (2012), 'Life after regions? The evolution of city-regionalism in England', *Regional Studies*, 46: 1243–59.

Jeffery, C., Wyn Jones, R., Henderson, A., Scully, R. & Lodge, G. (2014), 'Taking England seriously: the new English politics', Centre on Constitutional Change, https://www.centreonconstitutionalchange.ac.uk/sites/default/files/news/Taking%20England%20Seriously_The%20New%20English%20Politics.pdf, accessed 19 January 2018.

Kenealy, D., Eichhorn, J., Parry, R., Paterson, L. & Remond, A. (2017), *Publics, Elites and Constitutional Change in the UK* (London, Palgrave Macmillan).

Moreno, L. (2006), 'Scotland, Europeanization and the "Moreno Question"', *Scottish Affairs*, 54: 1–21.

Rallings, C. & Thrasher, M. (2014), 'Mayoral referendums and elections revisited', *British Politics*, 9: 2–28.

Rivers, D. & Wells, A. (2016), 'Polling error in the 2015 UK general election: an analysis of YouGov's pre and post-election polls', YouGov, https://d25d2506sfb94s.cloudfront.net/cumulus_uploads/document/x4ae830iac/YouGov%20%E2%80%93%20GE2015%20Post%20Mortem.pdf, accessed 19 January 2018.

Sandford, D. (ed.) (2009), *The Northern Veto* (Manchester, Manchester University Press).

Sandford, D. (2016), 'Devolution to local government in England', Briefing Paper 07029, House of Commons Library, http://researchbriefings.parliament.uk/ResearchBriefing/Summary/SN07029, accessed 19 January 2018.

Stoker, G. & Wolman, H. (1992), 'Drawing lessons from US experience: an elected mayor for Britain's local government', *Public Administration*, 70: 241–68.

Wyn Jones, R., Lodge, G., Henderson, A., & Wincott, D. (2012), *The Dog that Finally Barked: England as an Emerging Political Community* (London, Institute for Public Policy Research).

Wyn Jones, R., Lodge, G., Jeffery, C., Gottfried, G., Scully, R., Henderson, A. & Wincott, D. (2013), *England and its Two Unions: The Anatomy of a Nation and its Discontents* (London, Institute for Public Policy Research).

13

English Nationalism in Historical Perspective

MICHAEL KENNY

13.1 Introduction

One of the most striking aspects of the commentary generated by the referendum on the UK's membership of the European Union, held in June 2016, was a notable rise in interest in English nationalism. Presented by various commentators as a key dynamic behind the decision taken by a majority of the English to support Brexit (Jack 2016; O'Toole 2016), the provenance, character and implications of this national lineage have become questions of wide interest. Different explanations for its perceived emergence have been advanced and the connection routinely made with a rising tide of ethnic-majority nationalism across the Western world, culminating in the election to the US presidency of Donald Trump (*The Economist* 2016).

Such characterisations tend to overlook significant variations in the history and contexts of these currents. In the UK various substate nationalisms have long been a feature of the political landscape (most notably in Scotland), but the majority of UK citizens still identify to varying degrees with Britishness, the patriotism associated with the state, core institutions and laws. This undoubtedly complicates the question of whether English nationalism should be seen as a species of ethnic-majority nationalism. Equally, the comparative angle does not tell us much about why it is that nationalism in the English context aligns with scepticism towards EU membership but does not do so—to the same extent—in most other European countries. What exactly is it about the notion of Englishness that renders the conceptions of sovereignty and statehood it advances antithetical to the very idea of membership of the EU (Wellings 2012)?

Indeed, one of the most notable features of current debates over 'English nationalism' is an abiding confidence about the nature of the phenomenon which this term describes. But this assumption is in key respects misplaced as there are good reasons for seeing this as elusive and fluctuating, rather than transparent or settled, in character. This is partly because Englishness is framed in a variety of different political colours and also experienced and practised in a greater variety of ways (Aughey 2007; Kenny 2014). And it is also because its existence and character remain the subject of vigorous disagreement in scholarly circles and public commentary. There is still therefore a real need for a more dispassionate and informed understanding of this re-emerging form of national consciousness.

While much commentary relies upon survey data to promote an understanding of English attitudes (for instance Jeffery et al. 2014), I present the case here for a stronger sense of history as crucial to generating a deeper understanding of this form of national consciousness. In order to understand whether a particular form of collective identity has come to acquire greater weight and carry new meanings, a historical perspective that enables us to assess change or continuity over time is important (Mandler 2006). In the English case, there is particular merit in considering whether the current emphasis upon the novelty and disruptive character of Anglo-nationalism is appropriate, or whether this is better understood as a more continuous, or periodically recurrent, phenomenon. In this chapter, therefore, I seek to place some of our contemporary preoccupations in a historical light and juxtapose them with some of the main accounts of the provenance and character of political Englishness. I aim also to shed light on whether the arguments of those who seek to compare the English case with other nationalisms are sound and illustrate the prevalence within leading expressions of Englishness of exceptionalist ideas about the nation's historical development. I suggest, in conclusion, that unduly confident assumptions about what the English want should be replaced with an appreciation of how fractured and contested the interpretation of English nationalism has always been—and remains.

13.2 Interpreting English Nationalism: Challenges of Evidence and Interpretation

There are various reasons why the label 'English nationalist' tends to attract opprobrium rather than curiosity in liberal circles. Perhaps the most important is its lingering association with Enoch Powell, the last major political figure to identify himself wholeheartedly with this cause. English nationalism was the normative underpinning for the highly controversial stances he took, from the late 1960s, on immigration from the Commonwealth and the UK's attempts to join the Common Market (McLean 2001). Powellite thinking has left a considerable imprint upon subsequent assumptions about English nationalism (Nairn 1977). His commitment to the monocultural character of the nation, and his willingness to employ vernacular racism, as well as classical allusion, to make his rhetorical points, has done much to give the term a toxic political reputation. And its subsequent association with figures and groups on the far right cemented this reputation. A distinctly English form of nationalism informed Margaret Thatcher's political conception of nationhood (Lynch 1999). But whether current manifestations of Englishness fit into these patterns and whether contemporary claims about a putative English political community are, as Powell asserted, incompatible with a multicultural society, are questions that merit deeper investigation than they have typically received.

Enquiry in this area also requires more careful attention to questions of conceptual terminology. Is 'nationalism' an appropriate term to employ in this case, when there is considerable evidence of a growing sense of cultural expression and exploration and uncertainty about the political implications and constitutional forms associated with manifestations of English national sentiment (Kenny 2014: 21–3; see also Chapter 8 by Ford & Sobolewska)? Might it instead make more sense to talk of a reversion to an older sense of nationhood, rather than the sudden eruption of nationalism? At the same time, nationalism as a generic concept is interpreted variously by its historians and theorists. While some stress the integral importance of struggle and the projection of political ambitions (and for this reason doubt that nationalism has been born in England (English 2012)), other scholars emphasise the importance of culturally rooted forms of substate nationalist mobilisation, a model which has on occasions been employed in relation to Englishness (Hutchinson 1999). And now, in the last few years, a number of commentators, drawing upon polling data, maintain that new connections between a rooted sense of English identity and a set of distinctive political aspirations and beliefs have been established, and that a discernible pattern of thinking about sovereignty, national self-determination and self-government is apparent among many of those who define themselves as English, rather than British (for instance Henderson et al. 2017; Wyn Jones et al. 2012).

However, in both conceptual and empirical terms debate about this phenomenon is in its infancy. And some important questions need to be answered by those committed to the notion that a fully-fledged English nationalism has come into being. These include such issues as: How do new assertions of Englishness fit with long-established patterns of identification with Britain and Britishness? Has the habit of seeing the two as interchangeable fallen away entirely in the wider culture? And how much variation is there within the depiction of the English nation—between classes, ethnic groups and different regions? Analytically too there are still important issues to be pursued, such as whether 'nationalism' is being invoked in too encompassing a manner in this case and if various other members of the terminological family to which it belongs—national identity or nationhood for instance—might be more appropriate terms to employ in relation, for instance, to the growth of cultural expressions or the variety of ways in which Englishness is lived and manifested in daily life.

While a focus upon English nationalism has become familiar since the Brexit vote, in the years leading up to it the majority of politicians and many commentators were reluctant to believe that Englishness was becoming more salient or politically resonant (for instance Ormston 2012; see also Henderson et al. 2017). Most held to the premise that the English remained temperamentally indifferent to questions of institutional structure and constitutional order and inclined to see nationalism as an alien, exotic and decidedly unEnglish ideology. Repeated, pejorative references to the 'Leave' position as that espoused by 'little Englanders' from the 'Remain' camp during the campaign leading up to the referendum held on 23 June 2016 reflected the enduring power of this assumption (Cowell 2016). This is one reason why so many politicians and commentators were blindsided by the appeal of the idea of Brexit as an expression of national aspiration (Peck 2016). The rhetoric of the Leave campaign, including the ubiquitous claim that Brexit would enable citizens to 'take back control' and 'take their country back', appeared better tailored to this sensibility. And while the vote registered clear majorities for Remain in Scotland, Northern Ireland and London, the higher turnout among voters in all of the other regions testifies to the sense of righteous commitment which voting for Brexit came to acquire for many English voters. For many it appears to have represented an overdue opportunity to protest against the policies and priorities of the governing elites and to signal major concerns about the erosion of national sovereignty (Tombs 2016).

But what exactly, in institutional and constitutional terms, does this mean? Does 'taking back control' signal the reassertion of the familiar narrative of English constitutionalism—involving a reassertion of parliamentary sovereignty and the unitary state? Or might it now signal a more bounded and delineated conception of an English polity, operating in a more autonomous fashion from 'other' national communities within a remodelled UK? Writer Neal Ascherson (2016) is one of the few observers since the referendum to appreciate the nature of English ambiguity on this score:

> The slogan in the referendum was 'Take Back Control'. But of what and from whom? The establishment Leavers said: 'Take back the sovereignty of Parliament, the Ark of the English Covenant. England isn't England if Parliament can be overruled by anyone—least of all by foreigners.' But the mass of more plebeian Leavers asked something different: why should they obey laws they didn't want, made somewhere else by politicians they didn't elect? … It was the imagined rights of the nation they wanted to take back, not of Westminster.

Different social constituencies may have different ideas in mind when they assert the rights of the English nation. And this thought could be taken further still. Are there geographic differences which also shape different hopes and dreams in relation to 'England'? And, more concretely, does a growing divergence in national outlook between London and 'provincial' England represent a more fundamental political–territorial cleavage than that associated with other, familiar distinctions in English culture—including the fabled north–south divide (see Chapter 10)? Ascherson also poses the important question: What is the authority from which sovereignty is to be wrested in the English nation's pursuit of self-determination? In the context of the EU referendum, the dominant power against which it was mobilised was apparent. Yet, polling over the past decade or more suggests that the notion that English nationalism has been ignited primarily by the European Question is misleading. For the UK's membership of the EU appears to have diminished, not risen, in salience for many people in England over the last twenty years, even as it has become an issue of growing concern at elite level (Clements, Lynch & Whitaker 2013). Euroscepticism in general is certainly not a distinguishing characteristic of the English, as high levels of scepticism have also developed in Wales and, to a lesser extent, in Northern Ireland and Scotland (Curtice 2016). So, while it is certainly likely that feelings of national identity informed support for Brexit in a distinctive way in England (Clarke, Goodwin & Whiteley 2017), it remains open to question whether concerns over membership of the EU were a primary motivation for this shift in national mood.

Another reason for seeing the roots and implications of English nationalism as more uncertain than much commentary assumes is the notable absence of public debate about nationhood and constitution in relation to England and the dearth of focus on these issues among the UK's political parties. Comparison with the constitutional literacy and awareness of other national groups within the UK is instructive here. At the same time, the embryonic nature of popular discourse on these issues should not necessarily be conflated with indifference to questions touching upon the collective interest and identity of the English people and how these are affected by policy decisions and political processes. The importance of the latter was illustrated during the 2015 election campaign, when the Conservatives' focus upon the spectre of a Scottish National Party (SNP) coalition with Labour enabled it to lead the agenda and set the tone for the remainder of the campaign. As the largest people within a state that has long defined itself with reference to a patriotism focused upon the state and its institutions, the English have been encouraged to intermingle their own sense of nationhood with a patriotic allegiance to Britain and its traditions. The question now is whether they are still content to see things this way. This question lies at the heart of one of the most politically influential, historical interpretations of English nationalism—that offered by Tom Nairn, to which I now turn.

13.3 After Britain

One of the key sources for the conflation of English nationalism with the politics of Enoch Powell lies in the work of Tom Nairn, the leading Scottish theoretician of nationalism. His thinking has become widely influential in progressive circles since the late 1970s. It is discussed here as an illustration of two distinct tendencies in contemporary views of English nationalism: the belief that this is an inherently regressive form of ethnocultural nationalism, on the one hand, and the notion that it encodes a democratic demand for self-government on the other. Nairn's thinking, rather unusually, encompassed both of these positions, which makes it of particular interest.

In his *Break-Up of Britain* (1977), and various subsequent analyses, Nairn stressed the obfuscatory mystique fostered by the core institutions of the British state among the English. He argued that the state-sponsored patriotism which encompassed the distinct nationalities and territories of the UK had served to obscure the ossified nature of the class relationships over which the state presided in Britain and the arcane character of the institutions at its heart. But this settlement now faced a deepening structural dislocation, precipitated by the nationalist currents that were emerging in its peripheries. This gathering crisis could only be resolved in a moment of disruption 'at the level of the state, allowing the emergence of sharper antagonisms and a will to reform the old order root and branch' (Nairn 1977: 45). It was also increasingly clear, he suggested, that the underperforming British economy was being held back by the absence of a modern state system. Nairn was adamant that the portfolio of reforms circulating within the world of high politics—including ideas for devolution and greater autonomy for the English regions—amounted to 'ways of preserving the old state—minor alternations to conserve the antique essence of English hegemony' (1977: 51)—rather than representing meaningful attempts to grapple with the underlying situation.

He devoted considerable space in *Break-Up* to the nationalism of Enoch Powell. Powellism constituted a kind of 'comment on the absence of a normal nationalist sentiment, rather than an expression of nationalism' (1977: 78). Although it deployed the rhetoric and syntax of nationalist sentiment, this body of ideas represented something different altogether—a further, morbid symptom of the continuing power of the *ancien régime* state to divert and suppress the national will of the English. In a judgement that has been endlessly echoed by progressives when confronted with claims on behalf of an English *patria*, Nairn concluded that Powell's nationalism represented a kind of regressive fantasy, a 'conservative dream-world founded on an insular vein of English romanticism'. This, he declared, amounted to a 'Disney-like English world where the Saxon ploughs his fields and the sun sets to strains by Vaughan Williams' (1977: 261).

Nairn concluded in the late 1970s that the English need to rediscover who and what they are and to reinvent an identity of a more positive kind. Only when they forged a new national myth could their democratic energies and collective will be realised. This was a nation, he concluded in a later work, in the most curious of positions: having tended to take their hegemony over the archipelago they dominated for granted, and having not had to fight for their own nationhood, they had consented to a political system which provided precious little space for their own self-assertion (Nairn 2000). The tragedy of the English was that, having been at the centre of some of the key developments that had made the modern world, they had not been forced to think about who they were, as had other 'peripheral' peoples. Questions of identity never became political in this context as they did elsewhere. The precocity of English state formation meant that in England 'an unbeatable combination of factors turned "nationalism" into something theoretically alien' (Nairn 1993: 182). In a fateful, and influential, analysis he intimated that the national sensibilities of the English demanded critique from progressives. And it was only when this most conservative and hidebound of peoples could be shocked from their complacency and taught to become like other 'modern' nations that the hold of the past could be broken.

Stiff-backed Britishness represented a confected patriotism designed to shore up the ramshackle institutions of the state. His mocking accounts of 'Ukania'—a term borrowed from novelist Robert Musil's satirical account of the Habsburg Empire in its autumn years—have proved appealing to a host of writers and campaigners (Barnett 2000). The monarchy was a recurrent object of his critical ire, providing an emblematic instance of the 'folklore from above' (Nairn 1993: 174) which was offered in the place of authentic popular nationalism. Britain was still waiting for its own '1789' when a republican nationalism would replace Ukania's *ancien régime*, a conclusion that has been widely shared by later progressives and has flowed into the campaigning work of groups such as Charter 88. However, as the last century grew old and the political prospects of nationalism in the UK and elsewhere, he believed, were rosier, Nairn's thinking underwent a subtle, but notable, shift (see especially Nairn 2002, 2006). He now saw signs that the asymmetrical character and consequences of devolution were irking the English and a proto-democratic set of demands were starting to emerge in response. His developing thinking about Scottish nationalism inclined him to think that the English would now be forced to confront questions of identity and self-government as they were increasingly exposed as the last remaining people living under British rule.

The legacy of his thinking has ultimately been a dichotomous one. On the one hand, Nairn warned progressives off the veneration of the English cultural tradition and the British institutions that has been so important to dominant accounts of Englishness. But, on the other, he came to emphasise that a fully democratic nationalist consciousness might one day emerge and is most likely if the British state and domestic union come apart. This dualism has served to make many progressives distant from, and wary of, nearly all actual manifestations of Englishness (Kenny 2014: 241) and many have subscribed to the Nairnite fear of the English backlash—a resentful and regressive response among a people who are fundamentally devoid of national confidence and unsure of who they are.

This bifurcated approach to English nationalism has been widely replicated. It relies, however, upon a limited reading of Powell's thinking and the nature of his appeal, and it overstates his thinking as the exemplary expression of English nationalism. In fact, Powell's rise and political appeal were, in key respects, contingent reflections of the circumstances in which he arose. It was because of Powell's ability to reach into Labour's working-class vote in a period of relative economic decline, and the exhaustion of a floundering Labour Government, that he became such an important and destabilising force in British politics (Gamble 1986; Schofield 2013). He achieved this position because he spoke directly to feelings of anxiety about national identity and the erosion of the social compact that were increasingly widespread in the 1960s, with Commonwealth migrants being seen by many as undeserving beneficiaries of the state's largesse and a haven for rival cultural traditions and practices.

Powell raised the spectre of a populist nationalism fixated upon the recovery of an older England and illustrated the popular potential of a politics of class-based resentment among supporters of the Labour Party. He was himself unable to carry this politics forward, partly due to his swift marginalisation in the Conservative Party, but also because of his profound loyalty to the British parliamentary system (Heffer 2000). But he established a powerful template for a nationalism that might cut across existing party lines and speak for an increasingly pronounced sense of working-class alienation in the very particular circumstances of the 1960s and 1970s, as the UK's economy entered a downturn, as unemployment and economic insecurity rose and as the welfare state encountered a significant set of fiscal pressures (Whipple 2009).

Nairn's analysis of Powell was insensitive to these contextual considerations and tended to overlook the social issues and fears that have been a crucial seedbed for popular nationalism in the English case. Moreover, the 'civic-liberal' template which he and other proponents of progressive nationalism have sought to transpose to the English context, is belied both by the class-based character of English nationalism and by the distinctive composition of English national consciousness (Tombs 2014). Analyses which stipulate the ideal-typical forms in which Englishness must appear for it to count as authentic nationalism, or which understate the historical preference of most of the English to identify with the institutions of British democracy and government, have tended to reinforce an abiding sense of alienation from nearly all actual manifestations and expressions of Englishness.

13.4 After Empire

An important interpretative cousin of this perspective is the argument that it is Britain's post-imperial dilemma which supplies the key to the character and prospects of English nationalism. Nairn himself linked these arguments in *Break-Up*, seeing the end of empire as an important cause of the diminishing hold, and potential breakdown, of the British state. Nevertheless, the post-imperial interpretation pursues a rather different interpretive logic. It promotes the argument that empire and its aftermath are the defining experiences of the UK and its constituent peoples, and it suggests that the inability of the English to deal with the traumatic experience of imperial decline has conditioned the emergence of English national self-assertion. Versions of this position are widely echoed across the humanities and social sciences and reverberate in political circles too (for instance Gilroy 2007; Sarkar 2016). One of its leading academic exponents is historical sociologist Krishan Kumar, who has consistently argued that the singular character of English nationalism is best understood by considering the English as an 'imperial people'. To his mind, the appropriate comparator for England is those other former imperial peoples—the Russians, Austrians and Turks—who were also called to develop a 'missionary consciousness' in relation to empire and came to believe that they had a special mission to bring to bear in other parts of the world (Kumar 2006: 6, 2016: 37–8). These tasks required instilling in their national majority a degree of self-deprecation, or indeed denial, in order to develop a more encompassing and inclusive form of state-wide patriotism. In crucial respects these empire nations developed a sense of purpose that was couched in 'civilisational', rather than ethno-cultural, terms.

Kumar (2003) deploys this comparison to highlight the development of a state-sponsored patriotism in the British case, which relied upon the obfuscation of the boundaries between English and British identities and gave considerable scope to people from different national groupings to identify with the state's broader goals (see also Colley 2009). This position undergirds his distinctive contribution to ongoing debates about the origins of national consciousness among the English (Hutchinson et al. 2007). Towards the end of the 19th century, Kumar argues, a new case for the British state was required, reflecting the imperatives and challenges generated by the Industrial Revolution and the growing emphasis upon the role of the state in providing social welfare across the various territories of the kingdom. Under the sign of British patriotism, various different national projects were pursued—including the construction of a free trade economic order and the development of an overseas empire.

Kumar argues that these developments represented precursors to the birth of 'Englishness', which he links to the moment when sections of the British elite began to doubt that it was their destiny, as the leading imperial power, to pursue the missionary role associated with empire. And so, he and others maintain, English national consciousness was born out of deep anxiety triggered by, first, the decline of empire and then its dissolution. Empire represented a project into which the English willingly poured their sense of who they were (Kumar 2016). And this meant identifying with a 'universalist' conception of their own values and culture—as English institutions and liberty were depicted as the epitome of progress throughout the world—to ensure that other nations and cultures were, as Robert Young (2007) has put it, able to 'write' themselves into the English story. Englishness became deterritorialised, he suggests, and detached from the real places, institutions and narratives that had been its sources. It became a curiously 'empty' form of collective identity.

More prosaically, the tasks of running a large, complex empire which involved managing people of many races and nationalities also produced an imperative to suppress both the need and desire for an identity that celebrated the English nation (Kumar 2003). But following the end of empire, the lack of meaningful content within this national formation became increasingly apparent: 'With the change in England's condition, with its reduction to the status of a small nation off the European mainland, these myths cease to have much meaning but it has proved difficult to find or invent new ones' (2003: 215). A sense of existential angst about who they now were started to settle upon the English in the 1960s, when it was clear that the external empire was no longer tenable. After empire the English have been forced to reconsider their own future and locate a sense of national purpose.

Kumar's argument for the importance of colonial divestment and the inability of the UK's elites to deal with the challenges associated with post-imperial decline resonate widely in the social sciences and among contemporary historians, especially those influenced by post-colonial theory—for instance Paul Gilroy's (2007) suggestion that English national consciousness has taken the form of a deep-seated cultural melancholia. This interpretation rests, however, upon the contentious assumption that, in giving up its empire and losing its dominant power status, the United Kingdom has experienced the kind of psychic trauma and cultural fallout that typically beset imperial hegemons when they decline. There is, however, an extensive debate among historians about the adequacy of this reading of the effects of empire at both elite and popular levels, with some pointing to the dearth of obvious signs that empire's loss triggered the kind of national soul-searching and rising anxiety stressed by Kumar (Darwin 2011; Howe 2013).

This issue touches on a much more extensive, ongoing debate within British historiography about the impact of empire upon domestic politics and popular culture (Thompson 2005). The notion of Englishness as an inherently anxious and racially exclusionary form of national expression has travelled far and wide; it has shaped a deep wariness towards it within liberal circles and is directly connected to historical accounts of the lingering aftermath of empire. Yet the assumption that English nationalism is necessarily more exclusive, resentful and anxious than a Britishness that was formed by the imperial experience, or indeed than nationalisms elsewhere, is both telling and deserving of critical examination.

Equally, the imperial thesis can be employed to support a very different kind of conclusion: that it is the English—the last remaining subjects of the empire state—who are now turning against the ethos and assumptions of 'Greater Britain', rather than seeking comfort from a nostalgic reincarnation of it. The vote for Brexit, following a well-documented rise in disaffection with the systems of politics and governance under which the English live, may represent the expression of a national consciousness directed against the policy priorities and approaches of a British establishment which still hankers after great power status and favours a political economy rooted in the ideals of free trade and global markets. Far from representing a kind of extended nervous breakdown among a once-imperial people, English nationalism may represent the triumph of a long-established counter-view in British politics—one which reasserts the needs of industry over finance, regions over the capital and English particularity against the universal Englishness of empire (Bragg 2006; Light 1991).

13.5 After Evolution

Despite some notable points of difference, both of these broad perspectives place emphasis on discontinuities in recent British history in their presentations of English nationalism. They became especially prominent during the 1990s, a period when the notion that identities were 'invented' and malleable in kind, rather than primordial and given, became a prevailing motif of much historiography and social science and echoed trends in the political world too (Castells 1997; Giddens 1998). Such a contention was reflected in the hubristic thinking informing some of the Blair Government's early forays into the politics of national identity, including its unconvincing 'Cool Britannia' initiative. Such ideas seemed to betray an inability to appreciate the depth of, and sense of meaning supplied by, feelings of nationhood. In response, various historians and popular writers produced works that unearthed the deep sense of belonging and meaning associated with Englishness in particular (Bragg 2006; Scruton 2006). These arguments helped give life to an extended discussion, and sometimes celebration, of the exceptional and evolutionary nature of this form of identity.

This broad perspective has sustained a very different perspective upon the history and prospects of English nationalism, which is depicted as neither a manifestation of anxiety nor a response to a crisis of identity, but as the resumption of a pathway that was set to one side at some point in the modern era. It was given its most extended political elaboration in the late 1990s in the work of Conservative philosopher and campaigner Roger Scruton. His popular work *England: An Elegy* was written in the early months of the Blair Government and reflects a profound sense of political marginalisation and national pessimism: 'things had moved on so much that the whole concept of Britain had been thrown into disarray. It had become quite apparent that there is no such cultural entity any more' (Scruton 2006: 30). Instead, he turned his attention to the ideals, institutions and landscapes that had sustained and shaped a national lineage that was now on the verge of extinction. The natural, and eternal, focal point for expression of Englishness was the countryside, the locus of a resonant sense of home and belonging and now the object of the expressed hostility of a powerful government.

Scruton's invocation of a timeless, rooted Englishness drew upon a range of archetypical cultural elements and ideas, but also contained some novel political elements. These included a redoubtable critique of the contempt shown by the political elite—now fully empowered through the election of a Labour Government—towards the heritage of England. Additionally, inward migration into England was deliberately being promoted 'as a foil against the English by their enemies'. Immigration, he insisted, 'provides them with a very interesting way of delegitimizing England: the idea that it should be multicultural not monocultural, and it's not because of the intrinsic racism of the English' (cited in English, Hayton & Kenny 2009: 353). His characterisation of an England at the mercy of the interlocking processes of globalisation, immigration and Europeanisation, and increasingly unprotected by its political and economic leaders, spoke to an important shift in parts of the public mood during this period.

His characterisation of an endangered English tradition was, despite its elegiac tone, designed to spark recognition and prompt mobilisation among those of a conservative inclination. Importantly, in subsequent years, the same pattern of argument was offered by other writers moved by different political ambitions. Campaigner and writer Paul Kingsnorth (2008), coming from a left-wing anti-globalisation perspective, proposed a reclamation of the authenticity and sense of heritage associated with English folk culture. He and others argued for the recuperation of a long-running, but latterly forgotten, radical lineage which might sustain the construction of a progressive English patriotism in the present. Such a position was championed by a handful of English politicians in these years and has gradually come to acquire greater respectability in liberal circles (see Kenny (2014) for a discussion of this perspective).

These various ideological efforts to reappropriate a more deeply rooted sense of the English story built upon some notable historiographical contributions in the last few decades. These culminated in the celebration of national distinctiveness which underpinned the arguments of the 'Historians for Britain' group who campaigned in favour of Brexit in 2016 (Abulafia 2015). English exceptionalism had other roots too, drawing upon an established lineage of historical scholarship which has stressed both the longevity and the exceptional qualities of Englishness as a species of national consciousness. The English, according to historian Leah Greenfield (1992), were forerunners, not latecomers, in the development of nationalism. It was during the later medieval period that a distinctive sense of an English national community became prevalent—this was orchestrated by Henry VIII for his project of state centralisation and expansion. This work echoed the judgement of émigré intellectual Hans Kohn (1940), writing half a century beforehand. Whereas England had once been a poor, relatively backward country, under the twin influences of Henry VIII and the Reformation—he argued in an iconic essay published in 1940—it acquired a unique blend of cultural confidence and self-belief, much of which was rooted in the influence of a Protestant-inspired providentialism. The English were increasingly receptive to the notion that they were a 'people reborn', whose identity was interwoven with a sense of religious mission. Such ideas, he and other later historians maintained, were integral to the events leading up to the Civil War of the 17th century. For Anthony Smith (2013), notions of the elect status of the English and the sacred mission with which they had been endowed were an important crucible for an emergent, exceptionalist form of national self-understanding. This imprinted some important ideas—about election, providence and civilisational influence—within the English mindset.

These accounts have been of enduring significance, both in their stress upon the unique character of English national sentiment and their explanation of why the English mind seemed unmoved by the nationalist currents which swept across Continental Europe during the last decades of the 19th century. The English could not recognise in themselves what they recoiled from in their rivals, Kohn suggested, and while they increasingly turned away from the very idea of popular nationalism, they were actually cementing their own unique form of it, one that was rooted in liberal patterns of thinking about liberty and constitutional government.

While some of the constitutive elements of this lineage changed over time, the assumption that a historically embedded strain of nationhood is now coming back to life, casting off the different masks it has worn since the establishment of Britain and the pursuit of empire, has become a very familiar trope in contemporary debate—and figured prominently in some of the historical arguments that surfaced during debates about Brexit. This idea is at the heart of Robert Tombs' (2014) widely discussed history of the English people. In it he chronicled the evolution of the ways in which the English had, over time, conceived of their own sense of nationhood and connected these ideas to the early formation of the English state. He pointed also to the distinctive sense of historical memory—and indeed mythology—which have sustained a rich, evolving and adaptive Englishness over a considerable timespan. Tombs' book served to highlight some striking continuities of national sentiment and reflection, while also bringing to the fore the great array of territorial unions and alliances into which the English have been inserted.

The growing imperative, first apparent in the academy and then—during the 2000s—in the wider culture, to retell the English national story in bolder and more delineated terms, constitutes an important prelude to the emergence of a politically resonant Englishness. These popular works tended to push the British point of reference into the background, while also supplying accounts of England which were in many ways similar to those Whiggish tales which were, in earlier decades, told in Britain's name. Thus, columnist Simon Jenkins provided an accessible version of this narrative in his *A Short History of England* (2011). This, and various other similar popular histories, have played an important cultural role in shaping the sensibilities of audiences increasingly drawn towards the imaginative reconstruction of the English story. In his more recent historical essay, Robert Winder (2017) unfolds an entertaining argument about the singular importance of sheep-farming and the woollen trade for the formation of English national consciousness. In this genre of writing a contemporary moral is rarely hard to find. Jenkins, for instance, drew the conclusion that the English people might no longer be content to maintain their sense of nationality beneath the carapace of British citizenship, nor to subsume their identity and sovereignty within the EU.

As a growing number of writers and cultural practitioners, as well as a small number of politicians, have sought to derive various political conclusions from accounts which stress either the unique cultural disposition of the English or singular aspects of their geography and historical experience, an increasingly stark antinomy has emerged between those who see in their heritage an ancient line of descent and inspiration and those who see its political reappropriation as a threat to the project of establishing an overarching form of nationality for the whole of the United Kingdom. The restorationist approach sustains a very different national sensibility to the emphasis upon the anxiety associated with English nationalism. For its proponents, Englishness is framed as the overdue return of a forgotten or neglected lineage, not the invention of a brand-new identity. In the context of Brexit, the contention that a residual English rebelliousness—not a newly formed nationalism—might have played a key role in shaping the decisions of many of the English has been a notable feature of subsequent commentary (Kenny 2017; Taylor 2017).

As many different historians have observed, the English are far from unique in conceiving their own nationhood in exceptional terms (Özkırımlı 2011). And certainly the long tradition of seeking to distil the essence of the English character has for the most part ended in laments about the difficulties associated with definition. But accounts that highlight some of the key features of Britain's geography, political economy and territorial state have all pointed to significant singularities which have contributed to, or shaped, the very distinctive patterns of thought and feeling which are bound up with the national self-understanding of the English. And a focus upon these suggests the importance of longer-running developments and trends in the history of English nationalism.

13.6 English Nationalism through the Historical Lens

Engaging with these historiographical debates serves a number of different purposes. One is to remind us that whereas nationalism is typically referenced in contemporary political terms as the antithesis of a cosmopolitan liberalism identified with the perspectives of elites, the English nation has been painted in a range of different political colours in different historical periods. In her work, for instance, intellectual historian Julia Stapleton (1999) stresses the complex and shifting nature of England and Englishness as powerful themes within elite-level thinking a century ago and has identified their imbrication with liberal ideas of citizenship in the early decades of the 20th century. National liberals, such as Sir Ernest Barker, stressed the interaction of forms of continuity and change that were central to the English governing tradition and which found echo in the character of its people: 'this long slow movement of the character of England, has it not something enduring?' (1947: 575). Re-engagement with the variety of traditions and thinkers who engaged and argued over Englishness supplies an important counterpoint to the presumption that right-wing populists and illiberal nationalists are its most authentic and natural political exponents.

Reappraising historical interpretations of English nationalism is of value for another reason. Contemporary understandings of this pattern of sentiment tend to assume its incompatibility with other forms of identity and attachment. Critics routinely claim, for instance, that it is very likely to be the antithesis to the civic model of Britishness. But an understanding of the rich heritage of political thinking associated with Englishness suggests that other conceptual and normative possibilities have been, and can still be, explored. Multidimensional and pluralistic notions of the English nation, and the values it has been said to convey, have been advanced by a great many writers and thinkers over the course of the last century. And, at the popular level too, it is striking that most English people continue to feel an attachment to different forms of identity when given the choice to do so.

The notion of Englishness as an all-encompassing identity that crowds out other allegiances is also belied by an appreciation of the regional diversity which has long been an accompaniment to this form of national sentiment. In the contemporary debate there is a habitual tendency to see English nationalism as a rival to entrenched forms of local attachment. Yet historians have shown how regional and county loyalties have served as crucibles for, not alternatives to, powerful ideas of England. In his account, for instance, historian Robert Colls (2004) suggests that the 'identity' of England was built in multiple ways from a wide array of materials and local attachments. The variegated roots from which notions of England spring are a key source of the different kinds of Englishness which continue to be expressed and celebrated. A richer engagement with the historiography that has built up on the question of how the English have lived and intuited their sense of nationhood would do much to dispel some of the myths and fears associated with contemporary debate on English nationalism.

13.7 Conclusions

What the term English nationalism describes, and what it signifies in political terms, should be seen as more complicated questions than much current discourse on this topic allows. Given the salience of this form of national sentiment and its potential ramifications, at a moment of considerable uncertainty for the UK's territorial constitution, the case for a more measured, reflective and informed discussion of this phenomenon is particularly strong. The continuation of the established habit of conflating Englishness with the most notorious political variant of it—Powell's anti-immigrant and anti-EU nationalism—has undergirded a tendency to demonise and simplify English preferences in the context of the Brexit vote (O'Toole 2016). Taking the longer view affords valuable insight into the richness, regional diversity and political ecumenism which characterised ideas of England and the English since the late 19th century. In the more recent period there has been a significant narrowing of the imagination when this topic is pondered and a debilitating tendency to retreat behind established battle lines in offering judgements of this national lineage and its constitutional implications.

In this chapter I have sought to make a small contribution to these processes by suggesting the merits of re-engaging some of the major studies and theories of English national consciousness that have emerged in recent years. Each of the perspectives considered here sheds light on important aspects of English identity, offering explanations of its ethnocultural characteristics, democratic potential, post-imperial dimensions and evolutionary nature. These accounts compete and overlap in various respects and each has its critics and limitations. My intention here is not to make an argument for one over the others. Instead I seek to show that engaging with such characterisations has a wider value. First, it sheds light on the variety of influences and factors which have been pertinent to the renewal of English identities and dethrones the current preoccupation with Euroscepticism as the sole or main crucible for nationalism among the English. This enables us, secondly, to take a longer view on English nationalism and place current anxieties about it in perspective. As Linda Colley (2014) has observed, there is a venerable tradition of concern about who the English are, what kind of national consciousness they exhibit and whether the nation faces a spiral of inexorable decline, which has re-emerged on numerous occasions in the last few centuries, notably during moments of profound national danger or uncertainty.

It is important to appreciate, thirdly, that contrasting accounts of England's national-cultural character and geopolitical future have long been in play, drawing upon a rich and varied intellectual heritage. And this helps explain why this species of nationalism can seemingly be employed to sustain divergent, sometimes contrary, political arguments and programmes. In the current period, for instance, it is notable that England is invoked to support two potentially rival ideas: the notion of Brexit as a victory for a retreat from interdependency and wider entanglements and a falling back into the *habitus* of 'little England', on the one hand, and the claim that the English are now free to regain their 'global', trading and outward-facing heritage, on the other. Such divergences arise from competing views of the English and their histories and rival understandings of the relationship of this people to the tradition of British constitutional government and parliamentary democracy. Whether the English will continue to see themselves, in constitutional terms, as a people defined by the tenets of parliamentary sovereignty and the ethos of the United Kingdom, or will follow an emerging path towards asserting England as a site of political community and some form of self-government, is now one of the major questions at the heart of the UK's territorial politics.

A debate about these issues which is dominated by clichés and caricatures about English nationalism, or which follows the narrow tramlines of partisan political debate, is unlikely to illuminate or inform the momentous decisions that lie ahead for the English and their political representatives. It is in this spirit that we have gathered together the diverse scholarly contributions included in this volume and asked these authors to take a step back from contemporary debates about politics and constitution, in order to offer reasoned, evidenced and historically informed reflections on the key topics and issues associated with the governance of England.

References

Abulafia, D. (2015), 'Britain: apart from, or a part of, Europe?', *History Today*, 11 May, http://www.historytoday.com/david-abulafia/britain-apart-or-part-europe, accessed 4 June 2018.

Ascherson, N. (2016), 'England prepares to leave the world', *London Review of Books*, 17 November.

Aughey, A. (2007), *The Politics of Englishness* (Manchester, Manchester University Press).

Barker, E. (1947), *Character of England* (Oxford, Oxford University Press).

Barnett, A. (2000), 'Corporate populism', *New Left Review*, 3, https://newleftreview.org/II/3/anthony-barnett-corporate-populism-and-partyless-democracy, accessed 4 June 2018.

Bragg, B. (2006), *The Progressive Patriot; a Search for Belonging* (London, Bantam Press).

Castells, M. (1997), *The Power of Identity: The Information Age: Economy, Society, and Culture, Volume II* (Oxford, Blackwell).

Clarke, H., Goodwin, M. & Whiteley, P. (2017), 'Why Britain voted for Brexit: an individual-level analysis of the 2016 referendum vote', *Parliamentary Affairs*, 70: 439–64.

Clements, B., Lynch, P. & Whitaker, R. (2013), 'The low salience of European integration for British voters means that UKIP will have to expand their platform to gain more support', LSE EUROPP blog, 8 March, http://eprints.lse.ac.uk/50187/1/blogs.lse.ac.uk-The_low_salience_of_European_integration_for_British_voters_means_that_UKIP_will_have_to_expand_their.pdf, accessed 4 June 2018.

Colley, L. (2009), *Britons: Forging the Nation 1707–1837* (New Haven, CT, Yale University Press).

Colley, L. (2014), *Acts of Union and Disunion: What Has Held the UK Together—and What is Dividing it* (London, Profile).

Colls, R. (2004), *Identity of England* (Oxford, Oxford University Press).

Cowell, A. (2016), 'Great Britain or "Little England"? "Brexit" vote revives an old tension', *New York Times*, 26 June.

Curtice, J. (2016), *How Deeply Does Britain's Euroscepticism Run?* (London and Strathclyde, UK in a Changing EU/NatCen).

Darwin, J. (2011), *The Empire Project* (Cambridge, Cambridge University Press).

The Economist (2016), 'Trump's world: the new nationalism', 19 November.

English, R. (2012), *Is there an English Nationalism?* (London, IPPR).

English, R., Hayton, R. & Kenny, M. (2009), 'Englishness and the Union in contemporary conservative thought', *Government and Opposition*, 44(4): 343–65.

Gamble, A. (1986), *The Conservative Nation* (Basingstoke, Macmillan).

Giddens, A. (1998), *The Third Way: The Renewal of Social Democracy* (Cambridge, Polity).

Gilroy, P. (2007), *After Empire: Melancholia or Convivial Culture? Multiculture or Postcolonial Melancholia* (London, Routledge).

Greenfield, L. (1992), *Nationalism: Five Roads to Modernity* (Cambridge, MA, Harvard University Press).

Heffer, S. (2000), *Nor Shall my Sword: Reinvention of England* (London, Phoenix).

Henderson A., Jeffery, C., Wincott, D. & Wyn Jones, R. (2017), 'How Brexit was made in England', *British Journal of Politics and International Relations*, 19(4): 631–46.

Howe, S. (2013), 'Internal decolonization? British politics since Thatcher as post-colonial trauma', *Twentieth Century British History*, 14(3): 286–304.

Hutchinson, J. (1999), 'Re-interpreting cultural nationalism', *Australian Journal of Politics and History*, 45(3): 392–409.

Hutchinson, J., Reynolds, S., Smith, A. D., Colls, R. & Kumar, K. (2007), 'Debate on Krishan Kumar's *The Making of English National Identity*', *Nations and Nationalism*, 13(2): 179–203.

Jack, I. (2016), 'English nationalism has shattered my sense of belonging to Britain', *The Guardian*, 22 October.

Jeffery, C., Wyn Jones, R., Henderson, A. & Lodge, G. (2014), 'Taking England seriously: the new English politics', http://www.centreonconstitutionalchange.ac.uk/sites/default/files/news/Taking%20England%20Seriously_The%20New%20English%20Politics.pdf, accessed 4 June 2018.

Jenkins, S. (2011), *A Short History of England* (London, Profile).

Kenny, M. (2014), *The Politics of English Nationhood* (Oxford, Oxford University Press).

Kenny, M. (2017), 'E. P. Thompson: last of the English radicals', *Political Quarterly*, 88(4): 579–88.

Kingsnorth, P. (2008), *Real England: Battle Against the Bland* (London, Portobello).

Kohn, H. (1940), 'The genesis and the character of English nationalism', *Journal of the History of Ideas*, 1: 69–94.

Kumar, K. (2003), *The Making of English National Identity* (Cambridge, Cambridge University Press).

Kumar, K. (2006), 'Empire and English nationalism', *Nations and Nationalism*, 12(1): 1–13.

Kumar, K. (2016), *The Idea of Englishness: English Culture, National Identity and Social Thought* (London, Routledge).

Light, A. (1991), *Forever England: Literature, Femininity and Conservatism between the Wars* (London, Routledge).

Lynch, P. (1999), *The Politics of Nationhood: Sovereignty, Britishness and Conservative Politics* (Basingstoke, Macmillan).

McLean, I. (2001), *Rational Choice and British Politics: An Analysis of Rhetoric and Manipulation from Blair to Peel* (Oxford, Oxford University Press).

Mandler, P. (2006), 'What is "national identity"? Definitions and applications in modern British historiography', *Modern Intellectual History*, 3(2): 271–97.

Nairn, T. (1977), *Break-Up of Britain* (London, New Left Books).

Nairn, T. (1993), *The Enchanted Glass: Britain and its Monarchy* (London, Verso).
Nairn, T. (2000), *After Britain: New Labour and the Return of Scotland* (London, Granta).
Nairn, T. (2002), *Pariah* (London, Verso).
Nairn, T. (2006), *Global Nations* (London, Verso).
Ormston, R. (2012), 'The English Question: How is England responding to devolution?', NatCen, http://www.scotcen.org.uk/media/1026914/the-english-question-final-for-publication-280212pdf-2-.pdf, accessed 4 June 2018.
O'Toole, F. (2016), 'Brexit is being driven by English nationalism: and it will end in self-rule', *The Guardian*, 19 June.
Özkırımlı, U. (2011), *Theories of Nationalism* (London, Palgrave).
Peck, T. (2016), '"I was too focused on the economy" says Osborne', *The Independent*, 17 December.
Sarkar, M. (2016), *Englishness and Post-Imperial Space* (Newcastle upon Tyne, Cambridge Scholars Publishing).
Schofield, C. (2013), *Enoch Powell and the Making of Post-Colonial Britain* (Cambridge, Cambridge University Press).
Scruton, R. (2006), *England: An Elegy* (London, Continuum).
Smith, A. D. (2013), *The Nation Made Real: Art and National Identity in Western Europe, 1600–1850* (Oxford, Oxford University Press).
Stapleton, J. (1999), 'Resisting the centre at the extremes: "English" liberalism in the political thought of interwar Britain', *British Journal of Politics and International Relations*, 1(3): 270–92.
Taylor, J. D. (2017), 'The working class revolts', *New Statesman*, 7 February.
Thompson, A. (2005), *The Empire Strikes Back? The Impact of Imperialism on Britain from the Mid-Nineteenth Century* (Harlow, Pearson Longman).
Tombs, R. (2014), *The English and their History* (London, Allen Lane).
Tombs, R. (2016), 'The English revolt', *New Statesman*, 24 July, http://www.newstatesman.com/politics/uk/2016/07/english-revolt, accessed 4 June 2018.
Wellings, B. (2012), *English Nationalism and Euroscepticism: Losing the Peace* (London, Peter Lang).
Whipple, A. (2009), 'Revisiting the "rivers of blood" controversy: letters to Enoch Powell', *Journal of British Studies*, 48(3): 717–35.
Winder, R. (2017), *The Last Wolf: The Hidden Springs of Englishness* (London, Little, Brown).
Wyn Jones, R., Lodge, G., Henderson, A. & Wincott, D. (2012), *The Dog that Finally Barked: England as an Emerging Political Community* (London, IPPR).
Young, R. (2007), *The Idea of English Ethnicity* (London, Wiley-Blackwell).

Index